Progress in Psychobiology and Physiological Psychology

Volume 6

Contributors to This Volume

Linda M. Bartoshuk
Mark A. Berkley
Marion Frank
William Hodos
G. J. Mogenson
Carl Pfaffmann
A. G. Phillips
Paul Rozin
Thomas C. Snell
Edward M. Stricker
Michael J. Zigmond

Progress in
PSYCHOBIOLOGY AND
PHYSIOLOGICAL PSYCHOLOGY

Edited by JAMES M. SPRAGUE
Institute of Neurological Sciences
and Department of Anatomy
The School of Medicine
University of Pennsylvania
Philadelphia, Pennsylvania

and ALAN N. EPSTEIN
Leidy Laboratory
Department of Biology
University of Pennsylvania
Philadelphia, Pennsylvania

Volume 6

1976

ACADEMIC PRESS New York • San Francisco • London
A Subsidiary of Harcourt Brace Jovanovich, Publishers

ACADEMIC PRESS, INC.
111 Fifth Avenue, New York, New York 10003

United Kingdom Edition published by
ACADEMIC PRESS, INC. (LONDON) LTD.
24/28 Oval Road, London NW1

LIBRARY OF CONGRESS CATALOG CARD NUMBER: 66-29640

ISBN 0-12-542106-0

PRINTED IN THE UNITED STATES OF AMERICA

Contents

Coding Gustatory Information
in the Squirrel Monkey Chorda Tympani

Carl Pfaffmann, Marion Frank, Linda M. Bartoshuk, and Thomas C. Snell

Vision and the Visual System: A Bird's-Eye View

William Hodos

Cat Visual Psychophysics:
Neural Correlates and Comparisons with Man

Mark A. Berkley

Recovery of Function after Damage to
Central Catecholamine-Containing Neurons:
A Neurochemical Model for the Lateral
Hypothalamic Syndrome

Edward M. Stricker and Michael J. Zigmond

Motivation: A Psychological Construct in Search
of a Physiological Substrate

G. J. Mogenson and A. G. Phillips

The Evolution of Intelligence and
Access to the Cognitive Unconscious

Paul Rozin

Contents   vii

List of Contributors

Numbers in parentheses indicate the pages on which the authors' contributions begin.

Linda M. Bartoshuk, John B. Pierce Foundation Laboratory, New Haven, Connecticut (1)

Mark A. Berkley, Department of Psychology, Florida State University, Tallahassee, Florida (63)

Marion Frank, The Rockefeller University, New York, New York (1)

William Hodos, Department of Psychology, University of Maryland, College Park, Maryland (29)

G. J. Mogenson, Departments of Physiology and Psychology, University of Western Ontario, London, Ontario (189)

Carl Pfaffmann, The Rockefeller University, New York, New York (1)

A. G. Phillips, Department of Psychology, University of British Columbia, Vancouver, British Columbia, Canada (189)

Paul Rozin, Department of Psychology, University of Pennsylvania, Philadelphia, Pennsylvania (245)

Thomas C. Snell, The Meeting School, Rindge, New Hampshire (1)

Edward M. Stricker, Psychobiology Program, Departments of Psychology and Biology, University of Pittsburgh, Pittsburgh, Pennsylvania (121)

Michael J. Zigmond, Psychobiology Program, Departments of Psychology and Biology, University of Pittsburgh, Pittsburgh, Pennsylvania (121)

This volume, the sixth in a series covering progress in physiological psychology, has two changes. First, the format carries a new title, "Progress in Psychobiology and Physiological Psychology". Second, Eliot Stellar has relinquished his role as editor because of the responsibilities in becoming Provost, and his place has been taken by Alan Epstein, Professor of Biology, University of Pennsylvania. Our editorial policy will remain the same, namely to achieve a broad coverage of research fields bearing on various behaviors, and the brain mechanisms mediating them. We have attempted to provide a highly flexible context in which this research was presented, including critical reviews, syntheses based chiefly on work done in a single laboratory, presentations of original work, or various combinations of these. A major aim has been to achieve an updating of concepts, working hypotheses, and data for the use of a wide spectrum of professionals. Our belief has been that such publications would serve as nodal points of reference as well as catalysts in the development of these fields of research.

We wish to thank the authors for their outstanding contributions and Academic Press for the freedom they have continued to give us in the organization of these volumes.

James M. Sprague
Alan N. Epstein

Contents of Previous Volumes

Coding Gustatory Information in the Squirrel Monkey Chorda Tympani

Carl Pfaffmann,[1] Marion Frank,[1] Linda M. Bartoshuk,[2]
and Thomas C. Snell[3]

I. Introduction

The electrophysiological study of taste in mammals has focused on afferents in the chorda tympani because of their accessibility to surgical exposure, and the ease of stimulating their receptor fields on the anterior tongue dorsum, and because the sensory component of this nerve is almost exclusively gustatory. A wide variety of species—rat, mouse, rabbit, guinea pig, bat, hamster, cat, dog, pig, sheep, goat, cow, rhesus monkey, and man—have been studied; some only in the total nerve discharge, as in man, but most by single-fiber analysis as well (Andersson *et al.*, 1950; Beidler *et al.*, 1955; Bernard, 1964; Bradley and Mistretta, 1972; Gordon *et al.*, 1959; Kitchell, 1963; Ogawa *et al.*, 1972; Pfaffmann, 1941, 1955; Sato *et al.*, 1969; Zotterman, 1956, 1971). Species differences are notable. Although the chorda tympani of nearly all species studied shows good acid and salt responses, among the salts there are clear differences in effectiveness. Rodents show good responses to Na^+ salts but weak responses to K^+ salts, whereas cats and other carnivores show a good K^+ and poor Na^+ response. The response to distilled water is quite variable from species to species. Cats and rabbits show a clear water response, rats and man very little; but prior treatment of the tongue surface markedly influences the response to water. The response to quinine is sizable in the cat chorda tympani, but in most other species it is weak because afferents subserving this sensitivity travel largely in the IXth nerve. The chorda tympani of the cat shows relatively little response to sugars, that of

[1] The Rockefeller University, New York, New York.
[2] John B. Pierce Foundation Laboratory, New Haven, Connecticut.
[3] The Meeting School, Rindge, New Hampshire.

the rat only a moderate response compared to good responses in the dog, hamster, and guinea pig. This paper documents taste properties of the squirrel monkey's chorda tympani, especially its striking reactivity to sugars. Sugar elicits strong preference behavior in the squirrel monkey, as it does in a number of other mammals, and so permits close correlation of sensory physiology and behavior. Further, the order of preference of different sugars resembles the order of relative sweetness of sugars for man.

The single chorda tympani fibers reflect the sensitivity of the receptor cells of the taste buds on which the afferent nerve endings terminate. The individual afferent fibers branch a number of times both within each bud and among buds. In the rat, one of the few species in which detailed information on innervation is available, a single chorda tympani fiber may supply as many as 9 separate taste buds (4.5 on the average) each of which is located on the dorsum of a single fungiform papilla and separated from its neighbor by 0.5 to 3.5 mm. The tongue surface between papillae is insensitive to taste stimuli (Beidler, 1969; Wang and Frank, cited in Pfaffmann, 1970). Single taste fibers in all species studied so far display multiple sensitivity when representative stimuli of the four classic taste modalities (salt, sour, bitter, and sweet) are employed. Although some taste fibers respond to only one of the four, the majority respond to two, three, or all four stimulus classes. Usually one of the stimuli is the most effective; that is, it elicits the highest frequency impulse discharge and can be designated as the "best stimulus." Such multiple sensitivity, however, cannot be attributed to branching of the afferent fibers. Punctate stimulation of all the individual taste buds of single fiber's receptive field shows all to possess the same pattern of chemical sensitivity and usually the same best stimulus (Wang and Frank, cited in Pfaffmann, 1970; Oakley, 1972). Microelectrode recordings from individual sensory cells within the taste buds reveal multiple sensitivity of the receptor cells themselves. Thus the cell membrane of any one receptor cell appears to be a heterogeneous surface composed of many different types of chemically receptive sites. That sensitivity with the greatest number of sites probably corresponds to the "best stimulus" for the receptor cell and its associated afferent fibers. The pattern of chemical sensitivity of the branches tends to match that of the parent fiber. Taste receptor specificity, thus, can best be described as relative or quantitative rather than "all or none," but can be characterized in terms of a "best stimulus."

Because the largest body of single fiber data has been gathered from rats and hamsters, the lack of sharp specificity of the peripheral mammalian taste system may reflect largely the properties of rodent taste and be unrepresentative of higher mammals, such as primates. Prior studies of the monkey chorda tympani reported only the whole nerve response or on too few units for quantitative analyses (Fishman, 1959; Gordon *et al.*, 1959; Ogawa *et al.*,

1972). In the present paper, we compare total nerve with single fiber responses of the chorda tympani nerve of the squirrel monkey and discuss their relations to behavioral reactions to sugars.

The total nerve gives one seriation of effectiveness: fructose > sucrose > maltose > lactose > galactose > dextrose. Behavioral measures show a different order among three of these: sucrose > fructose > dextrose, the major discrepancy occurring in the relative positions of fructose and sucrose. Single units of fibers responsive to sugar varied in sucrose–fructose effectiveness. There was less variation in the effectiveness of the other sugars. In fact two classes of sugar fibers were found: one in which sucrose was more effective than fructose, in number of nerve impulses elicited per unit time for equimolar solutions; the second in which fructose was more effective. The first class, responding primarily to sugars, was labeled the S class; the second group, responding primarily to salts (NaCl and NH_4Cl) with a lesser but nevertheless significant response to sugar, was labeled the N class. The sucrose–fructose effectiveness of the S class corresponds with that of behavioral tests.

II. Method and Procedure

Twenty male squirrel monkeys, *Saimiri sciureus,* weighing between 600 and 850 gm, were used. They were first given an intramuscular injection of 1.7 mg/kg of the tranquilizer Sernylin (5 mg/ml), followed by an intraperitoneal injection of 0.2 ml of sodium pentobarbital (60 mg/ml) 20 or 30 minutes later. Additional doses of 0.05 ml of sodium pentobarbital were given when necessary, with an average of about 2.0 mg/kg per hour.

The left side of the face was shaved with electric clippers, and the animal was placed prone in a holder that grasped the head firmly between upper jaw and infraorbital ridges, leaving the tongue and lower jaw free. The animals were warmed with a hot water bottle or electric heating pad, and rectal temperature was monitored.

All operative procedures were carried out with the aid of a Zeiss dissecting microscope. The skin and skin muscles covering the left zygomatic arch and posterior portion of the mandible were removed. The temporalis muscle was detached from the zygomatic arch, and the arch was removed. The masseter muscle was extracted, exposing the coronoid process of the mandible, which was carefully separated from the surrounding tissue and removed with a rongeurs. A number of venus sinuses thus exposed were tied off and cut. The chorda tympani was cut close to its entrance into the bulla, and at least 1 cm of the nerve was freed from the surrounding tissue. The lingual nerve was cut 0.5 to 1 cm proximally to its junction with the chorda tympani to facilitate adjustment of the electrodes. Single fibers, judged by the appearance of spikes of constant height, were obtained by teasing apart the main nerve bundles after removing the sheath. The deep incision, when covered with strips of plastic wrap, formed a natural moist chamber for the nerve. Recording electrodes of nichrome wire sealed in glass tubing were mounted in a micromanipulator. A Grass P511 preamplifier, Tektronix 502 dual-beam oscilloscope, and a Grass camera were used for single-fiber response recording; and a Hewlett-Packard 450 AR amplifier, a R-C summator modified from Beidler (1953) and a Varian graphic recorder, in addition, were used for the recording of the whole nerve response. Single fiber data were stored on analog tape (Magnecord 1048 stereo tape recorder) to be photographed later and analyzed.

All solutions were prepared from reagent grade chemicals and distilled water with the exception of sucrose; commercial cane sugar is exceptionally pure. One molar stock solutions of all sugars were prepared within 3 days prior to each preparation and refrigerated until about 24 hours before use. At this time they were allowed to come to room temperature and concentration series were prepared by dilution. This ensured that sugar solutions had reached an equilibrium state of mutarotation. The four basic taste stimuli were 0.5 M sucrose, 0.3 M NaCl, 0.01 M HCl, and 0.003 M quinine hydrochloride. Also used were 0.3 M NH_4Cl, and 0.5 M fructose, maltose, lactose, dextrose (glucose), and galactose. All stimuli were presented by means of a gravity flow system to a glass flow chamber for the anterior tongue. A typical stimulus sequence is shown in Fig. 1.

Whole-nerve response magnitude was recorded in units of recorder deflection. The numbers were then converted into percentage of the response to the standard stimulus: 0.3 M NH_4Cl (see Fig. 1). The response measure used for single-fiber analysis, derived from photographic records (see Fig. 2), was the number of impulses in the first 5 seconds of a response.

III. Results

A. RESPONSES TO TASTE STIMULI

1. Whole Nerve

The response of the whole nerve to NH_4Cl was substantial, and for this reason, it was chosen as the standard. Of particular interest is the good response to sugars. Water produced a small but definite response upon initiation of flow after a prior water rinse (see Fig. 1). Water following other stimuli produced a response depending upon the particular chemical (note response to water after HCl in Fig. 1).

Figure 3 shows the median relative chorda tympani peak response (bars)

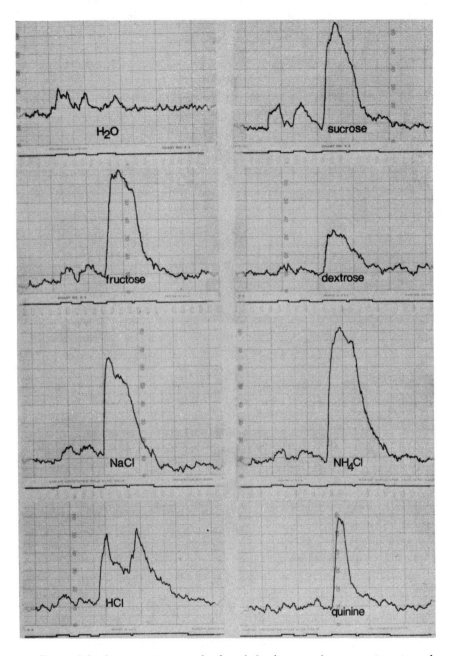

FIG. 1. Inkwriter summator records of total chorda tympani responses to water and taste stimuli applied to the anterior tongue. The first two deflections of marker signal flow of distilled water, the third deflection signals duration of stimulus flow, the fourth indicates rinse with distilled water. 1 division = 5 seconds.

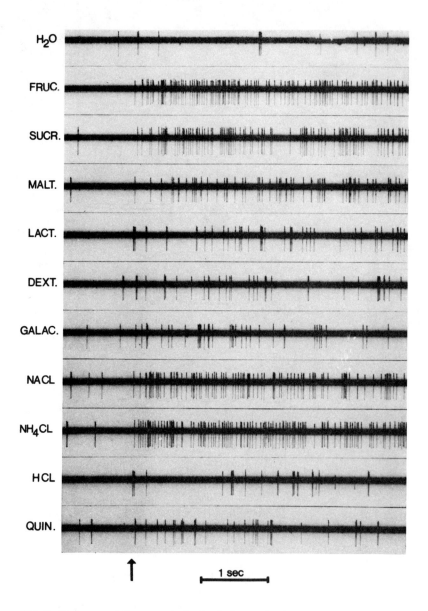

FIG. 2. Responses of the same single chorda tympani unit to sugars, to two salts, and to acid and quinine. Stimulus onset at arrow.

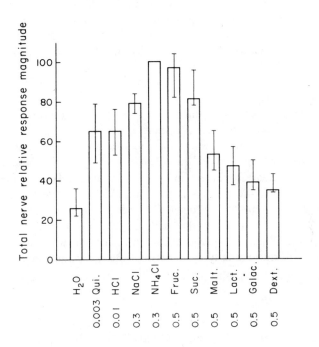

FIG. 3. Median values of total nerve responses relative to NH₄Cl in nine preparations. Bars indicate semi-interquartile ranges.

TABLE I
DISTRIBUTION OF RANK-ORDER CORRELATIONS OF
RESPONSE ACROSS NINE WHOLE CHORDA TYMPANI
NERVE PREPARATIONS

Correlation[a]	Frequency
+0.90 − +0.99	13
+0.80 − +0.89	12
+0.70 − +0.79	9
+0.60 − +0.69	1
+0.50 − +0.59	1

[a]Correlations $\geq \pm 0.75$, $p \geq 0.02$.

and semi-interquartile range (bracketed lines) to the standard stimuli for nine different nerve preparations. All preparations showed similar orderings of response size to the different chemicals. The median Spearman rank-order correlation between stimulus orderings by the nine preparations was +0.85, indicating a high consistency from preparation to preparation. Table I shows the distribution of the 36 rank-order correlations between all the possible pairs of the nine preparations.

Response magnitude is dependent on stimulus concentration, as shown in Fig. 4. Of the two salts, NH_4Cl is more effective than NaCl; and of the six sugars, fructose is more effective than sucrose and both are more effective than dextrose and, indeed, all the other sugars used, which produce smaller responses of similar size at equimolar concentrations. The quinine and HCl intensities were limited to no higher than 0.01 and 0.03 *M,* respectively, because these are both physiologically and behaviorally very strong taste stimuli. When used repeatedly they will lead to a rapid fall in neural response. The response functions in Fig. 4 can, thus, be taken as indices of taste responsivity of the chorda tympani nerve of the squirrel monkey.

2. Single-Fiber Analysis

A total of 48 single fibers were obtained by teasing apart the strands of the chorda tympani until the action potential record displayed by the oscillo-

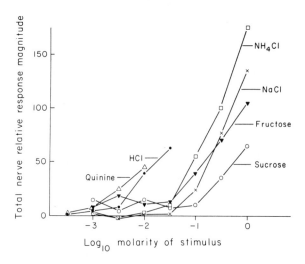

FIG. 4. Concentration functions of whole chorda tympani responses relative to NH_4Cl.

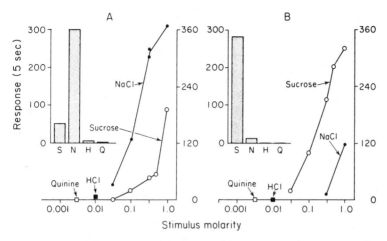

FIG. 5. (A and B) Single-unit intensity responses functions in impulses per 5 seconds for four basic taste stimuli in two different fibers. Inset is response histogram profile for 0.5 sucrose (S), 0.3 NaCl (N), 0.01 HCl (H), and 0.003 quinine hydrochloride (Q).

scope and subsequent photographic analysis showed the customary uniform pulse height of a single fiber (see Fig. 2). Of these, 13 were stimulated with a concentration series of the basic taste stimuli. Figures 5 and 6 give stimulus–response functions for four different fibers. Figure 5B illustrates the sensitivity of a fiber that was highly specific, responding primarily to sucrose and very little to the standard concentration of NaCl, although it did respond more to 1.0 M NaCl. Quinine and HCl elicited no response. The inset is a bar graph of responses to test concentrations of the basic taste compounds (0.5 M sucrose, 0.3 M NaCl, 0.01 M HCl, and 0.003 M quinine hydrochloride). Sucrose was the prime stimulus for this unit. Figure 5A shows the response profile of a unit predominantly sensitive to salt, with, however, a lesser response to sucrose over the physiologic range. No significant response occurred to HCl or quinine in this unit. In Fig. 6, C shows a unit primarily responsive to NaCl with low-level responses to acid and sucrose. In another acid-sensitive unit (not illustrated) the response to increasing concentrations of HCl was similar in shape, but the first detectable discharge appeared at 0.001 M with higher frequencies of discharge up to 228 impulses in 5 seconds at the highest concentration. The bar diagram C (Fig. 6) shows sensitivity to three basic stimuli: salt, sugar, and acid. Graph D (Fig. 6) shows a unit which responds best to quinine, but also responds to the other three basic stimuli. The overall frequency of discharge was lower in this case, and the response scale has been expanded on the graph. The bar graph illustrates a pattern of multiple sensitivity to four test stimuli. Such a range of specific to multiple sensitivity in different single taste fibers is like that commonly seen in earlier work on other species.

In addition to the 13 units stimulated with the concentration series, 30 other units were tested with all four of the basic tastes at the standard concentrations: 0.5 *M* sucrose, 0.3 *M* NaCl, 0.01 *M* HCl, and 0.003 *M* quinine hydrochloride. Since spontaneous activity varies from unit to unit, a response criterion of 1.5 times resting activity was employed. In 19 of the 43 fibers responses to all four of the basic tastes exceeded this response criterion; in 11 fibers, 3 did so; in 7, two; in 1, one. In 5 fibers none of the responses reached criterion. Multiple sensitivities to three or four of the four tastes, therefore, occurred in 30 of the 43 fibers (see column A in Table II). Column B shows the numbers to be expected if the four sensitivities were independent of each other and combined in fibers at random. The proportions of fibers responding to the test stimuli were as follows: 0.79 to sucrose, 0.86 to NaCl, 0.70 to HCl, and 0.53 to quinine. These proportions were used in determining the predicted frequencies. The obtained values deviate from those predicted by random association, but this analysis is addressed only to whether or not a response occurs (reaches a criterion) and does not discriminate among responses of different size.

Each of the response profiles in Figs. 5 and 6 shows that one of the test stimuli will yield a highest frequency of response. Therefore, it is possible to classify units by the stimulus that elicits the largest response; that is, by its

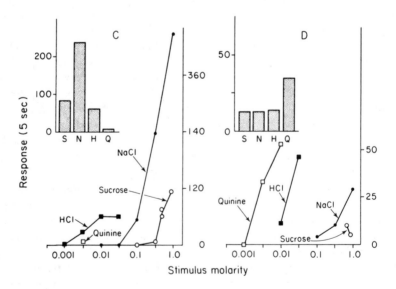

FIG. 6. (C and D) Same as Fig. 5 for two other units. Note lower scale values in (D).

TABLE II
DISTRIBUTIONS OF SENSITIVITIES
TO THE FOUR BASIC TASTE STIMULI IN 43 FIBERS

	Number of fibers		
Number of responses to basic tastes	A (criterion: 1.5 times resting)	B (A predicted from random combination)	C (criterion: best stimulus)
0	5	0.2	5
1	1	2.4	25
2	7	10.6	9
3	11	18.9	3
4	19	10.9	1

"best" stimulus. But to ensure that the "best" stimulus was considerably more effective than the others, an arbitrary criterion was adopted which required that the best stimulus frequency be at least double the frequency of responses to each of the other three stimuli; otherwise, the unit was designated as multiple. Using this method, 25 of the 43 units could unequivocally be classified by their best stimulus: 11 sucrose-best, 6 NaCl-best, 5 HCl-best, and 3 quinine-best. The responses of 5 units did not exceed the initial response criterion of 1.5 times resting level to any of the basic tastes. Thirteen units showed multiple sensitivity; that is, the largest response was not double the second largest (2 best stimuli), nor the second and third largest (3 best stimuli), nor twice any of the other three responses (4 best stimuli).

Figure 7 illustrates the variation found among the "best" stimulus contours. Line diagrams are used instead of bar graphs so that the response patterns of the several units across stimuli can be more easily followed. All acid-, salt-, and quinine-best units are shown, but only 6 of the 11 sucrose-best units and 8 of the 13 multiple units are shown to reduce confusion in the figures. The sucrose-best contours were arranged in order of size of response to sucrose, and every other unit was selected for representation in the figure. The omitted contours are very much like those depicted. Of the 13 multiple responders, the 6 with the largest responses and 2 representative weaker responders with flat contours are depicted. The 4 omitted contours are for units that did not discharge at rates greater than 50 impulses in 5 seconds to any of the 4 stimuli and yielded flat contours close to the baseline. Of the 8 multiple units shown, 5 responded best to 2 stimuli, 2 to 3 stimuli, and 1 to all 4 stimuli. A multiple contour does not necessarily reflect low absolute frequencies of response, but the converse is true; response frequencies of

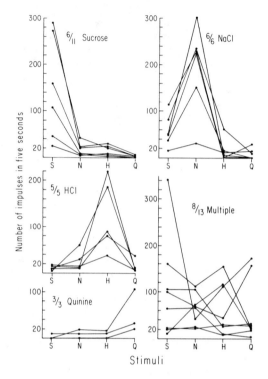

FIG. 7. Composite graph of single-unit response contours of the four stimulus classes responding best to sucrose, NaCl, HCl, quinine, respectively, and one multiple response class.

lesser absolute magnitude show less peaking and result in flatter contours. Column C in Table II gives the number of fibers having zero, one, two, three, or four "best" stimuli.

B. RESPONSES TO WATER

Responses to water after prior rinsing with water were observed in the total nerve (see Fig. 1) and in single fibers, but their magnitudes fluctuated markedly depending upon an apparent priming by the prior taste stimulus, even after several intervening water rinses. In fact, the response to water appeared at its greatest magnitude and with greatest consistency after priming by HCl. Accordingly, the response to water was systematically examined after 5–10 seconds of taste stimulation, at which time the taste response had adapted to a steady level of discharge. An increment of 5 more impulses per second above this steady-state level upon the application of water was defined as a water response.

Of 52 single fibers so analyzed, 24 gave no water response, 28 did so. Table III gives a tabulation of the 28 fibers responding to water as distributed among best stimulus classes and in terms of that basic stimulus which primed the largest water response. In 12 of the 28, water responses exceeded the response to any of the four basic taste stimuli. All classes of fibers showed some water responses. Eight of the 10 (80%) acid-best fibers gave the greatest proportion of water responders of any group. Salt, sucrose, and quinine best fibers followed in that order: 61%, 44%, and 33%, respectively. However, there is a clearer relation to the priming stimulus. The largest response to water in 19 of the 28 water responders was primed by HCl. Sucrose and quinine sometimes primed the largest water response of a fiber, but NaCl never did so. Therefore, there are different kinds of water responses. They are contingent responses, dependent upon what had been on the tongue previously.

C. RESPONSES TO SUGARS

1. Whole Nerve Response

The median magnitude of responses of 9 squirrel monkey chorda tympani nerves to three monosaccharides and three disaccharides yield the following order of effectiveness: fructose > sucrose > maltose > lactose > galactose > dextrose (Fig. 3). There is, however, considerable overlap among individual nerve responses to the last four sugars (note the interquartile ranges). The

TABLE III

DISTRIBUTION OF RESPONSES TO WATER
FOLLOWING THE FOUR BASIC TASTE STIMULI

Best taste stimulus	Largest water response after priming with				Number of water responders	Number of total fibers	% Water responders
	Sucrose	NaCl	HCl	Quinine			
Sucrose	2	0	7	1	10	23	61
NaCl	1	0	5	2	8	13	44
HCl	1	0	6	1	8	10	80
Quinine	1	0	1	0	2	6	33
	5	0	19	4	28	52	

relation fructose > sucrose > dextrose, however, is a consistent and reliable seriation that appeared in most total nerve preparations.

2. Single-Fiber Analysis

Single-fiber analysis, however, shows that individual nerve fibers responsive to sugars do not always show the same seriation. Some units respond more actively to sucrose, some to fructose, whereas the response to dextrose is usually the lowest of the three. In our sample, there were 31 cases where sucrose and fructose were both tested. In the 11 fibers where sucrose was the best stimulus (the sucrose response being twice the response to acid, salt, or quinine), the sucrose response exceeded the response to fructose in all cases (mean 5-second sucrose response: 117.8 impulses; mean fructose response: 88 impulses). Where NaCl was the best stimulus, the response to fructose exceeded the response to sucrose in 5 of 6 cases (mean sucrose response: 58.0 impulses; mean fructose response: 111.7 impulses). Among 5 other fibers in the sample, 2 were quinine-best, and 3 acid-best. The sucrose response was greater in 2 of these fibers, and the fructose greater in the other 3 cases (mean sucrose response: 14.0 impulses; mean fructose response: 18.2 impulses). Seven of the remaining fibers were multiple types, and 2 showed no response to any of the four basic tastes. Of the multiple types, 4 responded better to fructose, 2 to sucrose, and 1 equally to the two sugars. The relation, sucrose > fructose thus occurs in fibers primarily responsive to sugars, and fructose > sucrose is typical of those predominantly sensitive to salts.

In 8 instances of sugar-best and 5 of salt-best units, responses were obtained to all six sugars as well as the four basic tastes and NH_4Cl. Figure 8 is a more extended best stimulus plot: Fig. 8A shows the responses of the salt-best (N) and 8B the sucrose-best (S) fibers. Although there are variations in the exact shape of each of the curves, they all conform to general trends of their group. In the S class all other sugars stimulate to a lesser degree than sucrose and nonsugars are relatively ineffective. The N class, on the other hand, is maximally responsive to the salts, but each fiber does respond to sugars, with fructose the most effective and all others eliciting smaller responses except in one preparation, where response to lactose exceeds that to fructose. Thus, fibers that respond better to sugars are more sensitive to sucrose than to fructose, but fibers that respond better to salts than to sugars are more sensitive to fructose than to sucrose.

D. INTERRELATIONS AMONG SUGARS AND OTHER STIMULI

Following Erickson's (1963) lead, Pearson correlation coefficients were calculated for squirrel monkey chorda tympani fiber responses to all stimulus

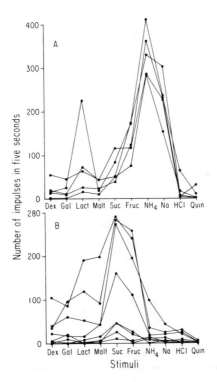

FIG. 8. (A) Expanded best stimulus contours for N (salt best) fibers. Sugars are arranged from right to left in order of increasing average magnitude of response to peak NH₄ Cl response. NaCl, HCl, and quinine are arranged as in Fig. 7. (B) Same for S (sucrose-best) group.

pairs. Figure 9 is a scatter-plot for responses to $0.3\,M$ NaCl and $0.3\,M$ NH₄Cl. Each point represents a particular unit's response to each of the two stimuli. The high positive correlation coefficient of $+0.94$ shows that the two salts stimulate the same group of units. As is seen in the response profiles in Fig. 8, the ammonium salt tends to elicit a higher frequency of discharge than NaCl, which is shown by the slope of the best-fit line through the points ($Y = 8.48 + 1.27X$). This corresponds to the higher overall chorda tympani response to NH₄Cl.

Table IV is the correlation matrix for all pairs of the stimuli used. Several points can be made. First, none of the basic taste stimuli are correlated with each other. Second, sucrose and fructose, indeed all sugars, are significantly correlated with each other. Third, sensitivities to the two salts are highly correlated and both salts are significantly correlated with only one of the six sugars: fructose.

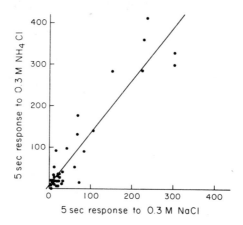

FIG. 9. Scattergram and correlation of response magnitudes of NaCl versus NH_4Cl. Each dot represents one single fiber preparation responding to both salts. $r = +0.94$; $Y = 8.48 + 1.27 X$.

TABLE IV

PEARSON CORRELATION COEFFICIENTS AMONG RESPONSES TO ALL
STIMULUS PAIRS

	Fructose	Maltose	Lactose	Dextrose	Galactose	NaCl	NH_4Cl	HCl	Quinine
Sucrose	+0.86*	+0.81*	+0.56*	+0.73*	+0.79*	+0.20	+0.23	+0.08	+0.27
(*n*)	(36)	(21)	(20)	(20)	(20)	(45)	(39)	(44)	(45)
Fructose		+0.71*	+0.75*	+0.76*	+0.79*	+0.55*	+0.56*	−0.18	0.00
(*n*)		(21)	(20)	(20)	(20)	(33)	(33)	(32)	(33)
Maltose			+0.62*	+0.92*	+0.76*	−0.08	−0.06	−0.10	−0.13
(*n*)			(20)	(20)	(20)	(21)	(21)	(20)	(21)
Lactose				+0.62*	+0.58*	+0.33	+0.40	+0.07	−0.20
(*n*)				(20)	(20)	(20)	(20)	(19)	(20)
Dextrose					+0.79*	+0.08	+0.05	+0.05	−0.09
(*n*)					(20)	(20)	(20)	(19)	(20)
Galactose						−0.09	−0.10	+0.22	+0.01
(*n*)						(20)	(20)	(19)	(20)
NaCl							+0.94*	+0.04	−0.01
(*n*)							(38)	(43)	(44)
NH_4Cl								−0.06	+0.07
(*n*)								(36)	(37)
HCl									+0.23
(*n*)									(44)

*$p < 0.01$.

IV. Discussion

The taste sensitivity of the chorda tympani of the squirrel monkey is not strikingly different from the taste sensitivity of the same nerve of such rodents as rat or hamster. The squirrel monkey chorda tympani resembles the hamster's in its well developed salt and sugar sensitivities. Its HCl sensitivity is definite but unremarkable and its quinine sensitivity is moderate. An analysis of the multiple sensitivities of the squirrel monkey chorda tympani fibers did not suggest the random distribution sometimes seen in rat taste nerves (Frank and Pfaffmann, 1969), but departures from random association of sensitivities had also been noted in other studies of rat and hamster chorda tympani fibers (Frank, 1973; Sato et al., 1969). The "best" stimulus classification of fibers shows no great discontinuity from rodent to squirrel monkey. Squirrel monkey taste fibers are not more specific than the hamster fibers. In fact, hamster chorda tympani fibers show less evidence of multiple sensitivity than do squirrel monkey fibers. Frank's analysis of hamster fibers required no multiple response class in order to completely categorize sensitivities of a sample of 79 units.

However, there are differences between the squirrel monkey and hamster chorda tympani. Table V compares correlations between responses to certain pairs of stimuli of the two species. In the hamster, the HCl response is significantly correlated with quinine and NaCl responses, but this is not so in the squirrel monkey. More striking is the lack of correlation between NaCl and $NH_4 Cl$ in the hamster as compared with the very strong correlation in the squirrel monkey. In the latter species a salt-best fiber is usually a $NH_4 Cl$-best fiber. In the rat these two salts are also uncorrelated ($r = +0.06$) (Erickson et al., 1965) suggesting a difference in electrolyte sensitivity mechanisms of rodent and primate. Finally, the positive correlation between fructose and both NaCl and $NH_4 Cl$ of the squirrel monkey does not occur in the hamster.

Squirrel monkey responses to water are dependent on the nature of the preceding or priming stimulus, as previously shown in rat and cat (Bartoshuk and Pfaffmann, 1965; Bartoshuk et al., 1971) and macaque monkey (Ogawa et al., 1972). Water following HCl stimulates more fibers than any other water contingency in squirrel monkey including fibers that respond best to sucrose, NaCl, HCl, and quinine. In man, water following HCl produces an intense, complex taste containing sweet, salty, and sour, as well as bitter. In fact, the best solute for the various water contingencies appears to be related to the taste quality evoked by that contingency in man with the exception of bitter water tastes. This latter may well result from the lack of quinine-best fibers in the squirrel monkey chorda tympani. This suggests that water does not produce any qualitatively new sensations, but rather that it mimics the sensations produced by conventional tastants.

TABLE V
CORRELATION COEFFICIENTS FOR SELECTED PAIRS OF HAMSTER
AND SQUIRREL MONKEY CHORDA TYMPANI FIBER RESPONSES

Stimulus pair	Hamster	Squirrel monkey	Stimulus pair	Hamster	Squirrel monkey
Sucrose, NaCl	−0.16	+0.20	HCl, quinine	+0.51*	+0.23
(*n*)	(79)	(45)	(*n*)	(79)	(44)
Sucrose, HCl	−0.24	+0.08	Sucrose, fructose	+0.80*	+0.86*
(*n*)	(79)	(44)	(*n*)	(47)	(36)
Sucrose, quinine	−0.13	+0.27	NaCl, NH₄Cl	+0.14	+0.94*
(*n*)	(79)	(45)	(*n*)	(47)	(38)
NaCl, quinine	+0.23	−0.01	NaCl, fructose	−0.18	+0.55*
(*n*)	(79)	(44)	(*n*)	(47)	(33)
NaCl, HCl	+0.49*	+0.04	NH₄Cl, fructose	+0.15	+0.56*
(*n*)	(79)	(44)	(*n*)	(46)	(33)

*$p < 0.01$.

In the early studies on the "water" fiber, Zotterman and his colleagues referred to one unitary fiber type (Cohen *et al.*, 1955; Gordon *et al.*, 1959; Zotterman, 1956). Some species (e.g., cat, dog, pig, monkey) had "water" fibers while others (e.g., man, rat) did not (Zotterman, 1956, 1971). The typical "water" fiber responded to water, HCl, and QHCl, but not to NaCl (Cohen *et al.*, 1955; Gordon *et al.*, 1959). In their experiments, they usually rinsed the tongue with Ringer's solution between stimuli. Thus they observed responses to water only from the group of fibers sensitive to water following Ringer's solution. In the early studies, the rat appeared to lack "water" fibers because the rat chorda tympani has few fibers responsive to water following NaCl while man appeared to lack "water" fibers because a distilled water rinse was used in the human studies rather than Ringer's.

In man the sweetness produced by water following HCl appears to result from stimulation of sweet receptor sites. *Gymnena sylvestre* (GS), which specifically abolishes sweetness at the receptor sites (Warren and Pfaffmann, 1959; Bartoshuk *et al.*, 1969), abolishes the sweet taste of water following HCl. In addition GS abolished both responses to sucrose itself and to water following HCl in a hamster chorda tympani fiber (Pfaffmann, 1970) and the responses to both saccharin and water following citric acid in the whole chorda tympani nerve of a human subject (Borg *et al.*, 1967). In these cases priming by acid appears to sensitize the sweet receptors to stimulation by water. It now seems likely that contingent water responses are relatively common across many species. The major difference across species seems to be in the number of fibers responsive to various contingencies.

The sugar sensitivities of the squirrel monkey appear to form a coherent group because all sugar responses are positively correlated with each other. Only one, fructose, shows a significant correlation with the salts. This requires further comment. Figures 8A and 8B show that there are at least two classes of units responsive to sugars: one (the S group) responds largely to sugars, and sucrose is the most effective sugar. The other (the N group) responds predominantly to the salts (NaCl and NH_4Cl) but also responds relatively well to sugars, but in this case fructose is more effective than sucrose or other sugars. This accounts for the positive correlation between fructose and salts. It also accounts for the larger response to fructose than sucrose of the whole nerve. The uniformly higher sucrose/fructose response ratio in the S class (mean ratio: 1.3, n = 11) contrasts with the lower sucrose/fructose ratio in N class units (mean ratio: 0.5, n = 6). The two fiber types (S and N) were both more sensitive to sucrose and fructose than the other four sugars. For most S or N type fibers stimulated with all six sugars (n = 16) sucrose and fructose yielded 28 of 32 possible ranks of 1 or 2 when responses to the six sugars were ranked from 1 to 6. The other four sugars fell into two less effective pairs: the disaccharides, maltose and lactose were usually the second most effective pair (21 of 32 possible ranks of 3 or 4), followed by the monosaccharides: galactose and dextrose as the least effective pair (22 of 32 possible ranks of 5 or 6). The exact order of effectiveness of the six sugars varied somewhat from fiber to fiber. Thus the single fiber data show the following relations:

$$S \text{ group: } S > F > M,L > D,G$$
$$N \text{ group: } F > S > M,L > D,G$$

For one exceptional N-type fiber, lactose was the most effective sugar, but the sucrose/fructose ratio was less than 1.

Our finding that fructose gave the largest chorda tympani whole nerve response of any 0.5 M sugar agrees with Andersen et al., (1962), who studied the sugar responses of the dog's chorda tympani. However, in their sample of 9 single fibers in which both sucrose and fructose were tested, fructose was more effective than sucrose in 7 instances, was equal to sucrose in 1, and less effective in 1 case. Their table does not give salt responses although they report that some sugar-sensitive fibers did respond to 0.5 M NaCl as well. One of their figures shows a unit responding to NaCl and sugars where fructose is more effective than sucrose. There are, however, species differences in the relative sensitivity of the whole chorda tympani nerve to different sugars. Where the order of effectiveness for the squirrel monkey and dog is fructose > sucrose > dextrose, the response of the whole chorda tympani of the rat (Tateda and Hidaka, 1966) shows the following order at equimolar concentrations of 1 M or less: sucrose > fructose > dextrose. Invertebrate single receptors of the flesh fly (Dethier and Hanson, 1965; Morita and Shiraishi, 1968) for concentrations below 0.3 M and butterfly (Takeda, 1961) show the order: sucrose > fructose > dextrose, whereas, for the blow fly the order is different, i.e., fructose > sucrose > dextrose.

The squirrel monkey, as a New World species, represents a distinct evolutionary line from Old World monkeys, which are closer to *Homo sapiens* (Jolly, 1972). Differences among the many monkey species might be expected. Although the single-fiber analysis on rhesus has been reported by other workers on a small number of preparations, there is evidence therein for multiple as well as specific sensitivity. A detailed quantitative and statistical analysis of a population of rhesus single units is much needed.

Tests of the relative sweetness of suprathreshold sugar solutions in man, either by matching (Cameron, 1947) or magnitude estimation (Moskowitz, 1971), show at equimolar concentrations that sucrose > fructose > maltose > lactose > dextrose > galactose; that is, sucrose > fructose > dextrose. Both these methods show sucrose sweeter than equimolar fructose (e.g., if sucrose = 0.1, the relative sweetness of fructose = 0.41 (Moskowitz, 1971)) and both are considerably sweeter than dextrose (relative sweetness = 0.19). These three sugars have been singled out because behavioral data related to their sensory effectiveness are available for the squirrel monkey. The squirrel monkey shows a stable and well defined preference for sugars over water in a typical two-bottle preference test, and the threshold concentration at which the preference is first apparent in an ascending series is sucrose > fructose > dextrose (Pfaffmann, 1970). This same order also results in operant behavior tests of relative reinforcing effectiveness (Ganchrow and Fisher, 1968). The animal will lick more rapidly and bar press at a higher rate for equimolar solutions of the sugars in the same order: sucrose > fructose > dextrose. Although one cannot operationally equate sweetness with such behavioral tests, the fact that the human infant shows a similar order in the strength of sucking and amount of these sugar solutions ingested (Desor *et al.,* 1973) is presumptive evidence of a correspondence between sweetness and preference, instrumental, and consummatory behavior.

At the very least, one correspondence seems clear. The order of effectiveness of only one class of sugar responsive fiber, the S fiber, correlates with effectiveness in behavioral situations. This is not true for the order of sugar effectiveness in the N fibers or in the total chorda tympani response. This suggests that there are two classes of sugar responsive fibers which signal different information to the CNS. Classifying a taste fiber by its best stimulus may indeed designate its functional modality or the quality it mediates; thus the "sugar-best" fibers would signal sweetness. The N fiber which also responds to sugars, but responds better to salt, may signal saltiness or another sensory quality. Its input does not drive the sugar preference behavior.

That the best stimulus for a sense organ defines its modality or submodality is a widespread assumption in most sensory studies: witness the label "red" receptors, touch receptors, warm receptors, best frequency of auditory units, etc. Zotterman (1967) over the years, and Wang and Bernard (1969) more recently, have done the same for taste. Our data and the correlation of the relative effectiveness of sugars for the S but not the N fibers with sugar preference agree with this point of view but caution upon doing so on an *a priori* basis without testing a broad range of stimuli.

The best stimulus classification, however, does not encompass all our fibers. A multiple sensitivity group remains that is not simply made up of low responding, nondifferentiated elements. Figure 7 shows fibers that are truly multiple in sensitivity, including one with the largest sucrose response of any in our sample and also the largest quinine response. Similarly, other multiple units in the figure show large responses to two or three basic stimuli. Some of the multiple units are low responders, but among the specific taste fiber groups there are also low responders. As noted in the introduction, multiple taste sensitivity does not appear to result from branching of afferent terminals to taste cells or taste buds of differing chemical sensitivity. The individual sense cells in a taste bud have heterogeneous sensitivities and respond to more than one basic taste to varying degrees in varying combinations (Kimura and Beidler, 1961; Sato and Ozeki, 1972; Sato, 1972). This heterogeneity, it can be said, carries over to the single afferent fibers. Afferent fiber branching may determine or change the relative proportions of the basic sensitivities, however.

The normal 7-day turnover of sense cells in the taste bud (Beidler and Smallman, 1965) presumably is associated with repeated making and breaking of afferent nerve–sense cell junctions. In this process, failure of all branches to make contact only with cells that match the parent fiber's chemical sensitivity might occur, leading to accidental multiple sensitivity. Such mismatching would make the system indiscriminate and "noisy." We do not think multiple sensitivity is a matching failure, but rather it provides a sensitivity pattern that could indeed serve a discriminatory function. Kawamura *et al.*, (1969), for example, attributed the "astringent" taste to multiple taste fibers which responded to 3% NaCl, 3% tartaric acid, 30% sucrose, 2% quinine, 5% tannic acid, and in one case to tartaric acid, quinine, and tannic acid. Application of 5% tannic acid not only stimulated this group of fibers but reduced their sensitivity to a second application of tannic acid and to the basic taste stimuli. Endings specific to only one basic taste, such as tartaric acid, neither responded to tannic acid nor were suppressed following tannic acid treatment. Quinine-specific or NaCl-specific fibers similarly were insensitive to and unaffected by tannic acid. Mechanosensitive and temperature sensitive endings in the tongue were not responsive to a 20% tannic acid solution. These authors conclude that such multiple taste fibers mediated the astringent taste.

In earlier reports from our own and other laboratories (Cohen *et al.*, 1955; Erickson *et al.*, 1965; Pfaffmann, 1941), the concept of across-fiber patterning has been invoked to resolve the problem of equivocal signal from fibers with multiple sensitivity. Where two or more stimuli of widely different taste quality activate any one receptor–fiber unit, the information from that unit by itself would be equivocal for these two stimuli. Such ambiguity could be resolved if an input in another parallel channel were simultaneously available for comparison. For example, in Fig. 5 either 1.0 M NaCl or 0.2 M sucrose will elicit a discharge of 120 impulses in fiber B. The uncertainty as to which of these is the actual stimulus can be resolved by comparing the discharge in A with that in B. Solving graphically, we find that 0.2 M sucrose arouses 60 impulses, 1.0 NaCl arouses 370 impulses (see Table VI). The relative ratio of A to B holds not only for these specific concentrations, but across the entire concentration range of both stimuli. Thus the relative activity in two or more parallel inputs could resolve the uncertainty of input coding as proposed by Pfaffmann (1941) and Erickson *et al.*, (1965). However, there is another equally logical possibility that each unit represents a labeled line which signals its unique quality whenever and however it is stimulated. The response functions of Fig. 5 define their best stimulus, *A* a salt-labeled line, *B* a sweet-labeled line. A 0.3 M or 1.0 M NaCl solution strong enough to stimulate B would, at the same time, drive A at from 300 to 350 impulses so that the input from A would predominate and lead to a sensation of saltiness. Correspondingly B can be fully activated only by sugar. We assume that dominant activity in any one set of labeled lines arouses its dominant sensory quality.

TABLE VI

Stimulus	Impulses in		Ratio
	A	B	
0.2 Sucrose	60	120	A < B
1.0 NaCl	370	120	A > B

Such an admixture of one predominant labeled line discharge with activity in other input channels seems reasonable when we remember that many taste stimuli have side qualitites if not mixed tastes. Whereas sucrose is sweet, glucose is reported to have a tart bitter–sour component, fructose sweet plus salty. NaCl is said to be the only salt yielding a pure salty taste, but in weak concentrations it is reported to taste sweet, then salty sweet, and then pure salty at a concentration of 0.2 M. KCl is reported as sweet, bitter, bitter–salty and then salty, bitter, and sour as concentration increases (cf. Renqvist, 1919, cited in Pfaffmann *et al.*, 1971). Except in the case of the highly specific receptors, which respond to only one taste quality, across-fiber information processing may include inhibition of the less dominant activity if one of the basic taste labeled lines is to register its major quality in the CNS. Funakoshi *et al.* (1972) have reported both inhibition and activation of cortical taste neurons by gustatory stimulation.

There are many stimuli we have not tested, including many natural chemical mixtures, as in foods, which must elicit composite responses across many fibers. Dethier (1974) has recently shown this to be the case with the three specific chemoreceptors for salt, sugar, and water of the blow fly. Clear preferences are displayed by this organism among natural foods, the chemical constituents of which discharge its three receptors to varying degrees so that a differential discharge pattern across fibers is elicited. Thus the well-known labeled line specificity may combine in an across-fiber pattern in the blow fly. Although specificity revealed by the best stimulus in the mammal may not be as sharp as that of blow fly receptors, we believe something of the same kind characterizes the vertebrate taste system. Information processing by means of both specific receptors and across fiber patterning can both occur simultaneously and are not incompatible.

Overall, we conclude that in mammals multiple sensitivity to taste stimuli clusters around certain modalities or labeled lines as revealed by the quality of their "best" stimulus. Two-thirds of our sample of taste units fall readily into one of the four classic taste categories with a peak at one basic taste stimulus. "Side bands" around such peaks produce a certain degree of multiple sensitivity. One-third of the responsive fibers, however, cannot be classified by a single "best stimulus" but appear to have broad multiple sensitivity.

V. Conclusions

1. Squirrel monkey taste system is not obviously more specific than rodent peripheral fiber taste systems.

2. Two-thirds of fibers can be classified into 4 classes, with the most effective or "best stimulus" as sugar, salt, acid, or quinine; but other basic

tastes may stimulate within each class to a lesser degree in a manner analogous to side bands of auditory single units. However, one-third of the units show a broader multiple sensitivity.

3. Response to water is not a unique sensitivity but occurs in 54% of the fibers and is primed by prior exposure or adaptation to taste stimuli, especially HCl.

4. Analysis of units responding to sugars reveals two classes. The S class is responsive to mono- and disaccharides, and relatively insensitive to other basic stimuli, with a characteristic response profile in which sucrose (S) is more effective than fructose (F), i.e., the S/F ratio is greater than 1.0. The N class, primarily reactive to salts is less so to sugars, with an S/F ratio of less than 1.0.

5. Behavioral and psychophysical evidence is discussed which correlates the function of the S class, not the N class, with preference behavior and reinforcement suggesting that the S class of fiber, but not the N class, signals sugar or "sweet" to the CNS as a labeled line.

6. Processing gustatory information by relatively specific classes of receptors with afferent labeled lines and across fiber patterning does not involve incompatible principles. Both may operate concurrently to extend the variety and range of discrimination.

Acknowledgments

Some of the total nerve recordings data derive from an unpublished thesis by T. C. Snell for the degree of Master of Science, Brown University, 1965. A preliminary account of the squirrel monkey single-unit data was given in a symposium at the Eastern Psychological Association (1973) and reported briefly in *Chemical Senses and Flavor* (Frank, 1974; Pfaffmann, 1974).

This research was supported by Grant Nos. GB-4198 and GB-25001 from the National Science Foundation.

Addendum

Since this paper was prepared, Professor M. Sato (1975) has reported that single taste units of macaque monkeys show greater specificity than do squirrel monkey units.

References

Andersen, H. T., Funakoshi, M., and Zotterman, Y. (1962). Electrophysiological investigation of the gustatory effect of various biological sugars. *Acta Physiologica Scandinavica* **56**, 362–375.

Andersson, B., Landgren, S., Olsson, L., and Zotterman, Y. (1950). The sweet taste fibres of the dog. *Acta Physiologica Scandinavica* 21, 105–119.

Bartoshuk, L. M., and Pfaffmann, C. (1965). Effects of pretreatment on the water taste response in cat and rat. *Federation Proceedings, Federation of American Societies for Experimental Biology* 24, 207.

Bartoshuk, L. M., Dateo, G. P., Vandenbelt, D. J., Buttrick, R. L., and Long, L. (1969). Effects of Gymnema sylvestre and Synsepalum dulcificum on taste in man. *In* "Olfaction and Taste III" (C. Pfaffmann, ed.), pp. 436–444. Rockefeller Univ. Press, New York.

Bartoshuk, L. M., Harned, M. A., and Parks, L. H. (1971). Taste of water in the cat: Effects on sucrose preference. *Science* 171, 699–701.

Beidler, L. M. (1953). Properties of chemoreceptors of tongue of rat. *Journal of Neurophysiology* 16, 595–607.

Beidler, L. M. (1969). Innervation of rat fungiform papilla. In "Olfaction and Taste III" (C. Pfaffmann, ed.), pp. 352–369. Rockefeller Univ. Press, New York.

Beidler, L. M., and Smallman, R. L. (1965). Renewal of cells within taste buds. *Journal of Cell Biology* 27, 263–272.

Beidler, L. M., Fishman, I. Y., and Hardiman, C. W. (1955). Species differences in taste responses. *American Journal of Physiology* 181, 234–239.

Bernard, R. A. (1964). An electrophysiological study of taste reception in peripheral nerves of the calf. *American Journal of Physiology* 206, 827–835.

Borg, G., Diamant, H., Oakley, B., Ström, L., and Zotterman, Y. (1967). A comparative study of neural and psychophysical responses to gustatory stimuli. *In* "Olfaction and Taste II" (T. Hayashi, ed.), pp. 253–264. Pergamon, Oxford.

Bradley, R. M., and Mistretta, C. M. (1972). The morphological and functional development of fetal gustatory receptors. *In* "Oral Physiology" (N. Emmelin and Y. Zotterman, eds.), pp. 239–253. Pergamon, Oxford.

Cameron, A. T. (1947). The taste sense and the relative sweetness of sugars and other sweet substances. *Sugar Research Foundation, Scientific Report Series* 9, 46.

Cohen, M. J., Hagiwara, S., and Zotterman, Y. (1955). The response spectrum of taste fibres in the cat. A single fibre analysis. *Acta Physiologica Scandinavica* 33, 316–332.

Desor, J. A., Maller, O., and Turner, R. E. (1973). Taste in acceptance of sugars by human infants. *Journal of Comparative and Physiological Psychology* 84, 496–501.

Dethier, V. G. (1974). The specificity of the labellar chemoreceptors of the blowfly and the response to natural foods. *Journal of Insect Physiology* 20, 1859–1869.

Dethier, V. G., and Hanson, F. E. (1965). Taste papillae of the blowfly. *Journal of Cellular and Comparative Physiology* 65, 93–100.

Erickson, R. P. (1963). Sensory neural patterns and gustation. *In* "Olfaction and Taste" (Y. Zotterman, ed.), Vol. 1, pp. 205–213. Pergamon, Oxford.

Erickson, R. P., Doetsch, G. S., and Marshall, D. A. (1965). The gustatory neural response function. *Journal of General Physiology* 49, 247–263.

Fishman, I. Y. (1959). Gustatory impulses of the white faced-ringtail monkey. *Federation Proceedings, Federation of American Societies for Experimental Biology* 18, 45.

Frank, M. (1973). An analysis of hamster afferent taste nerve response functions. *Journal of General Physiology* 61, 588–618.

Frank, M. (1974). The classification of mammalian afferent taste nerve fibers. *Chemical Senses and Flavor* 1, 53–60.

Frank, M., and Pfaffmann, C. (1969). Taste nerve fibers: A random distribution of sensitivities to four tastes. *Science* 164, 1183–1185.

Funakoshi, M., Kasahara, Y., and Kawamura, Y. (1972). Taste coding and central perception. *In* "Olfaction and Taste IV" (D. Schneider, ed.), pp. 336–342. Wiss. Verlagsges. MBH, Stuttgart.

Ganchrow, J., and Fisher, G. L. (1968). Two behavioral measures of the squirrel monkey's (*Saimiri sciureus*) taste for four concentrations of five sugars. *Psychological Reports* **22**, 503–511.

Gordon, G., Kitchell, R., Ström, L., and Zotterman, Y. (1959). The response pattern of taste fibers in the chorda tympani of the monkey. *Acta Physiologica Scandinavica* **46**, 119–132.

Jolly, A. (1972). "The Evolution of Primate Behavior." Macmillan, New York.

Kawamura, Y., Funakoshi, M., Kasahara, Y., and Yamamoto, T. (1969). A neurophysiological study on astringent taste. *Japanese Journal of Physiology* **19**, 851–865.

Kimura, L., and Beidler, L. M. (1961). Microelectrode study of taste receptors of rat and hamster. *Journal of Cellular and Comparative Physiology* **58**, 131–139.

Kitchell, R. (1963). Comparative anatomical and physiological studies of gustatory mechanisms. *In* "Olfaction and Taste" (Y. Zotterman, ed.), Vol. 1, pp. 235–255. Pergamon, Oxford.

Morita, H., and Shiraishi, A. (1968). Stimulation of the labellar sugar receptor of the fleshfly by mono- and disaccharides. *Journal of General Physiology* **52**, 559–583.

Moskowitz, H. R. (1971). The sweetness and pleasantness of sugars. *American Journal of Psychology* **84**, 387–406.

Oakley, B. (1972). The role of taste neurons in the control of the structure and chemical specificity of mammalian taste receptors. *In* "Olfaction and Taste IV" (D. Schneider, ed.), pp. 63–69. Wiss. Verlagsges. MBH, Stuttgart.

Ogawa, H., Yamashita, S., Noma, A., and Sato, M. (1972). Taste responses in the macaque monkey chorda tympani. *Physiology and Behavior* **9**, 325–331.

Pfaffmann, C. (1941). Gustatory afferent impulses. *Journal of Cellular and Comparative Physiology* **17**, 243–258.

Pfaffmann, C. (1955). Gustatory nerve impulses in rat, cat and rabbit. *Journal of Neurophysiology* **18**, 429–440.

Pfaffmann, C. (1970). Physiological and behavioural processes of the sense of taste. *Taste and Smell in Vertebrates, Ciba Foundation Symposium,* pp. 31–50.

Pfaffmann, C. (1974). Specificity of the sweet receptors of the squirrel monkey. *Chemical Senses and Flavor* **1**, 61–67.

Pfaffmann, C., Bartoshuk, L. M., and McBurney, D. H. (1971). Taste psychophysics. In "Handbook of Sensory Physiology" (L. M. Beidler, ed.), Vol. IV, Chemical Senses, Part 2, pp. 75–101, Springer-Verlag, Berlin, Heidelberg, New York.

Sato, M. (1975). Response characteristics of taste nerve fibers in macaque monkeys: Comparison with those in rats and hamsters. *In* "Olfaction and Taste, Vol. V" (D. Denton & J. Coghlan, eds.), pp. 23–26, Academic Press, New York.

Sato, M., and Ozeki, M. (1972). Transduction of stimuli into electrical events at the gustatory cell membrane in the rat fungiform papillae. *In* "Olfaction and Taste IV" (D. Schneider, ed.), pp. 252–258. Wiss. Verlagsges. MBH, Stuttgart.

Sato, M., Yamahita, S., and Ogawa, M. (1969). Afferent specificity in taste. *In* "Olfaction and Taste III" (C. Pfaffmann, ed.), pp. 470–487. Rockefeller Univ. Press, New York.

Sato, T. (1972). The electrical response of the frog taste cells as studied with the intracellular microelectrode. *In* "Olfaction and Taste IV" (D. Schneider, ed.), pp. 245–251. Wiss. Verlagsges. MBH, Stuttgart.

Takeda, K. (1961). The nature of impulses of single tarsal chemoreceptors in the butterfly, Vanessa indica. *Journal of Cellular and Comparative Physiology* **54**, 171–176.

Tateda, H., and Hidaka, I. (1966). Taste responses to sweet substances in rat. *Memoirs of the Faculty of Science, Kyushu University, Series E* **4**, 137–149.

Wang, M. A., and Bernard, R. A. (1969). Characterization and interaction of taste responses in chorda tympani fibers of the cat. *Brain Research* **15**, 567–570.

Warren, R. M., and Pfaffmann, C. (1959). Suppression of sweet sensitivity by potassium gymnemate. *Journal of Applied Physiology* **14**, 40–42.

Zotterman, Y. (1956). Species differences in the water taste. *Acta Physiologica Scandinavica* **37**, 60–70.

Zotterman, Y. (1967). The neural mechanism of taste. *Progress in Brain Research* **23**, 139–154.

Zotterman, Y. (1971). The recording of the electrical response from human taste nerves. *In* "Handbook of Sensory Physiology. Vol. IV: Chemical Senses" (L. M. Beidler, ed.), pp. 102–115. Springer-Verlag, Berlin.

Vision and the Visual System: A Bird's-Eye View

William Hodos

Department of Psychology,
University of Maryland,
College Park, Maryland

Consider the auk;
Becoming extinct because he forgot how to fly and could only walk.

Consider man, who may well become extinct
Because he forgot how to walk and learned how to fly before he thought.[1]

OGDEN NASH

I. Introduction

The study of vision and the visual system has been dominated by studies of mammals, mainly rats, cats, and rhesus monkeys. A principal cause of this concentration of effort was a belief that by studying these more or less close relatives of man we would gain a better understanding of the human visual system. Although this rationale has some merit, it is more an expression of hope than a statement of scientific reality. In this paper, I will attempt to point out some of the shortcomings of this approach and I will suggest some alternative approaches that offer additional avenues of attack on the general

[1] Copyright 1950 by Ogden Nash. From *Verses from 1929 on,* by Ogden Nash, by permission of Little, Brown and Co.

29

question of how the brain processes visual information and what the study of nonmammals may tell us about the human brain. I will begin with a discussion of the evolution of the visual system and will point out the various considerations that have led me to my present research on the avian visual system.

The rationale behind this project is that of the comparative method. Although I am not at present conducting comparative studies in the strict sense in my laboratory, I lean heavily on comparative data from other laboratories. The comparative method has two purposes: (1) to reconstruct evolutionary history; (2) to understand the relationship between structure and function. These two purposes are not mutually exclusive, but are complementary since changes in the relationship between structure and function are the basis of evolutionary trends. The power of the comparative method is that it can reveal relationships between structure and function that often cannot be detected by the continual study of a single species.

Vision is probably more important to birds than to any other class of vertebrates. Indeed, the optic tectum and other regions of the visual system of most birds are paragons of morphological differentiation and specialization. A dictum of the comparative approach is that if you want to know how a system works, study an animal that is highly specialized for the use of that system. Birds certainly qualify as visual specialists.

At the outset of this work I made the assumption that the avian nervous system was simpler and therefore would yield more readily to investigation. This was quickly proved wrong. The behavioral and anatomical studies to be described have shown that the avian visual system is not only as complicated as that of mammals, but contains many striking parallels to the mammalian visual system. The single-unit recording studies to be described also show a parallel to mammalian visual neurophysiology. These parallels do not appear to be coincidental, but most likely represent the common heritage of birds and mammals from their reptilian ancestors. This common heritage and common structural and functional arrangement strongly suggest common modes of information processing.

II. The Evolution of the Visual System

For the majority of vertebrates, vision is an important, if not the most important, distance sense. Consequently, for those interested in the evolution of the brain and behavior, the visual system has always held a particular fascination. Comparative studies of anatomy, physiology, and behavior involving vision have given rise to considerable speculation about the organization of the visual system in the earliest vertebrates and how it has become modified during the past half billion years. Until fairly recently, attempts at describing the evolutionary history of the visual system have been seriously handicapped by three main obstacles: (1) erroneous notions about the phylogenetic (i.e., genealogical) relationships among the various animals being compared, (2) lack of uniformity in selecting comparable features of the various animals for comparison, (3) lack of powerful experimental tools. This unfortunate combination of circumstance has plagued not only behaviorally oriented workers, but anatomists and physiologists as well. These handicaps have had a powerful effect on the development of evolutionary thought since they are intimately related to the fundamental questions involved in reconstructing evolutionary history: Which animals shall be compared? Which features of these animals shall be compared? Which techniques shall we use to compare these features? Recently, neural and behavioral scientists have shown increasing sophistication in their treatment of phyletic and comparative data. Moreover, a number of technical developments in these fields have yielded a rich store of valuable data.

A. SELECTION OF ANIMALS

The difficulties involved in selecting living animals to represent ancestral forms have recently been discussed by Hodos and Campbell (1969) and Hodos (1970a). These papers point out that many attempts to represent phylogenetic trends have been largely meaningless because the animals compared have not been descendants of a common evolutionary lineage. For example, rats, cats, and monkeys are often compared in order to point out evolutionary trends leading to man. Unfortunately, for such comparisons, no rodent was ever the ancestor of any carnivore and no carnivore was ever the ancestor of any primate. Each of these groups descended independently from ancestral insectivores. The insectivore line (represented today by moles, shrews, and hedgehogs) forms the central stem of the mammalian evolutionary tree from which all orders of placental mammals radiated (Romer, 1966, 1968b). Although all primates presumably radiated from a single insectivore stock, one cannot use just any primate to represent an ancestral condition in the human lineage. New World monkeys, for example, have led a long and independent existence from the Old World monkeys, which share a more immediate common lineage with the homonids (Simons, 1969). Even among our fairly close primate relatives, we must exercise caution in the choice of animals. For example, the rhesus monkey, which is so often used as a "stand-in" for humans in laboratory research, may not be the most appropriate animal in every circumstance. The differences in organization within the dorsal division of the lateral geniculate of various primates described by Kaas et al. (1972) may have functional significance and could affect the choice of primates. A strategy for dealing with such differences would be the study of a number of species of Old World monkeys and other anthropoids in order to determine the functional role of these differences and use the results of such a study for subsequent extrapolation to man.

Even with an appreciation of evolutionary relationships, assembling animals in a "quasi-evolutionary series" is a difficult undertaking because a number of important ancestral groups have become extinct without leaving any relatively unchanged descendants. An example of an important group of mammalian ancestors that are now extinct are the therapsids (mammal-like reptiles of the Triassic and Jurassic period (Romer, 1966, 1968b; Colbert, 1965).

Another problem stems from the fact that the paleontologists and taxonomists are not in universal agreement about a number of important relationships among living organisms. For example, the origin of the living orders of amphibians and their relationship to the earliest tetrapods is still unclear (Ørvig, 1968). Without an understanding of the relationship between living amphibians and the amphibian ancestors of reptiles, birds, and mammals, we are handicapped in our attempts to reconstruct the neural and behavioral evolution of the tetrapod lineage. Some theorists, for example Herrick (1948), have placed what may be excessive emphasis on extant amphibians as tetrapod "prototypes," i.e., living representatives of the earliest tetrapods.

B. HOMOLOGY AND EQUIVALENCE

In comparative studies, any aspect of two or more organisms can be compared for any purpose. However, if the purpose of the comparison is to reconstruct evolutionary history, a number of constraints are placed on the features to be compared. A term that is often encountered in such comparisons is "homology." Recently, Campbell and Hodos (1970) have described the communication problem that exists in some areas of comparative neuroanatomy because several, quite different, definitions of homology, based on different theoretical frameworks, are currently used by neuroanatomists. The confusion is further compounded by the fact that a number of anatomists use the term homology in an ambiguous way so that the reader is unable to determine in what sense the term is used. The origin of the term "homologue" (Owen, 1843) was in the context of structural correspondence, i.e., a similarity in comparable parts of the bodies of different species. Its use was predicated upon the pre-Darwinian concept of the immutability of species. Although many systematic biologists use the term "homolog" today to refer to structures of common phyletic origin (Bock, 1967, 1969), an apparently dwindling number still cling to the original structuralist usage (Boyden, 1969). Campbell and Hodos (1970) have suggested the following definition of phyletic homology as being useful for studies of neural evolution: "Structures and other entities are homologous when they could, in principle, be traced back through a genealogical series to a stipulated common ancestral precursor irrespective of morphological similarity." They have suggested that for the sake of uniform usage, the structuralist concept of homology be subsumed under the phylogenist concept of homoplasy: "Structures or entities that are morphologically similar but cannot, in principle, be traced back to a stipulated common precursor are homoplastic." These structural similarities are regarded as representative of such evolutionary processes are convergence, parallelism, etc.

To illustrate the differences between these concepts, let me pose a question that I have often been asked: "Does a pigeon have a lateral geniculate?" The question seems straightforward, but this is deceptive. The meaning of the question and hence its answer depend very much on the nature of the definition of homology. If by the question one means, "Does the pigeon have a cell group in the thalamus that resembles the lateral geniculate of a mammal?" then the question is being couched in structural correspondence terms. Of course the lateral geniculate varies quite widely among different orders of mammals, and even within orders the degree of variation is considerable (Kaas *et al.*, 1972; Campbell, 1972). This nonuniformity therefore would produce a counterquestion: "Which mammal?" However, no matter what the reply to this counterquestion, the answer would probably be "No." A rephrasing of the question in phylogenist terms would be, "Does a pigeon have a cell group in the thalamus that has the same pattern of connections with the retina and the telencephalon, the same cell-types, the same synaptology, histochemistry, etc., as the lateral geniculate of mammals, and can this cell group be traced through a series of extant animals that reasonably represent the mammalian and avian lineages from their common reptilian stock?" The answer to this question would be that we do not yet have sufficient data, but such evidence as we have at present leads me to offer a tentative answer, "Yes." However, any patterns of connections, etc., that were found in common between birds and mammals but that could not be traced through this genealogical series would be attributed to homoplasy and would be regarded as the result of common modes of adaptation to similar environmental challenges. The process that results in such similarities is called "convergence" in remotely related animals and "parallelism" in closely related forms.

The problem of behavioral homology poses many difficult questions. However, if the term "behavioral homology" is to have any meaning in the phyletic sense, it must be related to morphological homology (Atz, 1970; Hodos, in press). Thus, only behavior that can be related directly to homologous anatomical entities should be regarded as homologous.

C. RECENT TECHNICAL ADVANCES

Behavioral scientists have made great strides in the past two decades in improved laboratory methods for the study of animal behavior (Honig, 1966; Bitterman, 1965, 1969; Stebbins, 1970). However, only very recently have the powerful techniques of neurophysiology and neuroanatomy been diverted at all from their concentration on rats, cats, and monkeys to other orders of mammals and other classes of vertebrates. These powerful techniques include the use of microelectrodes for recording from individual neurons (e.g., Gaze and Jacobson, 1962; Jacobson, 1964; Rovainen, 1967a,b; Revzin, 1970; Llinas, 1969; Granda and Yazulla, 1971), the Nauta stain for degenerating axons and its variants for degenerating axon terminals (Riss et al., 1963; Fink and Heimer, 1967; Ebbesson, 1968; Karten, 1969), and the method of autoradiographic tracing (Meier et al., 1974). No doubt we will shortly see applications of the horseradish peroxidase tracing technique to nonmammalian material. The recent application of these methods to nonmammals in conjunction with the sophisticated techniques of modern behaviorism have opened the door to a fresh, new look at behavior and brain structure in a number of interesting, but generally neglected, groups of animals. These advances raise the possibilities for a new interpretation of evolutionary trends in the development of specific neural systems and their associated behaviors.

D. THE IMPORTANCE OF BIRDS FOR UNDERSTANDING VERTEBRATE EVOLUTION

The study of the nervous system and behavior of birds is of importance to those who are interested in vertebrate evolution in general and evolution of mammals in particular. This may seem like a paradoxical assertion, considering that no bird was ever an ancestor of any mammal. However, the following brief review of mammalian origins will hopefully resolve the paradox.

As mentioned earlier, the immediate reptilian ancestors of mammals, the therapsids, have become extinct, leaving no relatively unmodified descendants. Moreover, the cotylosaurs, which were the stem reptilian group, have also left no direct descendants that have remained substantially unchanged (Colbert, 1965; Romer, 1966, 1968a,b). Therefore, in order to draw inferences about the brain or behavior of the reptilian ancestors of mammals, we must study the other living descendants of the cotylosaurs: the turtles, crocodilians, lizards, and snakes. Of these, only the turtles and crocodilians are derived fairly directly from cotylosaurs. The snakes and lizards first appear in the fossil record at about the same time as placental mammals, and their relationship to the stem reptiles is quite speculative. The importance of birds for mammalian evolution lies in the fact that they are also descended from the stem reptiles and thus can play an important role in determining which characteristics of the brain and behavior of the living turtles and crocodilians represent the ancestral reptilian characteristics and which may be the derived (i.e., specialized) characteristics of the individual reptilian groups. Characteristics that are shared by crocodilians, turtles, birds, and mammals may reasonably be assumed to have existed in the cotylosaurs, which were the common ancestral group of all of them. Furthermore, birds have developed, quite independently, a number of characteristics in common with mammals in general and primates in particular: a strong pair bond, highly developed and extended parental care, complex vocal communication, bipedalism, complex social organization, endothermism, etc. (Welty, 1963; Wallace, 1963). Thus, comparison of birds and mammals can yield rich stores of information about the mechanism of convergence in behavior and the nervous system.

E. WHICH BIRDS SHALL WE STUDY ?

In my own research, I have for the present selected pigeons for study because of some theoretical considerations (mainly, their relative lack of specialization within the Class Aves), but primarily on practical grounds. The practical considerations are that pigeons are plentiful, readily obtainable, and easily maintained. A wealth of behavioral data and neuroanatomical data on pigeons has been collected. Also compelling among the practical factors is the existence of a stereotaxic atlas of the pigeon's brain (Karten and Hodos, 1967). Unfortunately, these practical considerations can exert a strong pressure in the direction of excessive concentration on a single avian species with the result that this species comes to be regarded as "the bird," just as for many years rats served as "the mammal" in comparative studies (Lockard, 1968). On the other hand, Romer (1966) has pointed out that although birds are divided into many different orders, the differences between a hummingbird and an albatross (which are in different orders) are much less than the differences between a seal and a cat, which are both members of the Order Carnivora. This is not to suggest that all birds are the same. Obviously owls and pigeons differ greatly in their visual behavior and anatomy. Rather, the foregoing is intended to point out the limitations inherent in basing evolutionary conclusions on data from a single species. Yet, despite these limitations there is considerable merit in carrying out an in-depth analysis of a single species as a basis for determining which types of variables may be the most appropriate for investigation in later comparisons across species. Since one cannot hope to carry out an extensive series of neural and behavioral investigations in a wide variety of species in the span of a single scientific career, this approach seems to have promise as a guide to future studies, which would be aimed at determining the extent to which the findings from pigeons could be generalized to the Class Aves as a whole.

F. ANATOMY AND PHYSIOLOGY OF THE AVIAN VISUAL SYSTEM

During the past decade, the first reliable information about the avian visual system, based on modern experimental technique, became available. A series of anatomical investigations of the visual system of pigeons by Cowan *et al.* (1961), Galifret (1966), Hirschberger (1967, 1971), Karten and Nauta (1968), and Meier *et al.* (1974) have disclosed a considerable amount of information about the terminations of the optic tract. These studies indicate that the optic tract terminates in (1) the optic tectum (which was known previously), (2) a complex of nuclei in the anterior, dorsal thalamus, collectively designated nucleus opticus principalis thalami (OPT), (3) in a laminated structure lying on the lateral floor of the dorsal thalamus, the nucleus geniculatus lateralis, pars ventralis, (4) the pretectal complex (area pretectalis and nucleus lentiformis mesencephali), (5) an accessory optic nucleus: the nucleus ectomammilaris, and (6) the nucleus suprachiasmaticus hypothalami. Their terminations are presented diagrammatically in Fig. 1.

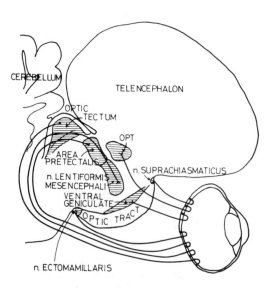

FIG. 1. Diagrammatic representation of the terminations of the optic tract in birds. Fiber pathways are indicated in solid lines. Cell groups are indicated by cross-hatching. OPT = nucleus opticus principalis thalami.

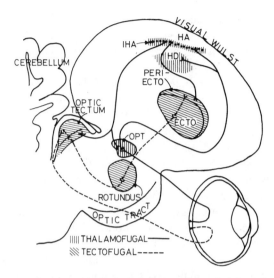

FIG. 2. Diagrammatic representation of the tectogufal and thalamofugal visual pathways. Fiber pathways are indicated by continuous and broken lines. Cell groups are indicated by cross-hatching. ECTO = ectostriatum; HA = hyperstriatum accessorium; HD = hyperstriatum dorsale; IHA = nucleus intercalatus hyperstriati accessorii; OPT = nucleus opticus principalis thalami; PERI-ECTO = peri-ectostriatal belt.

A related group of anatomical and physiological studies has charted the subsequent projections of the optic tectum and OPT (Karten and Revzin, 1966; Revzin and Karten, 1966–1967; Revzin, 1969; Karten and Hodos, 1970; Hunt and Webster, 1972; Karten et al., 1973; Meier et al., 1974). This latter series of investigations has disclosed the existence of two ascending visual pathways to the telencephalon. These pathways are represented diagrammatically in Fig. 2. The first pathway, designated the thalamofugal pathway, originates in the retina and passes to a complex of nuclei in the anterior, dorsal thalamus. This group of nuclei, the OPT, in turn, projects to a region in the medial, dorsal telencephalon designated as the "visual Wulst"[1a] by Karten et al. (1973). In pigeons, the fibers from OPT terminate mainly in a group of granule cells intercalated between the dorsal hyperstriatum (HD) and the accessory hyperstriatum (HA). This granule cell layer has been

[1a]The term "Wulst" is derived from the German der Wulst which means a bulge. In comparative neuroanatomy, the term refers to a prominent rostrocaudal protuberance along the dorsomedial aspect of the cerebral hemisphere of birds. Contained within the Wulst are such subdivisions of the telencephalon as the hyperstriatum accessorium and the hyperstriatum intercalatus superior. The visual Wulst is that region of the Wulst that is the telencephalic target of the OPT complex. For more detailed descriptions of the Wulst see Karten and Hodos (1967) and Karten et al. (1973).

designated nucleus intercalatus hyperstriati accessorii (IHA). To a lesser extent, fibers from OPT also terminate in the dorsal hyperstriatum. A comparable pathway exists in mammals and is called the geniculo-striate-cortical pathway. The visual Wulst sends efferent fibers to the optic tectum, OPT, and all other retinorecipient cell groups. The correspondence between the pigeon's thalamofugal visual pathway and the mammalian geniculo-striate-cortical pathway is further strengthened by Revzin's (1969) report that the cells of IHA have electrophysiological properties quite similar to those reported by Hubel and Wiesel (1962) for cells in the visual cortex of cats. Tempting as it might be, a conclusion that the cells of the thalamofugal pathway of pigeons are homologous to the cells of the geniculo-striate-cortical pathway of mammals as derivatives of a common cell group in ancestral reptiles is quite premature. Nevertheless, the possibility of such a relationship must be given serious consideration as a working hypothesis.

The second ascending visual pathway to the telencephalon, designated as the tectofugal pathway, passes from the retina to the optic tectum. From the tectum, a discrete fiber bundle passes to the nucleus rotundus, which is the largest and most prominent nucleus in the avian thalamus (Karten and Revzin, 1966; Revzin and Karten, 1966–1967). Fibers from nucleus rotundus terminate in the core region of the ectostriatum in the telencephalon (Karten and Hodos, 1970). The ectostriatal core probably projects to the surrounding peri-ectostriatal belt. The peri-ectostriatal belt also receives fibers from the visual Wulst. Thus, the two ascending pathways come into contact in the peri-ectostriatal belt. The target region of the efferent projections of the peri-ectostriatal belt is unknown at present.

G . EVOLUTIONARY HYPOTHESES

The optic tectum is generally conceded to be homologous with the retinorecipient layers of the mammalian superior colliculus since both seem to have been derived from the optic tectum of ancestral reptiles. Likewise a common phyletic origin of the nucleus lateralis posterior thalami of mammals and the nucleus rotundus thalami of birds is suggested by several recent lines of evidence: First, both these structures are the main thalamic recipients of the tectal efferents (Altman and Carpenter, 1961; Morest, 1965; Tarlov, 1965; Karten and Hodos, 1970; Hall and Ebner, 1970). Second, the descriptions by Schneider (1969) and Diamond and Hall (1969) of two ascending visual pathways to the telencephalon of mammals are strikingly similar to the descriptions of two ascending visual pathways to the telencephalon in birds (Karten, 1969; Karten and Hodos, 1970; Karten et al., 1973). Finally, the recent reports of a tectofugal visual pathway to the telencephalon in reptiles

(Hall and Ebner, 1970; Butler and Northcutt, 1971) add considerable strength to the suggestion that the nucleus rotundus of birds and reptiles is homologous with the nucleus lateralis posterior of mammals as derivatives of a common thalamic cell group in ancestral reptiles.

The significance of the term "striatum" as applied to the telencephalon of nonmammals requires some discussion at this point. The traditional view of the organization of the telencephalon of reptiles and birds, as described in the classic writings of Papez (1929) Ariëns Kappers et al. (1960), and Herrick (1948) is the "cortex" is virtually absent in these forms and the bulk of the cerebral mass consists of a greatly hypertrophied corpus striatum. Although various workers have used somewhat different designations for these telencephalic fields,[2] the suffix "–striatum" has been widely employed. Thus we have such subdivisions as neostriatum, hyperstriatum, paleostriatum, ectostriatum. However, the definition of cortex as a laminar arrangement of cells and fibers on the surface of the telencephalon may be too restricted a designation since the same populations of cells that are present in mammals also may be present in nonmammals, although not in a laminated arrangement (Karten, 1969; Nauta and Karten, 1970; Karten and Hodos, 1970; Zeier and Karten, 1971; Karten et al., 1973; Karten and Dubbledam, 1973). Thus, the relevant comparison may be not between all of the visual Wulst and all of striate cortex, but perhaps only between IHA and layer IV of striate cortex. If indeed much of what is currently regarded as striatum in avian and reptilian brains is found to contain populations of neurons comparable to those in specific neocortical fields, then the picture of cortical evolution in mammals would become much clearer. We would no longer have to deal with the perplexing de novo origin of the cerebral cortex in mammals. The cerebral cortex of mammals could then be seen in the context of an overall conceptual framework encompassing all amniotes and possibly anamniotes as well. This overall conception of the evolution of neocortex, as seen in the light of presently available data, is that many of the populations of neurons that are present in mammalian neocortex were present in ancestral vertebrates. The numbers of neurons in each population seem to have increased in the evolutionary line leading to birds and mammals in general and to primates in particular and the gross configurations of each population surely have changed. What has remained unchanged are their afferent and efferent relationships with other cell populations, cell types within the population, synaptology, histochemistry, and other fundamental characteristics that make each cell population a unique entity.

[2] See Karten and Hodos (1967) for a tabular comparison of the various telencephalic nomenclatures.

III. Behavioral Studies

A. EXPLORATIONS WITH COARSE DISCRIMINATIONS

Our early investigations used the discrimination of relatively coarse differences in the intensities or patterns of visual stimuli. These consisted of a 1.0
log unit difference in intensity and three pattern problems: vertical versus
horizontal bars, apex-up triangle versus apex-down triangle; and the same
triangles composed of small dots rather than solid contours. These stimuli are
shown in Fig. 3. The three pattern problems, which differed in luminous flux
by not more than 0.05 log unit, were intended to serve as a series of problems
graded in difficulty. The bars were learned at about the same rate as the
intensity problem, the solid triangles were learned more slowly, and the
dotted triangles were the most difficult. The stimuli were presented in a
conventional two-key operant conditioning chamber as shown in Fig. 4. The

FIG. 3. Stimuli used in the coarse discrimination experiments. The upper stimulus of
each pair was the positive stimulus. From Hodos and Karten (1966).

FIG. 4. Diagrammatic representation of the experimental chamber used in the coarse-discrimination experiments. From Hodos and Karten (1966).

pigeons were presented with all four problems in a quasi-random sequence 24 times per session for a total of 96 trials. A correction procedure was used. I will first discuss the effects of lesions in the tectofugal pathway, then the thalamofugal pathway, and finally the effects of combined interruption of both pathways.

Figure 5 shows the performance of three pigeons with lesions in the tectofugal pathway. These cases have been selected from our published reports (Hodos and Karten, 1966, 1970, 1974) and are typical of performance observed in these experiments. One pigeon had large bilateral lesions in the optic tectum, one had large bilateral lesions in nucleus rotundus, and one had large bilateral lesions of the ectostriatum. The left panel of each graph indicates the preoperative performance, and the right half indicates the postoperative performance. All three of these birds showed marked declines in discrimination performance to the chance level following damage to the tectofugal pathway. The deficit after tectal destruction is considerably more severe than that following lesions in the rostral components of the tectofugal pathway. Even after extensive retraining, no amelioration of the discrimination deficit occurred, as may be seen in the case shown in Fig. 5. In other cases, the birds' performance on the intensity or bars problem improved to the 90% level after prolonged retraining, but performance on the solid and dotted triangles remained at chance. Similar results were found by Jarvis (1974). The nucleus rotundus and ectostriatum lesions also show severe impairments in performance, but these impairments are milder than those following tectal lesions. The animals with these lesions were able to even-

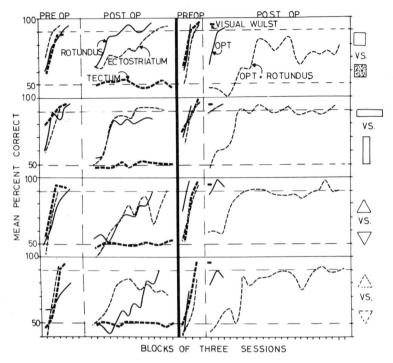

FIG. 5. Summary of the results of the coarse-discrimination experiments. The left half of the figure presents preoperative and postoperative performance curves of pigeons with representative lesions in various cell groups of the tectofugal pathway. Separate curves are shown for performance on each of the four discrimination problems. The right half of the figure presents comparable data for pigeons with lesions in the thalamofugal pathway. Also shown in the right half of the figure are data from a case with combined lesions of both tectofugal and thalamofugal pathways. OPT = nucleus opticus principalis thalami.

tually reach criterion levels of performance. A similar observation was made by Hodos and Fletcher (1974), who studied the effects of nucleus rotundus lesions on postoperative acquisition (rather than postoperative retention) and found essentially the same results. The effects of ectostriatum and nucleus rotundus lesions are very similar, and this similarity may be due to the fact that nucleus rotundus undergoes retrograde degeneration following destruction of ectostriatum. Nucleus rotundus lesions also result in deficits in color discrimination (Hodos, 1969).

    The larger deficit in performance after tectal lesions may result from several factors. First, the lesions occupy a greater volume of tissue than do those of nucleus rotundus or ectostriatum. Second, the tectum is a heterogeneous cell mass with numerous connections with other sensory systems, motor pathways, and "integrative" systems.

In contrast to the return to chance performance and slow rate of postoperative reacquisition of visual discriminations seen following lesions in the tectofugal pathway, lesions in the thalamofugal pathway result in little or no postoperative impairment. Hodos et al. (1973) reported that extensive bilateral destruction of OPT or IHA had little or no effect on performance of the intensity and pattern problems. Similar findings were reported by Pritz et al. (1970). However, combined lesions of the thalamofugal and tectofugal pathways resulted in more severe deficits than those following tectofugal pathway lesions alone (see Fig. 5). These findings are at variance with the report by Zeigler (1963) that lesions of the hyperstriatum result in intensity and pattern discrimination deficits. However, Zeigler's lesions included all the hyperstriatum, whereas those of Hodos et al. (1973) and Pritz et al. (1970) were confined to the visual Wulst. Thus, Zeigler may have destroyed the termination field of the efferents from the periectostriatal belt or possibly the target of a third visual pathway to the telencephalon.

The sparing of visual performance after thalamofugal pathway lesions is reminiscent of similar observations after lesions of the geniculo-striate-cortical pathway in a variety of mammals. Weiskrantz (1963), Hymphrey and Weiskrantz (1967), Weiskrantz and Cowey (1967), and Pasik and Pasik (1971) have reported sparing of visual discrimination performance after lesions confined to striate cortex in monkeys. Doty (1971) and Sprague et al. (1973) have reported sparing of visual function after removals of striate cortex in cats. Snyder and Diamond (1968) have described similar survival of visual discrimination after striate cortex ablation in tree shrews. The above studies also offer evidence that striate cortex lesions combined with destruction of other cell groups in the visual system do result in visual discrimination losses. A full discussion of the problem of sparing or loss after destruction of striate cortex in mammals is beyond the scope of this paper. However, these studies of mammals do indicate that sparing of vision after injury to the thalamofugal visual pathway is not a phenomenon that is unique to birds.

Recently, we have turned our attention to the other retinorecipient cell groups of the diencephalon and mesencephalon (Hodos and Bonbright, 1974). These include: (1) a bilaminate cell group located immediately ventral to nucleus rotundus and the OPT complex; (2) the nucleus geniculatus lateralis, pars ventralis (GLv), the so-called accessory optic nucleus, located medially in the floor of the mid-brain tegmentum; (3) the nucleus ectomammillaris, and a complex of nuclear groups located at the junction of the mesencephalon and diencephalon that seem to be roughly comparable to the mammalian pretectal complex; and (4) the nucleus lentiformis mesencephali and the area pretectalis. The nucleus pretectalis, located in the same general region, was not included in this group since it is a target of the optic tectum, not of the retina (Karten and Revzin, 1966). The behavioral procedure and stimuli were the same as were used to investigate the tectofugal and thalamo-fugal pathways in our earlier experiments.

The results of these studies are fairly simple to describe. Lesions of GLv or area pretectalis produced no deficit on any of the four problems. Lesions of nucleus ectomammillaris or nucleus lentiformis mesencephali resulted in slight performance decrements. Combined lesions of area pretectalis and nucleus lentiformis mesencephali resulted in an enhancement of this effect, but the impairment of performance was not nearly as severe as that seen after tectofugal pathway lesions.

An unexpected result of these studies was the effect of combined lesions of GLv and nucleus rotundus. Because Glv lies immediately ventral to nucleus rotundus for most of its rostrocaudal extent, our initial electrode trajectory was through nucleus rotundus. We knew from our previous studies that an electrode puncture of nucleus rotundus was not sufficient to produce a severe deficit. However, in a number of intended Glv cases, blood and other fluids, which could not easily penetrate the heavily myelinated fibers of the optic tract immediately ventral to Glv, followed the path of least resistance, which was back up the electrode track, and produced severe necrosis and chromatolysis in nucleus rotundus. We were quite startled to discover that these cases of extensive bilateral GLv destruction combined with massive bilateral damage to nucleus rotundus had little or no effect on discrimination performance. As may be seen in Fig. 6, such performance decrements as were observed were mainly limited to the intensity problem. This observation stands in sharp contrast to the effects described above of combined lesions of nucleus rotundus and another retinorecipient cell group, the OPT complex, in which case the effects of the combined lesions were greater than the effects of nucleus rotundus alone. The sparing of discrimination after combined lesions of nucleus rotundus and GLv is in some respects reminiscent of the findings of Sprague (1966) that lesions of the contralateral superior colliculus resulted in the restoration of visually guided behavior in cats with unilateral removal of occipital and temporal neocortex.

A further unexpected finding in the nucleus rotundus + Glv cases was that not all the cases showed this sparing of discrimination. A detailed comparison of the brains of those cases that showed the sparing and those that did not revealed that, in the pigeons that showed no sparing, the lesions had extended slightly more caudally to include the nucleus subpretectalis (SP). Figure 7 shows reconstructions of the lesions in two cases. Pigeons C-593 and C-616 have quite similar lesions, each involving roughly comparable amounts of destruction to nucleus rotundus, GLv, the dorsal thalamus, and the optic tract. The only difference that we could discern was that in C-616, which

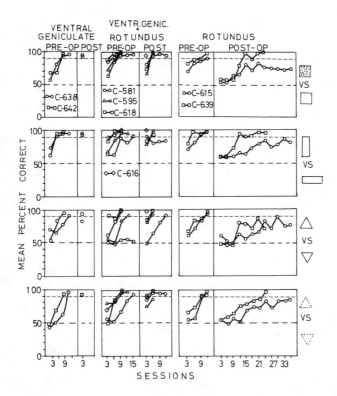

FIG. 6. Performance curves of pigeons with lesions of the ventral geniculate, nucleus rotundus, and combined lesions of the ventral geniculate and nucleus rotundus.

showed the sparing effect, the cells of SP appeared normal whereas in C-593, which did not show the sparing effect, extensive bilateral retrograde degeneration was seen in SP. Fortunately, we have knowledge of some of the anatomical relationships of SP. The cells of SP form a compact mass, situated within the fibers of the brachium of the superior colliculus as they assemble in the ventromedial quadrant of the optic lobe en route to the thalamus. Indeed the fibers of the brachium form a capsule around SP. Karten and Revzin (1966), using the Nauta method for silver impregnation of degenerating axons, reported that SP receives fibers from the optic tectum. Karten (personal communication) has confirmed this observation using the Fink–Heimer (1967) method for degenerating axon terminals. In view of these relationships, our present hypothesis is that SP is a part of the visual system. Unfortunately, nothing is known about the efferents of SP or GLv in birds. Recently, Swanson and Cowan (1973) have reported that in rats, GLv

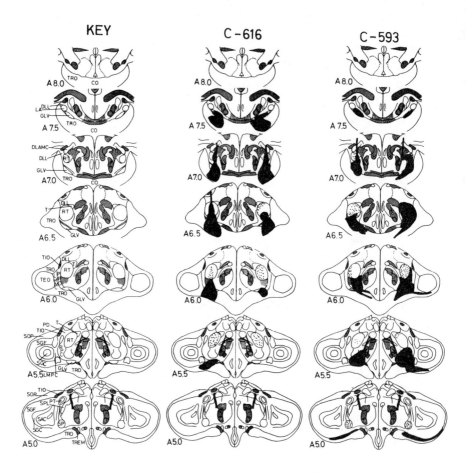

FIG. 7. Lesion reconstructions of two cases with combined lesions of nucleus rotundus and the ventral geniculate. The lesions have been reconstructed on drawings of transverse sections through the brainstem of *Columba livia*. The plates were derived from the atlas of Karten and Hodos (1967). The two cases have approximately the same amount of damage to nucleus rotundus and the ventral geniculate; however, the lesion in C-593 has resulted in retrograde degeneration in the subpretectal nucleus (plate A5.0), which is indicated with coarse stippling. At the left of the figure is a key that identifies a number of cell groups and fiber bundles in the plates. CO = chiasma opticum; DLAMC = nucleus dorsolateralis anterior thalami, pars magnocellularis; DLL = nucleus dorsolateralis anterior thalami, pars lateralis; GLV = nucleus geniculatus lateralis, pars ventralis; LA = nucleus lateralis anterior thalami; LMPC = nucleus lentiformis mesencephali, pars parvocellularis; PD = nucleus pretectalis diffusus; PPC = nucleus principalis precommisuralis; PT = nucleus pretectalis; RT = nucleus rotundus thalami; SAC = stratum album centrale; SGC = stratum griseum centrale; SGF = stratum griseum et fibrosum superficiale; SP = nucleus subpretectalis; SPL = nucleus spiriformis lateralis thalami; SOP = stratum opticum; T = nucleus triangularis thalami; TEO = tectum opticum; TIO = tractus isthmo-opticus; TREM = tractus ectomammillaris; TRO = tractus opticus.

projects to a number of other retinorecipient cell groups. Information about the efferents of GLv and SP in bird material is of crucial importance to understanding the nature of the deficit after tectofugal pathway lesions and the significance of the sparing of visual discrimination when a tectofugal lesion is combined with destruction of GLv.

A striking feature of the postoperative performance of pigeons with tectofugal pathway lesions is the eventual return to the preoperative level of performance after prolonged retraining. This apparent recovery of function occurs after all tectofugal pathway lesions, except cases with extensive destruction of the optic tectum (Hodos and Karten, 1966, 1970, 1974; Jarvis, 1974). The nature of the improvement in performance following an extensive period of postoperative retraining has been a persistent puzzle. One possible explanation might be some form of neuronal sprouting (Goodman and Horel, 1966; Moore *et al.*, 1974) and subsequent reorganization of the remainder of the visual system to process visual information differently than in an intact pigeon. Another possibility might be that the birds become more efficient in responding to the visual demands of the environment by utilizing properties of the stimuli to which an intact bird might not ordinarily attend. If lesions of the tectofugal pathway effectively increase the "noise" within the visual channel (a point to be discussed later), then the pigeons with tectofugal pathway lesions may be learning to become more efficient in detecting signals in a noisy channel. Still another line of speculation stems from our observations of the combined effects of nucleus rotundus lesions with lesions of GLv and GLv + SP. These findings suggest that the extent of sparing or loss following visual system injury may not necessarily be the result of a specific function of the injured cell group, but rather may be the result of the effects of the lesion on the total balance of excitatory and inhibitory mechanisms within the visual system as a whole. Pasik and Pasik (1971) have shown similar interactions between the effects of lesions of various components of the visual system in monkeys.

B. PSYCHOPHYSICAL STUDIES OF NORMAL PIGEONS

The finding that destruction of cells and fibers of a major visual pathway had little or no effect on visual discrimination was puzzling. One possible explanation of the sparing of visual performance is that the effects were subtle and discrimination of coarse differences in luminance or geometric patterns were not sufficiently sensitive to detect these deficits. Therefore, we decided to use psychophysical techniques to determine the limits of sensitivity of the pigeons. These limits could then be used as sensitive tests of the integrity of visual function

This approach has led to the development of psychophysical procedures for the evaluation of a variety of visual capacities: intensity differences, visual

acuity, and velocity detection. In addition to using these methods to evaluate
the effects of visual system injury, we have also used them to provide
normative data from intact subjects. The first of these procedures investigated
the ability of pigeons to detect small differences in the luminance of a visual
display (Hodos and Bonbright, 1972). Using a variation of the method of
constant stimuli, pigeons' difference thresholds for luminance were determined by requiring the birds to detect the presence or the absence of a series
of calibrated, neutral density filters in the path of a beam of light that
transilluminated a standard pigeon key. The pigeons had difference thresholds
ranging from approximately 0.05 to 0.20 log unit. The average difference
threshold was approximately 0.12 log unit. This is roughly equal to the
optical density of two microscope cover glasses.

A psychophysical analysis of discriminative capacity expresses sensory
capacity in terms of physical units, such as luminance, decibels, etc. Perhaps
greater insight into the visual world of a pigeon might be obtained from
expressing sensory capacity in psychological units. Such a transformation of
physical units into corresponding psychological units is termed "sensory
scaling." We have found in our recent experiments on pigeons (Hodos and
Bonbright, 1974) that a convenient sensory scale is one based on Fechner's
psychophysical law

$$\Delta S = k \log S$$

in which ΔS is the smallest increment in stimulus intensity that is reliably
detectable, i.e., the difference threshold, the just noticeable difference (JND);
S is the intensity of the standard stimulus against which the increments are
compared; and k is the constant of proportionality. When intensity is plotted
against the number of JNDs on semilogarithmic coordinates, Fechner's law is
represented by a straight line. Such a plot is shown in Fig. 8. In this figure,
the vertical broken line at the left represents the intensity of the dimmest
comparison stimulus. The space between these two broken lines represents
the stimulus continuum of the experiment. The point A indicates the origin
of the graph at zero JNDs. The point B represents the amount of luminance
in one JND (i.e., the size of the difference threshold). The slope of the line
AB represents the Fechner function. By extrapolating the line to the end of
the stimulus continuum to point C, we are able to specify the number of
JNDs in the contunuum. Thus the hypothetical subject shown in Fig. 8 would
have 7.5 JNDs in its continuum or, in other words, could fractionate the
intensity continuum from 58 to 318 cd/m^2 into approximately seven discriminable units.

This line of reasoning is predicated upon the assumption that a straight line
is the most appropriate description of the JND function in this intensity

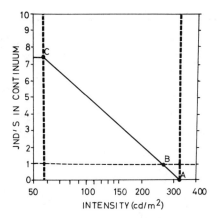

FIG. 8. Graphic representation of Fechner's law. The vertical broken lines indicate the extremes of the intensity continuum used in the intensity difference threshold study. Point A is the origin of the function at the standard. Point B is the location of the point of subjective equality [one just noticeable difference (JND) from the standard]. The slope of the Fechner function is given by the slope of line AB. Line BC is an extrapolation of the function to the end of the intensity continuum. Point C indicates the number of JNDs in the intensity continuum. From Hodos and Bonbright (1974). Copyright 1974 by the American Psychological Association. Reprinted by permission.

range. In order to determine whether the use of a linear JND scale is justified in this particular stimulus range, Sommers (1972) determined the intensity limits of the first JND as shown in Fig. 6. He then lowered the intensity of the standard by a value equivalent to the first JND and repeated the procedure to determine the value of the second JND. The standard was then lowered by a value equivalent to the second JND. This procedure was repeated for a total of five successive JNDs. The results of Sommers' experiment are shown in Fig. 9. The solid line represents the Fechner function based on the first JND. The fine broken lines represent ± 1 σ envelopes indicating the region in which the Fechner function might have fallen if the estimate of the first JND (upon which all else depended) were in error by ± 1 σ. The results suggest strongly that Fechner's law does hold within this stimulus range and that an extrapolation of the number of JNDs in the stimulus continuum from the first JND is not grossly in error.

Figure 10 shows the implications of Fechner's law for the analysis of threshold changes such as those that might follow some insult to the visual system, as in the case of surgical removal of tissue. The curve shown represents the changes in the slope of the Fechner function as a consequence of changing the magnitude of the first JND. The curve was generated empirically by plotting the number of JNDs in the stimulus continuum as a

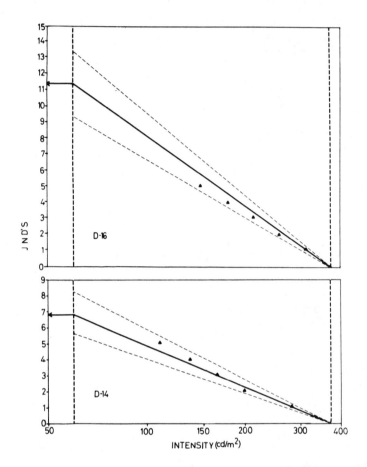

FIG. 9. Data from Sommers (1972) showing empirical Fechner functions (triangles) obtained from two pigeons. The solid lines represent the theoretical Fechner functions based on the first just noticeable difference (JND). The broken lines define boundaries within which the theoretical Fechner function would fall if the first JND were in error by ± 1 σ.

function of various magnitudes of the first JND. The curve indicates that for subjects that are very sensitive (very small difference thresholds), relatively small elevations of threshold result in rather large losses of sensory capacity (i.e., a large decrease in the number of discriminable units in the continuum). Thus, a subject that can reliably discriminate a difference of 0.05 log unit preoperatively and dropped to a difference threshold of 0.10 log unit post-operatively has dropped from a sensory capacity of 15 JNDs to one of about 7.5 JNDs. In other words, a seemingly trivial loss of 0.05 log unit actually represents a loss of about 50% of the subjects' sensory capacity. On the other hand, subjects that are relatively insensitive can tolerate much larger increases in the difference threshold without suffering such large losses in sensory capacity. For example, a subject with a preoperative difference threshold of 0.20 log unit (4 JNDs) and a postoperative difference threshold of 0.30 log unit (3 JNDs) has lost only 25% of its sensory capacity. In the study by Hodos and Bonbright (1974), the pigeons with lesions of the OPT complex lost 50–70% of their sensory capacity. However, the absolute numbers of JNDs that they retained was in the same range as the preoperative performance of some of the less sensitive birds in the experiment. Thus, a pigeon that has lost 75% of its sensory capacity, but can still fractionate the stimulus continuum into three discriminable units can discriminate "bright" from "moderately bright," "moderately bright" from "moderately dim," and "moderately dim" from "very dim." With such residual capacity, one should not be surprised to find good discrimination of relatively coarse differences in

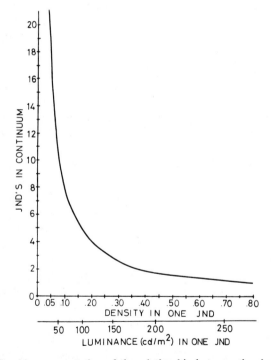

FIG. 10. Graphic representation of the relationship between the size of the first just noticeable difference (JND) and the number of JNDs in the intensity continuum of 54–318 cd/m². From Hodos and Bonbright (1974). Copyright 1974 by the American Psychological Association. Reprinted by permission.

intensity or geometric pattern. We have been very encouraged by the results of this scaling analysis and plan to use it in other psychophysical studies.

One may question whether a scale based on JNDs is the most appropriate to use, especially in view of the long history of controversy over the generality of Fechner's law. Several factors have led me to conclude that a JND scale is the most appropriate for use in studies of the effects of nervous system lesions. First, as shown by Sommers (1972) experiment, in which he empirically demonstrated that in the stimulus range that we used, Fechner's law can be used as the basis of a sensory scale. Second, techniques such as magnitude estimation generally depend upon such indicators as absolute response rate, as for example, in the procedure described by Herrnstein and Van Sommers (1962). Absolute response rates are too sensitive to the effects of motivational changes, motor effects and other nonsensory sequelae of central nervous system intervention, which could suggest a change in the sensory scale when in fact none had occurred. Finally, as Stevens (1971) indicated in his recent discussion of scaling, whichever scaling technique best satisfies the needs of the situation is the one to use.

In addition to studies of intensity resolution, we have also investigated the capacity of pigeons for spatial resolution (Hodos *et al.,* 1976a). Specifically, we used a method similar to that which we used to investigate intensity difference thresholds to measure the near-field visual acuity of pigeons. Pigeons use the central retina (corresponding to the lateral visual fields) for distance vision (beyond roughly 40 cm) and the posterior temporal retina (corresponding to the anterior visual fields) for near vision (Chard, 1939; Catania, 1964; Blough, 1971, 1973; Nye, 1973). The pigeons were required to look through a transparent pecking key at the stimulus, which was either a square-wave grating or a neutral density filter that transmitted the same amount of light as the grating. The pigeons were reinforced for pecking the right or left side-keys depending upon whether the grating or the neutral density filter had been present on that trial. After initial training, the subjects were exposed to progressively finer gratings using our variation of the method of constant stimuli (Hodos and Bonbright, 1972; Krasnegor and Hodos, 1974) in order to determine the limits of acuity. The filters and gratings were mounted in a motorized filter-wheel. Control tests indicated that the subjects were not using the vibration of the motor as a cue. We determined the visual angle subtended by the bars of each grating by using the most conservative estimate of the distance from the anterior nodal point of the eye to the surface of the target. This distance was the distance from the nodal point to the target when the beak was against the key and the key was maximally depressed. In order to measure this distance accurately, we took high-speed motion pictures (1000 frames/sec) of pigeons pecking during the discrimination of gratings from blanks. We found, to our surprise, that the pigeons closed their eyes when they pecked. Therefore, our conservative estimate of the target distance, which was approximately 43 mm, is probably meaningless since the birds' eyes are closed at that point. Therefore, we have used two other estimates of the distance to the target. One is the distance from the nodal point to the target when the bird's eyelid was half closed (approximately 51 mm). The other estimate is the distance from the nodal point to the target from the point at which the peck is initiated (approximately 62 mm). We feel that the 62 mm estimate is probably the most meaningful since the films suggest that inspection of the target occurs during the first seconds of the trial before any key-pecks occur. The pecks themselves appear to be ballistic responses that are released from the far point. Furthermore, measurements made from the films indicate that the 62 mm inspection distance is quite reliable from bird to bird. We then used the above psychophysical procedure to measure acuity over a wide luminance range. The results of this experiment are shown in Fig. 11. The data are presented in the form of decimal acuity, which is the reciprocal of the visual angle in minutes. The most intense target illuminant that the pigeons would not turn away from was approximately 1900 cd/m^2 (3.29 log cd/m^2). When this illuminant had been reduced by 4.0 log units with neutral density filters, the pigeons would not peck the key. Presumably, at this luminance, the key appeared dark to them. Thus the range of intensities that could be studied under photopic conditions spanned roughly 3.4 log units. The peak acuity (equivalent to 1.9 minutes of visual angle) occurred at 214 cd/m^2 (2.33 log cd/m^2). The slight falloff of acuity at higher luminance is probably due to glare. In a subsequent

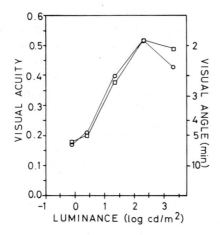

FIG. 11. Visual acuity (1/visual angle in minutes of arc) of two pigeons (□–□, C-412; o–o, D-27) as a function of the luminance of the stimulus.

study, Hodos and Leibowitz (1975) observed that when the spectral composition of the illuminant was varied, the acuity of the pigeons fell off sharply at the shorter wavelengths. Since the illuminant had been corrected for the pigeon's spectral sensitivity (Hodos, 1969) the most attractive explanation of this finding is that the birds may have fewer blue-sensitive receptors, which would result in a loss of resolution.

Another important property of a visual stimulus is its velocity. We have recently completed a long, tedious, and frustrating study of velocity detection in pigeons (Hodos *et al.,* 1976b). The behavioral procedure was essentially the same as we have used in our other psychophysical studies. The stimuli consisted of black bars on transparent 35 mm film, moving vertically in back of a transparent pecking key. The velocity of the film was controlled by a calibrated, variable-speed motor and was variable in the range 0–16 mm/sec, which corresponds to a retinal velocity of about 13 degrees of visual angle per second assuming a viewing distance of 71 mm. After five years of work, I have concluded that the technique is not readily adaptable to the study of lesion effects because pigeons are extremely difficult to train when stimulus movement is the relevant cue. Many months of training are necessary before most pigeons will discriminate either absolute or relative movement, even when the velocity difference is quite large. Moreover, subsequent psychophysical tests result in behavior that is highly variable. The results of our studies indicate that the absolute threshold for movement in pigeons is approximately 4°–5° of visual angle per second, with reference to an immobilized eye. The tip of the second hand of a man's watch (15 mm in length) at a distance of 15 cm from the eye would have a retinal velocity of 0.57°/sec. In order to produce a retinal velocity of 5°/sec, the second hand would have to make one revolution in 6.9 seconds. Since the pigeons were free to move their heads and eyes to track the target, the actual velocity of the retinal image may have been less than our estimate of 4°–5° per second. Although these velocities seem rather high, they are fairly consistent across subjects. Moreover, they do fit with Revzin's estimates of the minimal velocity that causes movement-sensitive cells in nucleus rotundus to discharge (Revzin, personal communication).

C. PSYCHOPHYSICAL STUDIES OF PIGEONS WITH VISUAL SYSTEM LESIONS

A major theme of my research during the past few years has been the use of these psychophysical techniques to investigate the same visual system structures that were explored previously using the coarse intensity and pattern discrimination tests. Most of our work to date used the intensity difference threshold technique. We have only recently completed the collection of normative data on visual acuity, and insufficient data on acuity changes after lesions are available at present. The motion detection procedure that I described is so prolonged and frustrating that I have abandoned it, for the time being, as a means of evaluating visual system functioning.

Our investigations of intensity difference threshold changes after visual system lesions have been largely confined to the thalamic components of the tectofugal and thalamofugal pathways, namely OPT and nucleus rotundus (Hodos and Bonbright, 1974). Postoperatively, the pigeons with destruction of the OPT complex showed small, but apparently permanent threshold elevations. These ranged from 0.10 to 0.15 log unit. The birds with destruction confined to nucleus rotundus showed larger initial threshold elevations, but with extended postoperative training, these deficits eventually returned to approximately the preoperative base line. A third group of pigeons, with combined destruction of OPT and nucleus rotundus, showed the largest threshold elevations, in excess of 0.80 log unit. After extended postoperative training, the performance of these birds improved to the level of the postoperative thresholds of the birds with damage of OPT alone. Thus, combined destruction of the two known visual inputs into the telencephalon produced an initial loss in sensitivity greater than either lesion alone. Moreover, after prolonged postoperative retraining, the residual deficit was equal to that of the birds with lesions confined to the OPT complex. A signal detection analysis indicated that the performance changes were largely attributable to sensory losses, not changes in response bias (Green and Swets, 1966; Hodos, 1970b). Our current speculation is that the deficits observed in these studies may represent an inability of the pigeons to filter out extraneous or irrelevant aspects of the visual world. Similar lines of speculation have been followed by Killackey and Diamond (1971) in their studies of extrastriate cortex in tree shrews, and Gross *et al.* (1971) in their investigations of foveal prestriate cortex in rhesus monkeys. In the paper by Hodos and Bonbright (1974) we speculated that a failure to filter extraneous stimuli could result in an increase in internal noise within the visual system. Such an increase in internal noise would reduce the signal-to-noise ratio and produce a decrease in detectability of stimuli that would be the same as though the noise level had remained unchanged but the signal strength had diminished.

The sensory scaling analysis provided some unexpected insights into the differences between the deficits of the birds with tectofugal lesions and those with thalamofugal lesions. Although the birds with thalamofugal lesions have smaller absolute losses in terms of JND size than birds with tectofugal lesions, their initial losses in terms of numbers of JNDs lost was the same as those of the tectofugal birds. Moreover, their permanent loss, in terms of the proportion of the preoperative sensory capacity remaining, was greater than that of the tectofugal birds. This suggests that perhaps one reason why birds with tectofugal pathway lesions show little or no deficit may be that their residual capacity is sufficient to succeed in the world of the experimental psychology laboratory. We have no idea how such animals would fare in their native environment. Ethological studies of birds with specific visual system destruction should prove to be quite valuable in assessing the role of these structures in visually guided behavior. Also of value would be the data on the ability of such birds to resolve spatial patterns, i.e., visual acuity. Other lesion targets in psychophysical studies now in progress are GLv, the pretectal complex, and the ectomammillary nucleus. In addition, we are attempting to replicate our GLv + nucleus rotundus effect using psychophysical methods.

IV. Overview and Implications

In this paper, I have discussed some of the advantages of studying birds in order to gain a better understanding of the neural substrate of visual information processing. I have also attempted to point out some of the pitfalls of the comparative and evolutionary approaches to brain function and behavior. The anatomical and physiological studies of the avian visual system that were described indicate a remarkable similarity in organization of the avian and mammalian visual systems. These similarities for the most part probably represent the common heritage of these two vertebrate classes from their reptilian ancestors.

The investigations that were carried out using coarse visual discrimination problems indicated that lesions of the tectofugal and thalamofugal pathways result in patterns of sparing and loss that are generally similar to effects obtained in comparable studies of mammals. The studies of lesions that involve more than one pathway of the visual system indicate that a failure to find a visual discrimination deficit after destruction of a retinorecipient cell group should not necessarily be interpreted as an indication that the cell group is not involved in visual information processing. The influence of such cell groups may only emerge when their destruction is combined with the destruction of other components of the visual system. In some circumstances the effect of the combined lesion may be to increase the magnitude of a discrimination deficit, as in the case of combined lesions of nucleus rotundus and OPT. Or, the effect of combined lesions may be to prevent the emergence of a deficit as in lesions of nucleus rotundus and GLv.

The studies using psychophysical procedures have enabled us to evaluate an animal at the limits of its performance ability. By presenting the strongest possible challenge to the information processing capabilities of the visual system, we have observed performance decrements that were undetectable with the use of the conventional method of coarse discrimination. The psychophysical approach also has enabled us to quantify the amount of sensory sparing and loss following brain lesions to an extent that is not possible with the trials to criterion measure that is typical of coarse discrimination experiments. In addition, the psychophysical approach has permitted us to make use of the powerful techniques of sensory scaling, which provide the means to express sparing and loss in psychological units rather than physical units. Thus we are able to evaluate performance changes as a percentage of the animals' preoperative sensory capacity. This type of evaluation has proved valuable in interpreting the effects of visual system lesions.

I believe that the research described here can contribute to our knowledge of brain–behavior relationships in three specific areas. First, these studies can aid in understanding the evolutionary heritage of the mammalian visual system by clarifying the relationship between the visual systems of mammals with those of birds and reptiles. The model of visual system evolution that we have been developing leads us to conclude that the differences between reptiles, birds, and mammals (and even within different orders of mammals) are not qualitative, but are quantitative. The relative degree of development between classes or even within orders of mammals, such as primates, seems to be a graduated adaptive response to environmental pressures rather than a series of quantal leaps forward. This view, if supported by further data, could have important implications for our generalization of findings from research on animals to man.

Second, such studies can advance our understanding of the mechanisms of visual information processing that are common to all amniotes (and perhaps to all vertebrates). The parallels in anatomy, unit responsiveness, and effects of lesions on behavior suggest very strongly that information is processed in comparable cell groups in birds and mammals in comparable ways. Since birds are highly adapted for vision, perhaps more than any other class of vertebrates, they are excellent subjects for studying visual information processing in the nervous system. Their common reptilian heritage with mammals makes the results of experiments on birds quite applicable to the interpretation of results in mammalian material. Because of the high degree of development of the visual system in birds, the study of visual mechanisms in these animals may offer a better means of understanding visual mechanisms than is now possible in mammals.

Finally, a challenging finding in our research is the varying recovery of function following destruction of different cell groups. Our behavioral and anatomical studies are directed, in part, to understanding the mechanisms for this recovery. Is it due to the availability of other parts of the visual system to carry out these functions by means of pathways not ordinarily utilized for this type of processing, or is it a reorganization of existing pathways to make more effective use of the restricted information available? Are the visual losses observed after visual system injury the result of the loss of a specific analyzer function that resides in the injured cells, or does it reflect a disruption of the balance between excitatory and inhibitory mechanisms in the visual system as a whole? If such were the case, could the surgical or chemical removal of a source of inhibition result in a restoration of function as some of our data and those of Sprague suggest? Hopefully, the foreseeable future will hold the answers to these questions.

References

Altman, J., and Carpenter, M. B. (1961). Fiber projections of the superior colliculus in the cat. *Journal of Comparative Neurology* 116, 157–178.
Ariëns Kappers, C. U., Huber, G. C., and Crosby, E. C. (1960). "The Comparative Anatomy of the Nervous System of Vertebrates, Including Man." Hafner, New York. (Reprint of 1936 edition.)
Atz, J. (1970). The application of the idea of homology to behavior. *In* "Development and Evolution of Behavior" (L. R. Aronson, E. Tobach, D. S. Lehrman, and J. S. Rosenblatt, eds.), pp. 53–74. Freeman, San Francisco, California.
Bitterman, M. E. (1965). Phyletic difference in learning. *American Psychologist* 20, 396–410.
Bitterman, M. E. (1969). Thorndike and the problem of animal intelligence. *American Psychologist* 24, 444–453.
Blough, P. M. (1971). The visual acuity of the pigeon for distant targets. *Journal of the Experimental Analysis of Behavior* 15, 57–67.
Blough, P. M. (1973). Visual acuity in the pigeon: II. Effects of target distance and retinal lesions. *Journal of the Experimental Analysis of Behavior* 20, 333–343.
Bock, W. J. (1967). Evolution and phylogeny in morphologically uniform groups. *American Naturalist* 97, 265–285.
Bock, W. J. (1969). Discussion: The concept of homology. *Annals of the New York Academy of Sciences* 167, 71–73.
Boyden, A. (1969). Homology and analogy. *Science* 164, 455–456.
Butler, A. B., and Northcutt, R. G. (1971). Ascending tectal efferent projections in the lizard, *Iguana iguana. Brain Research* 35, 397–601.
Campbell, C. B. G. (1972). Evolutionary patterns in mammalian diencephalic visual nuclei and their fiber connections. *Brain, Behavior and Evolution* 6, 218–236.
Campbell, C. B. G., and Hodos, W. (1970). The concept of homology and the evolution of the nervous system. *Brain, Behavior and Evolution* 3, 353–367.
Catania, A. C. (1964). On the visual acuity of the pigeon. *Journal of the Experimental Analysis of Behavior* 7, 361–366.
Chard, R. D. (1939). Visual acuity in the pigeon. *Journal of Experimental Psychology* 24, 588–608.
Colbert, E. H. (1965), "The Age of Reptiles." Newton, New York.
Cowan, W. M., Adamson, L., and Powell, T. P. S. (1961). An experimental study of the avian visual system. *Journal of Anatomy* 95, 545–563.
Diamond, I. T., and Hall, W. C. (1969). Evolution of neocortex. *Science* 164, 251–262.
Doty, R. W. (1971). Survival of pattern vision after removal of striate cortex in the adult cat. *Journal of Comparative Neurology* 143, 341–370.

Ebbesson, S. O. E. (1968). Retinal projections in two teleost fishes (*Opsanus tau* and *Gymothorax funebris*). An experimental study with silver impregnation methods. *Brain, Behavior and Evolution* 1, 134–157.

Fink, R. P., and Heimer, L. (1967). Two methods for selective impregnation of degenerating axons and their synaptic endings in the central nervous system. *Brain Research* 4, 369–374.

Galifret, Y. (1966). Le système visuel du pigeon: Anatomie et physiologie corrélations psychophysiologiques. Unpublished doctoral dissertation, Faculty of Sciences, University of Paris, Paris.

Gaze, R. M., and Jacobson, M. (1962). The projection of the binocular visual field on the optic tecta of the frog. *Journal of Experimental Physiology* 47, 273–280.

Goodman, D. C., and Horel, J. A. (1966). Sprouting of optic tract projections in the brain stem of the rat. *Journal of Comparative Neurology* 127, 71–88.

Granda, A. M., and Yazulla, S. (1971). The spectral sensitivity of single units in the nucleus rotundus of pigeon *(Columba livia)*. *Journal of General Physiology* 57, 363–384.

Green, D. M., and Swets, J. A. (1966). "Signal Detection Theory and Psychophysics." Wiley, New York.

Gross, C. G., Cowey, A., and Manning, F. J. (1971). Further analysis of visual discrimination deficits following foveal prestriate and inferotemporal lesions in rhesus monkeys. *Journal of Comparative and Physiological Psychology* 76, 1–7.

Hall, W. C., and Ebner, F. F. (1970). Thalamotelencephalic projections in the turtle *(Pseudemys scripta)*. *Journal of Comparative Neurology* 140, 101–122.

Herrick, C. J. (1948). "The Brain of the Tiger Salamander, *Ambystoma tigrinum.*" Univ. of Chicago Press, Chicago, Illinois.

Herrnstein, R. J., and Van Sommers, P. (1962). Method for sensory scaling with animals. *Science* 135, 40–41.

Hirschberger, W. (1967). Histologische Untersuchungen an den Primären Visuellen Zentren den Eulengehirnes und der Retinalen Repräsentation in Ihnen. *Journal für Ornithologie* 108, 187–202.

Hirschberger, W. (1971). Vergleichend Experimentell-Histologische Undersuchung zur Retinalen Repräsentation in den Primären Visuellen Zentren einiger Vogelarten. Unpublished doctoral dissertation, Johann Wolfgang Goethe-Universität, Frankfurt am Main.

Hodos, W. (1969). Color discrimination deficits after lesions of the nucleus rotundus in pigeons. *Brain, Behavior and Evolution* 2, 185–200.

Hodos, W. (1970a). Evolutionary interpretation of neural and behavioral studies of living vertebrates. *In* "The Neurosciences; Second Study Program" (F. O. Schmitt, ed.), pp. 26–39. Rockefeller Univ. Press, New York.

Hodos, W. (1970b). Nonparametric index of response bias for use in detection and recognition experiments. *Psychological Bulletin* 74, 351–354.

Hodos, W. (1975). The concept of homology and the evolution of behavior. *In* "Evolution, Brain and Behavior: Persistent Problems" (R. B. Masterton, W. Hodos, and H. Jerison, eds.). Lawrence Erlbaum Associates, Hillsdale, N.J. In press.

Hodos, W., and Bonbright, J. C., Jr. (1972). The detection of visual intensity differences by pigeons. *Journal of the Experimental Analysis of Behavior* 18, 471–479.

Hodos, W., and Bonbright, J. C., Jr. (1974). Intensity difference thresholds in pigeons after lesions of the tectofugal and thalamofugal visual pathways. *Journal of Comparative and Physiological Psychology* 87, 1013–1031.

Hodos, W., and Bonbright, J. C., Jr. (1975). Intensity and pattern discrimination after lesions of the pretectal complex, accessory optic nucleus and ventral geniculate in pigeons. *Journal of Comparative Neurology* 161, 1–18.

Hodos, W., and Campbell, C. B. G. (1969). *Scala Naturae:* Why there is no theory in comparative psychology. *Psychological Review* 76, 337–350.

Hodos, W., and Fletcher, G. V. (1974). Acquisition of visual discrimination after nucleus rotundus lesions in pigeons. *Physiology & Behavior* 13, 501–506.

Hodos, W., and Karten, H. J. (1966). Brightness and pattern discrimination deficits in the pigeon after lesions of nucleus rotundus. *Experimental Brain Research (Berlin)* 2, 151–167.

Hodos, W., and Karten, H. J. (1970). Visual intensity and pattern discrimination deficits after lesions of ectostriatum in pigeons. *Journal of Comparative Neurology* 140, 53–68.

Hodos, W., and Karten, H. J. (1974). Visual intensity and pattern discrimination deficits after lesions of the optic lobe in pigeons. *Brain, Behavior and Evolution* 9, 165–195.

Hodos, W., and Leibowitz, R. W. (1975). Spectral differences in the visual acuity of pigeons. Unpublished.

Hodos, W., Karten, H. J., and Bonbright, J. D., Jr. (1973). Visual intensity and pattern discrimination after lesions of the thalamofugal visual pathway in pigeons. *Journal of Comparative Neurology* 148, 447–468.

Hodos, W., Leibowitz, R. W., and Bonbright, J. C., Jr. (1976a). Near field visual acuity in pigeons: Effects of head position and stimulus luminance. *Journal of the Experimental Analysis of Behavior.* In press.

Hodos, W., Smith, L., and Bonbright, J. C., Jr. (1976b). Detection of the velocity of movement of visual stimuli by pigeons. *Journal of the Experimental Analysis of Behavior.* In press.

Honig, W. K. (1966). "Operant Behavior." Wiley, New York.

Hubel, D. H., and Wiesel, T. N. (1962). Receptive fields, binocular interaction and functional architecture in the cat's visual cortex. *Journal of Physiology (London)* 160, 106–154.

Humphrey, N. K., and Weiskrantz, L. (1967). Vision in monkeys after removal of the striate cortex. *Nature (London)* 215, 595–597.

Hunt, S. P., and Webster, K. E. (1972). Thalamo-hyperstriate interrelations in the pigeon. *Brain Research* 44, 647–651.

Jacobson, M. (1964). Spectral sensitivity of single units in the optic tectum of the goldfish. *Quarterly Journal of Experimental Physiology and Cognate Medical Sciences* 49, 384–394.

Jarvis, C. D. (1974). Visual discrimination and spatial localization deficits after lesions of the tectofugal visual pathway in pigeons. *Brain, Behavior and Evolution* 9, 197–232.

Kaas, J. H., Guillery, R. W., and Allman, J. M. (1972). Some principles of organization in the dorsal lateral geniculate nucleus. *Brain, Behavior and Evolution* 6, 253–299.

Karten, H. J. (1969). The organization of the avian telencephalon and some speculations on the phylogeny of the amniote telencephalon. *Annals of the New York Academy of Sciences* 167, 146–179.

Karten, H. J., and Dubbeldam, J. L. (1973). The organization and projections of the paleostriatal complex in the pigeon *(Columba livia)*. *Journal of Comparative Neurology* 148, 61–90.

Karten, H. J., and Hodos, W. (1967). "A Stereotaxic Atlas of the Brain of the Pigeon *(Columba livia)*." Johns Hopkins Press, Baltimore, Maryland.

Karten, H. J., and Hodos, W. (1970). Telencephalic projections of the nucleus rotundus in the pigeon *(Columba livia)*. *Journal of Comparative Neurology* 140, 35–52.

Karten, H. J., and Nauta, W. J. H. (1968). Organization of retino-thalamic projections in the pigeon and owl. *Anatomical Record* **160**, 373.

Karten, H. J., and Revzin, A. (1966). The afferent connections of the nucleus rotundus in the pigeon. *Brain Research* **2**, 368–377.

Karten, H. J., Hodos, W., Nauta, W. J. H., and Revzin, A. M. (1973). Neural connections of the "visual Wulst" of the avian telencephalon. Experimental studies in the pigeon *(Columba livia)* and owl *(Speotyto cunicularia)*. *Journal of Comparative Neurology* **150**, 253–278.

Killackey, H., and Diamond, I. T. (1971). Visual attention in the tree shrew: An ablation study of striate and extrastriate visual cortex. *Science* **171**, 696–699.

Krasnegor, N. A., and Hodos, W. (1974). The evaluation and control of acoustical standing waves. *Journal of the Experimental Analysis of Behavior* **22**, 243–249.

Llinas, R. (1969). "Neurobiology of Cerebellar Evolution and Development." AMA Educ. Res. Found.

Lockard, R. B. (1968). The albino rat: A defensible choice or a bad habit? *American Psychologist* **23**, 734–742.

Meier, R. E., Mihailovic, J., and Cuénod, M. (1974). Thalamic organization of the retino-thalamo-hyperstriatal pathway in the pigeon *(Columba livia)* *Experimental Brain Research (Berlin)* **19**, 351–364.

Moore, R. Y., Björklund, A., and Stenevi, U. (1974). Growth and plasticity of adrenergic neurons. *In* "The Neurosciences: Third Study Program" (F. O. Schmitt and F. G. Worden, eds.), pp. 961–977, MIT Press, Cambridge, Massachusetts.

Morest, D. K. (1965). Identification of homologous neurons in the posterolateral thalamus of cat and Virginia oppossum. *Anatomical Record* **151**, 390.

Nauta, W. J. H., and Karten, H. J. (1970). A general profile of the vertebrate brain with sidelights on the ancestry of cerebral cortex. *In* "The Neurosciences: Second Study Program" (F. O. Schmitt, ed.), pp. 7–26. Rockefeller Univ. Press, New York.

Nye, P. W. (1973). On the functional differences between frontal and lateral vision fields of the pigeon. *Vision Research* **13**, 559–574.

Ørvig, T., ed. (1968). "Current Problems of Lower Vertebrate Phylogeny," Fourth Nobel Symposium. Almqvist & Wiksel, Stockholm.

Owen, R. (1843). "Lectures on the Comparative Anatomy and Physiology of the Invertebrate Animals." Longman, Brown, Green & Longmans, London.

Papez, J. W. (1929). "Comparative Neurology." Crowell, New York.

Pasik, T., and Pasik, P. (1971). The visual world of monkeys deprived of striate cortex: Effective stimulus parameters and the importance of the accessory optic system. *In* "International Symposium on Visual Processes in Vertebrates" (T. Shipley and J. E. Dowling, eds.), Vision Research Supplement No. 3, pp. 419–435. Pergamon, Oxford.

Pritz, M. B., Mead, W. R., and Northcutt, R. G. (1970). The effects of Wulst ablations on color, brightness and pattern discrimination in pigeons *(Columba livia)*. *Journal of Comparative Neurology* **140**, 81–100.

Revzin, A. M. (1969). A specific visual projection area in the hyperstriatum of the pigeon *(Columba livia)*. *Brain Research* **15**, 246–249.

Revzin, A. M. (1970). Some characteristics of wide-field units in the brain of the pigeon. *Brain, Behavior and Evolution* **3**, 195–204.

Revzin, A. M., and Karten, H. J. (1966–1967). Rostral projections of the optic tectum and the nucleus rotundus in the pigeon. *Brain Research* **3**, 264–267.

Riss, W., Knapp, H. D., and Scalia, F. (1963). Optic pathways in *Cryptobranchus allegheniensis* as revealed by Nauta techniques. *Journal of Comparative Neurology* **120**, 31–43.

Romer, A. S. (1966). "Vertebrate Paleontology," 3rd Ed. Univ. of Chicago Press, Chicago, Illinois.

Romer, A. S. (1968a). "The Procession of Life." World Publ., Cleveland, Ohio.

Romer, A. S. (1968b). "Notes and Comments on Vertebrate Paleontology." Univ. of Chicago Press, Chicago, Illinois.

Rovainen, C. M. (1967a). Physiological and anatomical studies on large neurons of central nervous system of the sea lamprey *(Petromyzon marinus)*. I. Müller and Mauthner cells. *Journal of Neurophysiology* 30, 1000–1023.

Rovainen, C. M. (1967b). Physiological and anatomical studies on large neurons of central nervous system of the sea lamprey *(Petromyzon marinus)*. II. Dorsal cells and giant interneurons. *Journal of Neurophysiology* 30, 1024–1042.

Schneider, G. E. (1969). Two visual systems. *Science* 163, 895–902.

Simons, E. L. (1969). The origin and radiation of primates. *Annals of the New York Academy of Sciences* 167, 319–331.

Snyder, M., and Diamond, I. T. (1968). The organization and function of the visual cortex in the tree shrew. *Brain, Behavior and Evolution* 1, 244–288.

Sommers, D. I. (1972). The scaling of visual intensity differences by pigeons. Unpublished master's thesis, Univ. of Maryland, College Park.

Sprague, J. M. (1966). Interaction of cortex and superior colliculus in the mediation of visually guided behavior. *Science* 153, 1544–1547.

Sprague, J. M., Levy, J., DiBeradino, A., and Conomy, J. (1973). Effect of striate and extra-striate visual cortical lesions on learning and retention of form discrimination. *Program and Abstracts, Society for Neuroscience, San Diego, California*, p. 182.

Stebbins, W. C. (1970). "Animal Psychophysics." Appleton, New York.

Stevens, S. S. (1971). Issues in psychophysical measurement. *Psychological Review* 78, 426–450.

Swanson, L. W., and Cowan, W. M. (1973). Efferent connections of the ventral lateral geniculate nucleus (LGNv). *Proceedings of the Society for Neuroscience*, San Diego, California, p. 150. (Abstract.)

Tarlov, E. (1965). The distribution of ascending efferents of the superior colliculus in the brain of the rabbit. *Anatomical Record* 151, 425.

Wallace, G. J. (1963). "An Introduction to Ornithology." Macmillan, New York.

Weiskrantz, L. (1963). Contour discrimination in a young monkey with striate cortex ablation. *Neuropsychologia* 1, 145–164.

Weiskrantz, L., and Cowey, A. (1967). Comparison of the effects of striate cortex and retinal lesions on visual acuity in the monkey. *Science* 155, 104–106.

Welty, J. C. (1963). "The Life of Birds." Knopf, New York.

Zeier, H., and Karten, H. D. (1971). The archistriatum of the pigeon: organization of afferent and efferent connections. *Brain Research* 31, 313–326.

Zeigler, H. P. (1963). Effects of endbrain lesions upon visual discrimination learning in pigeons. *Journal of Comparative Neurology* 120, 161–182.

Cat Visual Psychophysics: Neural Correlates and Comparisons with Man

Mark A. Berkley

Department of Psychology,
Florida State University,
Tallahassee, Florida

I.	Introduction	63
II.	General Plan	65
	A. Stimulus Description	65
	B. Threshold Estimation	67
III.	Sensitivity of the Cat Visual System to Light	68
	A. Absolute Threshold	68
	B. Differential Intensity Thresholds (Increment Threshold)	71
	C. Dark Adaptation	73
	D. Spectral Sensitivity	75
	E. Color Vision	79
IV.	Temporal Response of the Cat Visual System	81
	A. Critical Fusion Frequency	81
	B. Temporal Modulation Sensitivity of the Cat	83
V.	Spatial Vision	87
	A. Visual Acuity	87
	B. Spatial Contrast Sensitivity Function	91
VI.	Complex Spatial Vision	94
	A. Form Vision	94
	B. Movement Sensitivity	98
VII.	Binocular Vision	100
	A. Visual Fields	100
	B. Cyclopean Vision	103
VIII.	Appendix	106
	A. Structural Comparisons of Cat and Man	106
	B. Feline Photometry	107
	References	111

I. Introduction

In attempts to understand the brain, numerous research strategies and tools have been used to good advantage. Among these, electrophysiological studies of single cells of the nervous system have been particularly revealing. Implicit in many of these studies is the assumption that the process being studied is the substrate of some behavior and, indeed, many of the published electrophysiological data provide tantalizing suggestions for understanding the neural substrates of behavior. However, it is not sufficient for a process to be an intuitively plausible or appealing substrate of behavior; it must be empirically demonstrated. How can neural substrates of behavior be explicitly discovered? The prime strategy for this discovery is the comparison (correlation) of data derived at various levels of inquiry, e.g., physiological, anatomical, and behavioral. When isomorphisms between various levels are found, the substrate for behavior is considered to be understood. To successfully apply this strategy, however, requires that explicitly stated hypotheses regarding the relationship between, for example, physiological and behavioral observations be made; linking hypotheses, as Brindley (1960) has called them. Further, Brindley (1960) has pointed out that at present there is only one acceptable linking hypothesis: two stimuli that produce indistinguishable neural signals will be reported by the subject to be indistinguishable. Because this linking hypothesis and its corollaries (e.g., Brindley, 1960; Boynton and Onley, 1962; Sekuler, 1974) are the only ones currently tenable, the types of data that are most useful in the evaluation of neural substrates are threshold measurements (Class A experiments—Brindley, 1960) derived both behaviorally and electrophysiologically. Thus, if a threshold response function of a neural element(s) is found to be isomorphic with the psychophysical threshold function, the neural element(s) is considered to be one of the substrates of the behavior. (An excellent example of the successful application of this strategy is the correlation between the rhodopsin action spectrum and scotopic spectral sensitivity.) A less emphasized aspect of this research strategy concerns the conditions under which the different classes of observations are made. Ideally, comparison of classes of data, e.g., electrophysiological and behavioral, should be derived under the same experimental conditions and obtained from the same organism, conditions often difficult, if not impossible to achieve. Nevertheless, the most promising and, to date, most successful area for the application of this strategy has been vision.

An important experimental subject in the pursuit of understanding vision has been the cat, this animal having the most extensively studied visual system of any vertebrate. The reasons for this popularity are many and varied: the cat is readily available, tractable, inexpensive, a convenient size, easy to keep and has a well-developed nervous system. While he is an obliging electrophysiological and anatomical subject, there are two major drawbacks in the use of the cat as an experimental subject: (1) he is, by repute, a poor subject for behavioral studies; and (2) his visual system differs significantly from that of primates, making simple extrapolations from feline data to human data somewhat tenuous.

Nevertheless, because of the rapid expansion of neurophysiological and anatomical data derived from the cat nervous system, and the explanatory power in the discovery of isomorphisms between behavioral and electrophysiological data, behavioral study of this animal offers a unique opportunity to expand our knowledge of the neural mechanisms underlying vision.

The present paper is an attempt to evaluate the areas of success in understanding vision in which the cat is used as the neural model. This evaluation will consist of comparing visual capacity estimates derived from various sources. There are two overall goals: (1) to evaluate the strategy of correlating behavioral and electrophysiological data, and (2) to describe what is known about feline vision in order to identify problem areas. Thus, the present paper brings together behavioral data gleaned from a variety of sources concerning the visual capacities of the cat. These findings are then compared with related electrophysiological and anatomical data. Where possible, comparisons are made with appropriate human data.

II. General Plan

Estimates of the visual capacities of the cat can be derived from three major sources: anatomy, physiology, and behavior. In this chapter, each visual capacity as measured behaviorally is considered with appropriate physiological and anatomical data subsequently presented. To facilitate this task, measurement units have been, where possible, converted to a single convention.

In addition, an appendix is included which contains several tables providing direct human—feline comparisons that may be useful to workers using the cat as an experimental subject. Also included are tables providing normative data on the cat visual system derived from scattered published sources.

The capacities described below follow, more or less, the general outline found in many books on human vision. Thus, the discussion will begin with the cat's absolute sensitivity to light. Before we can proceed with this topic, however, it is necessary to consider some problems in human—feline comparisons: the first concerns the choice of measurement units in the description of the visual stimulus, and the second concerns the definition of a threshold.

A. STIMULUS DESCRIPTION

For the most part, the measurement-unit conventions adopted for humans are appropriate for use with the cat. This is true only for those dimensions that do not depend on the unique characteristics of the human or cat eye. For example, units used to describe such stimulus dimensions as size (visual angle—minutes) and time, e.g., seconds, cycles/second (hertz), in human studies can safely be applied in feline studies. Stimulus intensity units, however, pose a problem because many of the units devised for use with humans cannot be used with the cat. The safest route in dealing with intensity is to simply describe the stimulus in physical terms, e.g., radiometric units, such as watts, ergs, quanta. Photometric units, such as millilamberts, foot-candles, candelas, cannot be used, in that, by definition, they depend on characteristics, e.g., spectral sensitivity, ocular media absorbance, unique to the human eye. Thus, it is incorrect to assume that two lights that appear identical to humans (photometrically equivalent) will be judged so by cats; nor is it correct to assume that two lights of equal physical energy will appear the same to cat and man. The use of photometric units, is therefore, not appropriate for use in animal studies (see discussion of this point by Rodieck, 1973, p. 285) but may be used with caution under certain circumstances if their limitations are understood. In this paper, the candela (cd/m^2) will be used in describing stimulus intensities. This unit was chosen for reasons described below and discussed by Rodieck (1973), as well as the fact that it has been widely used recently by many researchers.

Luminance (L) in candelas is defined as:

$$L_v = K_v \int_{400}^{700} L_{e\lambda} \, V_\lambda \, d\lambda \tag{1}$$

where L_v is luminance in candelas; $L_{e\lambda}$, the spectral radiance of the source in watts/m^2 per steradian; and V_λ, the relative spectral sensitivity of the human eye. K_v is a scaling constant relating the candela to a physical standard. (By definition, the luminance of a radiator at 2042°K is 6×10^5 cd/m^2.)

As can be seen from Eq. (1), luminance depends not only upon the spectral characteristics of the source ($L_{e\lambda}$), but upon the sensitivity of the eye to various wavelengths of light (V_λ). Because of this definition, different values will be derived depending on whether the spectral sensitivity of the light-adapted (V_λ) or dark-adapted eye (V'_λ) is used. Thus, there are photopic and scotopic candelas. Because the sensitivity of the feline eye is somewhat different from that of man, to be completely correct in using this unit in cat studies requires recomputation of candelas using the V_λ of the cat. When this is done (Table IIIA in the Appendix) for the dark-adapted cat eye (V'_λ), however, one finds only a small difference in the values derived from man and cat. The difference is small because of the great similarity of V'_λ between cat and man (see Fig. 3). Photopic candelas, however, do require recomputation for the cat. A comparison of these values and a description of the rationale are given in the Appendix, Table IIIA.

A more significant error is introduced in human–cat comparisons when considering the amount of *effective* light striking the retina of these two animals. In human studies, the traditional unit adopted to describe this quantity is the troland (td). A troland is simply defined as the retinal illumination produced by a 1 cd/m^2 source seen through a 1 mm^2 pupil. More simply, it is the product of the luminance of the light expressed in cd/m^2 multiplied by the area of the pupil (mm^2). Depending on whether scotopic or photopic candelas are used, one may have photopic or scotopic trolands.

$$td = L_v \times S \tag{2}$$

where L_v is luminance in candelas/m^2 and S is pupillary area in mm^2. Actually, since trolands are units of illumination, Eq. (2) should also contain terms representing the distance from the nodal point of the eye to the retina, the refractive index of the eye, and the size of the image as well as pupillary area. For the human eye, the factors other than pupil area are usually ignored. They cannot be ignored when considering the cat eye. Thus, trolands cannot be simply used in describing retinal illumination for the cat because: (1) the length of the cat eye is shorter than that of man so that the actual intensity of light (density) striking the feline retina is greater than in the human eyeball; (2) for the same given luminance, the aperture of the cat eye is different from that of man (under natural pupil conditions); and (3) the cat eye contains a reflector (tapetum lucidum) increasing the amount of light striking the receptors. Knowledge of the optical length of the cat eye as well as the pupillary area and tapetal reflectivity permits computation of a unit equivalent to the human troland for the cat, e.g., cat equivalent troland (CETd). These computations have been carried out for a range of luminances and are listed in Table IVA of the Appendix. Further details regarding the necessary assumptions and calculations are given there.

B. THRESHOLD ESTIMATION

While essentially arbitrary in nature, human psychophysical thresholds have well established definitions. One simple and often used definition may be stated as follows: threshold is that value of the stimulus which will be detected (or judged different) by the subject on 50% of the trials in which it is presented.

Application of this definition to animal studies would seem to be straightforward except that often the behavioral training methods used to determine the threshold are indirect and may be affected by variables that are not significant in human studies. For example, nonrandom manipulations of reward probability or order of stimulus presentation are often introduced in animal studies to deal with motivational difficulties or response strategies not present or significant in human studies. These manipulations produce effects that are difficult to evaluate in terms of simple response probabilities. To overcome some of these problems, a less stringent threshold definition is usually adopted, e.g., 75 or 80% correct choice. The use of criteria different from those in human studies and the unknown effects of motivation, attention, etc., make simple comparisons of thresholds between species tenuous at best. In this paper, motivational variables will be ignored, and differences in threshold criterion will be mentioned where they seem appropriate, but the reader should keep in mind the essentially arbitrary nature of threshold criteria.

While not without value, threshold estimates based on electrophysiological data are fraught with additional dangers. For example, data derived from single cells are currently impossible to evaluate in terms of behavioral thresholds because the role of the recorded cell in determining that threshold is unknown. Evoked potential data may be somewhat more useful because they are obtained by sampling the behavior of large cell populations. In any case, threshold comparisons between behavioral and electrophysiological estimates are always tenuous because of the arbitrary nature of threshold definitions. More useful are parametric functions relating neural response and some stimulus dimension. These types of data may be compared with similar behavioral data to establish isomorphisms because threshold criterion differences are relatively unimportant. Under these circumstances, it is sufficient to demonstrate close similarity in the shapes of the functional relationships.

III. Sensitivity of the Cat Visual System to Light

A. ABSOLUTE THRESHOLD

1. Behavioral Estimates

A number of behavioral determinations of the cat's absolute threshold to light have been made over the past 30 years. Using a two-choice discrimination procedure in which the cat had to approach one of two doors on which the stimulus appeared, Bridgeman and Smith (1942) reported a threshold of 2.6×10^{-7} cd/m^2. Using very similar procedures, Gunter (1951a) arrived at a value of 3.2×10^{-7} cd/m^2. In a study using a somewhat different testing procedure, which did not require a choice response but rather a simple approach (go—no go), and a flashed stimulus (4 μsec flash at 2/sec), Thorn (1970) reported a threshold value somewhat lower than that of the previously cited studies: 1.6×10^{-7} cd/m^2. The low value obtained by Thorn (1970) is most likely due to his flash presentation or calibration procedure because his human thresholds are also somewhat lower than are found by other investigators. The results of these studies are summarized in Table I below. All things considered, a reasonable estimate of absolute threshold for the cat derived from consideration of the above studies appears to be about 2.9×10^{-7} cd/m^2.

As discussed above, comparisons with classical human threshold studies are not strictly correct since stimulus configuration, criterion choice, and other

TABLE I

COMPARISON OF ABSOLUTE THRESHOLDS OF CAT AND MAN

Source	Cat threshold		Human threshold		Ratio of human/cat	
	cd/m²	Trolands[a]	cd/m²	Trolands	cd/m²	td
Bridgeman and Smith (1942)	2.6×10^{-7}	7.8×10^{-5}	1.8×10^{-6}	8.9×10^{-5}	6.9	1.1
Mead (1939, 1942)	4.1×10^{-7}	1.2×10^{-4}	(1.8×10^{-6})	8.9×10^{-5}	4.4	0.7
Gunter (1951a)	3.2×10^{-7}	9.6×10^{-5}	1.7×10^{-6}	8.4×10^{-5}	5.3	0.9
Thorn (1970)	1.6×10^{-7}	4.8×10^{-5}	1.3×10^{-6}	6.4×10^{-5}	8.1	1.3
LaMotte and Brown (1970)	–	–	–	–	3.2	

[a]To compare retinal illumination between cat and man, the human troland (td) unit was calculated for the cat. The rationale for this procedure was discussed in Section I,A, and details of the calculations and assumptions are given in the Appendix, Table IVA.

variables usually differ between animal and human studies. In several of the above studies, however, human thresholds were determined on the same apparatus and under similar conditions as the cat thresholds and are included in Table I for comparison. As can be seen in these studies, the cat is always found to be significantly more sensitive to light than man. Computation of the ratio of cat to human absolute sensitivities yields ratios of from 3.2 (LaMotte and Brown, 1970) to 8.1 (Thorn, 1970) times greater sensitivity. [While LaMotte and Brown (1970) did not report absolute thresholds, they did determine the difference in relative sensitivity of dark-adapted humans and cats, and this ratio is also listed in Table I.] It has been suggested (Bridgeman, 1938; Gunter, 1951a; Weale, 1954) that this difference can be attributed to the greater light-gathering ability of the feline eye, e.g., larger aperture, shorter optical length, and reflecting tapetum. If this is true, computation of the ratio of *retinal* (receptor) illuminance for cat and man should yield values near unity. To evaluate this hypothesis, the threshold luminance values in Table I have been converted to trolands (a unit of retinal illumination) and cat-equivalent trolands (see earlier section and Table IVA in Appendix). The last column of Table I lists the ratios of these values. Note that when ocular differences are equated, the ratios are near unity, indicating that cat and man are about equally sensitive. Thus, the ocular difference hypothesis is supported, and a second hypothesis follows: pigment densities in the cat and human eyes are equal (Weale, 1953b).

Absolute threshold should depend, to some extent, on the density of photopigment in the eye. Thus, the animal with the greater pigment density, everything else being equal, would be the more sensitive by virtue of having a greater probability of capturing a light quantum by the photopigment. Does the cat have a greater density of photopigment than man? The comparison made above suggests not.

Recent measures of pigment absorption in the living cat eye (Bonds and MacLeod, 1974) further support this view. In this study, it was shown that the pigment density in the cat eye is close to that of man (0.11 for the cat vs 0.09 for man). On the basis of these measures, and taking into account the differences in pupillary area, these authors concluded that if the human and cat eye were to absorb quanta at the same rate, the amount of light incident on the human eye should be about 9 times greater than that incident on the cat eye. This compares well with the 7–8 times greater absolute sensitivity reported in the behavioral studies. Thus, our previous conclusion that the retinal sensitivities of cat and man are essentially equal is further strengthened.

2. Electrophysiological Estimates

A few studies have attempted to estimate absolute thresholds from electro-physiological studies. In a study by Barlow et al. (1957), for example, the thresholds for light were determined for a number of retinal ganglion cells and were found to be considerably higher (5–100 times) than the absolute threshold as determined behaviorally by Gunter (1951a). [Other studies using the electroretinogram (ERG) (Granit, 1943; Pirenne, 1954) also reported threshold values much greater than those behaviorally determined.] The reasons for the higher estimates derived from the electrophysiological studies may be due to several factors: (1) the most sensitive elements in the retina were not sampled; (2) the subjective threshold estimation procedure used based on listening to (or looking at) the ganglion cell discharge or looking for minimal response is inappropriate; and (3) the intact animal uses information from a large number of inputs in making threshold responses (probability summation) while the researcher has available the responses of only a few neural elements. While the sampling problem cannot be eliminated in neurophysiological studies (except by recording from all neural elements), there have been attempts to make the threshold estimation procedure more objective. Heiss and Milne (1967), for example, attempted to use post-stimulus response histograms of ganglion cell responses to a brief flash to estimate threshold. Using this procedure, they were able to derive thresholds lower than previously reported in electrophysiological studies, but still some-what higher than the behavioral estimates. Good arguments, however, can be made against the simple use of average response histograms in estimating absolute thresholds in that signal averaging will always produce a measurable response if continued long enough so long as any response occurs on any of the trials (see Barlow and Levick, 1969a). Thus, at present it still has not been possible to adequately estimate absolute threshold from electrophysiological measures.

B. DIFFERENTIAL INTENSITY THRESHOLDS (INCREMENT THRESHOLD)

1. Behavioral Measures

Another dimension of sensitivity that relates to intensity of a visual stimulus is the capacity to detect a change in intensity (ΔI). This capacity, as is well known, is dependent on the absolute level (background) to which the increment is added (absolute threshold may be considered a special case when this level is zero). In an extensive behavioral study, Mead (1939) showed that the cat increment threshold (expressed as a Weber fraction, $\Delta I/I$) varied from a high of about 1.4 at a very low background luminance level (4.2×10^{-7} cd/m²) to a low of 0.34 at 684 cd/m². Hara and Warren (1961a) also obtained a value of 0.34, but at a much lower background luminance (4.1 cd/m²). In a more recent study, Thorn (1970) found a $\Delta I/I$ value of 0.116 for cats and a value of 0.114 for humans in the same apparatus. These measures were taken with a mean background luminance of 3.4×10^{-4} cd/m².

At present, it is difficult to say with certainty whether the cat is poorer than man in this capacity, although it probably is. Reports of human increment threshold suggest a greater sensitivity for man (smaller ratio) (LeGrand, 1968). In the study by Thorn (1970) in which both cats and humans were tested, man and cat appear to be very similar *at low luminance levels.* Similar results were obtained by Snigula and Grüsser (1968). With a target luminance of 1.43 cd/m², they determined the cat to have a $\Delta I/I$ ratio of 0.12, and humans tested on the same apparatus were only slightly better. It must be remembered, however, that the retinal illumination of the cat is nearly 1 log unit greater than in man with the same target luminance. Thus, it would be more reasonable to compare human and cat increment thresholds in which the human values are taken at a background level 1 log unit greater than used with the cat.

Figure 1 is a plot of the cat data obtained by Mead (1939, 1942) (filled circles) compared with human data derived from LeGrand (1968) (solid line). The human data were obtained with a target size and configuration similar to that used by Mead (1942) although the target separations were significantly different. Note that even shifting the cat function 1 log unit to the left does not yield good agreement. Except at low luminances, man appears to be superior. It is more likely, however, that Mead's (1942) data are not comparable to most human increment threshold studies because the separation between the "background" and the target was very large ($>5°$). The stimulus

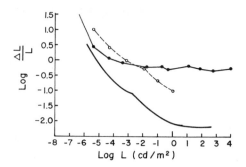

FIG. 1. Increment thresholds as a function of background luminance. ●———●, Points plotted from cat behavioral data obtained by Mead (1942); targets about 3° separated by ~12°. ———, Human data derived with 2.5° split-field targets (adapted from LeGrand, 1968). ○— — —○, Increment thresholds for a single ganglion cell (calculated from data of Sakmann and Creutzfeldt, 1969).

configuration employed by Mead (1942) consisted of two large panels, separated by a large septum. The cat's task was to choose the brighter (or dimmer) of the two panels. Thus, the large difference in sensitivity between the cat and human data shown in Fig. 1 may be more a reflection of the stimulus arrangements than in fundamental differences in sensitivity between the two. An adequate behavioral increment threshold study spanning a range of luminance values has not, as yet, been published. Nevertheless, an interesting feature of the cat data in Fig. 1 is the lack of an obvious rod–cone break as seen in the human function. The leveling off of the feline $\Delta I/I$ ratio at I values beyond −3 log cd/m² may be due, at least in part, to the efficiency of the feline pupil. We shall return to this point again when considering dark adaptation. Overall, there are insufficient data over a range of luminance values for the cat to permit a more fruitful comparison.

2. Electrophysiological Estimates

For the same reasons described in the section on absolute threshold, estimates of incremental threshold derived from electrophysiological data are questionable. A number of studies have examined the increment threshold of cat retinal ganglion cells (e.g., Barlow and Levick, 1969a,b; Sakmann and Creutzfeldt, 1969; Cleland and Enroth-Cugell, 1970). Snigula and Grüsser (1968) claimed good agreement of electrophysiological estimates (ganglion cell responses) with their behavioral data; they all show that $\Delta I/I$ decreases with increasing adaptation luminance. This agrees with both human and feline increment threshold data and suggests that "visual performance for luminance discriminations is mainly determined by retinal functioning" (Sakmann and Creutzfeldt, 1969). From the Sakmann and Creutzfeldt (1969) data, it is possible to obtain $\Delta I/I$ values for a number of adapting luminances for several ganglion cells. While comparison with behavioral data may be specious, these data are also plotted in Fig. 1 as the open circles. Note that the points have not been adjusted on either the X or Y axes.

A number of recent electrophysiological studies have concerned themselves with neural mechanisms that may govern the relationship between sensitivity and adaptation level (e.g., Barlow and Levick, 1969a,b; Cleland and Enroth-Cugell, 1970; Enroth-Cugell and Shapley, 1973a,b). Consideration of these models is beyond the scope of the present paper, and the reader is referred to these significant studies for a discussion of the gain mechanisms in the retina.

C. DARK ADAPTATION

1. Behavioral Measures

The time course, extent, and spectral properties of dark adaptation in the cat were recently studied successfully in a behavioral study by LaMotte and Brown (1970). In this study, a modified threshold-tracking procedure was used to follow the time course of threshold changes as a function of time in the dark. Thus, a response by the cat indicating that the stimulus was not seen increased the luminance of the target on the next trial while a successful detection decreased the luminance on the next trial. With this procedure, it was found that, under the appropriate light-adaptation conditions, the cat showed a dark-adaptation function similar to man's, including a rod—cone break. They also found that after intense light-adaptation to a white light, the cone adaptation segment lasted about 20 minutes when tested with a 604 nm light. Testing with blue light produced only a small cone segment. White light (3400°K color temperature) produced a 12—15-minute cone segment. Final threshold levels are shown out to 60 minutes, but they appear still to be declining somewhat (see Fig. 3 of LaMotte and Brown, 1970).

This study clearly demonstrated the magnitude and time course of dark adaptation in the cat. Compared to those for humans (solid line in Fig. 2), these data show that both the cone segment and the total adaptation time are somewhat longer for the cat. Thus, for a human light-adapted to a high intensity white light, complete dark adaptation rarely takes longer than 30—40 minutes. In the cat, this interval appears to be on the order of 50—70 minutes and possibly longer. A finding of equal significance in this study is that the cat is able to maintain his retina in a partially dark-adapted condition through constriction of his pupils. This pupillary mechanism is so efficient that even after exposure of a cat to lights of 2500 cd/m^2, the dark adaptation

74 Mark A. Berkley

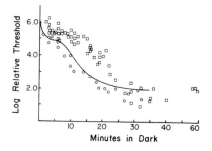

FIG. 2. Dark adaptation in cat and human. Behavioral thresholds as a function of time in the dark after exposure to 2500 cd/m² for 5 minutes for the cat. Each point is one threshold determination taken from different test sessions for 3 cats. Wavelength of test light 458 nm. ○, dark adaptation with natural pupils; □, data derived with dilated pupils (modified from LaMotte and Brown, 1970). ———, Human curve after 38.9×10³ trolands (about 12×10³ cd/m²) adaptation for 2 minutes and a <480 nm test light (modified from Hecht et al., 1937). Human curve is plotted so that final plateau is about 0.8 log unit above the final cat plateau, since this is about the difference in absolute threshold between cat and man.

record shows signs of partial dark-adaptation. The effects of this ability on the rate of dark adaptation are also shown in Fig. 2 (open circles). Note the significant increase in rate of dark adaptation under natural pupil conditions.

There has been only one study of pupil size vs light intensity reported for the cat. It shows that the cat's pupil has a larger dynamic range than that of man and closes down very rapidly at moderate levels of illumination (see Kappauf, 1943). A plot of these values is shown in Appendix Fig. 1A along with a comparable plot for man. Note that pupil widths, not diameters, are plotted for the cat because of the meridional asymmetry of the diameter of the cat pupil at moderate to high luminances.

2. Electrophysiological Studies

Relatively little electrophysiological work has been done on the *rate* of dark adaptation in the cat. Barlow et al. (1957), recording from ganglion cells in the retina, showed that sensitivity increased with time in the dark. They found a break in the function suggesting that rods and cones are connected to the same ganglion cells. They also reported that the cone segment of the dark adaptation curve for a single ganglion cell often extended out to 70 minutes and dark adaptation might not be complete even after 120 minutes in the dark. These values are extremely long both in comparison to those for man and to the results obtained with behavioral tests by LaMotte and Brown (1970). The long time course is apparently not due to anesthesia effects but could possibly be due to the disconnection of some efferent input to the retina, since the preparations were decerebrated.

It is more probable that at least some of the increased adaptation time is due to a feline photopigment regeneration process which is different from that in man. Retinal pigments have been studied *in situ* in the cat by several investigators (e.g., Weale, 1953b; Bonds and MacLeod, 1974). In these studies, regeneration of photopigment after pigment bleaches of known values have shown rhodopsin regeneration time in the cat to be about twice that in man (11 minutes for 50% regeneration for the cat vs 4.75 minutes for 50% regeneration for man) and may account for the extended adaptation times reported in both behavioral and electrophysiological studies (Bonds and MacLeod, 1974). In light of these findings, it would seem reasonable to say that complete dark adaptation in the cat (in which the pupil has been dilated) probably takes from 60 to 90 minutes depending on the level of bleaching. The rate of normal dark adaptation, however, is probably close to that for man when the cat can use its pupils to achieve a small degree of dark adaptation even in the presence of bright lights.

D. SPECTRAL SENSITIVITY

That the cat possesses a duplex retina has been known from anatomical studies for many years (e.g., Chievitz, 1889). Although many investigators have reported a preponderance of rods to cones in this retina (e.g., Leach *et al.*, 1961; Walls, 1942; Hollander and Stone, 1972), the number and distribution of these receptor elements was not adequately studied until a recent study by Steinberg *et al.* (1973). In this paper, counts of receptor types over most of the retina were made and plotted, and it provides the anatomical framework within which the spectral sensitivity of the cat will be considered.

The Steinberg *et al.* (1973) study revealed or confirmed several important features of the cat retina: (1) it is heavily dominated by rod receptors; (2) there is not a rod-free area of the retina homologous to a primate fovea; (3) the size of cones (diameter) is about the same as that of primates; (4) in the area centralis, the cat has about 6 times fewer cones than man has in his fovea; (5) the cat has about a 4 times greater density of rods than man in the region of maximum rod density (10° off-axis for the cat vs 15°–17° off-axis for man). This study, together with the less complete earlier works, confirms the presence of relatively large numbers of cones in the cat. A demonstration of the functional role of the cones, however, has been somewhat more difficult.

Several means may be employed to demonstrate the operation of rods and cones: (1) a nonmonotonic change in sensitivity with adaptation level (rod–cone break); or (2) different spectral sensitivity functions for each receptor system (Purkinje shift). Discrimination of stimuli differing in wavelength but having the same quantal efficiency (color vision) may also be used to test the role of cones, but it does not exclude the operation of rods. All these methods have been employed with the cat and will be briefly reviewed below.

1. Nonmonotonicity in Dark Adaptation

a. Behavioral Studies.   In humans, the function relating absolute sensitivity to time in the dark shows two plateaus, one early at about 7–10 minutes and another, much lower, at about 30–40 minutes (see solid line Fig. 2). These plateaus have been shown to be due to the operation of two distinct receptor systems (rods and cones), which differ in magnitude and time course of adaptation. The presence of two receptor types in the cat retina suggests that the cat, like man, should show a discontinuity in the dark adaptation function as the retina shifts from one receptor system to the other. The only behavioral study clearly showing the classic rod–cone break in the dark adaptation curve is that of LaMotte and Brown (1970). As mentioned earlier, these authors trained cats in a tracking paradigm and were able to follow the changes in threshold with time in the dark. With a white adaptation light of about 2500 cd/m^2, they found a rod–cone break after about 15 minutes in the dark. They also found that the dynamic range over which the cat adapts is about the same as in man (6 log units).

b. Electrophysiological Studies.   Electrophysiological evidence for a rod–cone break in the cat has come both from the early work of Granit (1943) as well as later single-cell studies. For example, the study of the responses of single ganglion cells in the cat retina during dark adaptation revealed this break demonstrating that both rods *and* cones are connected to many (but not all) ganglion cells (Barlow *et al.*, 1957). This result has been replicated many times (e.g., Daw and Pearlman, 1969; Andrews and Hammond, 1970a,b; Hammond and James, 1971).

2. Scotopic Sensitivity

a. Behavioral Studies.   Some success has been achieved in characterizing the spectral response of the different receptor systems in the cat retina. Using the same two-choice behavioral task used in his absolute threshold study (Gunter, 1951a), Gunter (1952) determined thresholds as a function of wavelength in dark-adapted cats to determine the sensitivity of the rod system. The function he derived had a peak sensitivity near 500 nm and matched the action spectrum of rhodopsin closely, with some small but significant deviations. These deviations appear to be due primarily to the effects of tapetal reflection and absorbance of the ocular media. Gunter

(1952) used correction factors (absorption of the ocular media and tapetal reflectance factors) inappropriate for the cat. More recent behavioral determinations of scotopic sensitivity in which appropriate corrections for ocular media absorption and tapetal reflection have been used (e.g., LaMotte and Brown, 1970; Loop, 1971) show good agreement with the absorption spectrum of rhodopsin. Examination of these data show that the cat scotopic sensitivity is very similar to human scotopic sensitivity. The ratio of cat to human scotopic luminosity is plotted in Fig. 4 (open circles). Gunter's (1952) curve, when adjusted with the proper lens absorption correction (Weale, 1954) is shifted toward the long wavelengths and suggests that his cats were partially light-adapted. All the behavioral functions published also show a slight elevation near 560 nm. This elevation is partially, but not entirely, due to tapetal reflectivity (see Weale, 1953a) which is maximal in this region of the spectrum.

   b. *Electrophysiological Estimates.* Electrophysiological estimates of scotopic sensitivity based on measurements of Granit (1943) are in excellent agreement with both the behavioral results and pigment chemistry (Weale, 1953b; Bonds and MacLeod, 1974). In an ERG study, Wirth (1953) also found excellent agreement with the rhodopsin absorption function. The fit was improved further by applying a correction for the absorbance of the feline ocular media (Weale, 1954). Thus, sensitivity of the cat to light at scotopic levels seems to be well understood and is very similar to that of man with two exceptions: (1) the absolute sensitivity of the cat is greater when comparisons are made by stimulus intensity, and (2) pigment regeneration appears to proceed at a slower rate in the cat than in man (Barlow *et al.,* 1957; Weale, 1953b; Bonds and MacLeod, 1974).

3. Photopic Sensitivity

   a. *Behavioral Studies.* Behavioral tests of the spectral sensitivity of the cat at relatively high luminance levels (photopic luminosity) have been made by a number of investigators. Thus, Gunter (1954a) reported a bimodal sensitivity function with peaks at 470 nm and 550 nm. Bonaventure (1962, 1964) also attempted to determine the cat's photopic sensitivity function but failed to find a difference in sensitivity from that of the dark-adapted cat. The failure to find a Purkinje shift in the cat was also reported by Piper (1905), using the ERG response. In light of subsequent studies, however, it would appear that either calibration or procedural difficulties produced the failure to observe the shift.

   Using the cone segments of their dark adaptation data, LaMotte and Brown (1970) reported a bimodal photopic sensitivity curve with peaks at about 510 and 565 nm. These data agree well with those of Granit (1943) and further

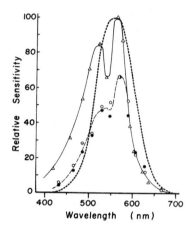

FIG. 3. Photopic spectral sensitivity of the cat and man. △, Cat behavioral data derived from cone plateaus of dark adaptation functions obtained after 5 minutes of 2500 cd/m² light adaptation. Data are the average of three cats. ○, ●, Spectral sensitivity derived from two neurons under photopic conditions (replotted from Daw and Pearlman, 1969; from Brown *et al.*, 1973). (Copyright 1973 by the American Psychological Association. Reprinted by permission.) Human photopic sensitivity is shown with dotted line (human data from CIE, 1931).

demonstrate the operation of a cone system. Figure 3 depicts the photopic spectral sensitivity of the cat compared with man. Note the relatively greater sensitivity of man to long wavelengths and the greater sensitivity of cats to short wavelengths. The latter effect appears to be due to the low absorbance of short wavelength light by the ocular media of the cat as compared to man

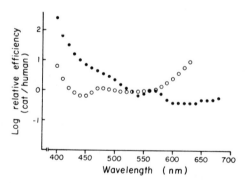

FIG. 4. Ratio of luminosities of cat and man. ●, Photopic luminosities V_λ(cat)/V_λ (human); ○, scotopic luminosities V'_λ (cat)/V'_λ (human). Cat photopic data are from LaMotte and Brown (1970); cat scotopic data, from Loop (1971); human photopic data from CIE (1931); scotopic data from CIE (1951).

(Weale, 1954). The ratio of cat to human photopic luminosity as a function of wavelength is shown in Fig. 4 (filled circles).

From these data, relative luminosity values may be calculated to permit adjustment of light intensities to be equally bright at or near threshold for cat and man. The values used in deriving the ratios in Fig. 4 are listed in Table IIA of the Appendix.

b. Electrophysiological Studies. Early studies by Granit (1943) showed a bimodal photopic sensitivity with peaks at about 507 and 560 nm, and these findings have been confirmed by Daw and Pearlman (1969) in a study of single cells. The data for two cells that they studied are included in Fig. 3 (open and filled circles) for comparison with the behavioral data. Whether the two peaks represent different cone types or an unusual interaction between cone pigment spectral sensitivity and tapetal reflectance is not certain.

E. COLOR VISION

1. Behavioral Studies

The demonstration that the cones in the cat retina are used in discriminating stimuli differing in wavelength (color vision) has been a most difficult task. Until recently, the results of these studies have been puzzling. In order to have color vision (the ability to discriminate between two lights on the basis of wavelength and independent of intensity) requires that at least two types of receptors be operating, e.g., two types of cones, two types of rods, or rods *and* cones. Numerous investigators reported failures to train cats to discriminate color (e.g., DeVoss and Ganson, 1915; Meyer *et al.,* 1954; Gunter, 1954b). Subsequent studies, however, have produced reliable demonstrations of the ability of cats to discriminate lights on the basis of wavelength (e.g., Bonaventure, 1962, 1964; Clayton, 1961; Clayton and Kamback, 1966; Mello and Peterson, 1964; Sechzer and Brown, 1964; Daw and Pearlman, 1970; Brown *et al.,* 1973). While all these studies show the cat to be able to discriminate wavelength, it is, apparently, an onerous task both for the cat and the investigator.

The bimodal photopic spectral sensitivity function described earlier suggests the possibility that cones and rods might have been operating in discriminating wavelength. In order to determine whether the cat has more than one cone type or uses rods *and* cones in making wavelength discriminations, it is necessary to be able to eliminate one of the receptor types, e.g., rods. Rods can be eliminated by using light levels high enough to saturate them. At these levels, presumably only cones are operating and discriminations based on wavelength would prove the existence of more than one cone type in the cat.

In a behavioral study, Daw and Pearlman (1970) determined the rod saturation threshold in cats and made their subsequent sensitivity measures above this level. Since they had believed that the cat had only one cone type (Daw and Pearlman, 1969), they were surprised to find that the cat could distinguish blue from orange since this indicated the presence of at least two cone types. The results of this study clearly demonstrated the existence of a cone whose sensitivity peaked in the blue end of the spectrum.

The findings of Daw and Pearlman (1970) have recently been extended in that a whole series of color pairs were used to evaluate the color discrimination capacity of the cat (Brown *et al.*, 1973). Brown *et al.* (1973) concluded that the cat can discriminate long (>570 nm) from medium (520–570 nm) from short (<520 nm) wavelengths. In addition to the two cone types suggested by Daw and Pearlman (1970), these authors believe that the cat probably has a third cone type with a peak near 570 nm. There is some support for this view in the electrophysiological data of Daw and Pearlman (1970). In any case, the cat has a poor absolute sense of color (Mello, 1968), apparently possessing only a weak ability to make relative wavelength discriminations.

A significant finding reported by LaMotte and Brown (1970) concerns the cat's capacity to keep the retina partially dark-adapted even under conditions of high illumination through efficient pupillary constriction. This fact, coupled with the weak sense of color the cat possesses, probably accounts for the varied results reported in experiments on cat color vision. Thus, at moderate to high light levels (10–1000 cd/m^2), the waking cat is probably in its mesopic range due to its efficient pupil.

2. Electrophysiological Studies

Daw and Pearlman (1969) electrophysiologically determined the light intensity necessary to produce rod saturation in lateral geniculate nucleus (LGN) cells and optic tract fibers. They then measured the spectral sensitivity of these cells at levels above rod saturation. All sampled cells had a peak sensitivity of about 556 nm. Since earlier studies had shown cats to be able to discriminate color, these authors suggested that the color discrimination ability of the cat was based on the response of rods *and* cones since they found only one type of cone. After their behavioral study which indicated a second cone type in the cat (Daw and Pearlman, 1970), they reexamined the LGN electrophysiologically and, after a heroic search, located 4 cells (out of a sample of 434) that had a peak sensitivity of about 445 nm (Daw and Pearlman, 1970; Pearlman and Daw, 1970). Thus, it would appear that the cat is a dichromat, and that his color sense is very weak.

On the basis of these and similar electrophysiological studies, several values for mesopic range and rod saturation have been reported (e.g., Barlow *et al.*, 1957; Daw and Pearlman, 1969; Hammond and James, 1971). The values reported by Daw and Pearlman (1969, 1970) and Hammond and James (1971) agree reasonably well. With a natural pupil, Daw and Pearlman (1969) estimated mesopic range to be $0.1-30$ cd/m^2 while Hammond and James (1971) estimated the range to be $0.1-40$ cd/m^2. Rod saturation was estimated to occur at about 30 cd/m^2, with the cone threshold about $0.1-2.5$ cd/m^2 for the cat. Human cone threshold is usually estimated to be 0.003 cd/m^2. Thus, the mesopic range appears to be narrower for cats than for humans, and cat cones to be less sensitive.

IV. Temporal Response of the Cat Visual System

Despite the many electrophysiological studies that have examined the temporal properties of portions of the cat visual system, a behavioral description of the cat's modulation sensitivity has only recently been reported (Loop and Berkley, 1975). Most behavioral estimates of the temporal properties of vision in cats have been concerned with critical fusion frequency (CFF), and these will be briefly reviewed before turning to modulation sensitivity.

A. CRITICAL FUSION FREQUENCY

1. Behavioral Studies

The earliest report of a behaviorally estimated fusion threshold (the rate of temporal intensity modulation at which a light appears fused or steady—CFF) is the work of Kappauf (1936). In this brief report, Kappauf, using a two-choice runway apparatus, found the cat's CFF to be 42 Hz at an average luminance of 6 cd/m^2, and 33 Hz at 0.06 cd/m^2. Few details of the training procedure and light stimulus are given, e.g., the light-dark ratio of the flicker. Kappauf did note, however, that at 9.4 cd/m^2 the cat's CFF was greater than 50 Hz. More recently, Pautler and Clark (1961), also using a two-choice runway apparatus, reported cats able to detect 55 Hz flicker at an average luminance of about 70 cd/m^2. In another study, at a light level which the authors described as "well below the customary limits for cone vision," Taravella and Clark (1963), using the same apparatus and stimulus as Pautler and Clark (1961), found the cat able to detect flicker at 65 Hz. Schwartz and Cheney (1966) found CFF values that ranged from 35 to 70 Hz at a luminance level of about 27 cd/m^2 using a two-choice apparatus. Finally, Loop and Berkley (1975), using a single stimulus method, found a CFF of 60

Hz with a sinusoidally modulated stimulus with an average luminance of only
0.03 cd/m^2. When compared with similar human data, these findings all
suggest that the cat has a higher CFF than man at equivalent target luminances. While simple comparisons between the human and feline studies are
always tenuous, it is noteworthy that all reported CFFs for the cat at low
luminances are high relative to man. Table II is a summary of behavioral CFF
estimates gathered from available sources.

2. Electrophysiological Estimates

Attempts to estimate CFF from electrophysiological data, in general, have
been only moderately successful. Two major approaches have been employed: single-cell recording and evoked-potential recording. While the single-
cell data are interesting and reveal much about temporal processing in the
visual system (e.g., Enroth, 1952; Grüsser and Creutzfeldt, 1957; Cleland and
Enroth-Cugell, 1966; Fukada et al., 1966; Hughes and Maffei, 1966; Maffei,
1968; Maffei et al., 1970; Fukada and Saito, 1971), it has not proved to be
particularly useful in evaluating the temporal response limit (CFF) of the
entire visual system. Gross potential studies of the retina (ERG), LGN, and
visual cortex are somewhat more useful in that the recorded response represents the sum of activity of a large number of neural elements and thus may
be more closely related to behavioral data. (The single-cell studies will be
considered in more detail in the section on modulation sensitivity.)

CFF estimates derived from ERGs have also been obtained in the cat (Dodt
and Enroth, 1953; van Hasselt, 1972). Dodt and Enroth (1953) found the
CFF using the ERG response a monotonically increasing function of target
luminance. They observed a break at about 65 cd/m^2 and 30 Hz. At 1600

TABLE II
COMPILATION OF CAT
CRITICAL FUSION FREQUENCY (CFF) ESTIMATES

Source	CFF (Hz)	Average luminance (cd/m^2)
	>50	9.4
Kappauf (1936)	42	6.0
	33	0.06
Pautler and Clark (1961)	55	70.0
Taravella and Clark (1963)	>65	–
Schwartz and Cheney (1966)	35–70	27.0
Loop and Berkley (1975)	~60	0.03

cd/m^2 they estimated the CFF to be near 70 Hz. In another ERG study, van Hasselt (1972) determined CFF as a function of luminance over a 5 log unit range. Since no absolute luminance calibration is given, comparison with other studies is not possible. However, two aspects of van Hasselt's data are interesting: (1) CFF increases with increases in average luminance (confirming Dodt and Enroth, 1953), and (2) there are two limbs to the luminance–CFF function, suggesting a rod and a cone segment.

Lindsley (1953) and Schwartz and Lindsley (1964) studied the temporal response of the cat visual system using evoked potentials and found that visual cortex exhibited lower frequency following characteristics (lower CFF) than more peripheral structures. In a similar study, Sturr and Shansky (1971) studied the amplitude of evoked responses to flash trains. They also report that subcortical structures follow higher frequencies of light flicker than visual cortex. Although they did not specifically estimate CFF in this study, their data suggest that the cat visual system is capable of following very high rates of flicker. However, the use of a gas-discharge flash stimulator makes the interpretation of these results somewhat difficult because of the changes in intensity that occur with changes in flicker rate, a problem the authors recognized.

In a more recent study in which averaged evoked potentials were employed, Berkley et al. (1975a) found that with a low luminance target (0.3 cd/m^2) and a sinusoidally modulated stimulus, CFF estimates ranged from 55 to 65 Hz. They also found, however, that their threshold estimation procedure could often produce very high CFF estimates. Details of the study and the threshold estimation procedure will be discussed in the next section.

B. TEMPORAL MODULATION SENSITIVITY OF THE CAT

1. Behavioral Studies

CFF is known to vary with average luminance and modulation depth (peak-to-trough intensity), yet few studies have been concerned with these variables. In addition, the frequent lack of luminance and modulation calibrations make construction of functions relating these factors difficult if not impossible. What is needed is a complete description of the temporal responsivity of the feline visual system in which luminance and modulation depth are studied.

A descriptive method derived from linear systems analysis has been used in studies of the temporal properties of the human visual system (deLange, 1954; Kelly, 1961) and provides a means for giving a complete description of the temporal properties of the system. With this method, the average luminance of a flickering target is held constant for a series of measurements while the modulation depth of the stimulus is varied. The modulation depth necessary to produce a report of flicker or fusion is determined for a number of modulation frequencies (but all at a fixed average luminance). A plot is then made of the percent modulation necessary to detect flicker (or fusion) at each of the temporal modulation frequencies. The procedure may then be repeated with different average luminances yielding a family of curves relating modulation sensitivity to average luminance and frequency. Usually (for mathematical simplicity), the waveform of the temporal intensity modulation is sinusoidal. The highest frequency seen as flickering at maximum modulation depth can be thought of as similar to the CFF. The great advantage of this descriptive method is that once the complete response function (transfer function) is known, the response of the visual system to any temporal luminance variation can be predicted.

Using a behavioral technique called conditioned suppression (for details, see Smith, 1970; Loop and Berkley, 1972), Loop and Berkley (1975) determined a temporal modulation function for the cat at one luminance level. The results of this study are shown in Fig. 5. It can be seen that the general shape of the function is similar to that of humans (dotted lines in Fig. 5B) but with two significant differences: (1) at the low mesopic luminance used in this study, the cat is able to detect flicker at a higher rate than man; and (2) the cat requires greater modulation depth to detect low frequency (<15 Hz flicker). Even after equating retinal illumination between cat and man (see

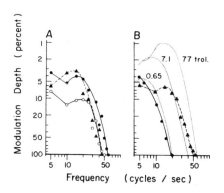

FIG. 5. Temporal modulation sensitivity of the cat and man. Modulation sensitivity for three cats (●, 18; ▲, Igor; ○, Moma) at average luminance of 0.03 cd/m². (B) ▲– – –▲, Average curve for three cats shown in (A) (8.2 eq. trolands). ●———●, Human threshold (1.1 trolands) obtained in same apparatus as that used with the cat; · · · ·, Human data from Kelly (1961) derived under similar conditions as the feline data. From Loop and Berkley (1975).

right side, Fig. 5), it was found that the cat still has greater high frequency sensitivity than man (for details, see Loop and Berkley, 1975). These data, as well as the CFF findings reviewed above, suggest that the cat may see as flickering many light sources man sees as fused, e.g., fluorescent lights, television, motion pictures.

2. Electrophysiological Estimates

Several studies have examined the temporal intensity modulation response of various parts of the cat visual system (e.g., Cleland and Enroth-Cugell, 1966; Hughes and Maffei, 1966; Maffei, 1968; Maffei et al., 1970). In these studies, the response of neural elements to light stimuli sinusoidally modulated in time are studied. As in the psychophysical studies, modulation thresholds are determined and transfer functions are constructed. Cleland and Enroth-Cugell (1966) and Maffei et al. (1970), for example, derived transfer characteristics for several retinal ganglion cells. Cleland and Enroth-Cugell (1966) found a small number of cells that showed a response linearly related to modulation depth over a limited range, and tuning characteristics similar in shape to human psychophysical transfer functions. Hughes and Maffei (1966) also reported a linear response between modulation depth and ganglion cell output, with an exponent for this relationship of 0.75. Maffei et al. (1970) used a stimulus that covered both the center and the surround of the receptive field of a ganglion cell, and described one "on" center cell showing a transfer characteristic that looked remarkably similar to the cat behavioral function found by Loop and Berkley (1975) except that the function covered a lower frequency range. While it is extremely unlikely that a single ganglion cell determines the transfer function of the entire visual system, this intriguing similarity beckons further study.

In an attempt to discover the role of visual cortex in temporal modulation sensitivity, Berkley et al. (1975a) recorded averaged potentials from the cortical surface of the cat in response to different modulation frequencies and depths. They found that the amplitude of the averaged response was a linear function of the log of modulation depth [as did Sternheim and Cavonius (1972) in similar human studies]. Using the extrapolation method described in Sections V, A and B (e.g., Campbell and Maffei, 1970; Berkley and Watkins, 1971, 1973; Sternheim and Cavonius, 1972), they obtained an estimate of the temporal modulation sensitivity of the cat visual system by extrapolating these functions to a baseline level. While the shape and general range of these functions agreed well with the behavioral estimates of Loop and Berkley (1975) (see Fig. 6), there was sufficient variability to warrant caution in making estimates of absolute sensitivity from data derived from anesthetized animals.

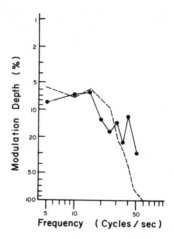

FIG. 6. Behavioral and evoked potential estimates of temporal modulation sensitivity in the cat. – – –, Average behavioral threshold for three cats. Average luminance of target 0.03 cd/m². ●——●, Evoked potential threshold modulation estimates obtained as described in text. Average luminance of target = 0.3 cd/m². Adapted from Berkley *et al.* (1975a).

The results described above suggest that, at some neural level in the visual sytem, there is a linear relationship between the logarithm of the modulation depth of the stimulus and the output of that neural structure. In the spatial domain, for example, it has been shown that cortical cells with simple receptive fields (Hubel and Wiesel, 1962) in cat striate cortex exhibit a linear relationship between discharge frequency and log spatial contrast while retinal ganglion cells, lateral geniculate cells and some complex cells in the cortex do not (Maffei and Fiorentini, 1973). Thus, these authors concluded that the neurons most likely performing the spatial contrast analysis are simple cells in striate cortex. Can a similar conclusion be drawn in the temporal domain? Hughes and Maffei (1966) reported that the discharge frequency of cat retinal ganglion cells is clearly related to the logarithm of stimulus modulation depth. Similar findings were reported by Sternheim and Cavonius (1972) in humans with the ERG as well as the visually evoked cortical potential.

While these results suggest that the frequency response of the visual system is determined by retinal mechanisms, the failure to find an ERG-derived transfer function that matched the psychophysical function by Sternheim and Cavonius (1972) as well as the lower CFF values derived from cortical studies strongly suggests the participation of other than retinal operators in determining the temporal response properties of the visual system. It appears likely, however, that neural mechanisms beyond the retina act simply as low pass filters.

V. Spatial Vision

Recent discoveries made in neurophysiological studies of the cat visual system concerning the processing of spatial stimuli (e.g., Hubel and Wiesel, 1962) make the cat's capacity to discriminate spatial stimuli extremely interesting and revealing, yet little is known about this capacity in the cat. To begin, we will consider the simplest spatial vision thresholds, e.g., visual acuity.

A. VISUAL ACUITY

1. Behavioral Measures

Visual acuity may be defined as the capacity to detect fine spatial details. The smaller the detail that can be seen, the greater the acuity. Because such variables as average luminance, target shape, contrast, and viewing time affect acuity measures, it is difficult to make simple comparisons between studies and/or animal species. Although there are many standard acuity targets, in the present discussion, visual acuity will be considered as the minimal detectable grating, expressed as the number of light-dark bar pairs per degree of visual angle (cycles/degree).

Several measures of the visual acuity of the cat have been made and, while not in exact agreement, are sufficiently similar to lend some confidence to their accuracy. Smith (1936) using a two-lane runway apparatus measured the visual acuity of cats using gratings and single lines as targets. He found that the animals could discriminate gratings of 5.5 minutes bar width. The average luminance of the targets was not reported, but from his description of the conditions of illumination, ~250 cd/m^2 appears to be a reasonable estimate. (Since Smith (1936) could not produce finer gratings, he used single lines as stimuli. With these targets, acuity ranged from 0.45 to 1.4 minutes for one subject and 1.1 to 3.3 minutes for the other.)

More recent behavioral acuity tests have yielded both higher and lower estimates of feline acuity. In a study of the effects of selective visual experience on visual acuity, Muir and Mitchell (1973) found that discrimination performance fell to chance levels at about 3.5 c/deg. They were able to improve this value only slightly with additional training (Muir and Mitchell, 1973). The average luminance of their targets was 75 cd/m^2.

Blake *et al.* (1974) determined the finest grating discriminable from a uniform field of equal luminance to be about 5.5 c/deg for the cat. Their target consisted of a grating with a sine wave luminance profile and an average luminance of 17.1 cd/m². In a similar study, Bisti and Maffei (1974) also using sine wave gratings, arrived at a value of 5.0–6.5 c/deg at an average luminance of 2 cd/m².

Using a two-choice discrimination paradigm, square wave gratings, and a modified tracking procedure, Berkley and Bloom (unpublished) have recently obtained acuity estimates for the cat. In this study, cats were rewarded for pressing a nose-key in front of a grating stimulus and not rewarded for pressing a nose-key in front of a uniform field stimulus. A correct choice reduced the size of the grating stimulus on the subsequent trial while an incorrect choice increased the size of the grating on the next trial. With this procedure and a target luminance of 15 cd/m², estimates ranged from 4.0 c/deg to 7.0 c/deg.

For ease of comparison, the acuity estimates described above are listed in Table III along with the average luminance of the targets employed.

Considering the differences in testing methods, criterion choice, and luminance differences, these studies are in excellent agreement. A complete acuity function for the cat has, as yet, not been reported, e.g., acuity over a range of luminance levels.

TABLE III
COMPILATION OF BEHAVIORAL ESTIMATES
OF CAT ACUITY

Source	Target	Luminance (cd/m²)	Acuity (c/deg)
Smith (1936)	Square wave grating	~250	5.5[a]
Smith (1936)	Single line	~250	0.45 minutes
Muir and Mitchell (1973)	Square wave grating	75	3.5
Blake et al. (1974)	Sine wave grating	30	5.5
Bisti and Maffei (1974)	Sine wave grating	2	5.5–6.5
Berkley and Bloom (unpublished)	Square wave grating	40	4.0–7.0

[a]The luminance value is estimated from the description given by Smith (1936). Finer gratings could not be made in this study, so it is not clear how much better the cats might have done.

2. Electrophysiological Measures

Since the size of retinal ganglion cell receptive field probably set the upper limits of acuity, numerous workers have attempted to relate the receptive field size to acuity. The studies that have measured the response of single-cell receptive fields stimulated with grating stimuli are of particular interest. At the level of the retina, Enroth-Cugell and Robson (1966) found several cells capable of responding to gratings up to 4 c/deg (sine wave gratings). Similar upper limit values were described for cells in the lateral geniculate (Wässle and Creutzfeldt, 1973). Lower values (e.g., 3 c/deg) were obtained in studies of visual cortex (Campbell et al., 1969a; Maffei and Fiorentini, 1973). Among all these studies, no cells have been described that respond to spatial frequencies above 5 c/deg. While sampling problems, optics, and the use of different average luminances may have contributed to this failure, it seems unusual that among all these studies cells with a higher frequency response escaped detection. If there are any, they must be few in number.

Using an evoked potential method, Berkley and Watkins (1971, 1973) were able to estimate the cats' acuity. Their method, modified from that used by Campbell and Maffei (1970) in humans, used the amplitudes of averaged responses evoked by phase-changed gratings of equal contrast and average luminance but different spatial frequencies. Plotting the amplitude of the response versus the log of the spatial frequency of the stimulus grating yielded a linear function which, when extrapolated to the zero response amplitude to determine the intercept, yielded an estimate of acuity. Values ranging from 3.1 to 6.9 c/deg were obtained with an average luminance of the gratings of 90 cd/m^2.

In a similar study of the cat by Campbell et al. (1973) in which response amplitude as a function of grating contrast was plotted, extrapolations yielded threshold contrast values. A plot of these values yielded a contrast sensitivity function (see next section). The high frequency intercept of this function represents an estimate of visual acuity. In this case, the intercept occurred between 12 and 15 c/deg despite the relatively low average luminance of their target grating (e.g., 2 cd/m^2). This value is considerably above any value found using behavioral techniques even at much higher luminance levels.

Because acuity depends so directly on the dioptrics of the eye, a number of investigators have evaluated the optics of the cat eye (Morris and Marriott, 1961; Wässle, 1971; Bonds et al., 1972). In general, these measurements compare the light distribution of the image plane (retina) with the light distribution in the object plane. When a single line is used as a target, a line-spread function is obtained that can be used to evaluate the quality of the optics. From such a line-spread function, Westheimer (1962) found the half-width of the retinal image to be 4–8 minutes with a 6 mm pupil. With a dilated pupil, Morris and Marriott (1961) obtained a value of 12 minutes. Bonds *et al.* (1972) reported similar values for a dilated pupil but found a significant narrowing of the line-spread function with a reduction in pupil size. Comparison with human line spread functions (Campbell and Gubisch, 1966) show the optics of the cat eye to be significantly poorer than that of man.

Wässle (1971) utilizing an optical transfer function (see next section) concluded that the upper limit for acuity in the cat should be about 5–6 c/deg. Taken together, the optical data suggest that the optics of the cat eye are 4–6 times poorer than those of man. Assuming that the grating acuity of man is 30 c/deg (1 minute stripe width), the cat grating threshold should fall between 5 and 7.5 c/deg. This range agrees well with the behavioral, and most of the electrophysiological, estimates described above.

A recent reevaluation of the optics of the cat eye by Enroth-Cugell and Robson (1974) has yielded a narrower line-spread function than previously reported, but the significance of this finding is difficult to evaluate at this time because the method employed in this study differs from that used by the earlier investigators and the method has not, as yet, been applied to the eye of man. The studies by Enroth-Cugell and Robson (1974) and Bonds *et al.* (1972) both suggested that the cat's acuity may be better than previously believed. The behavioral tests thus far reported have all used targets whose luminance was not sufficiently high to produce small pupils. Since significant image degradation has been reported in the cat eye with pupils larger than 4–5 mm (Bonds *et al.,* 1972) and all the behavioral studies used luminance values (<100 cd/m^2) that produced larger pupils, it is possible that the maximum acuity has as yet not been determined for the cat. Tests in which brighter targets are used, or in which small artificial pupils are used, should provide the answer.

In addition to optical limitations, certain limits on acuity must be imposed by the receptor mosaic. In primates, there is good evidence that grating acuity is closely related to intercone distance in foveal vision (Green, 1970). In the cat, minimum intercone distance in the area centralis is about 6.2 μm, subtending about 1.7 minutes of arc (Steinberg *et al.,* 1973), much smaller than the best acuity estimates would require. It is more likely, therefore, that ganglion cell size and distribution are more closely related to acuity than is receptor size. Anatomical studies of ganglion cells (dendritic spreads), which may be related to the size of the centers of ganglion cell receptive fields, have reported spreads of about 18 μm (Leicester and Stone, 1967). This diameter corresponds to a visual angle of approximately 5 minutes and agrees well with measures of acuity derived from other studies. Interganglion cell distance calculated from the data of Stone (1965) for small to medium-sized cells in area centralis is about 4 minutes.

B. SPATIAL CONTRAST SENSITIVITY FUNCTION

As mentioned above, the capacity for seeing details depends heavily on luminance and contrast. (Contrast is defined as the ratio of the difference in luminance between the light and dark portion of the target to the sums of the luminances.)

$$C = (L_{max} - L_{min})/(L_{max} + L_{min}) \qquad (3)$$

where L_{max} is luminance of the light part and L_{min} is luminance of the dark part. One could determine, for example, the finest resolvable grating at a given contrast for a series of spatial frequencies, but all at equal average luminances. Alternatively, the minimal contrast necessary to detect a grating of fixed frequency and average luminance could be determined. A plot of these data, using the reciprocal of threshold contrast vs spatial frequency, yields a function called contrast sensitivity function. For a complete description of the visual system, a series of such functions derived for different average luminances is plotted. This descriptive method, also borrowed from linear systems analysis, permits predicting the response of the system if the spatial frequency components of the stimulus are known (Schadé, 1956; Campbell and Robson, 1968).

1. Behavioral Studies

Two behavioral estimates of the cat's modulation transfer function have been reported. Blake et al. (1974) using sine wave target gratings of 17.1 cd/m² in space-average luminance, found a transfer function that peaked about 0.5 c/deg, falling rapidly both at lower and higher spatial frequencies. The high frequency cutoff was about 5–6 c/deg, in excellent agreement with the acuity estimates reported earlier by Smith (1936), Wässle (1971), and Berkley and Watkins (1971, 1973).

In another cat study, Bisti and Maffei (1974) determined a spatial contrast sensitivity function using behavioral methods. While their function is similar in general shape to that of Blake et al. (1974), it differs in that peak sensitivity is near 0.2 c/deg and the high-frequency cutoff is higher. Following the high-frequency leg to estimate the cutoff frequency yields a value near 12–15 c/deg. Since the luminance of the target in the Bisti and Maffei study was somewhat lower (2 cd/m²) than in the Blake et al. (1974) study (17 cd/m²), this discrepancy is even more difficult to understand. The results of these studies plus some comparable human data are shown in Fig. 7.

An interesting sidelight of visual acuity testing in humans is the finding that acuity is poorer when the test target contours are obliquely oriented than when they are vertical or horizontal (Taylor, 1963). This difference has been

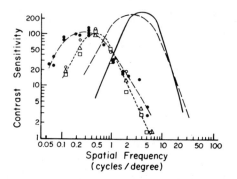

FIG. 7. Cat and human spatial contrast sensitivity functions. Two curves to the left are cat data obtained by behavioral tests: ●, Bisti and Maffei (1974) at 2 cd/m²; o, □, △, Blake *et al.* (1974) at 17.1 cd/m². The two curves to the right are comparable human data: – – –, Bisti and Maffei (1974) at 2 cd/m²; ——, O. Franzén and M. Berkley (unpublished) at 15 cd/m².

shown not to be due to optical factors (e.g., Mitchell *et al.*, 1967; Campbell and Green, 1965). Does the cat show a similar anisotropy? Current evidence suggests that the cat probably does not have an "oblique effect," in that contrast sensitivity measures derived both by behavioral and evoked potential methods have failed to reveal it (Campbell *et al.*, 1973; Bisti and Maffei, 1974).

2. Electrophysiological Measures

Enroth-Cugell and Robson (1966) have measured the spatial contrast transfer function for retinal ganglion cells in the cat using single-cell recording techniques. Employing grating stimuli, they measured the changes in the discharge pattern of ganglion cells as the gratings moved through the receptive field of the cell. By varying the contrast of the stimulus and noting the changes in discharge frequency, they were able to determine the minimal amount of contrast necessary to affect the firing pattern of the cell for different spatial frequencies of the grating. The threshold contrast was then plotted as a function of spatial frequency yielding a "contrast sensitivity function" for each cell. These findings were also related to previous reports of ganglion receptive field size, ganglion cell dendritic fields, visual acuity and the human contrast sensitivity function. The "contrast sensitivity functions" of ganglion cells were found to have the same general shape as the human contrast sensitivity function in that they show an optimal spatial frequency and reductions in sensitivity at both higher and lower spatial frequencies. Although the curves were similar in shape from one cell to another, the range of spatial frequency response and optimal frequency were different from cell to cell. Using the same general procedure and stimuli, Campbell et al. (1969a) measured the "contrast sensitivity" of cells in the lateral geniculate and visual cortex of cats. The results of this study are very similar to what was found for retinal ganglion cells in that similarly shaped functions were found although there may have been differences in visual field sites between these studies. Many of the cells studied, however, responded over a narrower frequency range than was observed at the retina and showed a more prominent decline in sensitivity at low spatial frequencies than was observed in the ganglion cell studies. The fact that the range and optimal spatial frequency were found to be different for different cells, however, supports the view that the contrast sensitivity function for the entire visual system may be the envelope of the individual cell responses.

Similar measures have also been made at other levels of the feline visual system. Thus, Maffei and Fiorentini (1973) described transfer functions for LGN and cortical cells and distinguished responses from simple and complex cells (Hubel and Wiesel, 1962) recorded from cat cortex—something earlier studies had neglected (e.g., Campbell et al., 1969a,b). The tuning curves of the LGN cells were similar to those described for ganglion cells but the tuning curves of simple cortical cells were very narrow in their bandpass, showing a very sharp low-frequency as well as high-frequency attenuation. The response range of these cells easily fits within the transfer function of the whole visual system as determined with behavioral methods (Blake et al., 1974; Bisti and Maffei, 1974). As mentioned earlier (Section IV, B), Maffei and Fiorentini (1973) also found that simple cells and some complex cells in visual cortex exhibited responses whose magnitude was linearly related to the log of the contrast of the grating targets. They did not find such a relationship for retinal ganglion cells or cells in the lateral geniculate nucleus and therefore concluded that, in the cat, spatial frequency is "analyzed" by simple cells in visual cortex.

It is logical to argue that single-cell studies can only yield a general, and possibly erroneous, view of the responsiveness of the visual system as a whole. The reasons for this have been discussed in Section II, B. Some of these difficulties may be eliminated by using an electrophysiological measure which samples large cell populations, including interactions between cells. The averaged evoked potential is such a measure. Using evoked potentials recorded from awake, paralyzed cats, Campbell et al. (1973) have derived an estimate of the contrast sensitivity of the cat. In this study, modified from a similar study in awake humans (Campbell and Maffei, 1970), potentials evoked by a phase-reversed grating were recorded for various modulation depths of the target grating. This was done for a variety of grating frequencies. Plots were then made of response amplitude vs log contrast and were found to be linear. Extrapolating these functions permitted the estimation of a contrast threshold for each spatial frequency. A plot of these threshold values (plotted as reciprocals of contrast) vs spatial frequency produced a sensitivity function which peaked near 0.2 c/deg, showing both a low-frequency as well as high-frequency roll-off. The surprising aspect of this function is the high-frequency portion which, when carried to its intercept of the frequency axis, suggests that the cat has a sine wave grating acuity of near 15 c/deg. In light of the behavioral studies reported above as well as the low luminance level of the targets used in this study (2 cd/m^2), it is difficult to interpret this finding, although it appears to agree with the behavioral estimates of Bisti and Maffei (1974).

Taken together, the findings of the cats spatial contrast sensitivity indicate that the cat operates in a lower frequency range than man, and, while humans can detect higher-frequency gratings than the cat, the cat is capable of seeing low-frequency gratings invisible to man.

VI. Complex Spatial Vision

A. FORM VISION

The most unique and salient aspect of vision is the ability to discriminate complex shapes and patterns. Little is known of neural mechanisms by which this remarkable capacity is achieved although recent discoveries have provided tantalizing glimpses of the underlying neural mechanisms. One difficulty in the study of form vision is the lack of parametric data related to this visual capacity. We have seen, for example, that numerous dimensions can be specified as being important in color vision, e.g., wavelength, adaptation level, retinal position. No such specification of relevant dimensions has as yet been achieved for form vision, although the recent Fourier models (e.g., Campbell and Robson, 1968) may be considered an attempt to do so. Consequently, most studies of form vision are little more than a catalog of discriminable form stimuli (Class B studies) without any simplifying scheme that would permit the performance of Class A studies on the underlying dimensions. This situation exists equally for cat and man.

1. Behavioral Studies

In the cat, most studies of form vision have been concerned with form categories and the effects of ablating various brain parts on form discrimination. For example, Sperry *et al.* (1955) showed that cats were able to discriminate small differences in the *shapes* of triangles. A variety of other more or less simple geometric shapes have also been shown to be discriminable by the cat (e.g., Hara and Warren, 1961b; Ganz and Fitch, 1968). A few studies have attempted to demonstrate complex form perception. For example, cats have been shown to possess size constancy (Gunter, 1951b) and the ability to generalize size and shape (Warren and Ebel, 1967). Thus, when trained to discriminate the larger of the two figures, and subsequently tested with a different size pair, cats were shown to choose the larger of the pair even though the absolute size was different from the initial training (size generalization) (Warren and Ebel, 1967). When trained to discriminate a pair of figures with a given set of contrast conditions (e.g., light against a dark background) cats will transfer the discrimination with a reversal of the contrast (dark on a light background) (Smith, 1935; Berkley, 1970). This type of equivalence testing is presumed to demonstrate that the animal is utilizing the shape of the figure in making the discrimination rather than some local light flux or spatial cue.

For the most part, such studies are little more than interesting exercises in that they do not suggest or evaluate underlying neural substrates of form vision. In an attempt to develop Class A studies of form vision, we have been examining a number of visual dimensions suggested by recent electrophysiological studies which may represent some fundamental parameters of this capacity. For example, we have trained cats to discriminate lines differing only in orientation in an attempt to determine contour orientation thresholds. In one study (Berkley and Warmath, 1974), two targets were presented (see Fig. 8) consisting of either two lines (one line on each target field), two line pairs (one parallel and the other not as shown in Fig. 8), or a parallel line pair and a pair in which one line is straight and the other is angled (bent) at its center. With single-line stimuli, the threshold angle to detect a difference in orientation was $10°-15°$ (Berkley and Warmath, 1974). Similar values have been reported in a study by Hirsch (1972) in which single stimuli were also used. With the line-pair stimuli as well as the bent-line stimuli, we have found the threshold to range from $3°$ to $5°$ (see Fig. 9) although one animal was able to consistently discriminate differences of only $2°$ (Berkley and Warmath, 1974). Comparable human studies have shown man able to discriminate orientation differences much smaller than this, but the values seem to depend heavily on stimulus configuration (Bouma and Andriessen, 1968; Lennie, 1972) so that simple comparisons are not possible.

Orientation sensitivity in humans has also been studied using masking or adaptation (e.g., Campbell and Kulikowski, 1966) paradigms. In these studies, the contrast necessary to detect one grating in the presence of another grating (or immediately after it is viewed) is determined for a number of angular differences between the two gratings. Threshold contrast (for the test grating) is then plotted as a function of the orientation difference between the test and masking (or adapting) grating. The half-width at half-height (bandpass) of

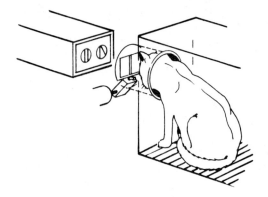

FIG. 8. Sketch of cat behavioral testing apparatus. Cat views the stimulus display through two transparent windows, which also serve as nose-keys. Device below nose-keys is beef baby food dispenser. Stimuli are electronically generated on an oscilloscope and controlled by computer. Display is 20 cm from nose-keys. Targets subtend about 5° at cat eye.

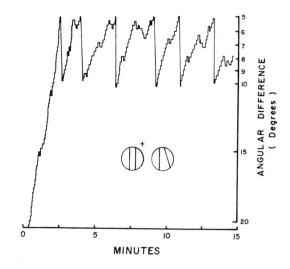

FIG. 9. Cat orientation tracking. Record, written out on an X-Y plotter, of angular difference between line pair shown at bottom of the figure. For each correct response, angular difference was reduced (upward on record) while for each incorrect response, angular difference was increased. To demonstrate the ease with which this animal could make the discrimination, the stimulus angle was reset to a 10° difference each time the cat reduced it to a 5° difference. From Berkley and Warmath (1974).

this function has been taken as an estimate of orientation tuning of orientation selective "channels" in the human visual system. The orientation bandpass values reported in these studies vary from 3° to 12°, depending on the test methods employed (Campbell and Kulikowski, 1966; Kulikowski, 1972; Kulikowski *et al.*, 1973). The relationship of these findings to the more direct contour orientation threshold measurements (e.g., Bouma and Andriessen, 1968) is currently unknown. Similar measurements of orientation sensitivity in cats would be most enlightening but, as yet, have not been reported.

2. *Electrophysiological Studies*

Single-cell studies of cat visual cortex have shown the importance of contour orientation as a trigger feature for many cortical cells (Hubel and Wiesel, 1962). Using drifting gratings as stimuli, Campbell *et al.* (1968) found, for the most tightly tuned cell, that a 50% reduction in response occurred with a 14° change in orientation of the test gratings from the preferred orientation. In a more recent study by Watkins and Berkley (1972, 1974) in which edges and slits were used as stimuli, it was found that: (1) simple cells (Hubel and Wiesel classification) were more tightly tuned for orientation than complex cells, and (2) orientation tuning was positively (but not perfectly) correlated with receptive field size; e.g., in general, the smaller the receptive field, the tighter the tuning for orientation. The most tightly tuned cell studied was a simple cell with a small receptive field in which a 50% reduction in response was achieved with a 6° deviation from the preferred orientation (orientation bandpass of 6°). Other studies (e.g., Blakemore *et al.*, 1972; Henry *et al.*, 1974; Rose and Blakemore, 1974), have also studied orientation selectivity of single cells and reported similar values. While absolute orientation thresholds cannot be estimated from these data, it is interesting to compare the tuning of orientation selective cells with our behavioral measures. If these cells subserve the capacity to discriminate orientation, one might expect that the cat should be able to discriminate differences in orientation of less than 10°. The behavioral studies show the cat able to perform this discrimination easily. A second prediction can be made from the Watkins and Berkley (1972, 1974) data: orientation discrimination capacity should be poorer in peripheral vision than in central vision because receptive fields representing the periphery are larger. Ablation studies in which the cortical representation of the central visual fields have been removed, sparing the peripheral fields, confirm this hypothesis (Berkley, 1971; Berkley, unpublished observations). In these studies it was found that lesions of cortex serving the central 10° of vision do not affect the animal's capacity to discriminate the classic test shapes (upright vs inverted triangle; circles vs square; vertical vs horizontal lines) but did reduce the orientation acuity of these animals.

Over the years, a great number of studies in which various brain parts have been ablated in order to discover their role in form vision have been performed on cats. A review of this vast literature will not be attempted here, but it is worthwhile to briefly consider some of the more recent ablation-behavior studies. Thus, cats appear to retain a remarkable degree of vision after removal of "visual cortex" (Spear and Braun, 1969; Winans, 1971; Doty, 1971; Sprague et al., 1973; Berlucchi et al., 1974). These studies all found cats able to discriminate various shapes, e.g., horizontal vs vertical stripes, upright vs inverted triangles. Since these studies removed most of the major cortical target zones of the projections from the LGN, they have been interpreted as indicating that either the geniculate–cortical system is not necessary for form vision or that other parts of the visual system, e.g., superior colliculus, pretectum, and their projection zones, are capable of mediating form vision (Doty, 1971; Sprague et al., 1973). Thus, these studies raise serious questions for current neural models of form vision. One major difficulty in interpreting these studies, however, is that the cues (features?) that these animals are using in making their discriminations are not known. Many of the stimuli used may more accurately be described as pattern (repetitive stripes, squares) than forms or shapes (triangles, crosses, etc.). There is some evidence that local flux cues (either spatial or temporal) may be used to discriminate such stimuli (Winans, 1971). Another complicating factor is the existence of cortical areas beyond striate cortex which receive geniculate input (e.g., areas 18 and 19; Glickstein et al., 1967; Berkley et al., 1967). These areas contain cells that have spatial contour-analyzing properties (Hubel and Wiesel, 1965) and may participate in form vision even after removal of area 17. It is also possible that cortical areas receiving a second-order input via superior colliculus (e.g., Graybiel, 1972) may also participate. In summary, these studies suggest that the geniculate–cortical system may not be necessary for some types of form vision, but the reasons why this is so are far from clear.

B. MOVEMENT SENSITIVITY

Electrophysiological studies of the cat visual system have shown that retinal image movement is important in activating many classes of cells (Hubel and Wiesel, 1962; Burns et al., 1962). Since most studies use paralyzed animals, it is not clear how much of image motion sensitivity is concerned with motion produced by eye movements or true stimulus movement. Nevertheless, retinal image motion is a potent dimension in activating many cortical cells, and the possibility of discovering correlations between neural properties and behavior appears particularly promising.

1. Behavioral Studies

a. Absolute Threshold. Relatively little is known of the cat's capacity to discriminate visual target motion. Early studies by Kennedy and Smith (1935) and Kennedy (1939) using a two-choice discrimination procedure and stationary vs rotating crosses as stimuli determined both the lower movement threshold as well as a relative movement threshold. These studies reported absolute thresholds ranging from 2.6 to 14.6 rotational degrees per second. For comparison with human studies as well as with available electrophysiological data, these values have been converted to tangential velocity at the outer tips of the rotating cross stimulus. This conversion yields a mean threshold of 1.12°/sec with a low value of 0.38°/sec and a high value of 2.18°/sec.

Using similar testing procedures (two-choice discrimination), Berkley *et al.* (1975b) determined absolute thresholds for linearly moving (oscillating) dots or lines generated on cathode ray tubes. The mean threshold value for 8 cats was 1.75°/sec with a range of 0.75°–2.8°/sec when a 50% detection criterion was used. The values were shifted upward to 2.8°–8.0°/sec when the criterion adopted by Kennedy and Smith (75% correct) was used. While the values arrived at in both these studies are similar, they are very much higher than similar measurements in man made at the same luminance (Leibowitz, 1955). These values are near 3–4 minutes/sec.

Since threshold has been shown to vary with viewing time (Brown and Conklin, 1954; Leibowitz, 1955), most human studies utilize a given exposure interval in which the stimulus is displayed. The reason is that movement is confounded with displacement. Thus, a very slowly moving stimulus could be detected simply by waiting long enough for the stimulus to have moved to a noticeably different location rather than by seeing it move. In the cat studies cited above, unlimited viewing time was permitted. Despite this fact, it is interesting that the cats in the Berkley *et al.* study described above, did not adopt a long-viewing time strategy. In this study, stimulus viewing time was recorded for each trial (time from start of stimulus presentation to response). Analysis of these data showed that viewing time did not increase with decreases in stimulus velocity. In fact, viewing time was found to be independent of stimulus motion, depending only on the animals' previous training experience. Since the animals were initially trained to discriminate a rapidly moving from a stationary stimulus and thus needed only a "short" viewing time to detect movement, they learned the discrimination using short viewing times. As the test stimulus was slowed, they made more and more errors but did not increase their viewing time. In subsequent testing which used a procedure in which errors were punished with electric shock, increased viewing times, decreased errors, and much lower thresholds (<20'/sec) were found. Even though these studies are suggestive, they were not performed in ways that permit simple comparison with human movement detection thresholds.

b. Differential Rate. Kennedy's (1939) article is the only behavioral study in which differential rate thresholds were determined in the cat. Using a standard of 80 angular deg/sec (40 linear deg/sec) he determined the cat's threshold for detecting a deviation from this velocity. Kennedy reported that the threshold of the cat was reached when the ratio of the standard to variable target velocity was 1.2:1. Other standard velocities were not used. Unfortunately, no other data exist regarding this capacity in the cat.

2. Electrophysiological Studies

The movement rate thresholds described above are within the optimal movement rates for one class of cortical neurons. Several studies have examined movement sensitivity for several classes of neurons (e.g., Pettigrew *et al.*, 1968; Watkins and Berkley, 1974). In these studies, it was found that simple cells responded best (on the average) to rates of 2°/sec or less while complex cells preferred more rapid rates, 5°–10°/sec. Since simple cells were often found to respond to extremely low movement rates; e.g., <0.2°/sec, thresholds for slow movement were not determined. Since it is not known which classes of neurons mediate the perception of slow movement, estimates of threshold cannot be derived from these data. However, recent single-cell studies have reported finding two general classes of cells in the retina, one that responds best to stationary patterns (X cells) while the other responds best to moving stimuli (Y cells) (Enroth-Cugell and Robson, 1966). There is good evidence that in visual cortex complex cells receive Y cell input and thus may be the cortical substrate of movement sensitivity (Hoffman and Stone, 1971; Maffei and Fiorentini, 1973). Since paradigms which attempt to differentiate between these two classes of cells in tests of movement discrimination (e.g., Tolhurst, 1973) have not yet been applied to the cat, the role of these cells is not understood, although a number of attractive hypotheses have been put forward (Keesey, 1972; Tolhurst, 1973; Kulikowski and Tolhurst, 1973).

VII. Binocular Vision

A. VISUAL FIELDS

1. Behavioral Estimates

Behavioral estimates of the extent of the visual field are based primarily on food or encounter perimetry (Sprague and Meikle, 1965). With this method, the cat is lightly held by one examiner and a "fixation object" (usually a piece of food held in a pair of forceps) is jiggled or tapped at some distance in front of the cat's nose to elicit fixation. A second stimulus (piece of food or other object) is then introduced at various positions, and the response of the cat is noted. Using these methods, Sprague and Meikle (1965) and Sherman (1973) reported that the horizontal extent of the binocular visual field is about 90°–100° either side of the visual axis (200° total).

Estimates of the extent of the visual field may also be obtained by determining the limits from which the pupil may be seen. Walls (1942) reported a total horizontal field of 287° for the cat with a binocular field of 130° (viz. extent of total field overlapped by each eye). Considering more recent measures, the lateral extent reported by Walls (1942) is probably an overestimate. Estimates made by Vakkur and Bishop (1963) based on optometric measurements made on excised feline eyes indicate that the cat has a total field of about 200° with a binocular field of 140°. The behavioral extents agree reasonably well except that the behaviorally determined binocular fields appear to be somewhat smaller ($\sim$90°) (Sherman, 1973) probably because of the limitations imposed by the nose. Given the uncertainties of the behavioral testing methods, the agreement is quite good. In man, the total extent of the field is usually given as 180° with about 90° binocular overlap (Walls, 1942; LeGrand, 1967). In comparison with man, the cat appears to have slightly greater peripheral extent of the visual fields and perhaps somewhat less binocular overlap.

2. Electrophysiological Estimates

Field extent estimates may also be derived from studies of single cells in dorsal lateral geniculate and visual cortex, e.g., determining the most lateral extent of visual field by estimating it from visual field position of receptive fields of LGN and cortex. (Binocular overlap may be similarly estimated.) Electrophysiological studies of LGN indicate that the region of binocular overlap extends at least for 40° either side of the midline (Bishop et al., 1962) confirming the behavioral and optical estimates of overlap. Subsequent studies are in excellent agreement with these estimates (Bishop et al., 1962; Sanderson, 1971; Hoffman et al., 1972). The lateral limits of the visual fields, however, have been little explored so it is difficult to estimate their extent with certainty. In addition, the possibility exists that the entire visual field is not represented in the geniculostriate system. There is electrophysiological evidence that the entire field is represented in striate cortex (Tusa, unpublished; Wilson and Sherman, 1974), but not in areas 18 and 19 (Tusa and Rosenquist, personal communication) even though these latter areas also receive direct input from the LGN (e.g., Glickstein et al., 1967; Berkley et al., 1967).

Data derived from measurement of receptive field positions of cortical neurons have been somewhat less useful in field extent estimates. In a visual field projection study (Bilge *et al.,* 1967; Kalia and Whitteridge, 1973), the most lateral edge of the field as represented by recorded cells extended to about 90°; but because of the great compression of the representation of the far periphery and the difficulty in mapping these cells, cells representing more lateral areas (if there are any) could easily have been missed.

The excellent agreement found between visual field estimates derived using behavioral, electrophysiological, optical, and anatomical methods provide the framework for considering some rules concerning the anatomical representation of the visual fields in visual cortex. Thus, topographic mapping of visual cortex (Bilge *et al.,* 1967) indicated that there is a larger representation of the central visual fields than peripheral fields, with less and less cortical area being devoted to greater and greater visual field eccentricities. The amount (linear millimeters) of cortex devoted to a given distance in visual space (e.g., degree of visual angle) has been expressed as the ratio (millimeters of cortex)/(degree of visual angle), and has been called the magnification factor (Daniel & Whitteridge, 1961). In central vision, this ratio is large, falling off precipitously with increasing eccentricity (Daniel and Whitteridge, 1961; Bishop *et al.,* 1962). Based on studies of the visual field representation in cat dorsal lateral geniculate, Bishop *et al.* (1962) postulated that this change in magnification factor was due to the nonuniform distribution of ganglion cells in the retina. Feline studies of ganglion cell density (Stone, 1965), magnification factor (Bilge *et al.,* 1967; Sanderson, 1971), and field representation (Bishop *et al.,* 1962) suggest the following relationship: the amount of cortical area representing a single ganglion cell is constant. An appropriate name for this relationship might be the Bishop–Whitteridge law. This relationship probably should be qualified to apply only to those ganglion cells that project to thalamus, since recent electrophysiological studies (Stone and Hoffman, 1972; Stone and Dreher, 1973; Stone and Fukuda, 1974) have shown that all ganglion cells do not project to thalamus.

In man, Weymouth (1958) showed that acuity declines with eccentricity at the same rate as ganglion cell density declines for eccentricities up to 30°. This was true despite the fact that he did not have the accurate ganglion cell counts of Van Buren (1963) but used the less accurate counts of Polyak (1957), and it suggests a simple relationship between acuity and magnification factor. Although this relationship has not been established directly in cats (because there are no peripheral acuity measures available for this animal), it has been shown to hold reasonably well in monkeys (Rolls and Cowey, 1970).

3. Anatomical Estimates

The amount of binocular overlap of the visual field has been said to be directly proportional to the percentage of uncrossed fibers in the optic chiasma (Walls, 1942). Walls called this relationship the Newton–Müller–Gudden law after the workers who proposed it. How well does it agree with the data on the cat for binocular overlap? We have seen that the cat has a binocular field of 90°–130° with a total field of about 200°. Thus, to obey the Newton–Müller–Gudden law, the cat should have from 40 to 50% of its optic nerve fibers uncrossed. Anatomical studies (Hayhow, 1958; Meikle and Sprague, 1964) indicate a somewhat lower value of 33%, although a quantitative study is yet to be done. Whether the behavioral estimates underestimate the extent of the visual field (which is highly possible), the Newton–Müller–Gudden law does not hold for the cat, or the anatomical estimates of percentage of uncrossed fibers are incorrect, cannot be decided with currently available data.

B. CYCLOPEAN VISION

Having frontally placed eyes and displaying conjugate eye movements, the cat is presumed to have cyclopean vision. That is, although it has two eyes, the world is seen as one. A second important aspect of significance in binocular vision is stereopsis. Stereopsis is usually defined as the capacity for seeing depth, using as depth cues retinal image disparity which is the result of binocular parallax. In the following section the two processes will be considered separately: (1) binocular single vision and (2) stereopsis.

1. Single Vision

As we have seen in a previous section, the visual field of each eye of the cat overlaps the other. Presumably, within this region of binocular overlap, the cat should experience single vision. While it is difficult to imagine otherwise, there is not and cannot be direct evidence that he does—only presumptive evidence. The evidence that the cat experiences single vision consists mainly of observations of the disjunctive eye movements of cats. In the normal human when a fixation object is at infinity, the visual axes of the two eyes are parallel. If a target object is closer than infinity, e.g., <20 feet, a degree of convergence (disjunctive eye movement—inward turning of both eyes) is necessary to reduce the retinal disparity and resultant diplopia that would exist without the vergence. Thus, one could conclude that if the cat makes vergence eye movements while fixating objects that are brought close to him, he is doing so to maintain single vision and, therefore, experiences single vision. On the other hand, single vision could also be experienced by suppressing the input from one eye. Presumably, if this mechanism of preserving single vision were used, no vergence eye movements would be seen.

While there has been some question as to the cat's capacity for making disjunctive eye movements (for review, see Hughes, 1972), current evidence suggests that cats are capable of making vergence eye movements but often do not (Hughes, 1972; Stryker and Blakemore, 1972). These investigators agree that the cat may be able to make a maximum vergence eye movement of 11°, corresponding to a fixation plane of about 20 cm. [Measures of accommodation also place the limits of near vision at about 20–25 cm (Elul and Marchiafava, 1964).] These data suggest that the cat has single vision maintained through the appropriate vergence eye movements but raise the interesting possibility that within the maximum vergence and accommodation distance (<20 cm), the cat may suffer from double vision.

2. Stereopsis

a. Behavioral Studies. Numerous cues are used in discriminating depth, many of them monocular. Having two frontally placed eyes, however, provides the basis for a unique cue to depth, e.g., spatial disparity of the images on the retina of each eye. Retinal disparity exists for all stimuli in front of or behind the fixation plane. Small differences in disparity have been shown to act as depth cues. Thus, even with the elimination of all visual cues except retinal disparity, the sensation of depth is possible (Julesz, 1971). The capacity to use disparity as a depth cue is called stereopsis. The question of whether the cat is capable of stereopsis has recently been examined experimentally. Fox and Blake (1971) using a shadow-casting apparatus, were able to show that the cat could discriminate two stimuli that produced differences in retinal disparity. Whether the resultant disparity produced the illusion of depth can only be inferred. However, since in the training procedure used by Fox and Blake (1971) the initial training targets differed in real depth, and the cats transferred their discrimination to the targets that offered only in a disparity cue, it would seem reasonable to assume that the cats experience stereopsis. No other direct tests of stereopsis have been made in the cat. Studies to determine the limits of this ability in the cat are clearly necessary.

b. Electrophysiological Studies. Several logical schemes for binocular vision have been proposed. For example, Cajal (as cited in Walls, 1942) suggested that there must exist in the brain a set of neurons that receive input from both eyes. He believed that such an arrangement could provide the basis of both single vision and stereopsis. Walls (1942), however, in his classic monograph, pointed out that such a scheme would require different sets of cells for different target depths in space, and he considered such an arrangement to be both inefficient and logically implausible. Recent electrophysiological studies, however, have shown Cajal to be correct.

Thus, recent studies on electrophysiology of single cells in cat visual cortex have provided the probable neural substrates both for binocular single vision and stereopsis in this animal. For single vision, for example, a class of cells with simple binocular input would be necessary. Hubel and Wiesel (1962)

have shown that there are many binocularly activated cortical cells in the cat.
More direct studies by Barlow *et al.* (1967) and by Blakemore (1969, 1970)
have also described binocularly activated cells, but with an additional property. They found cells sensitive to a range of retinal disparities. That is, they
found cells that responded maximally when there existed a retinal disparity
of the stimulus images, a condition naturally occurring when a stimulus is not
in the fixation plane. These authors suggested that these cells are the neural
substrate of stereopsis. Using quantitative measures derived from these
studies, Joshua and Bishop (1970) estimated the area in depth in which there
is single vision. By measuring the variance of disparity to which cells were
sensitive at increasing retinal eccentricities, they were able to estimate the
changes in the probable extent of this area of single vision in the cat with
changes in eccentricity. In human stereopsis studies, this area, called Panum's
area, has been shown to increase with eccentricity, e.g., the range within
which there is single vision increases with retinal eccentricity. Joshua and
Bishop (1970) showed that the depth range for single vision based on single
cell disparity studies increases at the same rate with eccentricity as Panum's
area has been shown to do in human vision. Figure 10 depicts these findings,
showing both the human psychophysical data (filled circles) as well as the
single cell data (open circles). (The reader is referred to the original report for
a more detailed discussion, which is beyond the scope of this paper.)

The remarkable series of experiments described briefly above has provided a
plausible neural substrate both for stereopsis and single vision. Because of the

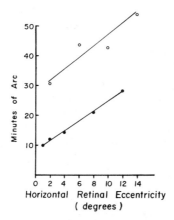

FIG. 10. Change in magnitude of human fusional area (depth in minutes) as a function
of retinal eccentricity compared with change in variance of horizontal disparities for
groups of cortical cells as a function of retinal eccentricity. ○, SD of receptive field
disparity (cat); •, dimensions of Panum's area (human). (From Joshua and Bishop, 1970.
Reprinted with permission.)

overwhelming face validity of these findings as well as their close correspondence with human psychophysical studies, the mechanisms suggested by these
workers are currently accepted even though no direct behavioral testing of
the cat has been done [except for the Fox and Blake (1971) study]. Because
threshold data are not available for the cat, human thresholds for stereopsis
will not be considered.

Other studies of cat visual cortex have revealed cells whose trigger features
correspond to various binocular vision features derived from psychophysical
studies in man and considerations based on geometric optics. For example,
cortical cells have been described that are said to be tuned to such unique
binocular vision features as interocular orientation differences (Blakemore *et
al.*, 1972) and visual direction (Blakemore, 1970). The validity of these
substrates is less well established and awaits behavioral testing of cats. In this
instance, electrophysiological study of the visual system has far surpassed
behavioral studies and has even suggested mechanisms and capacities for
psychophysical study.

Notable successes have been achieved in attempts to understand the neural
basis of vision, and the cat has provided much of the data. As long as the cat
remains a popular preparation for anatomists and physiologists, careful behavioral testing of this animal will continue to gain importance as the need for
Class A observations increases. It is hoped that the successes (and failures)
reported in this paper will be useful both as a reference source and as an
encouragement to workers to use the cat as a psychophysical subject.

VIII. Appendix

In the course of attempting to make comparisons between cat and man, it is
necessary to have certain normative data for both organisms. While such data
for man are easily available from any one of many reference sources (e.g.,
LeGrand, 1968; Graham, 1965; Davson, 1969), finding comparable feline
data is a more difficult task. Most of what is known about the cat visual
system is scattered in a variety of research journals. As an aid both in
evaluating human–cat comparisons and in having an accessible source for
normative feline data, a number of figures and tables have been included in
this paper as an appendix.

A. STRUCTURAL COMPARISONS OF CAT AND MAN

Table IA is a compilation of ocular and retinal measurements for cat and
man derived from the sources listed in the footnote.

To estimate retinal illumination, it is necessary to know the size of the
pupil (if artificial pupils are not used). The data in Fig. 1A comprise a plot of

TABLE IA
OCULAR AND RETINAL COMPARISONS[a]

Parameter	Man	Cat
Ocular		
Eye diameter	25 mm	22.3 mm
Posterior nodal distance	16.8 mm	12.5 mm
Total power of ocular optics	60 D	78 D
Retinal distance/minute of visual angle	4.9 μm	3.6 μm
Refractive indices		
Cornea	1.376	1.376
Aqueous	1.336	1.336
Lens	1.413	1.550
Vitreous	1.336	1.336
Pupil		
Maximum diameter	8 mm	14.2 mm
Maximum area	51 mm²	160 mm²
Minimum diameter	2 mm	<1 mm (width)
Interpupillary distance	62 mm	36 mm
Retina		
Maximum cone density	$146 \times 10^3/mm^2$	$26 \times 10^3/mm^2$
Cone diameter	2.5 μm	2.0–2.2 μm
Minimum intercone distance	2.5 μm	6.2 μm
Maximum rod density	$160 \times 10^3/mm^2$	$460 \times 10^3/mm^2$
Rod diameter	1–2.5 μm	1–2.5 μm
Position of maximum rod density	20°	10°–15°
Maximum ganglion cell density	$147 \times 10^3/mm^2$	$3 \times 10^3/mm^2$
Optic nerve and chiasma		
Total number of fibers	1,100,000	85,000
Percent decussation	53:47	66:33

[a]Ocular and pupillary values for man from LeGrand (1968); cat data from Vakkur *et al.* (1963) and Vakkur and Bishop (1963). Retinal values for man from Polyak (1957); for the cat from Steinberg *et al.* (1973). Optic nerve data from Kupfer *et al.* (1967) for man; for the cat, from Donovan (1967). Decussation value for man from Kupfer *et al.* (1967); for the cat from Walls (1942), Hayhow (1958), and Meikle and Sprague (1964).

the relationship of pupillary width to luminance level as determined by Kappauf (1943). Note that for the human, the pupil values are diameters whereas for the cat, width is used. This is because of the asymmetry of the shape of the cat pupil. More complete data on the true area of the feline pupil are currently not available.

B. FELINE PHOTOMETRY

As discussed in Section II,A, the use of luminance units (cd/m^2) in describing visual stimuli in cat studies is not correct since the spectral

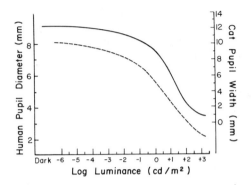

FIG. 1A. Pupil size as a function of luminance. Measurements were taken from photographs made of cats exposed to the light intensity indicated. ——, Data for cats (see scale on the right; note that scale on right is width, not diameter). – – –, Data for humans From Kappauf (1943). Copyright 1943, The Williams & Wilkins Co., Baltimore.

characteristic (V_λ) that enters into the computation of these units for man is different from that for the cat. To compute luminance (L_v) in cd/m², the following formula is used:

$$L_v = K_v \int_{400}^{700} L_{e\lambda} \, V_\lambda \, d\lambda \tag{A.1}$$

when $L_{e\lambda}$ is the spectral radiance of the source; V_λ is the spectral luminosity of the eye; and K_v is a scaling constant (see Section II, A).

In order to calculate "cat candelas," one must know the values of V_λ for the cat for photopic candelas and V'_λ for scotopic candelas. A listing of these values is given in Table IIA. The values of V_λ are derived from Brown et al. (1973), and those of V'_λ are from Loop (1971).

In Table IIIA, the scotopic and photopic scaling constants K_λ and K'_λ for candelas have been calculated for a full radiator with a color temperature of 2042°K $(L_{e\lambda})$ using the V_λ and V'_λ listed in Table IIA. The equivalent K_λ and K'_λ for man were computed using V_λ and V'_λ from CIE (1931) and CIE (1951), respectively. Note that the ratio of the cat to human K'_λ is about 1.0, indicating that scotopic candelas are about equivalent for cat and man. At photopic levels, however, a significant difference is seen between cat and man due to the differences in V_λ for the two eyes (See Figs. 3 and 4 in Section III, D).

The same computation was also carried out for illuminant A (rather than a full radiator at 2042°K), a light source more similar to commonly used tungsten sources. The color temperature of this source is 2854°K.

TABLE IIA
CAT PHOTOPIC AND SCOTOPIC
LUMINOUS EFFICIENCIES

λ (nm)	V_λ	V'_λ	λ (nm)	V_λ	V'_λ
400	0.09	0.06	560	1.00	0.32
410	0.12	0.08	570	0.95	0.23
420	0.13	0.11	580	0.71	0.17
430	0.19	0.16	590	0.40	0.12
440	0.23	0.21	600	0.28	0.09
450	0.27	0.29	610	0.19	0.06
460	0.34	0.46	620	0.14	0.05
470	0.42	0.79	630	0.11	0.03
480	0.49	0.93	640	0.65	0.01
490	0.61	0.995	650	0.05	
500	0.71	0.999	660	0.03	
510	0.79	0.97	670	0.02	
520	0.85	0.87	680	0.01	
530	0.82	0.77	690	0.00	
540	0.66	0.63	700	0.00	
550	0.79	0.46			

The ratios of the cat to human for this source are given in the lower portion of Table IIIA. As expected, scotopic candelas are similar for cat and man, but again a significant difference is seen for photopic candelas.

In Table IVA, the retinal illumination of cat and man have been computed for a range of luminance values. For man, retinal illumination was calculated as the product of luminance and pupillary area (trolands, td). The values used were derived from LeGrand (1968).

TABLE IIIA
HUMAN AND CAT CANDELAS
(FOR 2042°K SOURCE)

	Cat	Human	Ratio cat/human
Scotopic (K'_λ)	1611	1745	0.92
Photopic (K_λ)	918	680	1.35

(Ratio of candelas computed for illuminant A)

Scotopic candelas: cat/human = 0.97
Photopic candelas: cat/human = 0.80

TABLE IVA

COMPARISON OF RETINAL ILLUMINATION BETWEEN CAT AND MAN
UNDER NATURAL PUPIL CONDITIONS

Luminance L (cd/m^2)	Pupil area, S_H (mm^2)	Trolands, $L \times S_H$	Pupil area, S_c (mm^2)	"Trolands," $L \times S_c$	Eye size correction[a] ($\times$ 1.8)	Tapetal correction[b] $\times$ 1.4 (CETd)	Cat/human (td)
10^{-6}	49.6	5.0×10^{-5}	118.8	1.19×10^{-4}	2.1×10^{-4}	3×10^{-4}	6
10^{-5}	48.9	4.9×10^{-4}	116.9	1.17×10^{-3}	2.1×10^{-3}	3×10^{-3}	6.1
10^{-4}	47.4	4.7×10^{-3}	113.1	1.13×10^{-2}	2×10^{-2}	2.9×10^{-2}	6.2
10^{-3}	44.2	4.4×10^{-2}	107.5	1.1×10^{-1}	2×10^{-1}	2.9×10^{-1}	6.6
10^{-2}	38.4	3.8×10^{-1}	100.3	1.0	1.8	2.6	6.8
0.1	29.6	2.96	86.6	8.7	15.6	22.5	7.6
1	19.6	19.6	65.0	65.0	117	168.	8.6
10	11.7	117	32.2	322	580	835	7.1
10^2	7.1	710	5.3	530	954	1374	1.3
10^3	4.9	4910	0.8	800	1422	2016	0.4

[a] This correction taken as the ratio of the squares of the posterior nodal distances (PNDs) of cat and man $(PND_{cat})^2 / PND^2_{man} = 1.8$.

[b] This value is the average reflectance factor for a "yellow" tapetum over the visible spectrum empirically derived by Weale (1954). CETd = cat equivalent troland.

A similar calculation was performed for the cat, using pupillary areas estimated from Fig. 1A above. Since the cat pupil is asymmetrical, the areal values are only approximations, e.g., the pupil was considered circular for calculation purposes. At low luminance levels, this approximation is nearly correct, but with increasing luminance levels, a greater and greater error is introduced as the pupil takes on a more slitlike appearance. Thus, for values above 1 candela, the computed values underestimate retinal illumination by an increasing factor.

To equate for the differences in eye size between cat and man, a scaling factor that consists of the ratio of the squares of the posterior nodal distances (PND) was used. This value was calculated to be 1.8.

Finally, to estimate the effect of tapetal reflectivity, the average reflectance of the "yellow" tapetum as determined by Weale (1954) over the visible spectrum was used. This factor was 1.4.

Thus, to compute cat equivalent trolands (CETd), the following computation was performed:

$$CETd = L_v \times S_c \times P \times T_c \tag{A.2}$$

where L_v is luminance in cd/m^2; S_c is pupillary area in mm^2; P is the eye-size scaling factor (PND_c^2 / PND_H^2); and T_c is the tapetal reflectance factor.

The results of this calculation are listed in the next to last column (CETd) in Table IVA. In the last column, the ratio of cat (CETd) to human (td) trolands is given.

Acknowledgments

It is a pleasure to acknowledge the assistance of D. Warmath, K. Jones, and M. Bloom in collecting some of the data and in the preparation of several of the figures and tables; and of Ruth McCullough for the most patient and careful secretarial assistance. This work was supported by Grant 34166 from the National Science Foundation and Grant EY 00953 from the National Eye Institute.

References

Andrews, D. P., and Hammond, P. (1970a). Mesopic increment threshold spectral sensitivity of single optic tract fibres in the cat: Cone-rod interaction. *Journal of Physiology (London)* **209**, 65–82.

Andrews, D. P., and Hammond, P. (1970b). Suprathreshold spectral properties of single optic tract fibres in cat, under mesopic adaptation: Cone-rod interaction. *Journal of Physiology (London)* **209**, 83–103.

Barlow, H. B., and Levick, W. R. (1969a). Three factors limiting the reliable detection of light by retinal ganglion cells of the cat. *Journal of Physiology (London)* **200**, 1–24.

Barlow, H. B., and Levick, W. R. (1969b). Changes in the maintained discharge with adaptation level in the cat retina. *Journal of Physiology (London)* **202**, 699–718.

Barlow, H. B., Fitzhugh, R., and Kuffler, S. W. (1957). Dark adaptation, absolute threshold and Purkinje shift in single units of the cat's retina. *Journal of Physiology (London)* **137**, 327–337.

Barlow, H. B., Blakemore, C., and Pettigrew, J. D. (1967). The neural mechanism of binocular depth discrimination. *Journal of Physiology (London)* **193**, 327–342.

Berkley, M. (1970). Visual discriminations in the cat. *In* "Animal Psychophysics" (W. C. Stebbins, ed.), pp. 231–247. Appleton, New York.

Berkley, M. (1971). Line orientation discrimination deficits following partial ablation of the geniculo-cortical system in cats. *Society for Neuroscience, Washington, D.C.*

Berkley, M., and Warmath, D. S. (1974). Line orientation sensitivity in the cat: Behavioral measures. *Association for Research in Opthalmology, Sarasota, Fla.*

Berkley, M., and Watkins, D. W. (1971). Visual acuity of the cat estimated from evoked cerebral potentials. *Nature (London) New Biol.* **234**, 91–92.

Berkley, M., and Watkins, D. W. (1973). Grating resolution and refraction in the cat estimated from evoked cerebral potentials. *Vision Research* **13**, 403–415.

Berkley, M., Wolf, E., and Glickstein, M. (1967). Photic evoked potentials in the cat: evidence for a direct geniculate input to visual II. *Experimental Neurology,* **19**, 188–198.

Berkley, M., Loop, M., and Evinger, C. (1975a). Temporal modulation sensitivity in the cat. II. Evoked potential measures. *Vision Research* **15**, 563–568.

Berkley, M., Warmath, D., and Tunkl, J. (1975b). Discrimination of real movement by cats. In preparation.

Berlucchi, G., Lepore, F., and Simoni, A. (1974). Effects of lesions of the suprasylvian gyrus on visual discrimination learning and retention and on interhemispheric transfer in the cat. *Brain Research* **66**, 356.

Bilge, M., Bingle, A., Seneviratne, K. N., and Whitteridge, D. (1967). A map of the visual cortex in the cat. *Journal of Physiology (London)* **191**, 116P–118P.

Bishop, P., Kozak, W., Levick, W., and Vakkur, G. (1962). The determination of the projection of the visual field on to the lateral geniculate nucleus. *Journal of Physiology (London)* **163**, 503–539.

Bisti, S., and Maffei, L. (1974). Behavioral contrast sensitivity of the cat in various visual meridians. *Journal of Physiology (London)* **241**, 201–210.

Blake, R., Cool, S. J., and Crawford, M. L. J. (1974). Visual resolution in the cat. *Vision Research* **14**, 1211–1218.

Blakemore, C. (1969). Binocular depth discrimination and the nasotemporal division. *Journal of Physiology (London)* **205**, 471–497.

Blakemore, C. (1970). The representation of three-dimensional visual space in the cat's striate cortex. *Journal of Physiology (London)* **209**, 155–178.

Blakemore, C., Fiorentini, A., and Maffei, L. (1972). A second neural mechanism of binocular depth discrimination. *Journal of Physiology (London)* **226**, 725–749.

Bonaventure, N. (1962). Sensibilité spectrale et vision des couleurs chez le chat. *Psychologie Française* **1**, 75–82.

Bonaventure, N. (1964). La vision chromatique du chat. *Compte Rendu de l'Académie des Sciences* **259**, 2012–2015.

Bonds, A. B., and MacLeod, D. I. A. (1974). The bleaching and regeneration of rhodopsin in the cat. *Journal of Physiology (London)* **242**, 237–248.

Bonds, A. B., Enroth-Cugell, C., and Pinto, L. H. (1972). Image quality of the cat eye measured during retinal ganglion cell experiments. *Journal of Physiology (London)* **220**, 383–401.

Bouma, H., and Andriessen, J. (1968). Perceived orientation of isolated line segments. *Vision Research* **8**, 493–507.

Boynton, R., and Onley, J. (1962). A critique of the special status assigned by Brindley to "psychophysical linking hypothesis" of "Class A". *Vision Research* **2**, 383–390.

Bridgeman, C. S. (1938). The absolute brightness threshold and scotopic visibility curve of the cat's eye, 110 pp. Unpublished doctoral dissertation, Univ. of Rochester, Rochester.

Bridgeman, C. S., and Smith, K. U. (1942). The absolute threshold of vision in cat and man with observations on its relation to the optic cortex. *American Journal of Physiology* **136**, 463–466.

Brindley, G. S. (1960). "Physiology of the Retina and the Visual Pathway." Arnold, London.

Brown, J. L., Shively, F. D., LaMotte, R. H., and Sechzer, J. A. (1973). Color discrimination in the cat. *Journal of Comparative and Physiological Psychology* **84**, 534–544.

Brown, R., and Conklin, J. (1954). The lower threshold of visible movement as a function of exposure time. *American Journal of Psychology* **67**, 104–110.

Burns, B., Heron, W., and Pritchard, R. (1962). Physiological excitation of visual cortex in cat's unanesthetized isolated forebrain. *Journal of Neurophysiology* **25**, 165–181.

Campbell, F. W., and Green, D. (1965). Optical and retinal factors affecting visual resolution. *Journal of Physiology (London)* **181**, 576–593.

Campbell, F. W., and Gubisch, R. W. (1966). Optical quality of the human eye. *Journal of Physiology (London)* **186**, 558–578.

Campbell, F. W., and Kulikowski, J. (1966). Orientation selectivity of the human visual system. *Journal of Physiology (London)* 187, 437–445.

Campbell, F. W., and Maffei, L. (1970). Electrophysiological evidence for the existence of orientation and size detectors in the human visual system. *Journal of Physiology (London)* 207, 635–652.

Campbell, F. W., and Robson, J. (1968). Application of Fourier analysis to the visibility of gratings. *Journal of Physiology (London)* 197, 551–566.

Campbell, F. W., Cleland, G. F., Cooper, B. G., and Enroth-Cugell, C. (1968). The angular selectivity of visual cortical cells to moving gratings. *Journal of Physiology (London)* 198, 237–250.

Campbell, F. W., Cooper, G. F., and Enroth-Cugell, C. (1969a). The spatial selectivity of the visual cells of the cat. *Journal of Physiology (London)* 203, 223–235.

Campbell, F. W., Cooper, G. F., Robson, J. G., and Sachs, M. B. (1969b). The spatial selectivity of visual cells of the cat and the squirrel monkey. *Journal of Physiology (London)* 204, 120P–121P.

Campbell, F. W., Maffei, L., and Piccolino, M. (1973). The contrast sensitivity of the cat. *Journal of Physiology (London)* 229, 719–731.

Chievitz, J. H. (1889). Untersuchungen uber die Area centralis retinae. *Archiv für Anatomie und Entwicklungsgeschichte* pp. 139–196.

CIE (Commission Internationale de l'Eclairage) (1931). Proceedings of 8th Session, Cambridge University Press, Cambridge, England.

CIE (Commission Internationale de l'Eclairage) (1951). Proceedings of 12th Session, Bureau Central CIE, Paris, France.

Clayton, K. N. (1961). Color vision in the cat. *American Psychologist* 16, 415.

Clayton, K. N., and Kamback, M. (1966). Successful performance by cats on several colour discrimination problems. *Canadian Journal of Psychology/Review of Canadian Psychology* 20, 173–182.

Cleland, B., and Enroth-Cugell, C. (1966). Cat retinal ganglion cell responses to changing light intensities: Sinusoidal modulation in the time domain. *Acta Physiologica Scandinavica* 68, 365–381.

Cleland, B. G., and Enroth-Cugell, C. (1970). Quantitative aspects of gain and latency in the cat retina. *Journal of Physiology (London)* 206, 73–91.

Daniel, P., and Whitteridge, D. (1961). The representation of the visual field on the cerebral cortex in monkeys. *Journal of Physiology (London)* 159, 203–237.

Davson, H., ed. (1969). "The Eye," Vols. I–IV. Academic Press, New York.

Daw, N. W., and Pearlman, A. L. (1969). Cat colour vision: One cone process or several? *Journal of Physiology (London)* 201, 745–764.

Daw, N. W., and Pearlman, A. L. (1970). Cat colour vision: Evidence for more than one cone process. *Journal of Physiology (London)* 211, 125–137.

deLange, H. (1954). Relationship between critical flicker frequency and a set of low-frequency characteristics of the eye. *Journal of the Optical Society of America* 44, 380–389.

DeVoss, J. C., and Ganson, R. (1915). Color blindness of cats. *Journal of Animal Behavior* 5, 115–139.

Dodt, E., and Enroth, C. (1953). Retinal flicker response in cat. *Acta Physiological Scandinavica* 30, 375–390.

Donovan, A. (1967). The nerve fibre composition of the cat optic nerve. *Journal of Anatomy* 101, 1–11.

Doty, R. W. (1971). Survival of pattern vision after removal of striate cortex in the adult cat. *Journal of Comparative Neurology* 143, 341–370.

114   Mark A. Berkley

Elul, R., and Marchiafava, P. (1964). Accommodation of the eye as related to behavior in the cat. *Archives Italiennes de Biologie* **102**, 616–644.
Enroth, C. (1952). The mechanism of flicker and fusion studied on single retinal elements in the dark-adapted eye of the cat. *Acta Physiologica Scandinavica, Supplementum* **100**.
Enroth-Cugell, C., and Robson, J. G. (1966). The contrast sensitivity of retinal ganglion cells of the cat. *Journal of Physiology (London)* **187**, 517–552.
Enroth-Cugell, C., and Robson, J. G. (1974). Direct measurement of image quality in the cat eye. *Journal of Physiology (London)* **239**, 30–31P.
Enroth-Cugell, C., and Shapley, R. M. (1973a). Adapation and dynamics of cat retinal ganglion cells. *Journal of Physiology (London)* **233**, 271–309.
Enroth-Cugell, C., and Shapley, R. M. (1973b). Flux, not retinal illumination, is what retinal ganglion cells really care about. *Journal of Physiology (London)* **233**, 311–326.
Fox, R., and Blake, R. (1971). Stereoscopic vision in the cat. *Nature (London)* **233**, 55–56.
Fukada, Y., and Saito, H.-A. (1971). The relationship between response characteristics to flicker stimulation and receptive field organization in the cat's optic nerve fibers. *Vision Research* **11**, 227–240.
Fukada, Y., Motokawa, K., Norton, A. C., and Tasaki, K. (1966). Functional significance of conduction velocity in the transfer of flicker information in the optic nerve of the cat. *Journal of Neurophysiology* **29**, 698–714.
Ganz, L., and Fitch, M. (1968). The effect of visual deprivation on perceptual behavior. *Experimental Neurology* **22**, 639–660.
Glickstein, M., King, R. A., Miller, J., and Berkley, M. (1967). Cortical projections from the dorsal lateral geniculate nucleus of cats. *Journal of Comparative Neurology* **130**, 55–76.
Graham, C., ed. (1965). "Vision and Visual Perception," 637 pp. Wiley, New York.
Granit, R. (1943). The spectral properties of the visual receptors of the cat. *Acta Physiologica Scandinavica* **5**, 219–229.
Graybiel, A. M. (1972). Some extrageniculate visual pathways in the cat. *Investigative Ophthalmology* **11**, 322–332.
Green, D. (1970). Regional variations in the visual acuity for interference fringes on the retina. *Journal of Physiology (London)* **207**, 351–356.
Grüsser, O.-J., and Creutzfeldt, O. (1957). Eine neurophysiologische Grundlage des Brucke-Bartley, Effektes: Maxima der impulsfrequenz retinaler und corticaler neurone bei flimmerlicht mittlerer frequenzen. *Pfluegers Archiv für die Gesamte Physiologie des Menschen und der Tiere* **263**, 668–681.
Gunter, R. (1951a). The absolute threshold for vision in the cat. *Journal of Physiology (London)* **114**, 8–15.
Gunter, R. (1951b). Visual size constancy in the cat. *British Journal of Psychology* **42**, 288–293.
Gunter, R. (1952). The spectral sensitivity of dark-adapted cats. *Journal of Physiology (London)* **118**, 395–404.
Gunter, R. (1954a). The spectral sensitivity of light-adapted cats. *Journal of Physiology (London)* **123**, 409–415.
Gunter, R. (1954b). The discrimination between lights of different wave lengths in the cat. *Journal of Comparative and Physiological Psychology* **147**, 169–172.
Hammond, P., and James, C. R. (1971). The Purkinje shift in cat: Extent of the mesopic range. *Journal of Physiology (London)* **216**, 99–109.

Hara, K., and Warren, J. M. (1961a). Stimulus additivity and dominance in discrimination performance by cats. *Journal of Comparative and Physiological Psychology* 54, 86–90.

Hara, K., and Warren, J. (1961b). Equivalence reactions by normal and brain-injured cats. *Journal of Comparative and Physiological Psychology* 54, 91–93.

Hayhow, W. R. (1958). The cytoarchitecture of the lateral geniculate body in the cat in relation to the distribution of the crossed and uncrossed optic fibers. *Journal of Comparative Neurology* 110, 1–64.

Hecht, S., Haig, C., and Chase, A. (1937). The influence of light adaptation on subsequent dark adaptation of the eye. *Journal of General Physiology* 20, 831–850.

Heiss, W.-D., and Milne, D. C. (1967). Single fibers of cat optic nerve: "Thresholds" to light. *Science* 155, 1571.

Henry, G., Bishop, P., and Dreher, B. (1974). Orientation, axis and direction as stimulus parameters for striate cells. *Vision Research* 14, 767–777.

Hirsch, H. (1972). Visual perception in cats after environmental surgery. *Experimental Brain Research (Berlin)* 15, 405–423.

Hoffman, K.-P., and Stone, J. (1971). Conduction velocity of afferents to cat visual cortex: A correlation with cortical receptive fields. *Brain Research* 32, 460–466.

Hoffman, K.-P., Stone, J., and Sherman, S. M. (1972). Relay of receptive-field properties in dorsal lateral geniculate nucleus of the cat. *Journal of Neurophysiology* 35, 518–531.

Hollander, H., and Stone, J. (1972). Receptor pedicle density in the cat's retina. *Brain Research* 42, 497–502.

Hubel, D., and Wiesel, T. (1962). Receptive fields, binocular interaction and functional architecture in the cat's visual cortex. *Journal of Physiology (London)* 160, 106–154.

Hubel, D., and Wiesel, T. (1965). Receptive fields and functional architecture in two nonstriate visual areas (18 and 19) of the cat. *Journal of Neurophysiology* 28, 229–289.

Hughes, A. (1972). Vergence in the cat. *Vision Research* 12, 1961–1994.

Hughes, G. W., and Maffei, L. (1966). Retinal ganglion cell response to sinusoidal light stimulation. *Journal of Neurophysiology* 29, 333–352.

Joshua, D. E., and Bishop, P. O. (1970). Binocular single vision and depth discrimination. Receptive field disparities for central and peripheral vision and binocular interaction on peripheral single units in cat striate cortex. *Experimental Brain Research (Berlin)* 10, 389–416.

Julesz, B. (1971). "Foundations of Cyclopean Perception," 406 pp. Univ. of Chicago Press, Chicago, Illinois.

Kalia, M., and Whitteridge, D. (1973). The visual areas in the splenial sulcus of the cat. *Journal of Physiology (London)* 232, 275–283.

Kappauf, W. E. (1936). Flicker discrimination in the cat. *Psychological Bulletin* 33, 597–598.

Kappauf, W. E. (1943). Variation in the size of the cat's pupil as a function of stimulus brightness. *Journal of Comparative Psychology* 35, 125–131.

Keesey, U. (1972). Flicker and pattern detection: A comparison of thresholds. *Journal of the Optical Society of America* 62, 446–448.

Kelly, D. H. (1961). Visual responses to time-dependent stimuli. I. Amplitude sensitivity measurements. *Journal of the Optical Society of America* 51, 422–429.

Kennedy, J. (1939). The effects of complete and partial occipital lobectomy upon thresholds of real movement discrimination in the cat. *Journal of Genetic Psychology* 54, 119–149.

Kennedy, J., and Smith, K. (1935). Visual thresholds of real movement in the cat. *Journal of Genetic Psychology* **46**, 470–476.

Kulikowski, J. (1972). Orientation selectivity of human binocular and monocular vision revealed by simultaneous and successive masking. *Journal of Physiology (London)* **226**, 67P–68P.

Kulikowski, J. J., and Tolhurst, D. J. (1973). Psychophysical evidence for sustained and transient detectors in human vision. *Journal of Physiology (London)* **232**, 149–162.

Kulikowski, J., Abadi, R., and King-Smith, P. (1973). Orientation selectivity of grating and line detectors in human vision. *Vision Research* **13**, 1479–1486.

Kupfer, C., Chumbley, L., and Downer, J. (1967). Quantitative histology of optic nerve, optic tract and lateral geniculate nucleus of man. *Journal of Anatomy* **101**, 393–401.

LaMotte, R. H., and Brown, J. L. (1970). Dark adaptation and spectral sensitivity in the cat. *Vision Research* **10**, 703–716.

Leach, E., Marriott, F., and Morris, V. (1961). The distance between rods in the cat's retina. *Journal of Physiology (London)* **157**, 17P.

LeGrand, Y. (1967). "Form and Space Vision" (transl. by M. Millodot and G. Heath), pp. 58–63. Indiana Univ. Press, Bloomington.

LeGrand, Y. (1968). "Light, Colour and Vision," 2nd Ed., 564 pp. Chapman & Hall, London.

Leibowitz, H. (1955). The relation between the rate threshold for the perception of movement and luminance for various durations of exposure. *Journal of Experimental Psychology* **49**, 209–214.

Leicester, J., and Stone, J. (1967). Ganglion, amacrine, and horizontal cells of the cat's retina. *Vision Research* **7**, 695–705.

Lennie, P. (1972). The perception of orientation. Unpublished doctoral dissertation, Cambridge Univ., Cambridge, England.

Lindsley, D. B. (1953). Effect of photic stimulation on visual pathways from retina to cortex. *Science* **117**, 469.

Loop, M. S. (1971). An investigation of the scotopic luminosity function in the cat employing a modified conditioned suppression technique. Unpublished master's thesis, Florida State Univ., Tallahassee.

Loop, M. S., and Berkley, M. A. (1972). Conditioned suppression as a psychophysical technique for the cat. *Behavioral Research Methods & Instrumentation* **4**, 121–124.

Loop, M., and Berkley, M. (1975). Temporal modulation sensitivity in the cat. I. Behavioral measures. *Vision Research* **15**, 555–561.

Maffei, L. (1968). Spatial and temporal averages in retinal channels. *Journal of Neurophysiology* **31**, 283–287.

Maffei, L., and Fiorentini, A. (1973). The visual cortex as a spatial frequency analyzer. *Vision Research* **13**, 1255–1267.

Maffei, L., Cervetto, L., and Fiorentini, A. (1970). Transfer characteristics of excitation and inhibition in cat retinal ganglion cells. *Journal of Neurophysiology* **33**, 276.

Mead, L. C. (1939). The curve of visual intensity discrimination in the cat before and after removal of the striate area of the cortex. Unpublished doctoral dissertation, Univ. of Rochester, Rochester, New York.

Mead, L. C. (1942). Visual brightness in the cat as a function of illumination. *Journal of Genetic Psychology* **60**, 223–257.

Meikle, T., Jr., and Sprague, J. M. (1964). The neural organization of the visual pathways in the cat. *International Review of Neurobiology* **6**, 149–189.

Mello, N. K. (1968). Color generalization in cat following discrimination training on achromatic intensity and on wavelength. *Neuropsychologia* **6**, 341–354.

Mello, N. K., and Peterson, N. J. (1964). Behavioral evidence for color discrimination in cat. *Journal of Neurophysiology* **27**, 323–333.

Meyer, D. R., Miles, R. C., and Ratoosh, P. (1954). Absence of color vision in cat. *Journal of Neurophysiology* **17**, 289–294.

Mitchell, D., Freeman, R., and Westheimer, G. (1967). Effect of orientation on the modulation sensitivity for interference fringes on the retina. *Journal of the Optical Society of America* **57**, 246–249.

Morris, V. B., and Marriott, F. H. C. (1961). The distribution of light in an image formed in the cat's eye. *Nature (London)* **190**, 176.

Muir, D. W., and Mitchell, D. E. (1973). Visual resolution and experience: Acuity deficits in cats following early selective visual deprivation. *Science* **180**, 420–422.

Pautler, E. L., and Clark, G. (1961). The effect of chlorpromazine on the discrimination between intermittent photic stimulation and a steady light in normal and brain-damaged cats. *Journal of Comparative and Physiological Psychology* **54**, 493–497.

Pearlman, A. L., and Daw, N. W. (1970). Opponent color cells in the cat lateral geniculate nucleus. *Science* **167**, 84–86.

Pettigrew, J., Nikara, T., and Bishop, P. (1968). Responses to moving slits by single units in cat striate cortex. *Experimental Brain Research (Berlin)* **6**, 373–390.

Piper, H. (1905). Untersuchungen uber das electromotorische Verhalten der Netzhaut bei Warmblutieren. *Archiv für Anatomie und Physiologie, Physiologische Abteilung, Supplementum* **133**.

Pirenne, M. (1954). Absolute visual thresholds. *Journal of Physiology (London)* **123**, 40P.

Polyak, S. (1957). "The Vertebrate Visual System," 1390 pp. Univ. of Chicago Press, Chicago, Illinois.

Rodieck, R. W. (1973). "The Vertebrate Retina. Principles of Structure and Function." Freeman, San Francisco, California. p. 285ff.

Rolls, E., and Cowey, A. (1970). Topography of the retina and striate cortex and its relationship to visual acuity in rhesus monkeys and squirrel monkeys. *Experimental Brain Research (Berlin)* **10**, 298–310.

Rose, D., and Blakemore, C. (1974). An analysis of orientation selectivity in the cat's visual cortex. *Experimental Brain Research (Berlin)* **20**, 1–17.

Sakmann, B., and Creutzfeldt, O. (1969). Scotopic and mesopic light adaptation in the cat's retina. *Pfluegers Archiv* **313**, 168–185.

Sanderson, K. J. (1971). Visual field projection columns and magnification factors in the lateral geniculate nucleus of the cat. *Experimental Brain Research (Berlin)* **13**, 159–177.

Schadé, O. (1956). Optical and photoelectric analog of the eye. *Journal of the Optical Society of America* **46**, 721–739.

Schwartz, A. S., and Lindsley, D. B. (1964). Critical flicker frequency and photic following in the cat. *Boletin del Instituto de Estudios Médicos y Biólogicos [Universidad Nacional Autonoma de Mexico]* **22**, 249–262.

Schwartz, A. S., and Cheney, C. (1966). Neural mechanisms involved in the critical flicker frequency of the cat. *Brain Research* **1**, 369–380.

Sechzer, J. A., and Brown, J. L. (1964). Color discrimination in the cat. *Science* **144**, 427–429.

Sekuler, R. (1974). Spatial vision. *Annual Review of Psychology* **25**, 195–232.

Sherman, S. M. (1973). Visual field defects in monocularly and binocularly deprived cats. *Brain Research* **49**, 25–45.

Smith, J. C. (1970). Conditioned suppression as an animal psychophysical technique. *In* "Animal Psychophysics" (W. Stebbins, ed.), pp. 125–160. Appleton, New York.

Smith, K. U. (1935). Visual discrimination in the cat: II. A further study of the capacity of the cat for visual figure discrimination. *Journal of Genetic Psychology* **45**, 336–357.

Smith, K. U. (1936). Visual discrimination in the cat: IV. The visual acuity of the cat in relation to stimulus distance. *Journal of Genetic Psychology* **49**, 297–313.

Snigula, F., and Grüsser, O.-J. (1968). Vergleichende verhaltensphysiologische und neurophysiologische Untersuchungen am visuellen System von Katzen. I. Die simultane Helligkeitsschwelle. *Psychologische Forschung* **32**, 14–42.

Spear, P. D., and Braun, J. J. (1969). Pattern discrimination following removal of visual neocortex in the cat. *Experimental Neurology* **25**, 331–348.

Sperry, R., Miner, N., and Myers, R. (1955). Visual pattern perception following subpial slicing and tantalum wire implantations in the visual cortex. *Journal of Comparative and Physiological Psychology* **48**, 50–58.

Sprague, J., and Meikle, T. (1965). The role of the superior colliculus in visually guided behavior. *Experimental Neurology* **11**, 115–146.

Sprague, J., Levy, J., DiBerardino, A., and Conomy, J. (1973). Effect of striate and extra-striate visual cortical lesions on learning and retention of form discriminations. *Society for Neuroscience, San Diego, Calif.*

Steinberg, R. H., Reid, M., and Lacy, P. L. (1973). The distribution of rods and cones in the retina of the cat. *Journal of Comparative Neurology* **148**, 229–248.

Sternheim, C., and Cavonius, C. (1972). Sensitivity of the human ERG and VECP to sinusoidally modulated light. *Vision Research* **12**, 1685–1695.

Stone, J. (1965). A quantitative analysis of the distribution of ganglion cells in the cat's retina. *Journal of Comparative Neurology* **124**, 337–352.

Stone, J., and Dreher, B. (1973). Projection of X- and Y-cells of the cat's lateral geniculate nucleus to areas 17 and 18 of visual cortex. *Journal of Neurophysiology* **36**, 551–567.

Stone, J., and Fukuda, Y. (1974). The naso-temporal division of the cat's retina re-examined in terms of Y-, X- and W-cells. *Journal of Comparative Neurology* **155**, 377–394.

Stone, J., and Hoffman, K.-P. (1972). Very slow-conducting ganglion cells in the cat's retina: A major new functional type? *Brain Research* **43**, 610–616.

Stryker, M., and Blakemore, C. (1972). Saccadic and disjunctive eye movements in cats. *Vision Research* **12**, 2005–2013.

Sturr, J. F., and Shansky, M. A. (1971). Cortical and subcortical response to flicker in cats. *Experimental Neurology* **33**, 279–290.

Taravella, C. L., and Clark, G. (1963). Discrimination of intermittent photic stimulation in normal and brain-damaged cats. *Experimental Neurology* **7**, 282–293.

Taylor, M. (1963). Visual discrimination and orientation. *Journal of the Optical Society of America* **53**, 763–765.

Thorn, F. (1970). Detection of luminance differences by the cat. *Journal of Comparative and Physiological Psychology* **70**, 326–334.

Tolhurst, D. (1973). Separate channels for the analysis of the shape and the movement of a moving visual stimulus. *Journal of Physiology (London)* **231**, 385–402.

Vakkur, G. J., and Bishop, P. O. (1963). The schematic eye in the cat. *Vision Research* **3**, 357–381.

Vakkur, G. J., Bishop, P. O., and Kozak, W. (1963). Visual optics in the cat, including posterior nodal distance and retinal landmarks. *Vision Research* **3**, 289–314.

Van Buren, J. M. (1963). "The Retinal Ganglion Cell Layer," 143 pp. Thomas, Springfield, Illinois.

van Hasselt, P. (1972). The effects of ablation of visual cortical areas on the CFF of the electroretinogram of the cat. *Ophthalmological Research* 3, 160–165.

Walls, G. (1942). "The Vertebrate Eye and Its Adaptive Radiations," 785 pp. Cranbrook Inst., Bloomfield Hills, Michigan.

Warren, J., and Ebel, H. (1967). Generalization of responses to intermediate size by cats and monkeys. *Psychonomic Science* 9, 5–6.

Wässle, H. (1971). Optical quality of the cat eye. *Vision Research* 11, 995–1006.

Wässle, H., and Creutzfeldt, O. D. (1973). Spatial resolution in visual system: A theoretical and experimental study on single units in the cat's lateral geniculate body. *Journal of Neurophysiology* 36, 13–27.

Watkins, D., and Berkley, M. (1972). Orientation selectivity of single cells in cat visual cortex. *Association for Research in Vision and Ophthalmology, Sarasota, Fla.*

Watkins, D., and Berkley, M. (1974). Orientation selectivity of single neurons in cat striate cortex. *Experimental Brain Research (Berlin)* 19, 433–446.

Weale, R. A. (1953a). The spectral reflectivity of the cat's tapetum measured *in situ. Journal of Physiology (London)* 119, 30–42.

Weale, R. A. (1953b). Photochemical reactions in the living cat's retina. *Journal of Physiology (London)* 121, 322–331.

Weale, R. A. (1954). Light absorption in the crystalline lens of the cat. *Nature (London)* 173, 1049–1050.

Westheimer, G. (1962). Line-spread function of living cat eye. *Journal of the Optical Society of America* 52, 1326.

Weymouth, F. (1958). Visual sensory units and the minimum angle of resolution. *American Journal of Ophthalmology* 46, 102–113.

Wilson, J., and Sherman, S. M. (1974). Receptive field characteristics in cat striate cortex: changes with visual field eccentricity. *Society for Neuroscience, St. Louis, Mo.*

Winans, S. S. (1971). Visual cues used by normal and visual-decorticate cats to discriminate figures of equal luminous flux. *Journal of Comparative and Physiological Psychology* 74, 167–178.

Wirth, A. (1953). Electroretinographic evaluation of the scotopic visibility function in cats and albino rabbits. *Acta Physiologica Scandinavica* 29, 22–30.

Recovery of Function after Damage to Central Catecholamine-Containing Neurons: A Neurochemical Model for the Lateral Hypothalamic Syndrome

Edward M. Stricker and Michael J. Zigmond

Psychobiology Program,
Departments of Psychology and Biology,
University of Pittsburgh,
Pittsburgh, Pennsylvania

I. Introduction

One of the most dramatic effects of experimental damage to cerebral tissue is the total cessation of ingestive behaviors that occurs following bilateral lesions of the lateral hypothalamus (Anand and Brobeck, 1951). Animals with such lesions do not even accept food when it is placed in their mouths, and they starve to death within 6–10 days despite the presence of familiar and palatable diets. If kept alive by intragastric intubation of liquid nutrients, many of them begin to ingest some food again and eventually consume sufficient amounts for body weight maintenance (Morrison and Mayer, 1957; Teitelbaum and Stellar, 1954). Nevertheless, enduring deficits in their feeding and drinking responses to specific nutritional needs indicate that the animals have not recovered completely (Epstein, 1971; Teitelbaum and Epstein, 1962). The initial aphagia and adipsia, the progressive recovery of ingestive behaviors, and the persistent residual deficits in lesioned animals together form what has become known as the "lateral hypothalamic syndrome" (Teitelbaum and Epstein, 1962).

The critical effect of lateral hypothalamic lesions has traditionally been attributed to destruction of cell groups contained within the hypothalamus. This "hypothalamocentric" perspective has persisted through the years despite the fact that the most effective placements for the production of feeding and drinking deficits have consistently been localized in the far-lateral aspects of the tuberal hypothalamus (Anand and Brobeck, 1951; Morgane, 1961a; Oltmans and Harvey, 1972), a region consisting largely of ascending and descending fibers of passage rather than compact cellular masses (Morgane, 1969). Strong experimental support for considering the possible significance of extrahypothalamic structures to the control of ingestive behaviors can be found in parallel investigations in which either neuroanatomical issues or motivated behavior was the primary focus of concern. In the former, lateral hypothalamic damage has been found to produce neurochemical changes throughout the central nervous system (Andén et al., 1964; Heller et al., 1962; Heller and Moore, 1965); in the latter, aphagia and adipsia have been observed after lesions or knife cuts that spared the lateral hypothalamus (Albert et al., 1970; Ellison, 1968; Gold, 1967; Grossman and Grossman, 1973; Levine and Schwartzbaum, 1973; Morgane, 1961b). In an authoritative and comprehensive account of the lateral hypothalamic syndrome that appeared in a previous volume of this series, Epstein (1971) first integrated these findings and stated presciently that "the profound neurochemical deficiencies produced by the lesions must be related in some direct way to the deficits in feeding and to the motivational impairments of the syndrome" (p. 297).

This hypothesis has been examined recently in several laboratories concerned with the biological bases of behavior. Such studies have found that lateral hypothalamic lesions producing aphagia and adipsia in rats are associated with marked depletions of the brain catecholamines norepinephrine (NE) and dopamine (DA) (Fibiger et al., 1973; Oltmans and Harvey, 1972; Smith, 1973; Ungerstedt, 1971a; Zigmond and Stricker, 1972, 1973). On the basis of this and related work, plus consideration of the anatomical distribution and biochemical regulation of brain catecholamines, we have formulated a neurochemical model that we believe provides an explanation for the three basic mysteries of the lateral hypothalamic syndrome: (1) the initial aphagia and adipsia, (2) the subsequent recovery of function, and (3) the residual deficits in motivated ingestive behaviors. As well, it seems to provide a suitable perspective for viewing motivated behaviors in intact animals. This model is the subject of the present essay.

The following presentation is divided into four major sections. The first will consider recent evidence that central NE- and DA-containing neurons are involved in the lateral hypothalamic syndrome. The second section considers the functions of these neurons and the biochemistry of synaptic regulation within them. Our neurochemical model is presented in detail in the third section. Finally, some implications of this perspective as it relates to broader considerations of motivation and recovery of function are discussed briefly in the fourth section.

II. Brain Catecholamines and the Lateral Hypothalamic Syndrome

A. The Initial Loss of Ingestive Behaviors

Ungerstedt (1970) was the first to point out that lateral hypothalamic lesions, as well as most extrahypothalamic lesions that produced aphagia and adipsia, would interrupt DA-containing neurons of the nigrostriatal bundle as they coursed through the ventral diencephalon (Figs. 1 and 2). In order to separate damage to these fibers from damage to other tissue, Ungerstedt (1971c) injected the neurotoxin 6-hydroxydopamine (6-HDA) (Fig. 3) into various sites along the ascending dopaminergic pathways, including the lateral hypothalamus. He observed aphagia and adipsia in rats, in association with considerable damage to dopaminergic fibers of the nigrostriatal bundle (see also Fibiger et al., 1973; Marshall and Teitelbaum, 1973). Although his intracerebral injections of 6-HDA also damaged adjacent catecholamine (CA)-containing fibers, Ungerstedt emphasized the importance of striatal DA depletions because selective damage of other fiber tracts did not significantly affect ingestive behaviors.

For the past few years, we have been administering 6-HDA into the cerebrospinal fluid of rats via the lateral ventricles in order to selectively destroy central CA-containing pathways and study the consequent behavioral, physiological, and biochemical effects. Light and electron microscopic studies indicate a highly specific pattern of neuronal degeneration following 6-HDA treatment that is consistent with the distribution of CA-containing neurons (Bloom, 1971; Hedreen and Chalmers, 1972). The neurons that are most affected by the intraventricular treatments seem to be those located near cerebral ventricles or the subarachnoid space; fortunately, this includes most of the CA projections to the telencephalon (Schubert et al., 1973; Ungerstedt, 1971d), the pathways of greatest interest to us. Depletions of brain catecholamines are symmetrical, since 6-HDA administered into the lateral ventricles is distributed bilaterally throughout the brain. Furthermore, permanent depletions can be obtained in rats without damaging neurons containing such putative neurotransmitters as serotonin, acetylcholine, γ-aminobutyric

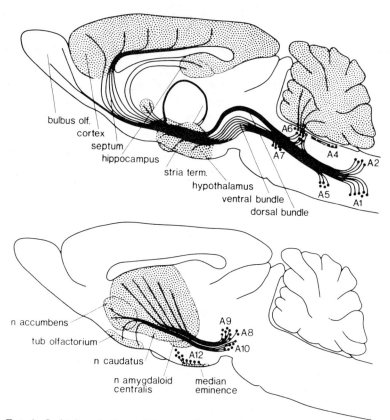

bulbus olf.
cortex
septum
hippocampus
stria term.
hypothalamus
ventral bundle
dorsal bundle

A6
A7
A4
A2
A5
A1

n accumbens
tub olfactorium
n caudatus
n amygdaloid centralis

A9
A8
A12
A10
median eminence

FIG. 1. Sagittal projections of the ascending norepinephrine (NE) and dopamine (DA) pathways in the rat brain (pathways descending to the cord are not included). The stippling indicates major nerve terminal areas. (Lower) The cell bodies of the DA-containing neurons include a group in the zona compacta of the substantia nigra (A9, according to the designations of Dahlstrom and Fuxe, 1964), a group that is situated slightly more caudally (A8), and a third, more ventromedial group which surrounds the interpeduncular nucleus (A10). Axons from A9 and A8 ascend in the ipsilateral crus cerebri and internal capsule through the globus pallidus to terminate in the caudate-putamen, forming a portion of the nigrostriatal projection. Axons from A10 ascend by an adjacent route and terminate in the basal telencephalon, including the nucleus accumbens and olfactory tubercle, forming a "mesolimbic" link. Recently, additional DA projections have been reported (not shown) that travel along a similar route, finally terminating in frontal and cingulate cortex (Lindvall and Björklund, 1974; Lindvall *et al.*, 1974). (Upper) There also are two major ascending neural pathways containing NE. One arises from cell groups in the medulla and pons (A1, A2, A5, A6, and A7), ascends in the medial lemniscus, and passes through the ventral tegmental area before continuing rostrally within the medial forebrain bundle. This "ventral bundle" of fibers gives rise to terminals which innervate the lower brain stem, hypothalamus, preoptic area, and septum. The other pathway arises from a more localized group of cell bodies in the region of the locus coeruleus (A6), ascends more dorsally in the reticular formation until it reaches the subthalamic nucleus, and then turns ventromedially to join the medial forebrain bundle. This "dorsal bundle" of fibers enters the hypothalamus intermingled with those of the ventral bundle (and, in more caudal areas, those of the DA-containing fibers of the nigrostriatal bundle) but continues beyond it and projects diffusely

acid, glutamic acid, and glycine in the brain (Bloom *et al.*, 1969; Breese and Traylor, 1970; Jacks *et al.*, 1972; Uretsky and Iversen, 1970) or reducing CA levels in the peripheral nervous system (Haeusler *et al.*, 1972). Dilution of the administered 6-HDA solution by ventricular fluid appears to minimize the nonspecific damage caused by the drug, which can be considerable when it is injected directly into brain parenchyma (Agid *et al.*, 1973b; Poirier *et al.*, 1972; Sotelo *et al.*, 1973; although see also Hökfelt and Ungerstedt, 1973: Simon *et al.*, 1974).

Despite its apparent specificity, the use of 6-HDA administered intra-ventricularly has been criticized. For example, in the cat 6-HDA has been shown to deplete serotonin as well as catecholamines (Petitjean *et al.*, 1972). Moreover, widespread nonspecific cellular damage has been observed in cat brain after the intraventricular injection of 500–3000 μg of 6-HDA (Poirier *et al.*, 1972), and similar observations have been made in the monkey (W. T. McKinney, A. J. Prange, and G. R. Breese, personal communication). Extensive nonspecific damage can be produced in rats, too, by administering very large doses of 6-HDA into the ventricles (Poirier *et al.*, 1972) or by injecting the drug very rapidly, but these problems can be avoided and we seldom obtain such unwanted effects with our treatments (Zigmond and Stricker, 1974). Furthermore, we find that similar behavioral effects are obtained when 6-HDA is administered by an intracisternal route rather than intraven-tricularly (although it takes more injections of 6-HDA to produce them), which presumably results in a different pattern of nonspecific ventricular damage (see also Breese *et al.*, 1973).

The effects of intraventricularly administered 6-HDA on food and water intakes of rats are as follows (Table I). (1) 6-HDA (two injections of 200 μg, into alternate ventricles, 3–4 days apart), without pretreatment, depletes 90–99% of the NE and 60–80% of the DA in the telencephalon, yet produces only transient hypophagia and hypodipsia.[1] (2) 6-HDA (2 × 200 μg), given 30 minutes after injections of pargyline (50 mg/kg, i.p.), a drug that inhibits monoamine oxidase, causes a 95–99% depletion of both NE and DA in the

[1] In no instance was hyperphagia observed. Recent evidence suggests that destruction of the ventral bundle of NE-containing neurons, that arises in the lower brain stem and projects to the hypothalamus and limbic system, leads to hyperphagia and obesity in rats (Ahlskog and Hoebel, 1973; Gold, 1973; Kapatos and Gold, 1973). Since our intra-ventricular 6-HDA treatments never produced more than 70–80% depletion of hypo-thalamic NE, it is possible that more complete damage to this pathway is necessary before hyperphagia results (see discussion of compensatory adjustments within residual neurons in Section IV,A).

throughout the telencephalon, including the neocortex. Note that there is also a lateral projection from the locus coeruleus that enters the cerebellum (adapted from Unger-stedt, 1971e). Not shown are additional ascending NE-containing projections observed recently (Lindvall and Björklund, 1974).

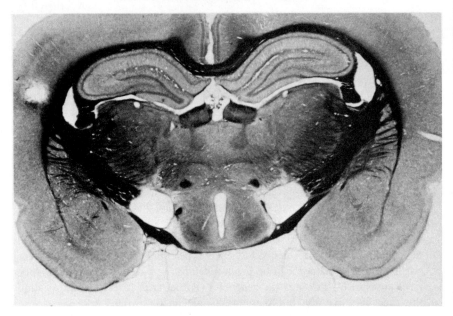

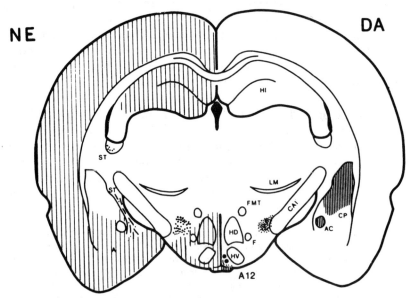

FIG. 2. (Top) Photomicrograph of a stained frontal section showing a representative lesion in the ventrolateral hypothalamus. Such large symmetrical lesions produced prolonged aphagia and adipsia (from Zigmond and Stricker, 1974). (Bottom) Drawing of a comparable section of the rat brain. The dots represent norepinephrine-containing axons in the left hemisphere and dopamine-containing axons on the contralateral side. The stripes indicate the major nerve terminal areas (adapted from Ungerstedt, 1971e).

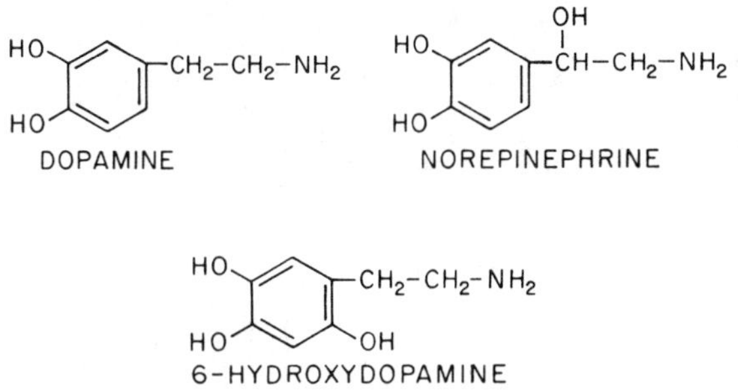

FIG. 3. The structural formulas of dopamine, 6-hydroxydopamine (6-HDA), and norepinephrine. Note that the drug 6-HDA is structurally similar to both of the naturally occurring catecholamines. Indeed, it is believed to gain preferential access into neurons containing these catecholamines through amine-specific uptake mechanisms in their axon terminals. Once within these neurons, metabolites are formed that destroy the nerve terminals (Heikkila and Cohen, 1971).

telencephalon and usually produces prolonged aphagia and adipsia. (3) 6-HDA (1 $\times$ 200 μg), given 30 minutes after injections of both pargyline (50 mg/kg, i.p.) and desmethylimipramine (DMI; 25 mg/kg, i.p.), a drug that appears to block the uptake of amines (such as 6-HDA) into the terminals of NE-containing neurons, causes 0–5% depletion of NE and 95–99% depletion of DA in the telencephalon and also produces prolonged aphagia and adipsia (Zigmond and Stricker, 1972, 1973; Stricker and Zigmond, 1974).

These findings are consistent with the important role of DA-containing nigrostriatal fibers in the central control of food and water intake that has been proposed. However, it is noteworthy that while 6-HDA only produced transient hypophagia and hypodipsia when 90% of telencephalic DA was depleted, complete disruption of ingestive behaviors often was associated with as little as 60% DA depletion when produced by electrolytic lesions of the lateral hypothalamus (Oltmans and Harvey, 1972; Zigmond and Stricker, 1973). There are several ways in which these findings might be interpreted. For example, if damage to a specific locus within the caudate was more significant than the degree of damage to the entire fiber bundle (cf. Sorenson and Ellison, 1970), then larger DA depletions after 6-HDA treatment might simply increase the possibility that this site will be damaged, while lateral hypothalamic lesions may interrupt the crucial nigrostriatal projections more readily. Alternatively, since feeding and drinking deficits can also be obtained with perifornical hypothalamic damage medial to the nigrostriatal bundle (Morgane, 1961a; Oltmans and Harvey, 1972), as well as with extrahypothalamic brain lesions which appear to lie outside of the nigrostriatal bundle (Gold, 1967; Lyon *et al.,* 1968; Parker and Feldman, 1967), it is possible that

TABLE I

EFFECT OF 6-HYDROXYDOPAMINE (6-HDA) TREATMENTS ON BRAIN CATECHOLAMINES AND INGESTIVE BEHAVIORS

Group[a]	Norepinephrine (μg/gm)[b]			Dopamine (μg/gm)[b]		Ingestive behavior
	Diencephalon	Brain stem	Telencephalon	Striatum	Telencephalon	
Control[c]	0.76 ± 0.04	0.38 ± 0.02	0.28 ± 0.01	8.27 ± 0.49	0.80 ± 0.11	Normal
6-HDA	0.14 ± 0.02	0.13 ± 0.02	<0.02[d]	3.44 ± 0.16	0.19 ± 0.03	Mild anorexia and hypodipsia
Pargyline + 6-HDA	0.09 ± 0.01	0.14 ± 0.01	<0.02[d]	<0.04[d]	<0.10[d]	Aphagia and adipsia
DMI, pargyline + 6-HDA	—[e]	—	0.25 ± 0.02	<0.04[d]	—	Aphagia and adipsia

[a] Male albino rats, 200–300 gm, were housed individually and maintained on Purina chow pellets and water. Drug-tested rats received 6-HDA (200 μg, intraventricularly), alone or 30 minutes after pretreatment with pargyline (50 mg/kg, i.p.) or pargyline and desmethylimipramine (DMI) (25 mg/kg, i.p.). Rats given 6-HDA alone or after pargyline pretreatment received two treatments, 48 hours apart; rats given 6-HDA after pargyline and DMI received a single treatment. Animals were killed at least 2 weeks after treatment, and tissues were prepared and analyzed spectrophotofluorometrically (see Stricker and Zigmond, 1974).

[b] Values are mean ± standard error of the mean for 4–10 animals, expressed as micrograms of catecholamine (CA) per gram of fresh brain weight.

[c] There was no significant effect on catecholamine concentrations of any vehicle injections or sham lesions, and control values have been pooled.

[d] Below the sensitivity of the assay.

[e] No data available.

other fiber pathways that are critically involved in motivated ingestive behaviors might also be damaged by lateral hypothalamic lesions, but not by intraventricular 6-HDA treatments.

To summarize, extensive depletion of telencephalic DA has been associated with aphagia and adipsia in rats following lateral hypothalamic damage. In order to determine the significance of this correlation, various attempts have been made in this and other laboratories to destroy the ascending dopaminergic neurons while minimizing less specific damage either to the lateral hypothalamus or to non-DA-containing pathways outside the diencephalon. Severe impairments of ingestive behavior were observed in each instance. Because these procedures produce different spectra of damage, the results obtained probably reflect the destruction of dopaminergic neurons that is common to all of them. Nevertheless, damage to other pathways also may contribute to the disruption of feeding and drinking behaviors that follows electrolytic lesions of the lateral hypothalamus.

B. RECOVERY OF FUNCTION

Teitelbaum and Stellar (1954) first observed that rats with lateral hypothalamic lesions may ultimately recover feeding and drinking behaviors if they are maintained by intragastric intubations of liquid diet during the immediate postoperative period. In later work, Teitelbaum and Epstein (1962) identified four distinct stages in the gradual recovery process: an initial stage of aphagia and adipsia, a second stage of anorexia and adipsia, a third stage in which animals can maintain body weight but are adipsic, and a fourth stage of apparent recovery. This general pattern of recovery was seen in all of their animals, although the duration of each stage was variable and seemed to depend on the size and symmetry of the lesions; that is, larger and more symmetrical lesions tended to be associated with more extended periods of recovery. Among a group of 50 representative animals, Epstein and Teitelbaum (1964) found that deficits ranged from no aphagia and less than 1 week of adipsia to 25 days of aphagia and more than a year of adipsia, with the modal animals requiring about 2–4 weeks to recover.

Rats given intraventricular injections of 6-HDA, following treatment with pargyline, show the same pattern of gradual recovery from aphagia and adipsia that is seen in rats with lateral hypothalamic lesions (Zigmond and Stricker, 1973); that is, they invariably eat palatable foods and fluids first, then accept dry chow, and finally drink water (Fig. 4). The range of effects produced by the biochemical lesion also resembles that which follows electrolytic lateral hypothalamic damage. For example, in a recent study of 43 rats given intraventricular 6-HDA after pargyline pretreatments (Stricker and Zigmond, 1974), 10 were observed to recover within 1–3 days, 17 never

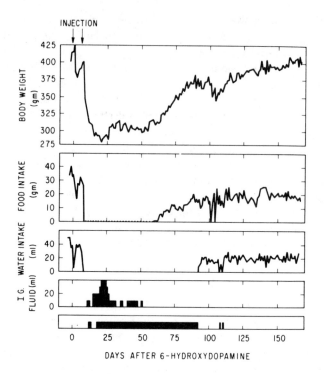

FIG. 4. Food and water intakes and body weight of a rat given two intraventricular injections of 6-hydroxydopamine (200 μg), each 30 minutes after pargyline (50 mg/kg, i.p.). Intragastric (I.G.) feedings are shown. The bottom line indicates access to highly palatable foods (from Zigmond and Stricker, 1973). Copyright 1973 by the American Association for the Advancement of Science.

ingested substantial amounts even of palatable foods and died within 1–8 weeks, but 16 animals recovered feeding and drinking behaviors according to the above sequence (Fig. 5).

There are several aspects of these data that should be noted. First, more prolonged initial periods of aphagia generally were associated with longer durations for recovery. The longest period of aphagia in this series of animals was 12 days (rat No. 14), although in other experiments we have observed periods as long as 64 days in which there was a complete cessation of all ingestive behaviors following intraventricular 6-HDA treatment. Second, whereas animals occasionally show only adipsia following lateral hypothalamic lesions (Andersson and McCann, 1956; Montemurro and Stevenson, 1957; Epstein and Teitelbaum, 1964), we have as yet never seen adipsia without a prior period of anorexia in any rat given 6-HDA intraventricularly.

Finally, it is evident that several animals spent an unusually long time in the early stages of recovery. A year after the 6-HDA treatments, one rat (No. 16) still required intragastric intubations in order to maintain its body weight while three others (Nos. 13–15) progressed only to the point of maintaining their body weights by the voluntary consumption of liquid diets and would not ingest Purina laboratory chow or drink water.

We have obtained the same pattern of recovery and range of effects following intraventricular 6-HDA injections given after pretreatment with both DMI and pargyline, which prevented damage to the central NE-containing neurons (Stricker and Zigmond, 1974), as well as following intracisternal 6-HDA injections. Similar results have also been reported after intracerebral 6-HDA (Marshall *et al.*, 1974; Myers and Martin, 1973) or knife cuts which may be expected to have interrupted the ascending dopaminergic projections (Albert *et al.*, 1970; Grossman and Grossman, 1973). It would appear that destruction of central DA-containing fibers provides the common basis for the aphagia and adipsia that is initially observed in each of these preparations.

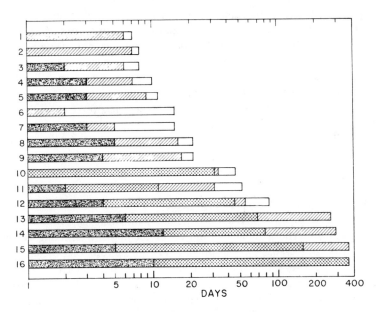

FIG. 5. The duration of aphagia (filled bar), anorexia requiring tube-feeding maintenance (hatched bar), anorexia not requiring tube-feeding maintenance (diagonal lines), and adipsia (open bar) for 16 rats given two intraventricular injections of 6-hydroxydopamine (200 μg), each 30 minutes after pargyline (30 mg/kg, i.p.). All but the last 4 rats ultimately recovered spontaneous consumption of Purina laboratory chow and water.

However, it is not immediately apparent how to account for recovery of ingestive behaviors since we have found that CA depletions are permanent (see also Moore and Heller, 1967; Ungerstedt, 1971a; Uretsky and Iversen, 1970). Three explanations may be suggested for this apparent paradox: (1) the initial aphagia may be due to CA depletions, while resumption of feeding results from functional recovery of this same pathway that is not detectable by measurements of amine concentrations; (2) the initial aphagia may be due to CA depletions, but resumption of feeding results from transfer of functions formerly served by the amines to another neurochemical pathway that is not affected by the lesions; (3) the initial aphagia may not be causally related to observed CA depletions but to another, as yet unknown, effect of the lesions that is more temporary.

The third hypothesis cannot yet be ruled out, although, as we have noted previously, concentrations of other putative transmitter substances do not appear to be decreased by intraventricular 6-HDA treatments. In order to differentiate between the first two hypotheses, we examined the effects of further disruption of central CA-containing neurons in animals which had recovered from the initial effects of intraventricular 6-HDA treatment or electrolytic lateral hypothalamic lesions. A single intraventricular injection of 200 µg 6-HDA reinstated aphagia and adipsia in both groups of rats, as did electrolytic lesions of the lateral hypothalamus (see also Teitelbaum and Epstein, 1962), but this time it was much more severe than it had been earlier; that is, rats did not ingest anything for at least 1 month after the treatment, more than 5 times the duration of the earlier period of aphagia. Similar, but more transient, effects were observed after CA synthesis was inhibited by administration of α-methyl-p-tyrosine (AMT) (Stricker and Zigmond, 1975; Zigmond and Stricker, 1973). These results suggest that the function of residual CA-containing neurons is critical for feeding and drinking behaviors in rats that have recovered from the initial disruptive effects of brain damage.

To summarize, rats may recover from the severe deficits produced by electrolytic or biochemical lesions despite permanent depletions of brain catecholamines. The gradual resumption of feeding and drinking behaviors follows the same course in each preparation and suggests that the underlying elements of recovery are similar. Furthermore, reinstatement of aphagia and adipsia after disruption of central CA function suggests that compensatory adjustments within the residual CA-containing neurons may be important in the observed recovery of function.

C. RESIDUAL DEFICITS

Detailed investigations have revealed distinctive residual deficits in rats recovered from lateral hypothalamic lesions, including (1) specific loss of the feeding response to insulin or 2-deoxy-D-glucose (2-DG, a drug that inhibits glycolysis) (Epstein and Teitelbaum, 1967; Wayner *et al.*, 1971), (2) chronic maintenance of body weight at subnormal levels (Powley and Keesey, 1970), (3) absent or considerably delayed responses to thirst stimuli (Epstein and Teitelbaum, 1964; Stricker, 1976; Stricker and Wolf, 1967), (4) impaired reflexive control of salivary flow (Rozkowska and Fonberg, 1972), leading to inefficient feeding (Kissileff and Epstein, 1969) and loss of thermoregulatory grooming in the heat (Hainsworth and Epstein, 1966; Stricker and Hainsworth, 1970), (5) loss of the specific hunger for sodium usually observed during sodium deficiency (Wolf, 1964; Wolf and Quartermain, 1967), and (6) poor learning to avoid a distinctly flavored solution associated with poison (Roth *et al.*, 1973).

Rats injected intraventricularly with 6-HDA, given with or without pargyline pretreatment, showed many of these same impairments (Stricker and Zigmond, 1974). The most consistent deficit observed was their failure to increase food intake following systemic administration of 2-DG (Table II). Not one of the lesioned rats consumed significantly more food during the 6-hour test sessions following intraperitoneal injection of 750 mg of 2-DG per kilogram than they had on prior control days, whereas all intact rats increased their intakes 2- to 3-fold. Even 6-HDA-treated rats which ultimately maintained their body weights within the normal range (see below) did not

TABLE II

FOOD (GM) AND WATER INTAKES (ML) OF BRAIN-DAMAGED RATS DURING ACUTE REGULATORY IMBALANCES[a]

Group	n	2-DG[b]	PG[c]	Isoprot.[d]	NaCl[e]
Control	10	+4.5 ± 0.3	8.6 ± 0.7	10.4 ± 0.8	16.6 ± 0.9
6-HDA	6	+0.8 ± 0.3*[f]	6.1 ± 0.8	10.3 ± 1.8	14.9 ± 1.3
6-HDA, pargyline (fast)	10	−0.2 ± 0.3*	4.2 ± 0.9*	11.2 ± 1.6	14.8 ± 1.5
6-HDA, pargyline (slow)	5	−0.6 ± 0.2*	0.0 ± 0.0*	5.1 ± 1.6*	0.6 ± 0.5*
LH lesions	8	−0.5 ± 0.05*	0.2 ± 0.1*	1.3 ± 0.7*	0.0 ± 0.0*
Post. MFB lesions	7	−1.3 ± 0.9*	1.0 ± 0.3*	0.5 ± 0.3*	0.0 ± 0.0*

[a]Values are mean ± standard error of the mean. Rats were given two intraventricular injections of 6-hydroxydopamine (6-HDA) (200 μg), or bilateral electrolytic lesions of the lateral hypothalamus (LH) or posterior medial forebrain bundle (MFB). Some 6-HDA-treated rats were pretreated with pargyline (50 mg/kg, i.p.); of these, some recovered feeding and drinking behaviors quickly and some recovered slowly.

[b]Food intakes during 6 hours after 750 mg/kg 2-deoxy-D-glucose (i.p.), relative to baseline values averaged over the preceding 3 days.

[c]Water intakes during 6 hours after 5 ml of 20% polyethylene glycol (s.c.). Food was not present. Baseline water intakes in these tests (and the others) were 0–1 ml.

[d]Water intakes during 3 hours after 0.33 mg of isoproterenol per kilogram (i.p.).

[e]Water intakes during 3 hours after 5 ml of 1.0 M NaCl (i.p.).

[f](*) indicates $p < 0.001$ in comparison to control rats.

respond behaviorally to this glucoprivic stimulus. In contrast, such autonomic glucoregulatory responses to 2-DG as hyperglycemia (resulting from epinephrine-induced glycogenolysis) and increased gastric acid secretion survived identical intraventricular treatments with 6-HDA (Stricker *et al.*, 1974; Zigmond and Stricker, 1974).

Like recovered laterals, 6-HDA-treated rats usually weighed considerably

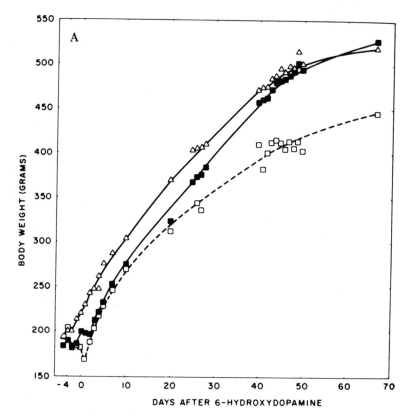

FIG. 6. (A) Effect of two intraventricular injections of 6-hydroxydopamine (6-HDA) (200 μg each, at −4 and 0 days) in representative rats whose body weights did (■) or did not (□) return to the levels of vehicle-treated rats (△) within 1–2 months. (B) (p. 135) Effect of two intraventricular injections of 6-HDA (200 μg each), after pargyline (50 mg/kg, i.p.) pretreatment, on the body weight of representative rats. One rat (■) was maintained by intragastric intubations of food until voluntary feeding recovered. The other two rats were not maintained by intragastric intubations; one (●) spontaneously recovered feeding, while the other (○) did not and died. The arrows denote the injections; the asterisk indicates terminal body weight. The smooth curve is the mean of 12 vehicle-injected rats (from Stricker and Zigmond, 1974). Copyright 1974 by the American Psychological Association. Reprinted by permission.

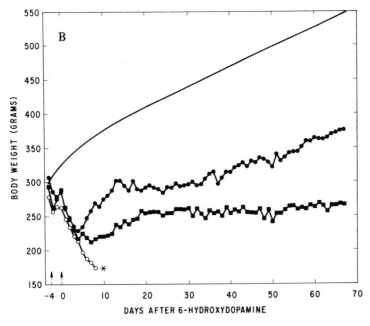

FIG. 6

less than control rats given the vehicle solution. Although there was marked variability in the levels at which body weights were being maintained, rats that recovered feeding and drinking behaviors within 1–3 days always maintained their body weights at more elevated levels than those that recovered slowly, while rats given intraventricular 6-HDA without any pretreatment, which had not become aphagic or adipsic at all, maintained their body weights at still higher levels (Fig. 6); indeed, about 20% of them ultimately increased their body weights to levels that fell within the range of control animals.

The 6-HDA lesioned rats also showed impaired responses to thirst stimuli which seemed to be proportional to the duration of recovery (Stricker and Zigmond, 1974, 1975). For example, intact rats given subcutaneous injections of 20% polyethylene glycol (PG) solution (which produced approximately a 20% loss of plasma fluid volume) usually increased their water intakes within the first hour after the onset of hypovolemia; in contrast, rats given intraventricular 6-HDA which had never been aphagic began drinking within 0–3 hours, rats which had recovered rapidly after 6-HDA given with pargyline pretreatment drank within 3–8 hours, and rats given pargyline plus 6-HDA that recovered slowly did not begin until 8–12 hours after the PG injection. Similar delays in drinking by 6-HDA-treated rats were observed following the administration of isoproterenol (0.33 mg/kg, s.c.) (which increases circulating angiotensin levels) or of 1 M NaCl (5 ml, i.p.) (which produces intracellular dehydration). Differences in intake 3—6 hours after the experimental injections (Table II) reflect the variable onsets of drinking that were observed.

As is the case following lateral hypothalamic lesions (Teitelbaum and Epstein, 1962), the impaired behavioral responses to thirst stimuli were not always permanent. For example, two rats drinking 0 ml and 2.5 ml of water in response to the injection of hypertonic NaCl solution 1 week after recovery from adipsia drank 18 ml and 14 ml, respectively, after receiving the same treatment 3 months later. The rats had required 88 and 34 days after the lesions, respectively, before they maintained themselves on laboratory chow and water.

The specific disruptions in glucoregulatory feeding, body weight maintenance, and thirst that were observed in rats following intraventricular 6-HDA after pargyline pretreatment have also been seen in 6-HDA-treated rats that had been pretreated with DMI and pargyline (Stricker and Zigmond, 1974) or with tranylcypromine (another monoamine oxidase inhibitor) (Fibiger *et al.*, 1973), in rats given intracisternal 6-HDA after pretreatment with pargyline (Breese *et al.*, 1973) and in rats given injections of 6-HDA directly into the substantia nigra or globus pallidus (Fibiger *et al.*, 1973; Marshall and Teitelbaum, 1973; Marshall *et al.*, 1974). In each of these studies a depletion of at least 80% of striatal DA was observed. In addition, the same persistent deficits in feeding and drinking behaviors were reported to occur following electrolytic lesions or parasagittal knife cuts along the anterolateral border of the lateral hypothalamus (Blass and Epstein, 1971; Grossman and Grossman, 1973), or electrolytic lesions of the posterior medial forebrain bundle caudal to the lateral hypothalamus (Table II) (Stricker, 1976) in rats that did not always show an initial period of aphagia and adipsia. Although biochemical assays were not performed in these studies, the lesions might be expected to have at least partially interrupted ascending dopaminergic fibers.

It should be emphasized, however, that not all of the residual deficits seen in recovered laterals have been observed in 6-HDA-treated rats (Stricker and Zigmond, 1974). For example, although many of these animals required weeks for recovery of ingestive behaviors, they did not show evidence of impaired reflex salivary secretions to food and thermal stimuli; that is, there was no prandial drinking or inefficient feeding, water intakes were substantial when food was withheld, and rats were able to thermoregulate during heat stress (see also Van Zoeren, 1974). Furthermore, all rats that recovered quickly following intraventricular 6-HDA after pargyline pretreatment showed sodium appetite in response to hypovolemia (see also Breese *et al.*, 1973) and learned to avoid toxic LiCl solution. (These latter experiments have not been repeated with rats that had required many weeks for recovery of function.)

To summarize, many but not all of the long-term impairments which characterize rats that have recovered from lateral hypothalamic lesions are seen in rats after intraventricular 6-HDA. Thus, this treatment seems to fractionate the lateral hypothalamic syndrome into a portion which is related to the CA depletions and a portion which may not be as dependent on an intact system of CA-containing neurons. That similar effects were obtained in rats treated with intraventricular 6-HDA after pargyline and DMI pretreatments, and in rats with 6-HDA lesions of the substantia nigra and globus pallidus, suggests that DA-containing neurons are necessary for animals to behave appropriately after the abrupt onset of large nutritional needs. Previously, the residual deficits have been interpreted as reflecting the disruption of specific regulatory systems. If this is so, then each of the affected behaviors must be mediated by a separate cluster of DA-containing neurons. Alternatively, it is possible that the same DA-containing neurons mediate some common aspect of each of these behaviors.

Despite the specificity of 6-HDA and the availability of biochemical assays, the individual CA projections whose damage was responsible for the observed effects have not yet been specified. The problem results from the facts that (1) all pathways utilizing the same CA are damaged more or less equally by 6-HDA when it is injected intraventricularly, and (2) the extensive overlap of these CA-containing pathways has made it difficult to separate them by electrolytic or 6-HDA lesions of intracerebral sites. In one of the few studies in which some separation has been attempted, Ungerstedt (1971c) reported that destruction of extranigrostriatal dopaminergic fibers (including the so-called mesolimbic projection) did not cause aphagia and adipsia. Unfortunately, the behavioral responses to acute nutritional needs were not examined in these animals. Furthermore, DA depletions were estimated from changes in histochemical fluorescence, and thus it is difficult to know whether all the fibers actually were damaged (Kopin et al., 1974). For example, it is conceivable that rats with lesions of the mesolimbic pathways would not respond to 2-DG, and thus resemble 6-HDA-treated rats with 90% loss of striatal DA which had not been aphagic immediately after 6-HDA treatment.

Finally, it should be noted that other neuronal pathways also might be necessary for mediating regulatory ingestive behaviors. For example, impaired feeding and drinking responses to acute regulatory demands have also been reported after damage to the frontal neocortex (Brandes, 1973), the lateral preoptic area (Black, 1971; Blass and Epstein, 1971; Blass and Kraly, 1974; Miselis and Epstein, 1971), or the perifornical area of the hypothalamus (Nicolaïdis and Meile, 1972; Sclafani et al., 1973). Although biochemical assays were not performed, damage to these neural structures would not be expected to disrupt a major portion of the ascending dopaminergic fibers. On the other hand, the dorsal bundle of noradrenergic fibers might well have been interrupted in each of these studies. Indeed, we have observed recently that 4 rats with perifornical lateral hypothalamic lesions recovered rapidly following an initial period of aphagia and adipsia, but did not increase feeding after systemic injections of 2-DG and showed considerable delays in drinking after the onset of hypovolemia or acute cellular dehydration. These rats had no detectable telencephalic NE but only 0–30% depletion of DA.[2]

III. Characteristics of Brain Catecholamines

Thus far, we have used biochemical measurements of brain catecholamines as merely a convenient way to quantify damage to apparently critical neural pathways, much as neuroanatomists have recently used histochemical fluorescence to trace pathways in the central nervous system (e.g., Andén *et al.*, 1964; Lindvall and Björklund, 1974; Ungerstedt, 1971a). For this purpose, any other means of identification would have been adequate, and little would have changed had other putative central neurotransmitters been found responsible for these effects. However, we believe that it is not coincidental that brain catecholamines play so important a role in mediating motivated behaviors. Indeed, we believe that a neurochemical model of the lateral hypothalamic syndrome becomes readily apparent after considering, first, the functions that can be provided by CA-containing neurons because of their anatomical organization, and second, the biochemical bases for regulation of their synaptic activities. It is to these characteristics of brain catecholamines that we will now turn.

A. FUNCTION

1. Arousal and Motivation

One of the prominent features of mammalian life is the constancy of the internal environment. This regulation is largely achieved by complementary

---

[2] These findings are generally consistent with traditional arguments for involvement of central NE-containing neurons in the control of ingestive behaviors that are based on studies in which intracerebral injections of NE increased food intake in rats (e.g., Booth, 1968; Grossman, 1960; Slangen and Miller, 1969). However, one must be cautious in interpreting such reports because it is difficult to determine whether exogenous NE administered in relatively large doses altered behavior by influencing neural firing or by disturbing cellular metabolism (e.g., by mobilizing neuronal glycogen reserves); moreover, it is unclear whether the NE acted on adrenergic receptor sites that are normally innervated by NE-containing neurons, and, if it did, whether these sites are within central neural pathways or part of the peripheral sympathetic control of the cerebral vasculature.

activities of the autonomic nervous system, the pituitary–adrenal axis, and motivated behavior. A significant aspect of the physiological contributions to homeostasis is the tendency for a generalized sympathetic activation to occur under any condition of extreme stress or excitement, thereby providing for the mobilization of energy reserves, increased oxygenation of the blood, cardiac acceleration, diversion of blood to skeletal muscles, and other such responses that combine to defend the internal milieu (Cannon, 1929). Activation of the adrenal cortex by ACTH promotes additional resistance, which again is similar regardless of whether the stress be homeostatic imbalance, physical trauma, or emotional alarm. The motivated behaviors that are associated with these emergencies, or lesser conditions of need, also have a broad, nonspecific component of arousal, which may be characterized by increased alertness, sensitivity to relevant sensory stimuli, and, frequently, locomotor activity. Reticular activation appears to be essential for the motivational responses, since stimuli cease to provoke electrocortical arousal and behavior when the reticulocortical input is depressed by anesthesia even though primary sensory pathways to the cortex are unimpaired (French *et al.*, 1953).

The reticular formation is strategically located for receiving sensory input from many sources. Consistent with its nonspecific function, heterogeneous afferent impulses have been shown to converge upon single reticular units (Amassian and DeVito, 1954; Scheibel *et al.*, 1955) and to activate the arousal system in a similar fashion regardless of the sense modality (Albe-Fessard *et al.*, 1960; French *et al.*, 1952; Starzl *et al.*, 1951). Although in most of the early electrophysiological studies sensory stimulation was confined to somatic, visual, or auditory systems, other work has clearly demonstrated that visceral sensations (e.g., from baroreceptors or chemoreceptors) also contribute to reticular activity (e.g., Dell, 1952; Grastyan *et al.*, 1952). For example, EEG desynchronization has been demonstrated to occur during hunger and thirst, whereas satiety is associated with slow electrocortical activity and drowsiness (Anokhin, 1961; Hockman, 1964; Steiner, 1962). In addition, the electrocortical effects of sensory input appear to be intensified and prolonged by circulating NE or epinephrine, as would result from the peripheral sympathetic discharge associated with pain, fear, cold stress, and other emergency states (Bonvallet *et al.*, 1954; Rothballer, 1956). Thus, reticular activity can result from the combined effects of exteroceptive, interoceptive, and humoral stimuli.

Catecholamines appear to play a critical role in the reticular activating system, as they do within the sympathoadrenal system (and perhaps in the control of anterior pituitary function; Fuxe and Hökfelt, 1969). Their contribution to central arousal was first indicated by psychopharmacological studies, which demonstrated that both electrocortical activation and behavioral responsiveness are decreased by drugs that depress activity in central catecholaminergic synapses whereas the reverse effects are obtained with drugs that augment activity in those synapses (see review by Jouvet, 1972). Specific increases in locomotor activity following administration of DA receptor agonists, and akinesia following selective blockade of DA receptors, also have been observed (e.g., Andén *et al.*, 1970; Ernst, 1967).

Although neurochemical identification of the critical fibers in such studies is often not available, two groups of CA-containing neuronal projections originating in the midbrain reticular formation have been recently identified which appear to be jointly responsible for these effects. They are the NE-containing projections from the locus coeruleus of the dorsolateral pontine tegmentum (the so-called "dorsal NE bundle") and the DA-containing projections from the substantia nigra and ventral tegmental area (Fig. 1). Each of these fiber tracts seems to be necessary for the initiation, maintenance, and proper execution of motivated acts, although their individual contributions are not identical. Thus, extensive damage to the NE-containing neurons increases the synchrony of EEG activity and allows only brief periods of behavioral orientation to sensory stimulation, whereas destruction of the DA-containing projections eliminates behavioral responsiveness despite the presence of normal desynchronous EEG activity (e.g., Feldman and Waller, 1962; Jones *et al.*, 1973). These observations, and related drug studies (Bradley and Elkes, 1957; Wikler, 1952), emphasize the independence of the systems mediating tonic cortical waking and those mediating more phasic behavioral arousal (see also Bolme *et al.*, 1972; Routtenberg, 1968). As might be expected, interruption of both ascending pathways leads to prolonged somnolence and coma (see Lindsley *et al.*, 1950; Nauta, 1946; Swett and Hobson, 1968).

The anatomical organization of the dorsal NE bundle clearly resembles the distribution of the adrenergic neurons in the sympathetic nervous system, in that both pathways project to an exceptionally large number of diverse structures from only a few cell groups (Dahlström and Fuxe, 1964; Ungerstedt, 1971a). This arrangement, whereby long axons and collaterals originating in the locus coeruleus can spread nervous activity simultaneously to practically all portions of the cerebral and cerebellar cortices, is consistent with the postulated function of the dorsal noradrenergic fibers in mediating tonic electrocortical arousal and alertness. Similarly, the DA-containing neurons arising from the substantia nigra innervate the corpus striatum, thus providing an anatomical basis for their influence on phasic extrapyramidal motor activities (see also Section III,A,2). Since CA-containing neurons generally exert long-lasting inhibitory postsynaptic effects (Bloom and Hoffer, 1973; Connor, 1970; Hoffer *et al.*, 1973), it would seem that nervous

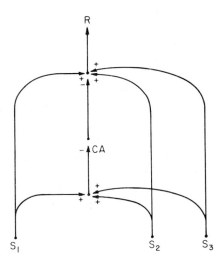

FIG. 7. Schematic representation of neural mechanisms by which sensory stimuli (S) might elicit an appropriate behavioral response (R). Arrows indicate neuronal pathways (which are not necessarily monosynaptic), plus signs indicate excitatory influences, minus signs indicate inhibitory influences, CA indicates synapses of catecholamine-containing terminals.

impulses in these pathways permit arousal by depressing activity in structures normally exerting an inhibitory influence.

A preliminary formulation of our thoughts on the function of these pathways is diagrammed schematically in Fig. 7. Each sensory stimulus is seen as having two effects: a specific one that activates neurons that are involved in eliciting some appropriate motivational state, and a nonspecific one that removes an inhibitory influence and thereby permits such responses to actually occur. Note that a stimulus would not evoke a behavioral response if either the specific (cf. Sprague *et al.*, 1961) or the nonspecific (i.e., the CA-containing neurons of the reticular formation) pathways were interrupted. Given the multiplicity of stimuli that impinge on an animal at any given time, we presume that the overt motivated response (for example, feeding = R) will be the one that is associated with the prepotent stimulus (in this case, decreased utilizable fuels = S_1). Additional stimuli (e.g., gustatory and olfactory cues associated with food = S_2 and S_3) would tend to augment the nonspecific arousal component, due to multisensory convergence onto single reticular neurons, and thereby facilitate responding (unless they were large enough to elicit competing motivational responses). Thus, a weak stimulus for hunger might still elicit feeding when combined with the incentive arousal from highly palatable food.[3,4]

In this context, it does not seem remarkable that animals sustaining extensive damage to both the noradrenergic and dopaminergic fiber systems, as occurs following lateral hypothalamic lesions or intraventricular 6-HDA treatments (without DMI), show increases in cortical EEG synchronization (Hansen and Whishaw, 1973; Laguzzi et al., 1972; Wampler, 1970), and generally appear to be unaware of interoceptive stimuli arising from homeostatic imbalances. Their initial aphagia and adipsia probably reflects the more fundamental problem they have of sustaining arousal in response to sensory stimulation. In fact, deficits in responding to olfactory and gustatory stimuli parallel the ineffectiveness of regulatory stimuli in provoking feeding and drinking, and probably contribute to the early disappearance of those behaviors (Marshall and Teitelbaum, 1974; Marshall et al., 1971). Nevertheless,

---

[3] This model proposes that central CA release generally disinhibits all behavior. Consistent with this formulation are common observations of behavioral arousal following treatment with amphetamine, an adrenergic agonist which increases the availability of catecholamines at receptor sites. In light of such findings, it may seem paradoxical that amphetamine also has anorexigenic effects. However, we believe that there exists an optimal level of CA activity for response to a particular stimulus, and that too much activity would permit stimuli other than the prepotent one to unduly influence the animal and thereby disrupt behavior (see Fig. 7). In this regard, we have observed that the reduction in food intake which follows the administration of amphetamine is paralleled by an increase in motor activity, and that both effects can be antagonized either by the selective destruction of DA terminals or by the administration of spiroperidol, a drug that blocks DA receptors (Heffner et al., 1975).

[4] This scheme is plainly oversimplified. Reticular activity is not determined solely by afferent stimulation, since it is well known that significant input into the reticular formation is mediated by descending pathways, such as those issuing from the cerebral cortex or neostriatum (e.g., French et al., 1955; Krauthamer and Albe-Fessard, 1965). Nor is cerebral arousal determined solely by activity in central CA-containing neurons. For example, there is considerable evidence that neurons containing serotonin are active during slow-wave sleep and inhibit the dorsal NE pathway (e.g., Jouvet, 1969; Pujol et al., 1971), whereas serotonin-containing neurons seem to be inhibited by dorsal NE-containing neurons during arousal (e.g., Petitjean and Jouvet, 1970; Pujol et al., 1973). A similar relationship between the nigrostriatal DA neurons and fibers containing acetylcholine or γ-aminobutyric acid also has been suggested on the basis of neurochemical, electrophysiological, and behavioral evidence (e.g., Carlton, 1963; Frigyese and Purpura, 1967; Hornykiewicz, 1971; Jasper et al., 1965; Javoy et al., 1974; McGeer et al., 1973; Olivier et al., 1970). While these considerations are critical to most discussions of sleep and motivational or attentional processes (e.g., Jouvet, 1972; Morgane, 1969; Morgane and Stern, 1974), we have neglected them in order to limit the scope of this paper and to focus attention on the changes that occur in catecholaminergic function following hypothalamic lesions, which we believe are predictive of most of the significant features of the lateral hypothalamic syndrome.

although the absence of consumatory behaviors may be the alterations that are most conspicuous to the investigator and are of gravest consequence to the experimental animals, it should be clear that their impairments are not limited to motivated ingestive behaviors but would include any voluntary activity that demands orientation to sensory stimuli and sustained alertness (cf. Avar and Monos, 1969; Caggiula *et al.,* 1973; Cooper *et al.,* 1972b; Satinoff and Shan, 1971).

2. Extrapyramidal Motor Function

In addition to their demonstrated involvement in central arousal mechanisms, there is persuasive evidence that the DA-containing neurons of the nigrostriatal pathway are fundamentally involved in mediating extrapyramidal motor activity. The critical findings in support of this argument are that (a) the corpus striatum, which forms an essential part of the extrapyramidal system, is densely innervated by DA-containing neurons ascending from the substantia nigra, (b) extreme hypokinesia, muscular rigidity, and tremor, are associated with degeneration of the nigrostriatal dopaminergic pathway in Parkinson's disease, experimental lesions that interrupt the nigrostriatal bundle, or drugs that reduce activity at striatal DA receptors, and (c) treatment with L-dopa increases DA levels in the striatum and reverses the symptoms that had been associated with its reduction in clinical patients and experimental animals (see review by Hornykiewicz, 1966).[5]

With regard to the lateral hypothalamic syndrome, gross motor impairments have been observed in rats that become aphagic and adipsic following electrolytic or 6-HDA lesions along the nigrostriatal dopaminergic bundle (Balagura *et al.,* 1969; Baillie and Morrison, 1963; Levine and Schwartzbaum, 1973; Marshall and Teitelbaum, 1974; Stricker and Zigmond, 1974; Turner, 1973; Ungerstedt, 1971c). These dysfunctions, including forelimb disuse and disabilities in biting, chewing, and lapping, have obvious implications for the initial absence of ingestive behaviors that is observed in these animals. Even after feeding and drinking resumes, we have observed that several 6-HDA-treated rats which never would ingest liquids when they were presented in a drinking tube with a standard nozzle would readily consume them from a

---

[5] As with arousal, the extrapyramidal functions of brain DA involve interactions with other neuronal pathways. For example, Parkinsonian symptoms can be produced or aggravated by cholinergic agents as well as by DA antagonists, and can be eliminated both by anticholinergic agents and by drugs stimulating DA activity (Hornykiewicz, 1971). Thus, Parkinsonism can be viewed as the result of an imbalance between activity of dopaminergic synapses in the striatum and activity of some opposing cholinergic projection.

wide and shallow dish (Stricker and Zigmond, 1974), and similar observations have also been reported in studies of rats with electrolytic or 6-HDA lesions of the lateral hypothalamus (Rodgers et al., 1965), the caudal subthalamic region (Wolf, 1971), or the substantia nigra (Marshall et al., 1974). Furthermore, it cannot be assumed that motor abilities that appear to be normal under basal conditions remain so during the severe regulatory imbalance that occurs during the tests for behavioral regulation; indeed, we often notice a sudden deterioration of sensory-motor functions in intraventricular 6-HDA-treated rats during such tests. On the basis of these findings, as well as certain theoretical considerations (see Section IV,B,3), we believe that the contribution of motor impairments to all stages of the lateral hypothalamic syndrome may be considerable.

3. Affect

In recent years there has been increasing speculation regarding a possible basis for human affective disorders in altered metabolism of central biogenic amines. Such theories have been derived largely from neuropharmacological studies elucidating the mechanisms of action of drugs that had proved to be therapeutic. For example, depression has been related to decreased activity at central CA receptors, since effective antidepressants have been found to increase the availability of CA to these receptors. Similarly, certain forms of schizophrenia have been attributed to excessive activity in central catecholaminergic pathways, since neuroleptics have been found to block CA receptors (see reviews by Matthysee, 1974; Snyder et al., 1974). Inferences about the affective state of experimental animals can be made from their behavior only with considerable caution. Nevertheless, the recent observations by Fonberg (1969) are so striking that they bear scrutiny. In animals with lateral hypothalamic lesions, she reports that not only is there " . . . loss of the specific alimentary drive, loss of hunger, but at the same time a lack of some kind of general drive, absence of energy, loss of the 'joy of life'. The dogs were sad, indifferent, did not jump, did not play, did not greet the experimenters. This general look of sadness was very striking and reminiscent of patients during the depressive state of schizophrenia." This description suggests apathy rather than somnolence, and adds another dimension to our interpretation of aphagia and adipsia following lateral hypothalamic lesions.

Lack of affect has also been inferred in studies of rats. For example, Roth et al. (1973) reported that recovered laterals would not avoid a specific flavored diet that was paired either with electric shock or poison. Since the lesioned animals did not engage in displacement activities suggesting conflict, the authors concluded that the rats did not fear punishment. This explanation is consistent with other reports that, after lateral hypothalamic lesions or intraventricular 6-HDA treatment, rats fail to learn to avoid or escape shock normally (Balinska, 1968; Cooper *et al.,* 1972b; Coscina and Balagura, 1970; Runnels and Thompson, 1969).

As noted earlier (Section II,C), we have observed that rats given intraventricular 6-HDA treatments which had not been aphagic or adipsic would learn to avoid a toxic LiCl solution normally (Stricker and Zigmond, 1974). In a more recent study, we deprived rats of water for 23 hours and gave them 0.15 *M* LiCl solution and then water in successive 30-minute periods. Whereas control rats were almost continually agitated when LiCl solution was present (i.e., they bit the drinking nozzle or the front mesh wall of the cage, groomed often, and were generally very active), and sampled the test fluid repeatedly, rats injected intraventricularly with 6-HDA (2 $\times$ 200 μg, no pretreatments) simply took a few initial licks of the test fluid and then retired quietly to the back of the cage until water was presented, at which time they drank. The lesioned rats clearly had learned to recognize and avoid the poisoned fluid, yet showed no signs of excitement or displacement behavior when it was available despite their evident thirst.

4. Summary

To summarize Section III,A, brain catecholamines appear to serve a variety of critical functions which must be considered in evaluating the neurological basis for the lateral hypothalamic syndrome. We have emphasized their contributions to arousal, motor function, and affect. In each of these dimensions, rats which become aphagic after lateral hypothalamic lesions seem to be severely deficient. Thus, despite increasing starvation they probably are not aware that they need food, they probably could not find the food even if they did feel hungry, and they probably could not ingest the food, and would not care to, even if they could find it. When you take into account additional deficits that do not seem to involve brain catecholamines, such as an impaired ability to digest food (Glavcheva *et al.,* 1970; Rozkowska and Fonberg, 1970) and to mobilize body energy reserves during severe need (Colin-Jones and Himsworth, 1970; Himsworth, 1970), the lateral hypothalamic syndrome becomes very complex indeed. In fact, it might be more appropriate to consider the syndrome as an amalgamation of many overlapping syndromes that together determine the outstanding disruptions in behavior that are observed. For the purpose of simplicity, we shall continue to focus on the impairments that are obtained both by biochemical lesions and by electrolytic lesions of the lateral hypothalamus, and therefore we shall discuss only those features of the syndrome that seem to be attributable to a deterioration in the function of brain catecholamines.

B. BIOCHEMICAL REGULATION

The life cycle of brain catecholamines has been the subject of considerable research (Fig. 8). Many aspects of this cycle appear to be regulated in response to changes in the rate of transmitter utilization (see reviews by Fleming *et al.*, 1973; Stjarne, 1973; Thoenen, 1974; Udenfriend and Dairman, 1971; Weiner *et al.*, 1973). These regulatory processes may be separated into two groups: those that tend to maintain constant the intracellular concentration of catecholamines and those that tend to maintain a constant level of postsynaptic activity.

1. Regulation of Intracellular CA Concentration

Studies in microorganisms have led to a generally accepted model for homeostatic regulations of the biosynthesis of particular compounds (see review by Nierlich, 1974). According to this scheme, the end product of a pathway can control its synthesis by inhibiting the initial enzymic step in the sequence. Several different types of studies suggest that end-product inhibition may also participate in the regulation of CA levels in mammalian tissues. While most of this evidence comes from studies utilizing peripheral tissue, a similar scheme is also supported for the brain. The evidence is as follows: (a) Exogenous catecholamines inhibit tyrosine hydroxylation, the initial step in CA synthesis, when added to *in vitro* systems containing sympathetic nerve terminals (Nagatsu *et al.*, 1964) or synaptosome-rich homogenates of brain tissue (Karobath, 1971). (b) Drugs that appear to increase cytoplasmic levels of catecholamines inhibit CA synthesis within a few minutes both in peripheral tissue and in brain (Besson *et al.*, 1971; Spector *et al.*, 1967; Weiner *et al.*, 1972). (c) Electrical stimulation of peripheral sympathetic nerve fibers produces an increase in CA synthesis (Sedvall *et al.*, 1968), resulting from a marked reduction in the susceptibility of tyrosine hydroxylase to inhibition by NE (Morgenroth *et al.*, 1974). Similar observations have been made in the brain of intact animals following the stimulation of both NE- and DA-containing cell groups (Murrin *et al.*, 1974; Roth *et al.*, 1974). (d) Acute exposure to stressful stimuli, such as electric foot shock, immobilization, exercise, or cold, increases CA turnover and biosynthesis, both in peripheral and central nervous systems (e.g., Bliss, 1973; Gordon *et al.*, 1966; Thierry *et al.*, 1968).

Thus, the immediate increase in synthesis during neural activity appears to result from an elevated rate of tyrosine hydroxylation that is permitted by a decrease in the inhibitory influence of the end product. However, even when all inhibition is removed and maximum velocity is attained, the ability of synthesis to compensate for increased release and destruction of transmitter is

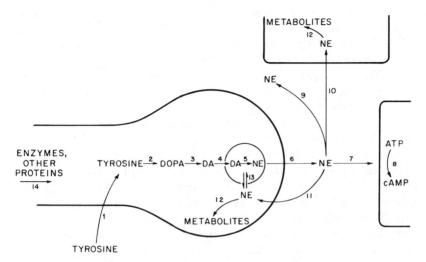

FIG. 8. The life cycle of norepinephrine (NE). Tyrosine is transported into the nerve terminal (1) where it is converted first to dopa (catalyzed by tyrosine hydroxylase) (2), then to DA (by dopa decarboxylase) (3), and finally, following the transport of DA into vesicles (4), to NE (by dopamine-β-hydroxylase) (5). NE is released into the synaptic cleft by exocytosis (6). There, it acts on the postsynaptic membrane (7), perhaps by influencing adenylate cyclase, an enzyme which catalyzes the conversion of adenosine triphosphate (ATP) to adenosine 3′,5′-cyclic monophosphate (cAMP) (8). NE is removed from the synapse either by diffusion (9) or by uptake into surrounding cells (10), the most important of which are the NE-containing terminals themselves (11). Once within the cytoplasm, NE can either be metabolized (by one of several routes, involving the enzymes monoamine oxidase and catechol-O-methyltransferase) (12) or taken up and stored in vesicles for reuse (13). The enzymes involved in the synthesis or catabolism of NE are formed in cell bodies and transported to their sites of action, as are various other proteins that may be important in the construction of vesicles, cell membranes, transport systems, and receptors (14). Note that while the figure is drawn for NE-containing neurons, the scheme is essentially the same for DA except that dopamine-β-hydroxylase is not present in the vesicles.

limited by the amount of available enzyme. For example, in the rat, maximal increases in NE synthesis of about 2-fold have been estimated (Sedvall *et al.,* 1968; see also Besson *et al.,* 1971), with further increases in utilization, such as occur during severe stress, producing an exhaustion of transmitter stores (e.g., Maynert and Levi, 1964; Vogt, 1954; Zigmond and Harvey, 1970).

The activation of enzyme by increased product utilization in microorganisms often is accompanied by the gradual induction of enzyme synthesis, permitting new, higher rates of product turnover without depletion. While the precise mechanism has not been worked out for mammalian CA-synthesizing cells, continuous or repeated exposure to conditions such as cold or insulin hypoglycemia is accompanied within 0.5–14 days by an apparent increase in the amount of peripheral tyrosine hydroxylase (e.g., Thoenen, 1970; Weiner and Mosimann, 1970); similar results have also been observed in central CA-containing neurons (e.g., Mandell, 1973; Thoenen, 1970; Zigmond et al., 1974). These new enzymes are synthesized in the cell body and travel by axonal transport to the terminal region, where they increase the biosynthetic capacity of the cell (Dairman and Udenfriend, 1970) and thereby expand the range over which turnover can be altered without a depletion of CA reserves (see Zigmond and Harvey, 1970).

In summary, short-term control of function in peripheral or central CA-containing neurons appears to occur in part through modulation of the activity of the initial, rate-limiting enzyme tyrosine hydroxylase, while longer-term control is achieved by changes in the amount of available enzyme. Within limits, such controls permit the utilization of catecholamines at a rate dictated by demand without disruption of function due to depletion of amines or the unnecessary accumulation of CA stores.

2. Regulation of Receptor Activity

The activity of postsynaptic neurons is proportional to the availability of CA which, in turn, is determined by the amount of CA released and the amount that is removed. For example, in the striatum receptors appear to monitor the concentration of DA in the synapse and influence its release so as to maintain a particular level of activity in the postsynaptic neurons. Thus, under basal conditions, chlorpromazine, a DA receptor antagonist, produces a rapid increase in the turnover and firing rate of DA-containing neurons, whereas apomorphine, a receptor agonist, has the reverse effects (e.g., Andén et al., 1970; Bunney et al., 1973; Nybäck et al., 1968). Comparable relationships at central noradrenergic synapses also have been reported (Andén et al., 1970; Farnebo and Hamberger, 1971), extending the well-documented phenomenon observed at peripheral adrenergic synapses (see review by Starke, 1973).

Removal of CA from the synapse is accomplished by uptake into CA terminals and other adjacent cells, by diffusion, and by enzymic degradation. The importance of reuptake for determining the postsynaptic response to nerve stimulation is suggested by the exaggerated response to exogenous CA that follows the administration of cocaine or other drugs that block uptake (Trendelenburg, 1966). Like release, the rate of removal of CA from the synaptic cleft also is influenced by the amount of amine present (Iversen, 1967). Thus, an increase in the availability of CA is, within limits, immediately followed by an increase in the rate of inactivation, since the uptake processes are not normally saturated, while reduced CA concentration should lead to a slower rate of removal from the synapse.

Further homeostatic control of synaptic transmission in CA-containing neurons is achieved by changes in postsynaptic sensitivity to catecholamines under varying conditions of use. For example, long-term disruption of sympathetic function in the periphery, by drugs such as AMT and reserpine or by surgical decentralization, leads to an increase in the responsiveness of the innervated tissue to exogenous NE, which can be prevented by the chronic infusion of receptor agonists. The extent of this "disuse supersensitivity" depends on the species and tissue under investigation and can range from 2- to 25-fold, developing over 3–28 days (see review by Fleming *et al.*, 1973). In the central nervous system, increased responsiveness to adrenergic agonists has also been observed following chronic treatment with AMT or reserpine (Dominic and Moore, 1969; Geyer and Segal, 1973).

To summarize, the modulation of synaptic transmission by changes in release and receptor sensitivity tends to maintain activity of CA-containing pathways within a desired range under basal conditions and to dampen the synaptic response to abrupt changes in input. [Similar regulatory processes appear to function in other synapses as well, including those utilizing serotonin and some of those using acetylcholine (see reviews by Mandell *et al.*, 1974; Szerb, 1972).] These characteristics would not be suited for the transmission of primary sensory information, or messages in a final somatic motor pathway, in which rapid, high-fidelity transmission is necessary. However, they do seem appropriate to neural pathways subserving homeostasis and motivation, since transient changes in input must be ignored while sustained changes must evoke a gradual, coordinated response.

IV. A Neurochemical Model of the Lateral Hypothalamic Syndrome

The capacity of the brain to recover from neurological damage has both fascinated and perplexed investigators for many years. Recovery of function often has been taken to indicate "equipotentiality" or "plasticity" for large areas of brain, and it has been suggested that brain functions could be transferred from one area to another (e.g., Lashley, 1929). However, we believe that the functions of the central CA-containing pathways, like those of the adrenergic sympathoadrenal system in the periphery, are unique and not transferable. We have already described data that suggest that in animals recovered from damage to central CA pathways, residual CA-containing neurons are critical to the maintenance of function. We believe that this can occur because within a given projection there does exist a large amount of equivalence, with CA-containing neurons receiving similar input and acting on overlapping postsynaptic receptive fields, and that therefore the adaptive processes just described can compensate for the decrease in activity that follows partial damage to these pathways.

A. THE MODEL

The following description summarizes our conception of the specific steps and mechanisms in the recovery process (Fig. 9). Immediately after subtotal damage to a bundle of CA-containing fibers, CA will be released due to terminal degeneration (and, following 6-HDA administration, displacement of CA from storage sites). Soon thereafter, CA release from the residual neurons will represent only a fraction of that which occurred before the lesion, and the rate of receptor activation will consequently be lower than normal. These decreases in CA release and receptor stimulation should lead to immediate increases in CA synthesis and release from residual neurons. If demand is large enough, synthesis rates will be inadequate and CA stores will be depleted. However, subsequent increases in the availability of tyrosine hydroxylase should progressively raise the capacity for sustained increases in CA turnover. In addition, the efficacy of released CA should increase, due, for example, to loss of uptake sites and enhanced sensitivity of the postsynaptic mem-

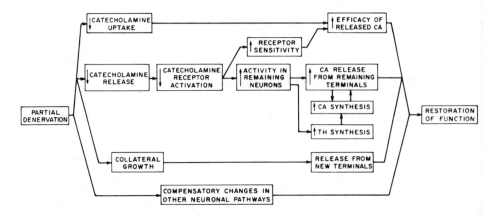

FIG. 9. A model for recovery of function following subtotal damage to central catecholamine (CA)-containing neurons. All changes (except for those in the lower portion) occur within pathways of residual catecholamine-containing neurons. In addition to these processes, recovery of function might be aided by the reversal of certain secondary effects of the lesions (e.g., vasomotor changes, hemorrhage, edema, the proliferation of glial cells). In the case of 6-hydroxydopamine-induced damage, reversal of receptor blockade (Haeusler, 1971), and repletion of catecholamines within central neurons that were depleted but not destroyed (Bartholini *et al.*, 1970), might also play a role in recovery.

brane. Finally, it is possible that the recovery process is aided by new neuronal growth, including collateral sprouting from intact axons and regenerating terminals, and by functional adjustments within interrelated pathways utilizing other neurotransmitters.

While we are still in the process of collecting much of the information necessary to adequately test this model, there already is a considerable amount of data which support it.

1. CA Release and Receptor Activation Increases during the Period Immediately Following Damage to CA-Containing Neurons

In the sympathetic nervous system, contraction of the nictitating membrane has been observed following transection and degeneration of the sympathetic postganglionic innervation of this tissue (Langer, 1966). Similarly, there are numerous reports of increased motor activity and other manifestations of CA release within 1–3 days after the administration of 6-HDA or electrolytic lesions along central CA pathways (Fibiger et al., 1972; Longo, 1973; Morrison, 1968).

2. Subtotal Damage to CA-Containing Neurons Increases Turnover and Synthesis in Neurons Remaining in the Same Pathway

Adrenal medullary secretion of catecholamines appears to be increased after a peripheral sympathectomy which leaves the innervation of the adrenal intact, thus compensating, in part, for the loss of NE that normally is released from adrenergic nerve terminals (see Thoenen et al., 1969). Similarly, turnover of DA in residual neurons increases after damage to the nigrostriatal bundle (Agid et al., 1973a; Sharman et al., 1967).

Our recent observations that feeding and drinking behaviors are more readily interrupted by AMT after lateral hypothalamic lesions or intraventricular 6-HDA treatments are consistent with such results (Fig. 10) (cf. Cooper et al., 1972a; Harvey, 1965; Schoenfeld and Zigmond, 1973). Since the amount of CA depletion, and thus the extent of functional impairment, following AMT seems to depend on the rate of CA turnover (Malmfors, 1964), these data may indicate that an increase in CA turnover occurs in residual neurons after brain damage. As might be expected from this hypothesis, those animals requiring the longest period of time for recovery were the most sensitive to AMT. For example, a dose of only 16–32 mg/kg (rather than 75 mg/kg; see Fig. 10) produced almost complete suppression of food and water intakes in 3 rats that had required more than 6 months for recovery (not included in Fig. 10). Although other explanations for these results are possible (see Zigmond and Stricker, 1973), it should be noted that

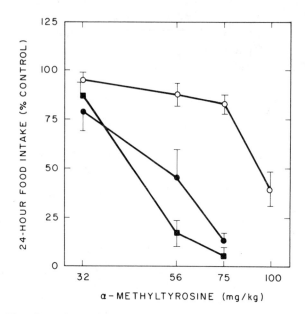

FIG. 10. The effect of α-methyl-*p*-tyrosine (AMT) on 24-hour food intake in control rats (o) and rats with either two pargyline (50 mg/kg, i.p.) plus 6-hydroxydopamine (200 μg, intraventricularly) treatments (■) or bilateral electrolytic lesions of the far-lateral hypothalamus (●). AMT was given intraperitoneally at 8 a.m., 4 p.m., and midnight, and food intake was measured during the 24 hours following the first injection. Each point represents the mean ± the standard error of the mean for 4–8 rats (32, 56, and 100 mg/kg doses) or 8–12 rats (75 mg/kg). We observe that 4 hours after the administration of AMT to control rats, the conversion of tyrosine-^{3}H to dopamine-^{3}H in striatum is reduced in proportion to the administered dose (from Zigmond and Stricker, 1973). Copyright 1973 by the American Association for the Advancement of Science.

they do not represent a generally heightened responsiveness to anorexic agents, since we have observed that similarly treated rats are less sensitive to the effects of amphetamine (see also Carlisle, 1964; and footnote 3).

3. The Amount of Enzyme Available for CA Synthesis in Remaining Neurons Increases after Subtotal Damage to CA-Containing Neurons

A 75% increase in the *in vitro* activities of both tyrosine hydroxylase and dopamine-β-hydroxylase has been observed in the adrenal medulla within 3 days after peripheral sympathectomy (Brimijoin and Molinoff, 1971). Thus far, there have been no long-term studies of tyrosine hydroxylase levels in residual neurons after extensive damage to brain CA neurons, although *in vitro* tyrosine hydroxylase activity has been found to be disproportionately high when compared to NE and DA depletions in rat brain 16–25 days after intraventricular 6-HDA treatment (Iversen and Uretsky, 1970).

4. CA Reuptake Is Retarded after Subtotal Damage to CA-Containing Neurons

The uptake of exogenous NE by peripheral tissue is virtually abolished within a few hours after surgical denervation (Hertting *et al.,* 1961) or intravenously administered 6-HDA (de Champlain, 1971). In the central nervous system, we have observed a decrease in NE uptake which was detectable within 6 hours after lateral hypothalamic lesions (Fig. 11) (Zigmond *et al.,* 1971). This decrease appeared to result from a reduced affinity of the residual terminals for NE as well as a reduction in number of axon terminals (Zigmond and Stricker, 1974). We also find decreased uptake of NE and DA after intraventricular 6-HDA (see also Iversen and Uretsky, 1970).

The functional significance of changes in CA uptake is suggested by the increase in motor activity that is elicited by L-dopa following the selective depletion of DA (Fig. 12) (see also Schoenfeld and Uretsky, 1973; Thornburg and Moore, 1975; Ungerstedt, 1971b). This increase can be detected within 24 hours after 6-HDA administration and is roughly proportional to the loss

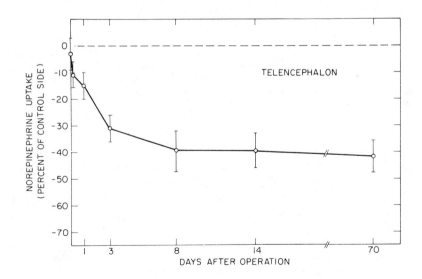

FIG. 11. Uptake of norepinephrine-^{3}H *in vitro* after unilateral lateral hypothalamic lesion. Uptake into the ipsilateral telencephalon is shown as a percentage of the control, contralateral side. Each point represents the mean ± the standard error of the mean for 4–12 rats (from Zigmond *et al.,* 1971). Copyright 1971 The Williams & Wilkins Co., Baltimore.

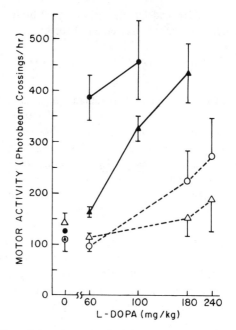

FIG. 12. The effect of dopa on motor activity in control rats (△) or in rats that had been given desmethylimipramine (25 mg/kg, i.p.) and 75 μg (○), 150 μg (▲), or 200 μg (●) of 6-hydroxydopamine intraventricularly. (These treatments had little effect on brain norepinephrine, but produced striatal dopamine depletions of 11, 42, and 86%, respectively.) Dopa was administered 5 minutes prior to testing and 30 minutes after pretreatment with RO4-4602 (50 mg/kg, i.p.), a peripheral decarboxylase inhibitor. Motor activity was measured as the number of photobeam crossings during the first hour of testing. Each point represents the mean ± the standard error of the mean for 4–6 rats.

of DA. Postsynaptic changes may play a role in the enhanced sensitivity to DA formed from the administered dopa; however, on the basis of a comparison between the effects of dopa and apomorphine (see below), we believe that the primary factor in the increased sensitivity to dopa is the retarded rate of DA inactivation which results from a decrease in DA uptake.

5. Postsynaptic Receptor Sensitivity Gradually Increases after Subtotal Damage to CA-Containing Neurons

There is a marked increase in the effector response to NE following surgical or chemical destruction of peripheral adrenergic neurons (see review by Fleming et al., 1973). A comparable phenomenon has long been postulated to

occur in the central nervous system (see Stavraky, 1961). Consistent with
this hypothesis, we have observed an increase in the amount of motor activity
that is elicited in rats by apomorphine (0.01–1.0 mg/kg, i.p.), a direct-acting
DA receptor agonist, following the selective depletion of telencephalic DA (1
X 200 μg of 6-HDA, 30 minutes after 25 mg of DMI per kilogram) (Zigmond
and Stricker, 1975; see also Schoenfeld and Uretsky, 1972; Ungerstedt,
1971b). Assuming that apomorphine is not primarily inactivated by uptake
into CA terminals, its effects, unlike those of dopa, probably reflect a change
in the postsynaptic membrane. In further contrast, sensitivity to apomorphine develops somewhat more slowly than does sensitivity to dopa, and is
readily apparent only in rats with lesions that deplete DA by at least 80% (see
also Thornburg and Moore, 1975).

Electrophysiological evidence for an increased sensitivity to DA after damage to the nigrostriatal bundle has been reported (Feltz and de Champlain,
1972), and, in collaboration with Dr. Alessandro Guidotti at the NIMH, we
have observed a 3-fold increase in the responsiveness of striatal adenylate
cyclase to DA (see legend, Fig. 8) after lesions which deplete DA by 85–95%
(Zigmond and Stricker, 1975; see also Mishra et al., 1974). An increase in the
enzyme's responsiveness to NE has also been reported to occur in the
telencephalon within 3 days after the intraventricular administration of
6-HDA (Kalisker et al., 1973; Palmer, 1972).

6. Increased Growth of CA Terminals May Occur after Damage

New growth of adrenergic fibers can be detected a few days after sympathetic nerve terminals have been destroyed by a peripheral injection of
6-HDA, and regeneration is complete within 1–3 months (de Champlain,
1971; Finch et al., 1973). Regenerative sprouting has also been observed in
central CA-containing pathways and is first detectable within 7 days of the
lesion (Björklund et al., 1971; Katzman et al., 1971). Although it is doubtful
that dopaminergic fibers could form functional connections in the telencephalon after their transection in the hypothalamus, reinnervation could be
provided by collaterals from adjacent, intact axons (Jonsson et al., 1974), as
in the periphery (Edds, 1953). The fact that telencephalic DA levels often are
only 1–2% of control values in rats that had recovered feeding and drinking
behaviors months after intraventricular 6-HDA treatment does not suggest
conspicuous growth of DA terminals; however, a 2- to 3-fold increase in DA
content in this range (which might be functionally significant) would go
undetected with our present methods.

Despite this support of our model, it should be recognized that a considerable amount of basic information still is lacking. First, there are few data

concerning biochemical regulation within central DA-containing neurons. In developing our model, we have assumed that these neurons (indeed, that all central CA neurons) function analogously to peripheral adrenergic fibers, and, as indicated, there is accumulating evidence that this may be true. However, an unfortunate gap exists in the information that is most relevant to our model: the physiological conditions under which central DA turnover is increased and the effect that such an increase might have on tyrosine hydroxylase.

Second, we can only speculate as to the relative importance of various neurochemical events that may provide a basis for recovery of function. In addition, although we have been focusing on possible changes within CA-containing neuronal pathways, it must be recognized that alterations in the function of interrelated neurons utilizing other neurotransmitters may be significant as well. For example, the turnover of serotonin has been shown to increase considerably during the first few days after central CA depletion (Blondaux et al., 1973), as would be expected if reciprocal inhibition characterized the relationship between serotonin- and CA-containing neurons. Increased serotonin turnover would be expected to suppress activity in residual CA-containing neurons in the lesioned pathway and thereby interfere with their function. However, later compensation within serotonin-containing neurons (e.g., by decreased turnover or subsensitivity of receptors) might be expected and, if it occurred, could provide an important mechanism for facilitating recovery of function by decreasing inhibition of CA-containing neurons. Unfortunately, the long-term effects of central CA depletion on the function of serotonin-containing neurons have not yet been described. Further experimentation is clearly necessary in order to determine whether this postulated mechanism, or any of the others that were discussed previously, really is critical to recovery and, if so, how much damage is necessary before it is initiated and what its time course is.

B. SOME IMPLICATIONS OF THE MODEL

We believe that the sequence of neurochemical events described in Fig. 10 may provide for recovery of function within a bundle of damaged CA-containing neurons because of the great potential for compensation that is present in these and interrelated pathways, and because of the nonspecific nature of the message that is probably conveyed by adjacent CA-containing neurons within these fiber tracts. There are three features inherent in this formulation that should be specified and considered in some detail because they provide a framework for a working model of the lateral hypothalamic syndrome.

1. Pathways of CA-Containing Neurons Can Sustain Extensive Damage before Basal Function Is Disrupted

Damage to CA-containing neurons should proportionately diminish the initial activity of the neural pathway, with the need for compensatory processes increasing correspondingly. As noted above, a 2-fold increase of NE turnover in the terminals of residual neurons can occur immediately, and an even greater potential for increased synthesis may exist in central dopaminergic terminals (Lovenberg and Bruckwick, 1975). Thus, it would take damage to at least 50% of the CA-containing neurons before this potential was exhausted. The rapid enhancement of the efficacy of CA, due first to retarded inactivation of CA and later to an increase in the sensitivity of the postsynaptic membrane, could extend considerably the damage from which recovery is possible. For example, the 5-fold increase in sensitivity to dopa that is observed 1 day after a lesion (Schoenfeld and Uretsky, 1973), together with a doubling of DA turnover, would provide for the restoration of basal function within 24 hours after destruction of 90% of the DA fibers. Additional changes in turnover made possible by the induction of tyrosine hydroxylase, and further enhancement of the efficacy of released neurotransmitter, would permit recovery from still larger lesions after only slightly longer periods of recovery. In short, apparent recovery of function might be expected to occur within a few hours or days after a lesion unless the residual fibers represent only a very small fraction of the original pathway.

These considerations suggest that central CA pathways have a relatively large capacity to maintain function despite extensive and irreversible damage. Consistent with this formulation are the reports that conspicuous behavioral impairments are absent after electrolytic lesions (Harvey, 1965; Heller et al., 1962) or 6-HDA treatments (Bloom et al., 1969; Breese and Traylor, 1970; Laverty and Taylor, 1970; Schoenfeld and Zigmond, 1973; Uretsky and Iversen, 1970) which leave intact 10–50% of the central CA stores; that behavioral and electrocortical arousal is not affected by any but the most complete lesions of the central CA-containing neurons (Jones et al., 1973; Jouvet, 1972); and that aphagia and adipsia in rats do not result from intraventricular 6-HDA treatment unless at least 90% of striatal DA has been lost, and does not last for more than a few days unless the depletion is greater than approximately 95% (Stricker and Zigmond, 1974; Zigmond and Stricker, 1972).

2. Animals with Damaged CA-Containing Neurons Will Be Less Sensitive to Weak Sensory Stimuli

We have proposed that recovery of function following damage to central CA-containing neurons is based, in large part, on increased turnover in residual neurons acting on receptors that have become supersensitive. Different behavioral effects of the lesions might be predicted depending on the relative contribution of each of these two factors. For example, if compensation resulted from receptor supersensitivity exclusively, then sensory stimuli would have normal effects on behavior in recovered animals because neurotransmitter release from residual neurons would elicit a response from the receptor that was exaggerated in exact proportion to the magnitude of damage to the terminals. On the other hand, if increased CA turnover contributed to recovery of function, as seems probable, then sensory signals would not be as effective in activating postsynaptic receptors in lesioned animals as in intact animals because there is no reason to expect that a given sensory input would increase neural activity disproportionately so as to compensate for the reduction in nerve terminals.

Two important implications derive from these considerations. First, rats recovered from extensive damage to central CA-containing neurons should be less responsive to ordinary laboratory noises or specific experimental stimuli than are intact controls. They should also be less responsive to interoceptive stimuli. For example, it should take a more intense stimulus for hunger to activate CA-containing neurons sufficiently for feeding behavior to occur. If the threshold for feeding is raised, then lesioned rats should eat less frequently than controls and should stop sooner when they do eat. This will inevitably lead to maintenance of body weight at levels below those of control rats. If the threshold was high enough, then lesioned animals might not be able to eat frequently enough to maintain their body weights, and tube feeding by the experimenter would be required for their survival. If the threshold was still higher, then lesioned animals might not eat at all. Since this threshold would tend to decrease as receptor supersensitivity developed, it should be greatest soon after the lesion and progressively diminish thereafter, although it should remain elevated so long as increased CA turnover in residual neurons provides some significant contribution to recovery of function. These considerations are obviously consistent with observations that there is an initial aphagia after extensive damage to CA-containing neurons, that it usually does not last more than a few days, that subsequent intermeal intervals gradually become shorter, and that there are long-term reductions in body weight maintenance after apparent recovery.

The second implication of this formulation is that nonspecific stimuli should be much more important to the activation of CA-containing neurons in lesioned animals than intact rats, since the extra stimulation might be critical in providing sufficient arousal for motivation and behavior. The importance of incentives in providing arousal might therefore account for the extreme finickiness of rats that are anorexic after lateral hypothalamic lesions or intraventricular 6-HDA treatment (cf. Teitelbaum and Epstein, 1963). If so, then it is not surprising that the meals taken are of relatively short duration, since as they proceed arousal from regulatory stimuli would decrease (owing to negative feedback from ingested food), arousal from the available diet would decrease (owing to sensory adaptation), and CA release from residual neurons would decrease (because synthesis rates could not support such elevated rates of CA turnover; see below). With recovery of function in CA-containing neurons, more arousal could be provided by regulatory stimuli, and thus the dependence of lesioned rats on highly palatable diets would be expected to decrease. Indeed, rats with lateral hypothalamic lesions eventually feed themselves by direct intubation of liquid diet through an intragastric fistula in the absence of any oropharyngeal or olfactory stimulation (Rodgers et al., 1965), and accept progressively smaller concentrations of sucrose solution. Nevertheless, as might be expected, food-related stimuli continue to play a larger than usual role in guiding consumatory behaviors and thereby influencing body weight maintenance (Mufson and Wampler, 1972; Teitelbaum and Epstein, 1962).

If the need for arousal is in fact a critical problem for rats in the early stages of recovery, then other sources of nonspecific stimulation also should be effective in promoting food ingestion, so long as nutrient needs provide the prepotent stimuli for behavior. This is exactly what seems to occur. For example, we have observed that with anorexic rats that had been given intraventricular 6-HDA after pretreatment with pargyline and DMI, or pargyline alone, the handling that is involved in measuring body weight or gastric intubation often is sufficient to promote feeding when rats are returned to their home cages (Stricker and Zigmond, 1974). Similarly, a painful tail clamp has been reported to stimulate feeding in anorexic rats with hypothalamic islands (which would include transection of the ascending CA-containing fibers) (Ellison et al., 1970) or with 6-HDA lesions of the substantia nigra (Marshall et al., 1974).

More recently, we have observed that amphetamine, which is known to enhance CA release and reduce reticular arousal thresholds (Bradley and Key, 1958; Glowinski and Axelrod, 1965), increased the food intake of 6 anorexic rats that had been given intraventricular 6-HDA and pargyline treatment or electrolytic lateral hypothalamic lesions. One rat ate continuously for 45 minutes after being given 5 mg/kg of d-amphetamine, and consumed 3.9 gm of Purina laboratory chow. Another rat given the same dose of drug would not eat dry food pellets but did eat Pablum continuously for 2 hours, consuming 45 gm. The other 4 rats ate smaller amounts of food (at least 1.0 gm of pellet or 22 gm of Pablum), and spent much of their time grooming or in restless movement about the cage. It is interesting to note that the general appearance and motor behavior of each animal improved dramatically after amphetamine treatment but then abruptly reverted back to the hunched posture and akinesia that had characterized them previously. Thus, amphetamine temporarily reversed other CA-dependent functions that also had been impaired by the lesions. These observations are consistent with other reports that amphetamine stimulates feeding in anorexic cats bearing lateral hypothalamic lesions (Wolgin and Teitelbaum, 1974), improves visual placing behavior in rats that had been given intrahypothalamic injections of 6-HDA (Sechzer *et al.*, 1973), and reverses the impaired sexual behavior of female rats after electrolytic lesions of the anterior hypothalamus (Herndon and Neill, 1973).

As yet, we have never seen an increase in the consumption of water by handling, amphetamine, or any other treatment that stimulates feeding in anorexic rats after lateral hypothalamic lesions or intraventricular 6-HDA. This suggests that hunger stimuli are more pronounced than thirst stimuli in these animals, as might be expected since rats receive considerable amounts of fluid when they are maintained on a liquid diet. These considerations, together with the probability that water provides much less incentive arousal than most foods, might explain why intake of water recovers later than ingestion of any other nutrient except those presented in unpalatable diets (which provide even less incentive).

Comparable improvements in other behaviors of brain-damaged rats can be seen to follow other procedures which also should generate considerable sensory stimulation. For example, in collaboration with Dr. John Marshall of the University of Pittsburgh, we have observed that aphagic or anorexic 6-HDA-treated rats that were akinetic in their individual home cages showed normal motor activity and exploratory behavior when placed in a group cage with other rats or in a shallow ice bath, and swam normally when placed in a large tank of tepid water. Similar observations have also been made of rats with electrolytic or 6-HDA lesions of the ascending dopaminergic pathways (Levitt and Teitelbaum, 1975; Robinson and Whishaw, 1974; Ungerstedt, 1974). These findings may be related to the observation that following reserpine or chlorpromazine, drugs which decrease central CA activity, rats no longer respond to a warning tone but will escape subsequent foot shock (Cook and Weidley, 1957). They also are reminiscent of numerous reports that Parkinsonian patients suddenly behave normally when confronted with emergencies (Schwab and Zieper, 1965). In each case, a higher threshold of arousal appears to be required in order to initiate the appropriate behavior.

3. Animals with Damaged CA-Containing Neurons Will Be Less Tolerant of Strong Sensory Stimuli

Following damage to central CA-containing neurons, we have proposed that there will be increased release from residual neurons, accompanied by increased CA synthesis. However, in the absence of a proportionate increase in tyrosine hydroxylase, the neurons would then have less of a reserve with which to increase CA synthesis still further when a stimulus provokes additional release. Consequently, strong stimuli might increase neuronal activity so much that CA synthesis could not keep up with release, CA levels in the terminal would be depleted, and the resultant decrease in receptor stimulation would reestablish aphagia and adipsia. Regression to an earlier stage of recovery should be most likely when CA depletions are extensive and the stress employed is particularly severe and prolonged.

Consistent with this formulation, we have observed that rats requiring several months or longer to recover water drinking following intraventricular 6-HDA plus pargyline treatment, or electrolytic lateral hypothalamic lesions, do not drink at all after severe hypovolemia produced by subcutaneous 30% PG treatment, even during a 24-hour drinking test, and do not eat when food is returned to their cages subsequently (Stricker, 1976; Stricker and Zigmond, 1974). Comparable effects have also been observed when CA-depleted rats are exposed to heat (Van Zoeren, 1974) or cold stress (Marshall *et al.*, 1974), or experience acute hypoglycemic shock (Epstein and Teitelbaum, 1967).

These considerations may account for many of the impairments in feeding and drinking behaviors that have been observed in recovered laterals and other animals with extensive damage to central CA-containing neurons. The experimental treatments that have revealed residual deficits typically involve the abrupt onset of large nutritional needs, often stimulating maximal behavioral responses in intact rats (as in Table II). Such treatments would be expected to produce stimuli that are well above the range that damaged catecholaminergic systems can accommodate without compromising their function. Consequently, the failure of lesioned rats to eat or drink under such circumstances would seem to reflect their general inability to behave appropriately after acute and profound stress, rather than the ineffectiveness of specific regulatory stimuli for hunger or thirst.

In light of these arguments, there appear to be three general procedures that would increase the probability that CA-depleted rats would respond to a severe regulatory imbalance: (a) decrease the magnitude of the imbalance, (b) decrease the magnitude of concomitant background stress, or (c) increase the capacity or efficacy of released CA in the lesioned animals. With regard to the first, we have recently observed that rats depleted of 60–80% striatal DA that are unresponsive to 750 mg/kg of 2-DG may increase their food intakes when a 375 mg/kg dose is employed (see also Levitan, 1974), or when glucoprivation is produced more gradually by chronic treatment with increasing doses of protamine zinc insulin (Fig. 13). Similarly, rats with comparable brain damage which decreased their food intakes when they were shaved and then exposed to 5°C for 48 hours were found to increase their food intakes when

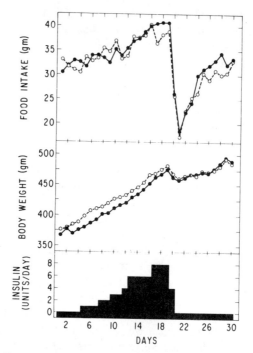

FIG. 13. The effects of daily injections of protamine zinc insulin on food intakes and body weights in control rats (o– – –o) and rats that had received two intraventricular injections of 6-hydroxydopamine (6-HDA) (200 μg each) (●———●). Each point represents the mean of 5 animals. Not shown are findings that 1 week prior to the onset of insulin treatments, 6-HDA-treated rats did not increase food intakes after 750 mg/kg injection of 2-deoxy-D-glucose whereas control rats did (from Stricker et al., 1975). Copyright 1975 by the American Association for the Advancement of Science.

the cold stress was less intense (Stricker et al., 1975). Thus, the inability of lesioned rats to respond behaviorally to severe homeostatic imbalances does not imply that they will be unable to respond appropriately to more moderate and gradually developing stimuli for hunger and thirst, such as arise when meals are taken ad libitum.

There is little systematic evidence pertaining to the second alternative, although sometimes we have noticed a striking improvement in feeding behavior of rats in the initial stages of recovery when they are housed in pairs and maintained in an environment closer to their thermoneutral range (approximately 28–32°C for males), instead of being housed singly in an air-conditioned room. These observations suggest that the postoperative environment may have a substantial influence on recovery of function. Endogenous stress also may contribute to behavioral deficits when destruction of central

CA-containing neurons is extensive. For example, the pronounced nutritional needs of aphagic and adipsic animals that have lost considerable amounts of body weight should increase CA release in the residual neurons and thereby tax the neuron's capacity to support any behavioral function. Consistent with this hypothesis, we have found that anorexic animals, but not intact controls, have much more pronounced sensory-motor dysfunctions when they are maintained 30–40% below preoperative body weight levels than when they are given more tube feedings so that body weight loss is only 10–20%. Similarly, rats with unilateral electrolytic lesions of the lateral hypothalamus, which are aphagic for only a few postoperative days and lose relatively little body weight during this time (Gold, 1966; Gray and Everitt, 1970), seem to recover sensory-motor functions much more rapidly than rats with bilateral lesions (Marshall and Teitelbaum, 1974).

As for the third alternative, there is some evidence that the capacity of central CA-containing neurons for neurotransmitter release may be much greater in the dark than during daylight hours (cf. Zigmond and Wurtman, 1970). In this regard, recovered laterals that were injected with hypertonic NaCl solution in the late morning have been reported to begin drinking within 1–2 hours after the lights were extinguished (Stricker, 1976). Furthermore, Rowland (1976) has recently observed that recovered laterals drank rapidly when they were injected with hypertonic saline during the dark period. These results suggest that the behavioral capacities of rats with central CA depletions might not be constant throughout the day but show a circadian rhythm, with a peak occurring when it is dark. This hypothesis is consistent with previous observations that recovered laterals take their meals only at night (Kissileff, 1970; Kakolewski et al., 1971).

Observations that some residual deficits in thirst disappear after several months (see Section II,C; also, Roth et al., 1973) also demonstrate an improved ability of CA-depleted rats to tolerate regulatory imbalances; this improvement may have been provided by gradual increases in the capacity for CA turnover. In addition, we have recently observed that many lesioned rats, especially those with less extensive CA depletions, eat to 2-DG after having received daily injections of insulin or being exposed to 5°C for several weeks (Stricker et al., 1974), stimuli that might be expected to further increase tyrosine hydroxylase activity (e.g., Thoenen, 1970; Weiner and Mosimann, 1970; Zigmond et al., 1974). Moreover, the improvement disappeared gradually after the chronic stimulation was withdrawn (Table III), as would be expected from the long half-life of tyrosine hydroxylase (Brimijoin and Molinoff, 1971).

Finally, we have recently observed that rats recovered from the initial effects of intraventricular 6-HDA, which would not increase feeding after systemic injections of 2-DG or increase drinking within 6 hours after the subcutaneous injection of 30% PG solution, would respond normally when they were pretreated with caffeine or theophylline (Zimmerman and Stricker 1975; Stricker and Zigmond, 1976). These drugs inhibit the enzyme responsible for the catabolism of cyclic AMP and thus should produce a temporary increase in the sensitivity of postsynaptic receptors to released CA (see Fig. 8).

4. Summary

We have proposed a neurochemical model for the lateral hypothalamic syndrome on the basis of the apparent contribution of central CA-containing neurons to behavior and their ability to function over a wide range of stimulus intensities and durations. The latter properties permit compensatory

TABLE III
EFFECT OF CHRONIC INSULIN
TREATMENT ON FEEDING DURING
ACUTE GLUCOPRIVATION[a]

	Food intake (gm)	
	Controls	6-HDA
Before stress		
Baseline	2.8 ± 0.5	2.1 ± 0.9
2-DG	7.4 ± 0.3^b	2.6 ± 0.8
After stress		
Baseline	4.1 ± 0.2	2.6 ± 0.5
2-DG (2 weeks)	6.8 ± 0.5^b	5.0 ± 0.8^b
2-DG (4 weeks)	6.0 ± 0.2^b	4.4 ± 1.0^b
2-DG (6 weeks)	6.9 ± 1.1^b	3.2 ± 0.9

[a]Values are mean ± standard error of the mean. Rats were given two intraventricular injections of 6-hydroxydopamine (200 μg) or the vehicle solution ($n = 5, 5$). Food intakes during 6 hours after 2-deoxy-D-glucose (2-DG) treatment (750 mg/kg, i.p.) are presented and are compared with baseline values averaged over control 6-hour periods during the preceding 3 days. Increasing doses of protamine zinc insulin (from 1 to 8 units) were administered daily for 3 weeks (see Fig. 13). 2-DG was given 2, 4, and 6 weeks after termination of the insulin injections. Baseline values preceding each of these feeding tests were similar and have been combined.
[b]$p < 0.01$.

changes to occur within these neural pathways following subtotal damage, but at the cost of certain impairments in their functional capacity. The impairments underlie most of the curious symptoms that are observed in rats after lateral hypothalamic damage. Thus, rats with moderate amounts of brain damage appear to behave normally in the limited environment of the laboratory, but specific examinations reveal that they have become less sensitive to simple stimuli and have lost their ability to behave normally in stressful situations. Rats with more extensive brain damage are readily detected because they cannot survive without assistance even in the controlled conditions of the laboratory. In other words, increasing damage to central CA-containing neurons proportionately truncates the range of stimuli that can be accommodated, and rats become both less sensitive to weak stimuli and less tolerant of strong ones. The progressive return of motivated behaviors that is observed reflects the fact that the functional range can be widened, while residual deficits in behavior indicate that recovery is not complete.

V. General Summary and Conclusions

A. HOMEOSTASIS AND MOTIVATION

Peripheral sympathectomy precludes autonomic arousal and results in the well-known intolerance of animals to even minor stress. Similarly, extensive damage to the CA-containing projections in the brain eliminates both tonic alertness and phasic behavioral arousal, and is inevitably followed by prolonged somnolence and coma. CA-containing neurons thus appear to be essential to physiological and behavioral activities that help to maintain the internal environment, and their functions cannot be readily transferred to other neural pathways.

The anatomical and biochemical organization of CA-containing neurons in the central nervous system suggest their involvement in the broad, nonspecific arousal component of the physiological and behavioral responses to homeostatic imbalance. The central neurons, like those of the periphery, are organized to transmit information to large areas in response to input to a few, localized groups of cells. These cells are found primarily in the lower brain stem, intermingled among sensory afferents and motor nuclei, and their thin unmyelinated axons fan out to innervate all the areas that have been implicated in studies of motivated behavior, including the hypothalamus, basal ganglia, limbic forebrain, and association cortex. These fibers transmit at a slow velocity and frequency and generally exert a long-lasting inhibitory influence which appears to modulate the effects of other inputs to the postsynaptic cells.

Several feedback loops exist which help to maintain a constant basal level of synaptic transmission. These include changes at CA synapses, such as altered CA release and receptor sensitivity, as well as changes which modulate sensory input into the reticular system, including the adaptation of sensory receptors and the centrifugal inhibition of afferent activity from them. Such processes, together with corticofugal controlling mechanisms, are adaptive in that they allow habituation of routine and repetitive sensory input and thereby permit selective attention to more significant signals (see reviews by Dell, 1963; Hernández-Peón, 1961). However, it would be disastrous if the same mechanisms suppressed or modified interoceptive sensory messages signaling homeostatic imbalances for long periods of time, and an alternative multilevel process for dealing with that input seems to occur instead. Thus, mild regulatory needs elicit compensatory physiological responses in the autonomic nervous system that tend to reduce the initial stimulus without involving cerebral arousal or behavior (see Smith *et al.,* 1972). Larger imbalances create greater input, both neural and endocrine, and seem to be associated with the emergence of hypothalamopituitary responses. At this stage cortical alertness occurs, but the animal should still be free of the demands of motivated behavior. Still larger stimuli ultimately evoke appropriate motivated activities that are designed to correct the homeostatic imbalance. We believe that different groups of CA-containing neurons (i.e., the adrenergic fibers of the sympathetic nervous system, the central NE- and DA-containing neurons) become sequentially involved in mediating these autonomic, physiological, and behavioral contributions to regulation. At any level, synaptic transmission in CA-containing neurons is not restored to its basal state until the irritating stimulus has been removed.

The hypothalamus has traditionally been assigned a pivotal role in directing the behavioral contributions to homeostasis. This concept arose from observations of prolonged aphagia and adipsia following destruction of the ventrolateral diencephalon (Anand and Brobeck, 1951; Montemurro and Stevenson, 1957; Teitelbaum and Stellar, 1954) and was supported by numerous subsequent reports that electrical stimulation of the same lateral hypothalamic area would evoke consumption of food or water (e.g., Mogenson and Stevenson, 1967; Steinbaum and Miller, 1965). However, as we have emphasized in the present paper, aphagia and adipsia have also been observed following electrolytic or biochemical lesions of various sites in the basal ganglia, limbic forebrain, or midbrain tegmentum, while stimulation of the same extrahypothalamic structures elicits feeding and drinking (e.g., Robinson and Mishkin, 1968; Wyrwicka and Doty, 1966). In retrospect, the effective sites in most of these studies can be projected along CA-containing pathways from lower brain stem to telencephalon. Consistent with this observation, recent investigations in which those neural pathways were specifically damaged have revealed clear deficits in feeding and drinking behaviors. On the basis of that evidence, plus additional considerations of the anatomy, function, and bio-chemistry of these ascending reticular fibers, it seems probable that these CA-containing neurons, rather than the lateral hypothalamic area they tra-verse, may be the critical neural tissue that is involved in controlling moti-vated ingestive behaviors.

We have emphasized homeostatic motivated behaviors in the present discus-sion, but only because they have been most extensively studied in rats with lateral hypothalamic damage. As might be expected, animals with extensive damage to the central ascending CA-containing neurons also show disruption in a much wider range of activities, including mating, maternal and thermo-regulatory behaviors, and avoidance of punishment; indeed, their disabilities transcend most discussions of feeding and drinking and involve more funda-mental dysfunctions, such as somnolence, hypokinesia, apathy, and sensory neglect. Thus, it seems probable that these neural systems participate in motivation more generally, perhaps by mediating components of arousal, affect, and motor function that are common to all voluntary behavior. It is in this context that we interpret the considerable evidence that stimulation of central CA-containing neurons, either by handling, peripheral stress, sym-pathomimetic drugs, or direct passage of electrical current, serves to augment any of a variety of motivated responses, apparently depending, in part, on the array of internal needs and environmental opportunities that are then avail-able (e.g., Caggiula, 1972; Devor et al., 1970; Valenstein et al., 1968).

To summarize, CA-containing neurons appear to have some basal level of function that provides a set point of arousal. Excessive sensory input elicits interdependent biochemical, neural, physiological, and behavioral responses that remove the stimulus or attenuate its effects, while restriction of input leads to the opposite compensatory changes. In this form, our conceptual framework is clearly an extension of well-known formulations presented previously by Hebb (1955), Lindsley (1951), Dell (1958), Morgane (1969), and many others who have postulated that there is a nonspecific arousal component of motivated behavior and that much of behavior can be under-stood as an attempt to attain an optimal level of arousal.

B. RECOVERY OF FUNCTION FOLLOWING BRAIN DAMAGE

A significant amount of functional recovery is possible after subtotal damage to central CA-containing neurons. This appears to be due in large part to compensatory changes that occur within residual neurons and their post-synaptic receptors, presumably in response to the initial decrease in CA activity that follows the lesions. The specific processes seem to include increased CA release and synthesis, increased synthesis of tyrosine hydroxylase, and increased receptor sensitivity; collateral sprouting and adjustments within other neuronal systems that are functionally interrelated with the CA-containing neurons also may be important. In other words, many of the same adaptive mechanisms that help to maintain constancy during normal fluctuations in the utilization of these pathways, or following their disruption by various drugs, appear to serve a similar function when they are damaged.

Some of these compensatory processes can occur rapidly and thereby permit animals to sustain large lesions without loss of basal function. For example, we have observed that aphagia and adipsia in rats do not last more than a few days unless 95% of the telencephalic terminals containing DA are destroyed by intraventricular 6-HDA treatment. Since total damage affords no opportunity for recovery within the system, it should be clear that there is only a narrow range of DA levels (perhaps 2–5% of control) that are associated with profound initial deficits yet can later support recovery of function. With depletions within that range, animals are stuporous and/or inactive and may remain so for weeks or longer. As might be expected, the rate of recovery appears to depend on the size of the lesion and consequent need for compensation, with bigger depletions generally associated with more prolonged periods of recovery.

The recovery process may also be significantly influenced by certain pre- or postoperative treatments that seem to affect the biochemical mechanisms at the synapse. For example, several procedures known to increase CA turnover or tyrosine hydroxylase levels (Friedman et al., 1973; Glick and Greenstein, 1973; Korf et al., 1973; Weiner and Mosimann, 1970) have been shown to promote recovery following lateral hypothalamic lesions, including pretreatment with systemic insulin injections (Balagura et al., 1973), prior food deprivation (Powley and Keesey, 1970), lesions of the frontal cortex (Glick and Greenstein, 1972), or electrical stimulation of neurons adjacent to the lesioned area (Harrell et al., 1974). Recovery from the aphagia and adipsia following lateral hypothalamic lesions has also been hastened by pretreatment with AMT (Glick et al., 1972), which should increase the sensitivity of receptors to CA (Geyer and Segal, 1973), as well as by posttreatment injections of nerve growth factor (Berger et al., 1973), a substance that induces the synthesis of tyrosine hydroxylase (Thoenen et al., 1971) and enhances postlesion neuronal growth (Bjerre et al., 1973). Finally, it should be noted that recovery of function can also be facilitated by allowing time for the compensatory processes to occur within residual neurons following a unilateral lesion before the contralateral side is damaged (see review by Finger et al., 1973).

The significance of the residual neurons for recovery had been suspected by Teitelbaum and Epstein (1962), who found that a more prolonged aphagia and adipsia would be reinstated in recovered laterals when areas adjacent to the damaged tissue were destroyed by enlarging the lesions. More recently, Teitelbaum (1971) has suggested that recovery is supported only in part by the reversal of certain side effects of the electrolytic lesions, which had temporarily disrupted function in undamaged neurons surrounding the lesion site. In addition, he proposed that, after lateral hypothalamic lesions, animals "regress" to an amotivational state in which only reflexive feeding occurs, and that recovery of regulatory ingestive behaviors represents a progressive reencephalization of function. In support of this provocative idea, Teitelbaum (1971) cited findings that unusually prolonged aphagia and adipsia are re-established in recovered laterals after functional decortication by spreading cortical depression (Balinska et al., 1967; Teitelbaum and Cytawa, 1965), and that there is a striking parallel between details of the lateral hypothalamic syndrome and the ontogenetic development of feeding and drinking behaviors in weanling rats (Cheng et al., 1971; Teitelbaum et al., 1969). On the other hand, it is also possible to interpret these studies in terms of neural activity in central dopaminergic fibers. For example, spreading cortical depression causes a substantial increase in DA release in the striatum (Keller et al., 1972), which may have exceeded the capacity for increased synthesis in the residual neurons and thereby depressed their function (much like any large stress; see Section IV,C,3). Moreover, the development of regulatory controls at weaning parallels the gradual appearance of DA terminals in the striatum (Loizou, 1972; Olson et al., 1972), and Dr. Mark Friedman, in our laboratory, has recently observed a sensitivity to the anorexic effects of AMT in 18-day-old rats that is similar to the response of adult lesioned animals (Friedman, 1974). In short, encephalization described by Teitelbaum may actually reflect the increasing functional capacity of central DA-containing neurons, with the four stages of recovery representing recognizable landmarks along a continuum of function rather than discrete levels of cerebral control.

Despite recovery of motivated ingestive behaviors sufficient for survival on an ad libitum maintenance regime, it is clear that lesioned animals can no longer respond appropriately during severe homeostatic imbalances. Because they rarely encounter such situations in the protected laboratory environment, these inadequacies should not be disabling; indeed, they frequently go unnoticed unless specific examinations are conducted. In contrast, their behavioral impairments before recovery could be readily detected, even while they remained in their home cages. Thus, the range of their behavioral capabilities is severely compressed immediately after the lesion, when animals are most insensitive to weak stimuli and intolerant of intense ones, but reexpands gradually over time as compensatory neurochemical processes develop. Consequently, the deficits produced by lesions must be defined and continually redefined by the interaction between the current functional capacity of the CA-containing projections and the complexity of the environment in which the lesioned animals live (cf. Lashley, 1929).

We believe that this conceptual framework is also relevant to problems of human mental health and cerebral dysfunctions. For example, like rats with lateral hypothalamic lesions, there is a loss of neostriatal DA in patients with Parkinson's disease but an absence of prominent symptoms until depletions reach 70–80% (Hornykiewicz, 1973). Because of the considerable compensation that is possible within the residual neurons, degeneration of nigrostriatal fibers may go unnoticed until some stressful incident precipitates the symptoms. In fact, such "traumatic Parkinsonism" is a well known clinical phenomenon (see Schwab and England, 1968). It is easy to imagine how this could happen, and how the latent problem could have gone undetected. According to our present model, early diagnosis of Parkinson's disease and related disorders would be very difficult unless tests included an examination of performance on some complex behavioral task during acute stress (psychological or physiological) or after treatment with drugs that affect central CA-containing neurons. However, classical neurological tests for this disease are conducted with safeguards against the possible disruptive effects of stress. Such tests should be reevaluated in light of recent advances in the understanding of the effects produced by experimental damage to the nigrostriatal dopaminergic fibers, and the processes by which recovery of function may occur.

C. FINAL SUMMARY

1. Like the peripheral adrenergic neurons in the sympathetic nervous system, central neurons containing the catecholamines norepinephrine (NE) and dopamine (DA) project diffusely to a large number of neural structures from only a few cell groups. This anatomical organization is consistent with the apparent contribution of these neurons to the broad, nonspecific components of arousal that are associated with homeostatic imbalance and other conditions of excitement or alarm.

2. Dopamine-containing neurons traverse the far lateral aspects of the hypothalamus, ascending to regions throughout the telencephalon from cell bodies in the mesencephalon. Specific destruction of 90% or more of these DA terminals, such as follow intraventricular administration of the neurotoxin 6-hydroxydopamine, leads to aphagia, adipsia, akinesia, and sensory neglect in rats. Although the individual DA-containing projections whose damage was responsible for these effects have not yet been specified, it seems probable that these fibers are the critical tissue that is damaged by large

lateral hypothalamic lesions, which are well known to abolish motivated behavior.

3. Animals suffering damage to DA-containing neurons may be characterized by an apparent insensitivity to relatively weak sensory stimuli and an intolerance of relatively intense ones. We believe that the former results from a reduction in number of nerve terminals, with a greater increase in stimulus intensity now being needed to produce an equivalent increase in total DA turnover, while the latter may result from the decreased ability of the residual neurons to increase synthesis and thereby support major increases in DA release. These changes contract the range of stimuli which the lesioned animals can respond to, and underlie their specific behavioral deficits.

4. Gradual recovery of ingestive behaviors and sensory-motor functions occurs in most brain-damaged animals within a few weeks after lesioning. Recovery of function appears to be due, in part, to compensatory processes that occur within residual neurons of the damaged pathway. For example, increased release of catecholamines from the remaining intact terminals, together with an increased efficacy of released neurotransmitter, helps to restore basal function despite permanent catecholamine depletions. As these and other neurochemical compensations proceed, the functional range widens. Nevertheless, even after the resumption of voluntary feeding and drinking behaviors, "centrally sympathectomized" animals maintain body weight at much lower levels than controls and fail to respond appropriately during marked homeostatic imbalances. These residual deficits in behavior indicate that recovery is not complete.

5. Because of the great potential for compensation that is present in catecholamine-containing neurons, and because of the nonspecific nature of the message that is probably conveyed by adjacent neurons within these fiber tracts, pathways of catecholamine-containing neurons can sustain extensive damage before basal function is disrupted. However, even when brain damage is moderate, the neurochemical compensations that are required to maintain function result in a narrowing in the range of the animal's behavioral capabilities. These changes are much less prominent than when brain damage is severe and may go unnoticed unless specific examinations are conducted. These relatively subtle behavioral dysfunctions have obvious relevance for human mental health, and provide a conceptual framework for evaluating the striking symptomatology that can be precipitated by stress in people with subclinical degeneration of brain catecholamine-containing neurons.

6. In sum, we believe that models based on biochemical and neuropharmacological principles can be constructed which provide an appropriate perspective for analyzing motivated behavior in intact animals as well as recovery of function following brain damage.

Acknowledgments

We are grateful for the colleagueship of our students and associates: Dr. Mark Friedman, Mr. Thomas Heffner, Mr. Gregory Kapatos, Ms. Deborah Levitan, Ms. Debra Rubinstein, Mr. Charles Saller, Ms. Janet Van Zoeren, Ms. Suzanne Wuerthele, Ms. Jen-shew Yen, Dr. Libby Yunger, and Mr. Mark Zimmerman. We also thank Mr. Hilton Adler, Ms. Kathleen Moran, and Mr. Ronald Szymusiak for their assistance in the laboratory, and Dr. John Marshall and Dr. Ronald Schoenfeld for their helpful comments about this manuscript. We are additionally indebted to Dr. Philip Teitelbaum, whose unique ability to consider the lateral hypothalamic syndrome in broad terms and from many perspectives has served as an invaluable model for our multidisciplinary approach, and who has generously provided us with intellectual stimulation, encouragement, and good counsel over the years.

Our research has been supported by grants from the U. S. National Institute of Mental Health (MH-20620 and MH-25341), the U. S. National Science Foundation (GB-22830), Eli Lilly and Co., and Smith Kline and French Co.

References

Agid, Y., Javoy, F., and Glowinski, J. (1973a). Hyperactivity of remaining dopaminergic neurones after partial destruction of the nigro-striatal dopaminergic system in the rat. *Nature (London), New Biology* **245**, 150–151.

Agid, Y., Javoy, F., Glowinski, J., Bouvet, D., and Sotelo, C. (1973b). Injection of 6-hydroxydopamine into the substantia nigra of the rat. II. Diffusion and specificity. *Brain Research* **58**, 291–301.

Ahlskog, J. E., and Hoebel, B. G. (1973). Overeating and obesity from damage to a noradrenergic system in the brain. *Science* **182**, 166–169.

Albe-Fessard, D., Rocha-Miranda, C., and Oswaldo-Cruz, E. (1960). Activités évoquées dans le noyau caudé du chat en réponse à des types divers d'afférences. II. Étude microphysiologique. *Electroencephalography and Clinical Neurophysiology* **12**, 649–661.

Albert, D. J., Storlien, L. H., Wood, D. J., and Ehman, G. K. (1970). Further evidence for a complex system controlling feeding behavior. *Physiology & Behavior* **5**, 1075–1082.

Amassian, V. E., and DeVito, R. V. (1954). Unit activity in reticular formation and nearby structures. *Journal of Neurophysiology* **17**, 575–603.

Anand, B. K., and Brobeck, J. R. (1951). Hypothalamic control of food intake in rats and cats. *Yale Journal of Biology and Medicine* **24**, 123–140.

Andén, N. E., Carlsson, A., Dahlstrom, A., Fuxe, K., Hillarp, N. A., and Larsson, K. (1964). Demonstration and mapping out of nigro-neostriatal dopamine neurons. *Life Sciences* **3**, 523–530.

Andén, N. E., Butcher, S. G., Corrodi, H., Fuxe, K., and Ungerstedt, U. (1970). Receptor activity and turnover of dopamine and noradrenaline after neuroleptics. *European Journal of Pharmacology* **11**, 303–314.

Andersson, B., and McCann, S. M. (1956). The effect of hypothalamic lesions on the water intake of the dog. *Acta Physiologica Scandinavica* **35**, 312–320.

Anokhin, P. K. (1961). The multiple ascending influences of the subcortical centers on the cerebral cortex. *In* "Brain and Behavior" (M. A. B. Brazier, ed.), Vol. 1, pp. 139–170. Amer. Inst. Biol. Sci., Washington, D.C.

Avar, A., and Monos, E. (1969). Behavioural changes in pregnant rats following farlateral hypothalamic lesions. *Acta Physiologica Academiae Scientiarum Hungaricae* **35**, 295–303.

Baillie, P., and Morrison, S. D. (1963). The nature of the suppression of food intake by lateral hypothalamic lesions in rats. *Journal of Physiology (London)* **165**, 227–245.

Balagura, S., Wilcox, R. H., and Coscina, D. V. (1969). The effect of diencephalic lesions on food intake and motor activity. *Physiology & Behavior* **4**, 629–633.

Balagura, S., Harrell, L., and Ralph, T. (1973). Glucodynamic hormones modify the recovery period after lateral hypothalamic lesions. *Science* **182**, 59–60.

Balinska, H. (1968). The hypothalamic lesions: Effects on appetitive and aversive behavior in rats. *Acta Biologiae Experimentalis (Warsaw)* **28**, 47–56.

Balinska, H., Buresova, O., and Fifkova, E. (1967). The influence of cortical and thalamic spreading depression on feeding behavior of rats with lateral hypothalamic lesions. *Acta Biologiae Experimentalis (Warsaw)* **27**, 355–363.

Bartholini, G., Pletscher, A., and Richards, J. (1970). 6-hydroxydopamine-induced inhibition of brain catecholamine synthesis without ultrastructural damage. *Experientia* **26**, 598–600.

Berger, B. D., Wise, C. D., and Stein, L. (1973). Nerve growth factor: enhanced recovery of feeding after hypothalamic damage. *Science* **180**, 506–508.

Besson, M. J., Cheramy, A., and Glowinski, J. (1971). Effects of some psychotropic drugs on dopamine synthesis in the rat striatum. *Journal of Pharmacology and Experimental Therapeutics* **177**, 196–205.

Bjerre, B., Björklund, A., and Stenevi, U. (1973). Stimulation of growth of new axonal sprouts from lesioned monoamine neurones in adult rat brain by nerve growth factor. *Brain Research* **60**, 161–176.

Björklund, A., Katzman, R., Stenevi, U., and West, K. A. (1971). Development and growth of axonal sprouts from noradrenaline and 5-hydroxytryptamine neurons in the rat spinal cord. *Brain Research* **31**, 21–33.

Black, S. L. (1971). Hypothalamic lesions, hypovolemia, and the regulation of water balance in the rat. Unpublished doctoral dissertation, McMaster Univ., Hamilton, Ontario, Canada.

Blass, E. M., and Epstein, A. N. (1971). A lateral preoptic osmosensitive zone for thirst in the rat. *Journal of Comparative and Physiological Psychology* **76**, 378–394.

Blass, E. M., and Kraly, F. S. (1974). Medial forebrain bundle lesions: Specific loss of feeding to decreased glucose utilization in rats. *Journal of Comparative and Physiological Psychology* **86**, 679–692.

Bliss, E. L. (1973). Effects of behavioral manipulations upon brain serotonin and dopamine. *In* "Serotonin and Behavior" (J. Barchas and E. Usdin, eds.), pp. 315–324. Academic Press, New York.

Blondaux, C., Juge, A., Sordet, F., Chouvet, G., Jouvet, M., and Pujol, J. F. (1973). Modification du métabolisme de la sérotonine (5-HT) cérébrale induite chez le rat par administration de 6-hydroxydopamine. *Brain Research* **50**, 101–114.

Bloom, F. E. (1971). Fine structural changes in rat brain after intracisternal injection of 6-hydroxydopamine. *In* "6-Hydroxydopamine and Catecholamine Neurons" (T. Malmfors and H. Thoenen, eds.), pp. 135–150. North-Holland Publ., Amsterdam.

Bloom, F. E., and Hoffer, B. J. (1973). Norepinephrine as a central synaptic transmitter. *In* "Frontiers in Catecholamine Research" (E. Usdin and S. H. Snyder, eds.), pp. 637–642. Pergamon, Oxford.

Bloom, F. E., Algeri, S., Groppetti, A., Revuelta, A., and Costa, E. (1969). Lesions of central norepinephrine terminals with 6-OH-dopamine: biochemistry and fine structure. *Science* 166, 1284–1286.

Bolme, P., Fuxe, K., and Lidbrink, P. (1972). On the function of central catecholamine neurons–their role in cardiovascular and arousal mechanisms. *Research Communications in Chemical Pathology & Pharmacology* 4, 657–697.

Bonvallet, M., Dell, P., and Hiebel, G. (1954). Tonus sympathique et activité électrique corticale. *Electroencephalography and Clinical Neurophysiology* 6, 119–144.

Booth, D. A. (1968). Mechanism of action of norepinephrine in eliciting an eating response on injection into the rat hypothalamus. *Journal of Pharmacology and Experimental Therapeutics* 160, 336–348.

Bradley, P. B., and Elkes, J. (1957). The effects of some drugs on the electrical activity of the brain. *Brain* 80, 77–117.

Bradley, P. B., and Key, B. J. (1958). The effect of drugs on arousal responses produced by electrical stimulation of the reticular formation. *Electroencephalography and Clinical Neurophysiology* 10, 97–110.

Brandes, J. S. (1973). Recovery of ingestive behavior following frontal neocortical ablations in the rat. *Eastern Psychological Association Meeting, Washington, D.C.*

Breese, G. R., and Traylor, T. D. (1970). Effect of 6-hydroxydopamine on brain norepinephrine and dopamine: Evidence for selective degeneration of catecholamine neurons. *Journal of Pharmacology and Experimental Therapeutics* 174, 413–420.

Breese, G. R., Smith, R. D., Cooper, B. R., and Grant, L. D. (1973). Alterations in consumatory behavior following intracisternal injection of 6-hydroxydopamine. *Pharmacology, Biochemistry and Behavior* 1, 319–328.

Brimijoin, S., and Molinoff, P. B. (1971). Effects of 6-HDA on the activity of tyrosine hydroxylase and dopamine-β-hydroxylase in sympathetic ganglia of the rat. *Journal of Pharmacology and Experimental Therapeutics* 178, 417–424.

Bunney, B. S., Walters, J. R., Roth, R. H., and Aghajanian, G. K. (1973). Dopaminergic neurons: effect of antipsychotic drugs and amphetamine on single cell activity. *Journal of Pharmacology and Experimental Therapeutics* 185, 560–571.

Caggiula, A. R. (1972). Shock-elicited copulation and aggression in male rats. *Journal of Comparative and Physiological Psychology* 80, 303–307.

Caggiula, A. R., Antelman, S. M., and Zigmond, M. J. (1973). Disruption of copulation in male rats after hypothalamic lesions: a behavioral, anatomical and neurochemical analysis. *Brain Research* 59, 273–287.

Cannon, W. B. (1929). "Bodily Changes in Pain, Hunger, Fear and Rage," 2nd Ed. Appleton, New York.

Carlisle, H. J. (1964). Differential effects of amphetamine on food and water intake in rats with lateral hypothalamic lesions. *Journal of Comparative and Physiological Psychology* 58, 47–54.

Carlton, P. L. (1963). Cholinergic mechanisms in the control of behavior by the brain. *Psychological Review* 70, 19–39.

Cheng, M. F., Rozin, P., and Teitelbaum, P. (1971). Starvation retards development of food and water regulations. *Journal of Comparative and Physiological Psychology* 76, 206–218.

Colin-Jones, D. G., and Himsworth, R. L. (1970). The location of the chemoreceptor controlling gastric acid secretion during hypoglycaemia. *Journal of Physiology (London)* 206, 397–409.

Connor, J. D. (1970). Caudate nucleus neurons: correlation of the effects of substantia nigra stimulation with iontophoretic dopamine. *Journal of Physiology (London)* 208, 691–704.

Cook, L., and Weidley, E. (1957). Behavioural effects of some psychopharmacological agents. *Annals of the New York Academy of Sciences* **66**, 740–752.

Cooper, B. R., Breese, G. R., Howard, J. L., and Grant, L. D. (1972a). Enhanced behavior depressant effects of reserpine and α-methyltyrosine after 6-hydroxydopamine treatment. *Psychopharmacologia* **27**, 99–110.

Cooper, B. R., Breese, G. R., Howard, J. L., and Grant, L. D. (1972b). Effect of central catecholamine alterations by 6-hydroxydopamine on shuttle box avoidance acquisition. *Physiology & Behavior* **9**, 727–731.

Coscina, D. V., and Balagura, S. (1970). Avoidance and escape behavior of rats with aphagia produced by basal diencephalic lesions. *Physiology & Behavior* **5**, 651–657.

Dahlstrom, A., and Fuxe, K. (1964). Evidence for the existence of monoamine-containing neurons in the central nervous system. I. Demonstration of monoamines in the cell bodies of brainstem neurons. *Acta Physiologica Scandinavica, Supplementum* **232**, 1–55.

Dairman, W., and Udenfriend, S. (1970). Increased conversion of tyrosine to catecholamines in the intact rat following elevation of tissue tyrosine hydroxylase levels by administered phenoxybenzamine. *Molecular Pharmacology* **6**, 350–356.

de Champlain, J. (1971). Degeneration and regrowth of adrenergic nerve fibers in the rat peripheral tissues after 6-hydroxydopamine. *Canadian Journal of Physiology and Pharmacology* **49**, 345–355.

Dell, P. (1952). Corrélations entre le système végétatif et le système de la vie de relation. Mesencéphale, diencéphale et cortex cérébral. *Journal of Physiology (Paris)* **44**, 471–557.

Dell, P. (1958). Some basic mechanisms of the translation of bodily needs into behaviour. *Neurological Basis of Behavior, Ciba Foundation Symposium, 1957*, pp. 187–201.

Dell, P. (1963). Reticular homeostasis and critical reactivity. *In* "Brain Mechanisms" (G. Moruzzi, A. Fessard, and H. H. Jasper, eds.), pp. 82–103. Elsevier, Amsterdam.

Devor, M. G., Wise, R. A., Milgram, N. W., and Hoebel, B. G. (1970). Physiological control of hypothalamically elicited feeding and drinking. *Journal of Comparative and Physiological Psychology* **73**, 226–232.

Dominic, J. A., and Moore, K. E. (1969). Supersensitivity to the central stimulant actions of adrenergic drugs following discontinuation of a chronic diet of α-methyltyrosine. *Psychopharmacologia* **15**, 96–101.

Edds, M. V., Jr. (1953). Collateral nerve regeneration. *Quarterly Review of Biology* **28**, 260–276.

Ellison, G. D. (1968). Appetitive behavior in rats after circumsection of the hypothalamus. *Physiology & Behavior* **3**, 221–226.

Ellison, G. D., Sorenson, C. A., and Jacobs, B. L. (1970). Two feeding syndromes following surgical isolation of the hypothalamus in rats. *Journal of Comparative and Physiological Psychology* **70**, 173–188.

Epstein, A. N. (1971). The lateral hypothalamic syndrome: Its implications for the physiological psychology of hunger and thirst. *In* "Progress in Physiological Psychology" (E. Stellar and J. M. Sprague, eds.), Vol. 4, pp. 263–317. Academic Press, New York.

Epstein, A. N., and Teitelbaum, P. (1964). Severe and persistent deficits in thirst produced by lateral hypothalamic damage. *In* "Thirst in the Regulation of Body Water" (M. J. Wayner, ed.), pp. 395–406. Pergamon, Oxford.

Epstein, A. N., and Teitelbaum, P. (1967). Specific loss of the hypoglycemic control of feeding in recovered lateral rats. *American Journal of Physiology* **213**, 1159–1167.

Ernst, A. M. (1967). Mode of action of apomorphine and desamphetamine on gnawing compulsion in rats. *Psychopharmacologia* **10**, 316–323.

Farnebo, L. O., and Hamberger, B. (1971). Drug-induced changes in the release of ³H-monoamines from field stimulated rat brain slices. *Acta Physiologica Scandinavica Supplementum* **371**, 35–44.

Feldman, S. M., and Waller, H. J. (1962). Dissociation of electrocortical activation and behavioural arousal. *Nature (London)* **196**, 1320–1322.

Feltz, P., and de Champlain, J. (1972). Enhanced sensitivity of caudate neurons to microiontophoretic injections of dopamine in 6-hydroxydopamine treated cats. *Brain Research* **43**, 601–605.

Fibiger, H. C., Lonsbury, B., Cooper, H. P., and Lytle, L. D. (1972). Early behavioural effects of intraventricular administration of 6-hydroxydopamine in rat. *Nature (London), New Biology* **236**, 209–211.

Fibiger, H. C., Zis, A. P., and McGeer, E. G. (1973). Feeding and drinking deficits after 6-hydroxydopamine administration in the rat: similarities to the lateral hypothalamic syndrome. *Brain Research* **55**, 135–148.

Finch, L., Haeusler, G., Kuhn, H., and Thoenen, H. (1973). Rapid recovery of vascular adrenergic nerves in the rat after chemical sympathectomy with 6-HDA. *British Journal of Pharmacology* **48**, 59–74.

Finger, S., Walbran, B., and Stein, D. G. (1973). Brain damage and behavioral recovery: serial lesion phenomena. *Brain Research* **63**, 1–18.

Fleming, W. W., McPhillips, J. J., and Westfall, D. P. (1973). Postjunctional supersensitivity and subsensitivity of excitable tissues to drugs. *Ergebnisse der Physiologie, Biologischen Chemie und Experimentellen Pharmakologie* **68**, 55–119.

Fonberg, E. (1969). The role of the hypothalamus and amygdala in food intake, alimentary motivation and emotional reactions. *Acta Biologiae Experimentalis (Warsaw)* **29**, 335–358.

French, J. D., Von Amerogen, F. K., and Magoun, H. W. (1952). An activating system in brain stem of monkey. *AMA Archives of Neurology and Psychiatry* **68**, 577–590.

French, J. D., Verzeano, M., and Magoun, H. W. (1953). A neural basis of the anesthetic state. *AMA Archives of Neurology and Psychiatry* **69**, 519–529.

French, J. D., Hernández-Peón, R., and Livingston, R. B. (1955). Projections from cortex to cephalic brain stem (reticular formation) in monkey. *Journal of Neurophysiology* **18**, 74–95.

Friedman, E., Starr, N., and Gershon, S. (1973). Catecholamine synthesis and the regulation of food intake in the rat. *Life Sciences* **12**, 317–326.

Friedman, M. I. (1974). Ontogeny of feeding and drinking: catecholamine involvement in the weaning process. *Eastern Psychological Association Meeting, Philadelphia, Pa.*

Frigyese, T. L., and Purpura, D. (1967). Electrophysiological analysis of reciprocal caudato-nigral relations. *Brain Research* **6**, 440–456.

Fuxe, K., and Hökfelt, T. (1969). Catecholamines in the hypothalamus and the pituitary gland. *In* "Frontiers in Neuroendocrinology, 1969" (W. F. Ganong and L. Martini, eds.), pp. 47–96. Oxford Univ. Press, London and New York.

Geyer, M. A., and Segal, D. S. (1973). Differential effects of reserpine and alphamethyl-p-tyrosine on norepinephrine and dopamine induced behavioral activity. *Psychopharmacologia* **29**, 131–140.

Glavcheva, L., Rozkowska, E., and Fonberg, E. (1970). The effect of lateral hypothalamic lesions on gastric motility in dogs. *Acta Neurobiologiae Experimentalis (Warsaw)* **30**, 279–293.

Glick, S. D., and Greenstein, S. (1972). Facilitation of recovery after lateral hypothalamic damage by prior ablation of frontal cortex. *Nature (London), New Biology* **239**, 187–188.

Glick, S. D., and Greenstein, S. (1973). Possible modulating influence of frontal cortex on nigrostriatal function. *British Journal of Pharmacology* **49**, 316–321.

Glick, S. D., Greenstein, S., and Zimmerberg, B. (1972). Facilitation of recovery by α-methyl-p-tyrosine after lateral hypothalamic damage. *Science* **177**, 534–535.

Glowinski, J., and Axelrod, J. (1965). Effect of drugs on the uptake, release, and metabolism of H^3-norepinephrine in the rat brain. *Journal of Pharmacology and Experimental Therapeutics* **149**, 43–49.

Gold, R. M. (1966). Aphagia and adipsia produced by unilateral hypothalamic lesions in rats. *American Journal of Physiology* **211**, 1274–1276.

Gold, R. M. (1967). Aphagia and adipsia following unilateral and bilaterally asymmetrical lesions in rats. *Physiology & Behavior* **2**, 211–220.

Gold, R. M. (1973). Hypothalamic obesity: the myth of the ventromedial nucleus. *Science* **182**, 488–490.

Gordon, R., Spector, S., Sjoerdsma, A., and Udenfriend, S. (1966). Increased synthesis of norepinephrine and epinephrine in the intact rat during exercise and exposure to cold. *Journal of Pharmacology and Experimental Therapeutics* **153**, 440–447.

Grastyan, E., Hasznos, T., Lissak, K., Molnar, L., and Ruzsonyi, Z. (1952). Activation of the brain stem activating system by vegetative afferents. *Acta Physiologica Academiae Scientiarum Hungaricae* **3**, 103–122.

Gray, R. H., and Everitt, A. V. (1970). Hypophagia and hypodipsia induced by unilateral hypothalamic lesions in the rat. *American Journal of Physiology* **219**, 398–402.

Grossman, S. P. (1960). Eating or drinking elicited by direct adrenergic or cholinergic stimulation of hypothalamus. *Science* **132**, 301–302.

Grossman, S. P., and Grossman, L. (1973). Persisting deficits in rats "recovered" from transections of fibers which enter or leave hypothalamus laterally. *Journal of Comparative and Physiological Psychology* **85**, 515–527.

Haeusler, G., Gerold, M., and Thoenen, H. (1972). Cardiovascular effects of 6-hydroxydopamine injected into a lateral brain ventricle of the rat. *Naunyn-Schmiedeberg's Archiv für Pharmakologie und Experimentelle Pathologie* **274**, 211–228.

Haeusler, H. (1971). Short and long term effects of 6-hydroxydopamine on peripheral organs. *In* "6-Hydroxydopamine and Catecholamine Neurons" (T. Malmfors and H. Thoenen, eds.), pp. 193–204. North-Holland Publ., Amsterdam.

Hainsworth, F. R., and Epstein, A. N. (1966). Severe impairment of heat-induced saliva-spreading in rats recovered from lateral hypothalamic lesions. *Science* **153**, 1255–1257.

Hansen, M. G., and Whishaw, I. Q. (1973). The effects of 6-hydroxydopamine, dopamine and dl-norepinephrine on food intake and water consumption, self-stimulation, temperature and electroencephalographic activity in the rat. *Psychopharmacologia* **29**, 33–44.

Harrell, L. E., Raubeson, R., and Balagura, S. (1974). Acceleration of functional recovery following lateral hypothalamic damage by means of electrical stimulation in the lesioned areas. *Physiology & Behavior* **12**, 897–899.

Harvey, J. A. (1965). Comparison between the effects of hypothalamic lesions on brain amine levels and drug action. *Journal of Pharmacology and Experimental Therapeutics* **147**, 244–251.

Hebb, D. O. (1955). Drives and the C.N.S. (conceptual nervous system). *Psychological Review* **62**, 243–254.

Hedreen, J. C., and Chalmers, J. P. (1972). Neuronal degeneration in rat brain induced by 6-hydroxydopamine; a histological and biochemical study. *Brain Research* **47**, 1–36.

Heffner, T. G., Zigmond, M. J., and Stricker, E. M. (1975). Brain dopamine involvement in amphetamine-induced anorexia. *Federation Proceedings, Federation of American Societies for Experimental Biology* **34**, 348.

Heikkila, R., and Cohen, G. (1971). Inhibition of biogenic amine uptake by hydrogen peroxide: a mechanism for toxic effects of 6-OHDA. *Science* **172**, 1257–1258.

Heller, A., and Moore, R. Y. (1965). Effect of central nervous system lesions on brain monoamines in the rat. *Journal of Pharmacology and Experimental Therapeutics* **150**, 1–9.

Heller, A., Harvey, J. A., and Moore, R. Y. (1962). A demonstration of a fall in brain serotonin following central nervous system lesions in the rat. *Biochemical Pharmacology* **11**, 859–866.

Hernández-Peón, R. (1961). Reticular mechanisms of sensory control. *In* "Sensory Communication" (A. Rosenblith, ed.), pp. 497–520. MIT Press, Cambridge, Massachusetts.

Herndon, J. G., and Neill, D. B. (1973). Amphetamine reversal of sexual impairment following anterior hypothalamic lesions in female rats. *Pharmacology, Biochemistry and Behavior* **1**, 285–288.

Hertting, G., Axelrod, J., Kopin, I. J., and Whitby, L. G. (1961). Lack of uptake of catecholamines after chronic denervation of sympathetic nerves. *Nature (London)* **189**, 66.

Himsworth, R. L. (1970). Hypothalamic control of adrenaline secretion in response to insufficient glucose. *Journal of Physiology (London)* **206**, 411–417.

Hockman, C. H. (1964). EEG and behavioral effects of food deprivation in the albino rat. *Electroencephalography and Clinical Neurophysiology* **17**, 420–427.

Hökfelt, T., and Ungerstedt, U. (1973). Specificity of 6-hydroxydopamine induced degeneration of central monoamine neurones: an electron and fluorescence microscopic study with special reference to intracerebral injection on the nigrostriatal dopamine system. *Brain Research* **60**, 269–297.

Hoffer, B. J., Siggins, G. R., Oliver, A. P., and Bloom, F. E. (1973). Activation of the pathway from locus coeruleus to rat cerebellar Purkinje neurons: Pharmacological evidence of noradrenergic central inhibition. *Journal of Pharmacology and Experimental Therapeutics* **184**, 553–569.

Hornykiewicz, O. (1966). Dopamine (3-hydroxytyramine) and brain function. *Pharmacological Reviews* **18**, 925–964.

Hornykiewicz, O. (1971). Neurochemical pathology and pharmacology of brain dopamine and acetylcholine: rational basis for the current drug treatment of parkinsonism. *In* "Recent Advances in Parkinson's Disease" (F. H. McDowell and C. H. Markham, eds.), pp. 33–65. Davis, Philadelphia, Pennsylvania.

Hornykiewicz, O. (1973). Parkinson's disease: from brain homogenate to treatment. *Federation Proceedings, Federation of American Societies for Experimental Biology* **32**, 183–190.

Iversen, L. L. (1967). "The Uptake and Storage of Noradrenaline in Sympathetic Nerves." Cambridge Univ. Press, London and New York.

Iversen, L. L., and Uretsky, N. J. (1970). Regional effects of 6-hydroxydopamine on catecholamine containing neurons in rat brain and spinal cord. *Brain Research* **24**, 364–367.

Jacks, B. R., de Champlain, J., and Cordeau, J. P. (1972). Effects of 6-hydroxydopamine on putative transmitter substances in the central nervous system. *European Journal of Pharmacology* 18, 353–360.

Jasper, H. H., Khan, R. T., and Elliott, K. A. C. (1965). Amino acids released from the cerebral cortex in relation to its state of activation. *Science* 147, 1448–1449.

Javoy, F., Agid, Y., Bouvet, D., and Glowinski, J. (1974). Changes in neostriatal DA metabolism after carbachol or atropine microinjections into the substantia nigra. *Brain Research* 68, 253–260.

Jones, B. E., Bobillier, P., Pin, C., and Jouvet, M. (1973). The effect of lesions of catecholamine-containing neurons upon monoamine content of the brain and EEG and behavioral waking in the cat. *Brain Research* 58, 157–177.

Jonsson, G., Pycock, C., Fuxe, K., and Sachs, C. (1974). Changes in the development of central noradrenaline neurons following neonatal administration of 6-HDA. *Journal of Neurochemistry* 22, 419–426.

Jouvet, M. (1969). Biogenic amines and the states of sleep. *Science* 163, 32–41.

Jouvet, M. (1972). The role of monoamines and acetylcholine-containing neurons in the regulation of the sleep-waking cycle. *Ergebnisse der Physiologie, Biologischen Chemie und Experimentellen Pharmakologie* 64, 166–307.

Kakolewski, J. W., Deaux, E., Christensen, J., and Case, B. (1971). Diurnal patterns in water and food intake and body weight changes in rats with hypothalamic lesions. *American Journal of Physiology* 221, 711–718.

Kalisker, A., Rutledge, C. O., and Perkins, J. P. (1973). Effect of nerve degeneration by 6-hydroxydopamine on catecholamine-stimulated adenosine $3',5'$-monophosphate formation in rat cerebral cortex. *Molecular Pharmacology* 9, 619–629.

Kapatos, G., and Gold, R. M. (1973). Evidence for ascending noradrenergic mediation of hypothalamic hyperphagia. *Pharmacology, Biochemistry and Behavior* 1, 81–87.

Karobath, M. (1971). Catecholamines and the hydroxylation of tyrosine in synaptosomes isolated from rat brain. *Proceedings of the National Academy of Sciences, United States* 68, 2370–2373.

Katzman, R., Björklund, A., Owman, C., Stenevi, U., and West, K. A. (1971). Evidence for regenerative axon sprouting of central catecholamine neutrons in the rat mesencephalon following electrolytic lesions. *Brain Research* 25, 579–596.

Keller, H. H., Bartholini, G., Peiri, L., and Pletscher, A. (1972). Effects of spreading depression on the turnover of cerebral dopamine. *European Journal of Pharmacology* 20, 287–290.

Kissileff, H. R. (1970). Free feeding in normal and "recovered lateral" rats monitored by a pellet-detecting eatometer. *Physiology & Behavior* 5, 163–173.

Kissileff, H. R., and Epstein, A. N. (1969). Exaggerated prandial drinking in the "recovered lateral" rat without saliva. *Journal of Comparative and Physiological Psychology* 67, 301–308.

Kopin, I. J., Palkovits, M., Kobayashi, R. M., and Jacobowitz, D. M. (1974). Quantitative relationship of catecholamine content and histofluorescence in brain of rats. *Brain Research* 80, 229–236.

Korf, J., Roth, R. H., and Aghajanian, G. K. (1973). Alterations in turnover and endogenous levels of norepinephrine in cerebral cortex following electrical stimulation and acute axotomy of cerebral noradrenergic pathways. *European Journal of Pharmacology* 23, 276–282.

Krauthamer, G., and Albe-Fessard, D. (1965). Inhibition of nonspecific sensory activities following striopallidal and capsular stimulation. *Journal of Neurophysiology* 28, 100–124.

Laguzzi, R., Petitjean, F., Pujol, J. F., and Jouvet, M. (1972). Effets de l'injection intraventriculaire de 6-hydroxydopamine. II. Sur le cycle veille-sommeils du chat. *Brain Research* 48, 295–310.

Langer, S. Z. (1966). The degeneration contraction of the nictitating membrane in the unanesthetized cat. *Journal of Pharmacology and Experimental Therapeutics* 151, 66–72.

Lashley, K. S. (1929). "Brain Mechanisms and Intelligence." Univ. of Chicago Press, Chicago, Illinois.

Laverty, R., and Taylor, K. M. (1970). Effects of intraventricular 2, 4, 5-trihydroxy-phenylethylamine (6-hydroxydopamine) on rat behaviour and brain catecholamine metabolism. *British Journal of Pharmacology* 40, 826–846.

Levine, M. S., and Schwartzbaum, J. S. (1973). Sensorimotor functions of the striatopallidal system and lateral hypothalamus and consumatory behavior in rats. *Journal of Comparative and Physiological Psychology* 85, 615–635.

Levitan, D. E. (1974). Effects of intraventricular 6-hydroxydopamine on the ingestive behaviors of rats during glucopenia or hypovolemia. Unpublished master's thesis, Univ. of Pittsburgh, Pittsburgh, Pennsylvania.

Levitt, D. R., and Teitelbaum, P. (1975). Somnolence, akinesia, and sensory activation of motivated behavior in the lateral hypothalamic syndrome. *Proceedings of the National Academy of Sciences, United States* 72, 2819–2823.

Lindsley, D. B. (1951). Emotion. *In* "Handbook of Experimental Psychology" (S. S. Stevens, ed.), pp. 473–516. Wiley, New York.

Lindsley, D. B., Schreiner, L. H., Knowles, W. B., and Magoun, H. W. (1950). Behavioral and EEG changes following chronic brain stem lesions in the cat. *Electroencephalography and Clinical Neurophysiology* 2, 483–498.

Lindvall, O., and Björklund, A. (1974). The organization of the ascending catecholamine neuron systems in the rat brain as revealed by the glyoxylic acid fluorescence method. *Acta Physiologica Scandinavica, Supplementum* 412, 1–48.

Lindvall, O., Björklund, A., Moore, R. Y., and Stenevi, U. (1974). Mesencephalic dopamine neurons projecting to neocortex. *Brain Research* 81, 325–332.

Loizou, L. A. (1972). The postnatal ontogeny of monoamine-containing neurons in the central nervous system of the albino rat. *Brain Research* 40, 395–418.

Longo, V. G. (1973). Central effects of 6-hydroxydopamine. *Behavioral Biology* 9, 397–420.

Lovenberg, W., and Bruckwick, E. A. (1975). Mechanisms of receptor mediated regulation of catecholamine synthesis in brain. *In* "Pre- and Postsynaptic Receptors" (E. Usdin and W. E. Bunney, Jr., eds.), pp. 149–169. Dekker, New York.

Lyon, M., Halpern, M., and Mintz, E. (1968). The significance of the mesencephalon for coordinated feeding behavior. *Acta Neurologica Scandinavica* 44, 323–346.

McGeer, E. G., Fibiger, H. C., McGeer, P. L., and Brooke, S. (1973). Temporal changes in amine synthesizing enzymes of rat extrapyramidal structures after hemitransections or 6-hydroxydopamine administration. *Brain Research* 52, 289–300.

Malmfors, T. (1964). Release and depletion of the transmitter in adrenergic terminals produced by nerve impulses after the inhibition of nonadrenaline synthesis or reabsorption. *Life Sciences* 3, 1397–1402.

Mandell, A. J. (1973). Redundant macromolecular mechanisms in central synaptic regulation. *In* "New Concepts in Neurotransmitter Regulation" (A. J. Mandell, ed.), pp. 259–277. Plenum, New York.

Mandell, A. J., Knapp, S., and Hsu, L. L. (1974). Some factors in the regulation of central serotonergic synapses. *Life Sciences* 14, 1–17.

Marshall, J. F., and Teitelbaum, P. (1973). A comparison of the eating in response to hypothermic and glucoprivic challenges after nigral 6-hydroxydopamine and lateral hypothalamic electrolytic lesions in rats. *Brain Research* 55, 229–233.

Marshall, J. F., and Teitelbaum, P. (1974). Further analysis of sensory inattention following lateral hypothalamic damage in rats. *Journal of Comparative and Physiological Psychology* 86, 375–395.

Marshall, J. F., Turner, B. H., and Teitelbaum, P. (1971). Sensory neglect produced by lateral hypothalamic damage. *Science* 174, 523–525.

Marshall, J. F., Richardson, J. S., and Teitelbaum, P. (1974). Nigrostriatal bundle damage and the lateral hypothalamic syndrome. *Journal of Comparative and Physiological Psychology* 87, 808–830.

Matthysee, S. (1974). Dopamine and the pharmacology of schizophrenia: the state of the evidence. *Journal of Psychiatric Research* 11, 107–113.

Maynert, E. W., and Levi, R. (1964). Stress-induced release of brain norepinephrine and its inhibition by drugs. *Journal of Pharmacology and Experimental Therapeutics* 143, 90–97.

Miselis, R. R., and Epstein, A. N. (1971). Preoptic-hypothalamic mediation of feeding induced by cerebral glucoprivation. *American Zoologist* 11, 624.

Mishra, R. K., Gardner, E. L., Katzman, R., and Makman, M. H. (1974). Enhancement of dopamine-stimulated adenylate cyclase activity in rat caudate after lesions in substantia nigra: evidence for denervation supersensitivity. *Proceedings of the National Academy of Sciences, United States* 71, 3883–3887.

Mogenson, G. J., and Stevenson, J. A. F. (1967). Drinking induced by electrical stimulation of the lateral hypothalamus. *Experimental Neurology* 17, 119–127.

Montemurro, D. G., and Stevenson, J. A. F. (1957). Adipsia produced by hypothalamic lesions in the rat. *Canadian Journal of Biochemistry and Physiology* 35, 31–37.

Moore, R. Y., and Heller, A. (1967). Monoamine levels and neuronal degeneration in rat brain following lateral hypothalamic lesions. *Journal of Pharmacology and Experimental Therapeutics* 156, 12–22.

Morgane, P. J. (1961a). Medial forebrain bundle and "feeding centers" of the hypothalamus. *Journal of Comparative Neurology* 117, 1–25.

Morgane, P. J. (1961b). Alterations in feeding and drinking behavior of rats with lesions in globi pallidi. *American Journal of Physiology* 210, 420–428.

Morgane, P. J. (1969). The function of the limbic and rhinic forebrain-limbic midbrain systems and reticular formation in the regulation of food and water intake. *Annals of the New York Academy of Sciences* 157, 806–848.

Morgane, P. J., and Stern, W. C. (1974). Chemical anatomy of brain circuits in relation to sleep and wakefulness. *In* "Advances in Sleep Research" (E. Weitzman, ed.), Vol. 1, pp. 1–131. Spectrum Publ., New York.

Morgenroth, V. H., Boadle-Biber, M., and Roth, R. H. (1974). Tyrosine hydroxylase: activation by nerve stimulation. *Proceedings of the National Academy of Sciences, United States* 71, 4283–4287.

Morrison, S. D. (1968). The relationship of energy expenditure and spontaneous activity to the aphagia of rats with lesions in the lateral hypothalamus. *Journal of Physiology (London)* 197, 325–343.

Morrison, S. D., and Mayer, J. (1957). Adipsia and aphagia in rats after lateral subthalamic lesions. *American Journal of Physiology* 191, 248–254.

Mufson, E. J., and Wampler, R. S. (1972). Weight regulation with palatable food and liquids in rats with lateral hypothalamic lesions. *Journal of Comparative and Physiological Psychology* 80, 382–392.

Murrin, L. C., Morgenroth, V. H., and Roth, R. H. (1974). Activation of striatal tyrosine hydroxylase by increase in impulse flow. *Pharmacologist* **16**, 213.

Myers, R. D., and Martin, G. E. (1973). 6-OHDA lesions of the hypothalamus; interaction of aphagia, food palatability, set-point for weight regulation, and recovery of feeding. *Pharmacology, Biochemistry and Behavior* **1**, 329–345.

Nagatsu, T., Levitt, M., and Udenfriend, S. (1964). Conversion of L-tyrosine to 3,4-dihydroxyphenylalanine by cell-free preparations of brain and sympathetically innervated tissues. *Biochemical and Biophysical Research Communications* **14**, 543–549.

Nauta, W. J. H. (1946). Hypothalamic regulation of sleep in rats. An experimental study. *Journal of Neurophysiology* **9**, 285–316.

Nicolaïdis, S., and Meile, M. H. (1972). Cartographie des lésions hypothalamiques supprimant la réponse alimentaire aux injections intracardiaques du 2-déoxy-d-glucose. *Journal of Physiology (Paris)* **65**, 150A.

Nierlich, D. P. (1974). Regulation of bacterial growth. *Science* **184**, 1043–1050.

Nybäck, H., Borzecki, Z., and Sedvall, G. (1968). Accumulation and disappearance of catecholamines formed from tyrosine-^{14}C in mouse brain: Effect of some psychiatric drugs. *European Journal of Pharmacology* **4**, 395–403.

Olivier, A., Parent, A., Simard, H., and Poirier, L. J. (1970). Cholinesterasic striatopallidal and striatonigral efferents in the cat and the monkey. *Brain Research* **18**, 273–282.

Olson, L., Seiger, A., and Fuxe, K. (1972). Heterogeneity of striatal and limbic dopamine innervation: highly fluorescent islands in developing and adult rats. *Brain Research* **44**, 283–288.

Oltmans, G. A., and Harvey, J. A. (1972). LH syndrome and brain catecholamine levels after lesions of the nigrostriatal bundle. *Physiology & Behavior* **8**, 69–78.

Palmer, G. C. (1972). Increased cyclic AMP response to norepinephrine in the rat brain following 6-hydroxydopamine. *Neuropharmacology* **11**, 145–149.

Parker, S. S., and Feldman, S. M. (1967). Effect of mesencephalic lesions on feeding behavior in rats. *Experimental Neurology* **17**, 313–326.

Petitjean, F., and Jouvet, M. (1970). Hypersomnie et augmentation de l'acide 5-hydroxyindolacétique cérébral par lésion isthmique chez le cat. *Comptes Rendus Hebdomadaires des Séances de la Société de Biologie* **164**, 2288–2293.

Petitjean, F., Laguzzi, R., Sordet, F., Jouvet, M., and Pujol, J. F. (1972). Effets de l'injection intraventriculaire de 6-hydroxydopamine. I. Sur les monoamines cérébrales du chat. *Brain Research* **48**, 281–293.

Poirier, L. J., Langelier, P., Roberge, A., Boucher, R., and Kitsikis, A. (1972). Nonspecific histopathological changes induced by the intracerebral injection of 6-hydroxy-dopamine (6-OH-DA). *Journal of Neurological Sciences* **16**, 401–416.

Powley, T. L., and Keesey, R. E. (1970). Relationship of body weight to the lateral hypothalamic feeding syndrome. *Journal of Comparative and Physiological Psychology* **70**, 25–36.

Pujol, J. F., Buguet, A., Froment, J. L., Jones, B., and Jouvet, M. (1971). The central metabolism of serotonin in the cat during insomnia. A neurophysiological and biochemical study after administration of p-chlorophenylalanine or destruction of the raphe system. *Brain Research* **29**, 195–212.

Pujol, J. F., Stein, D., Blondaux, C., Petitjean, F., Froment, J. L., and Jouvet, M. (1973). Biochemical evidences for interaction phenomena between noradrenergic and serotoninergic systems in the cat brain. *In* "Frontiers in Catecholamine Research" (E. Usdin and S. H. Snyder, eds.), pp. 771–772. Pergamon, Oxford.

Robinson, B. W., and Mishkin, M. (1968). Alimentary responses to forebrain stimulation in monkeys. *Experimental Brain Research (Berlin)* **4**, 330–366.

Robinson, T. E., and Whishaw, I. Q. (1974). Effects of posterior hypothalamic lesions on voluntary behavior and hippocampal electroencephalograms in the rat. *Journal of Comparative and Physiological Psychology* **86**, 768–786.

Rodgers, W. L., Epstein, A. N., and Teitelbaum, P. (1965). Lateral hypothalamic aphagia: motor failure or motivational deficit? *American Journal of Physiology* **208**, 334–342.

Roth, R. H., Salzman, P. M., and Morgenroth, V. H. (1974). Noradrenergic neurons: allosteric activation of hippocampal tyrosine hydroxylase by stimulation of the locus coeruleus. *Biochemical Pharmacology* **23**, 2779–2784.

Roth, S. R., Schwartz, M., and Teitelbaum, P. (1973). Failure of recovered lateral hypothalamic rats to learn specific food aversions. *Journal of Comparative and Physiological Psychology* **83**, 184–197.

Rothballer, A. B. (1956). Studies on the adrenaline-sensitive component of the reticular activating system. *Electroencephalography and Clinical Neurophysiology* **8**, 603–621.

Routtenberg, A. (1968). The two-arousal hypothesis: Reticular formation and limbic system. *Psychological Review* **75**, 51–80.

Rowland, N. (1976). Circadian rhythms and the partial recovery of regulatory drinking in rats after lateral hypothalamic lesions. *Journal of Comparative and Physiological Psychology* (in press).

Rozkowska, E., and Fonberg, E. (1970). The effects of lateral hypothalamic lesions on food intake and instrumental alimentary reflex in dogs. *Acta Neurobiologiae Experimentalis (Warsaw)* **30**, 59–68.

Rozkowska, E., and Fonberg, E. (1972). Impairment of salivary reflexes after lateral hypothalamic lesions in dogs. *Acta Neurobiologiae Experimentalis (Warsaw)* **32**, 711–720.

Runnels, P., and Thompson, R. (1969). Hypothalamic structures critical for the performance of a locomotor escape response in the rat. *Brain Research* **13**, 328–337.

Satinoff, E., and Shan, S. Y. Y. (1971). Loss of behavioral thermoregulation after lateral hypothalamic lesions in rats. *Journal of Comparative and Physiological Psychology* **77**, 302–312.

Scheibel, M., Scheibel, A., Mollica, A., and Moruzzi, G. (1955). Convergence and interaction of afferent impulses on single units of reticular formation. *Journal of Neurophysiology* **18**, 309–331.

Schoenfeld, R. I., and Uretsky, N. J. (1972). Altered response to apomorphine in 6-hydroxydopamine-treated rats. *European Journal of Pharmacology* **19**, 115–118.

Schoenfeld, R. I., and Uretsky, N. J. (1973). Enhancement by 6-hydroxydopamine of the effects of dopa upon the motor activity of rats. *Journal of Pharmacology and Experimental Therapeutics* **186**, 616–624.

Schoenfeld, R. I., and Zigmond, M. J. (1973). Behavioural pharmacology of 6-hydroxydopamine. *In* "Frontiers in Catecholamine Research" (E. Usdin and S. H. Snyder, eds.), pp. 695–700. Pergamon, Oxford.

Schubert, P., Kreutzberg, G. W., Reinhold, K., and Herz, A. (1973). Selective uptake of ^{3}H-6-hydroxydopamine by neurons of the central nervous system. *Experimental Brain Research (Berlin)* **17**, 539–548.

Schwab, R. S., and England, A. C. (1968). Parkinson syndromes due to various specific causes. *In* "Handbook of Clinical Neurology" (P. J. Vinken and G. W. Bruyn, eds.), pp. 227–247. Wiley, New York.

Schwab, R. S., and Zieper, I. (1965). Effects of mood, stress and alertness on the performance in Parkinson's disease. *Psychiatria et Neurologia* 150, 345–357.

Sclafani, A., Berner, C. N., and Maul, G. (1973). Feeding and drinking pathways between medial and lateral hypothalamus in the rat. *Journal of Comparative and Physiological Psychology* 85, 29–51.

Sechzer, J. A., Ervin, G. N., and Smith, G. P. (1973). Loss of visual placing in rats after lateral hypothalamic microinjections of 6-hydroxydopamine. *Experimental Neurology* 41, 723–732.

Sedvall, G. C., Weise, V. K., and Kopin, I. J. (1968). The rate of norepinephrine synthesis measured *in vivo* during short intervals; influences of adrenergic nerve impulse activity. *Journal of Pharmacology and Experimental Therapeutics* 159, 274–282.

Sharman, D. F., Poirier, L. J., Murphy, G. F., and Sourkes, T. L. (1967). Homovanillic acid and dihydroxyphenylacetic acid in the striatum of monkeys with brain lesions. *Canadian Journal of Physiology and Pharmacology* 45, 57–62.

Simon, H., Le Moal, M., Galey, D., and Cardo, B. (1974). Selective degeneration of central dopaminergic systems after injection of 6-hydroxydopamine in the ventral mesencephalic tegmentum of the rat: Demonstrations by the Fink-Heimer stain. *Experimental Brain Research (Berlin)* 20, 375–384.

Slangen, J. L., and Miller, N. E. (1969). Pharmacological tests for the function of hypothalamic norepinephrine in eating behavior. *Physiology & Behavior* 4, 543–552.

Smith, G. P. (1973). Introduction: Neuropharmacology of thirst. *In* "The Neuropsychology of Thirst: New Findings and Advances in Concepts" (A. N. Epstein, H. R. Kissileff, and E. Stellar, eds.), pp. 231–241. Winston, Washington, D.C.

Smith, G. P., Gibbs, J., Strohmayer, A. J., and Stokes, P. E. (1972). Threshold doses of 2-deoxy-D-glucose for hyperglycemia and feeding in rats and monkeys. *American Journal of Physiology* 222, 77–81.

Snyder, S. H., Banerjee, S. P., Yamamura, H. I., and Greenberg, D. (1974). Drugs, neurotransmitters, and schizophrenia. *Science* 184, 1243–1253.

Sorenson, C. A., and Ellison, G. D. (1970). Striatal organization of feeding behavior in the decorticate rat. *Experimental Neurology* 29, 162–174.

Sotelo, C., Javoy, F., Agid, Y., and Glowinski, J. (1973). Injection of 6-hydroxydopamine in the substantia nigra of the rat. I. Morphological study. *Brain Research* 58, 269–290.

Spector, S., Gordon, R., Sjoerdsma, A., and Udenfriend, S. (1967). End-product inhibition of tyrosine hydroxylase as a possible mechanism for regulation of norepinephrine synthesis. *Molecular Pharmacology* 3, 549–555.

Sprague, J. M., Chambers, W. W., and Stellar, E. (1961). Attentive, affective, and adaptive behavior in the cat. *Science* 133, 165–173.

Starke, K. (1973). Regulation of catecholamine release: α-receptor mediated feed-back control in peripheral and central neurones. *In* "Frontiers in Catecholamine Research" (E. Usdin, and S. H. Snyder, eds.), pp. 561–565. Pergamon, Oxford.

Starzl, T. E., Taylor, C. W., and Magoun, H. W. (1951). Collateral afferent excitation of reticular formation of brain stem. *Journal of Neurophysiology* 14, 479–496.

Stavraky, G. W. (1961). "Supersensitivity following Lesions of the Nervous System." Univ. of Toronto Press, Toronto.

Steinbaum, E. A., and Miller, N. E. (1965). Obesity from eating elicited by daily stimulation of hypothalamus. *American Journal of Physiology* 208, 1–5.

Steiner, W. G. (1962). Electrical activity of rat brain as a correlate of primary drive. *Electroencephalography and Clinical Neurophysiology* 14, 233–243.

Stjarne, L. (1973). Mechanisms of catecholamine secretion: Dual feedback control of sympathetic neurotransmitter secretion; role of calcium. *In* "Frontiers in Catecholamine Research" (E. Usdin and S. H. Snyder, eds.), pp. 491–496. Pergamon, Oxford.

Stricker, E. M. (1976). Drinking by rats after lateral hypothalamic lesions: a new look at the lateral hypothalamic syndrome. *Journal of Comparative and Physiological Psychology* (in press).

Stricker, E. M., and Hainsworth, F. R. (1970). Evaporative cooling in the rat: Effects of hypothalamic lesions and chorda tympani damage. *Canadian Journal of Physiology and Pharmacology* 48, 11–17.

Stricker, E. M., and Wolf, G. (1967). The effects of hypovolemia on drinking in rats with lateral hypothalamic damage. *Proceedings of the Society for Experimental Biology and Medicine* 124, 816–820.

Stricker, E. M., and Zigmond, M. J. (1974). Effects on homeostasis of intraventricular injection of 6-hydroxydopamine in rats. *Journal of Comparative and Physiological Psychology* 86, 973–994.

Stricker, E. M., and Zigmond, M. J. (1975). Brain catecholamines and thirst. *In* "Control Mechanisms of Drinking" (G. Peters, J. T. Fitzsimons, and L. Peters-Haefeli, eds.), pp. 55–61. Springer-Verlag, Berlin and New York.

Stricker, E. M., and Zigmond, M. J. (1976). Brain catecholamines and the lateral hypothalamic syndrome. *In* "Hunger: Basic Mechanisms and Clinical Implications" (D. Novin, W. Wyrwicka, and G. A. Bray, eds.), pp. 19–32. Raven, New York.

Stricker, E. M., Zigmond, M. J., Friedman, M. I., and Redgate, E. S. (1974). The contribution of central catecholamine-containing neurons to several glucoregulatory mechanisms. *Federation Proceedings, Federation of American Societies for Experimental Biology* 33, 564.

Stricker, E. M., Friedman, M. I., and Zigmond, M. J. (1975). Glucoregulatory feeding by rats after intraventricular 6-hydroxydopamine or lateral hypothalamic lesions. *Science* 189, 895–897.

Swett, C. P., and Hobson, J. A. (1968). The effects of posterior hypothalamic lesions on behavioral and electrographic manifestations of sleep and waking in cats. *Archives Italiennes de Biologie* 106, 283–293.

Szerb, J. C. (1972). The effect of atropine on the metabolism of acetylcholine in the cerebral cortex. *Progress in Brain Research* 36, 159–165.

Teitelbaum, P. (1971). The encephalization of hunger. *In* "Progress in Physiological Psychology" (E. Stellar and J. M. Sprague, eds.), Vol. 4, pp. 319–350. Academic Press, New York.

Teitelbaum, P., and Cytawa, J. (1965). Spreading depression and recovery from lateral hypothalamic damage. *Science* 147, 61–63.

Teitelbaum, P., and Epstein, A. N. (1962). The lateral hypothalamic syndrome: Recovery of feeding and drinking after lateral hypothalamic lesions. *Psychological Review* 69, 74–90.

Teitelbaum, P., and Epstein, A. N. (1963). The role of taste and smell in the regulation of food and water intake. *In* "Olfaction and Taste" (Y. Zotterman, ed.), Vol. 1, pp. 347–360. Pergamon, Oxford.

Teitelbaum, P., and Stellar, E. (1954). Recovery from the failure to eat produced by hypothalamic lesions. *Science* 120, 894–895.

Teitelbaum, P., Cheng, M. F., and Rozin, P. (1969). Development of feeding parallels its recovery after hypothalamic damage. *Journal of Comparative and Physiological Psychology* 67, 430–441.

Thierry, A. M., Javoy, F., Glowinski, J., and Kety, S. S. (1968). Effects of stress on the metabolism of norepinephrine, dopamine and serotonin in the central nervous system of the rat. I. Modifications of norepinephrine turnover. *Journal of Pharmacology and Experimental Therapeutics* **163**, 163–171.

Thoenen, H. (1970). Induction of tyrosine hydroxylase in peripheral and central adrenergic neurones by cold-exposure of rats. *Nature (London)* **228**, 861–862.

Thoenen, H. (1974). Trans-synaptic enzyme induction. *Life Sciences* **14**, 223–235.

Thoenen, H., Mueller, R. A., and Axelrod, J. (1969). Trans-synaptic induction of adrenal tyrosine hydroxylase. *Journal of Pharmacology and Experimental Therapeutics* **169**, 249–254.

Thoenen, H., Angeletti, P. U., Levi-Montalcini, R., and Kettler, R. (1971). Selective induction by nerve growth factor of tyrosine hydroxylase and dopamine-β-hydroxylase in the rat superior cervical ganglia. *Proceedings of the National Academy of Sciences, United States* **68**, 1598–1602.

Thornburg, J. E., and Moore, K. E. (1975). Supersensitivity to dopamine agonists following unilateral, 6-hydroxydopamine-induced striatal lesions in mice. *Journal of Pharmacology and Experimental Therapeutics* **192**, 42–49.

Trendelenburg, U. (1966). Mechanisms of supersensitivity and subsensitivity to sympathomimetic amines. *Pharmacological Reviews* **18**, 629–640.

Turner, B. H. (1973). Sensorimotor syndrome produced by lesions of the amygdala and lateral hypothalamus. *Journal of Comparative and Physiological Psychology* **82**, 37–47.

Udenfriend, S., and Dairman, W. (1971). Regulation of norepinephrine synthesis. *In* "Advances in Enzyme Regulation" (G. Weber, ed.), Vol. 9, pp. 145–165. Pergamon, Oxford.

Ungerstedt, U. (1970). Is interruption of the nigrostriatal dopamine system producing the "lateral hypothalamic syndrome"? *Acta Physiologica Scandinavica* **80**, 35A–36A.

Ungerstedt, U. (1971a). Stereotaxic mapping of the monoamine pathways in the rat brain. *Acta Physiologica Scandinavica, Supplementum* **367**, 1–48.

Ungerstedt, U. (1971b). Postsynaptic supersensitivity after 6-hydroxydopamine induced degeneration of the nigro-striatal dopamine system. *Acta Physiologica Scandinavica, Supplementum* **367**, 69–93.

Ungerstedt, U. (1971c). Adipsia and aphagia after 6-hydroxydopamine induced degeneration of the nigro-striatal dopamine system. *Acta Physiologica Scandinavica, Supplementum* **367**, 95–122.

Ungerstedt, U. (1971d). Histochemical studies on the effect of intracerebral and intraventricular injections of 6-hydroxydopamine on monoamine neurons in the rat brain. *In* "6-Hydroxydopamine and Catecholamine Neurons" (T. Malmfors and H. Thoenen, eds.), pp. 101–127. North-Holland Publ., Amsterdam.

Ungerstedt, U. (1971e). Use of intracerebral injections of 6-hydroxydopamine as a tool for morphological and functional studies on central catecholamine neurons. *In* "6-Hydroxydopamine and Catecholamine Neurons" (T. Malmfors and H. Thoenen, eds.), pp. 315–332. North-Holland Publ., Amsterdam.

Ungerstedt, U. (1974). Brain dopamine neurons and behavior. *In* "The Neurosciences, Third Study Program" (F. O. Schmitt and F. G. Worden, eds.), pp. 695–703. MIT Press, Cambridge, Massachusetts.

Uretsky, N. J., and Iversen, L. L. (1970). Effects of 6-hydroxydopamine on catecholamine containing neurones in the rat brain. *Journal of Neurochemistry* **17**, 269–278.

Valenstein, E. S., Cox, V. C., and Kakolewski, J. W. (1968). Modification of motivated behavior elicited by electrical stimulation of the hypothalamus. *Science* **159**, 1119–1121.

Van Zoeren, J. (1974). The contribution of central norepinephrine-containing neurons to thermal homeostasis in the rat. Unpublished doctoral dissertation, Univ. of Pittsburgh, Pittsburgh, Pennsylvania.

Vogt, M. (1954). The concentration of sympathin in different parts of the central nervous system under normal conditions and after the administration of drugs. *Journal of Physiology (London)* **123**, 451–481.

Wampler, R. S. (1970). Changes in sleep and arousal accompanying the lateral hypothalamic syndrome in rats. Unpublished doctoral dissertation, Univ. of Pennsylvania, Philadelphia.

Wayner, M. J., Cott, A., Millner, J., and Tartaglione, R. (1971). Loss of 2-deoxy-D-glucose induced eating in recovered lateral rats. *Physiology & Behavior* **7**, 881–884.

Weiner, N., and Mosimann, W. F. (1970). The effect of insulin on the catecholamine content and tyrosine hydroxylase activity of cat adrenal glands. *Biochemical Pharmacology* **19**, 1189–1199.

Weiner, N., Cloutier, G., Bjur, R., and Pfeffer, R. I. (1972). Modification of norepinephrine synthesis in intact tissue by drugs and during short-term adrenergic nerve stimulation. *Pharmacological Reviews* **24**, 203–221.

Weiner, N., Bjur, R., Lee, F. L., Becker, G., and Mosimann, W. F. (1973). Studies on the mechanism of regulation of tyrosine hydroxylase activity during nerve stimulation. *In* "Frontiers in Catecholamine Research" (E. Usdin and S. H. Snyder, eds.), pp. 211–221. Pergamon, Oxford.

Wikler, A. (1952). Pharmacologic dissociation of behavior and EEG "sleep patterns" in dogs: Morphine, n-allylmorphine, and atropine. *Proceedings of the Society for Experimental Biology and Medicine* **79**, 261–265.

Wolf, G. (1964). Effect of dorsolateral hypothalamic lesions on sodium appetite elicited by desoxycorticosterone and by acute hyponatremia. *Journal of Comparative and Physiological Psychology* **58**, 396–402.

Wolf, G. (1971). Neural mechanisms for sodium appetite: Hypothalamus positive-hypothalamofugal pathways negative. *Physiology & Behavior* **6**, 381–389.

Wolf, G., and Quartermain, D. (1967). Sodium chloride intake of adrenalectomized rats with lateral hypothalamic lesions. *American Journal of Physiology* **212**, 113–118.

Wolgin, D. L., and Teitelbaum, P. (1974). The role of activation and sensory stimuli in the recovery of feeding following lateral hypothalamic lesions in the cat. *Eastern Psychological Association Meeting, Philadelphia, Pa.*

Wyrwicka, W., and Doty, R. W. (1966). Feeding induced in cats by electrical stimulation of the brain stem. *Experimental Brain Research (Berlin)* **1**, 152–160.

Zigmond, M. J., and Harvey, J. A. (1970). Resistance to central norepinephrine depletion and decreased mortality in rats chronically exposed to electric foot shock. *Journal of Neurovisceral Relations* **31**, 373–381.

Zigmond, M. J., and Stricker, E. M. (1972). Deficits in feeding behavior after intraventricular injection of 6-hydroxydopamine in rats. *Science* **177**, 1211–1214.

Zigmond, M. J., and Stricker, E. M. (1973). Recovery of feeding and drinking by rats after intraventricular 6-hydroxydopamine or lateral hypothalamic lesions. *Science* **182**, 717–720.

Zigmond, M. J., and Stricker, E. M. (1974). Ingestive behavior following damage to central dopamine neurons: Implications for homeostasis and recovery of function. *In*

"Neuropsychopharmacology of Monoamines and Their Regulatory Enzymes" (E. Usdin, ed.), pp. 385–402. Raven Press, New York.

Zigmond, M. J., and Stricker, E. M. (1975). Compensatory changes after intraventricular administration of 6-hydroxydopamine: A neurochemical model for recovery of function. *In* "Chemical Tools in Catecholamine Research" (T. Malmfors, O. Almgren, A. Carlsson, J. Engel, G. Jonsson, and C. Sachs, eds.), North-Holland, Amsterdam.

Zigmond, M. J., and Wurtman, R. J. (1970). Daily rhythm in the accumulation of brain catecholamines synthesized from circulating H^3-tyrosine. *Journal of Pharmacology and Experimental Therapeutics* 172, 416–422.

Zigmond, M. J., Chalmers, J. P., Simpson, J. R., and Wurtman, R. J. (1971). Effect of lateral hypothalamic lesions on uptake of norepinephrine by brain homogenates. *Journal of Pharmacology and Experimental Therapeutics* 179, 20–28.

Zigmond, R. E., Schon, F., and Iversen, L. L. (1974). Increased tyrosine hydroxylase activity in the locus coeruleus of rat brain stem after reserpine treatment and cold stress. *Brain Research* 70, 547–552.

Zimmerman, M. B., and Stricker, E. M. (1975). Evidence for a contribution of cyclic-AMP to glucoregulatory feeding. *Eastern Psychological Association Meeting, New York, N.Y.*

Motivation: A Psychological Construct in Search of a Physiological Substrate

G. J. Mogenson and A. G. Phillips

Departments of Physiology and Psychology,
University of Western Ontario, London, Ontario,
and Department of Psychology, University of British
Columbia, Vancouver, British Columbia, Canada

I. Introduction

Nervous systems are built for actions.... Actions are directed towards goals (Livingston, 1967).

Movements are parts of actions, and actions have to satisfy the needs of the organism and secure the survival of the species. Therefore, they must be guided by messages from the internal milieu as well as from the environment (Kornhuber, 1974).

One of the most prominent features of the behavior of animals is that it is goal directed. Animals seek food or water, move to a shady place, or explore a novel feature of the environment; man turns up the thermostat when it is cold, works overtime in order to buy a new car, or gets up early on Sunday morning to play golf. Psychologists use the term motivation to designate those inferred processes that account for the initiation of such behaviors. It is the task of the physiological psychologist and of other neuroscientists to discover the physiological mechanisms that subserve motivational processes. "We will not fully understand our basic phenomenon (drinking behavior, or feeding behavior, etc.) if we do not continuously confront the fact of motivation and the elusive neurological problem it poses" (Epstein, 1973, p. 329).

Major developments in the study of neural mechanisms of motivated behavior have occurred during the last two or three decades. They resulted from the application of stereotaxic techniques to investigate the effects of lesions and stimulation of various brain structures on the behavior of animals, made possible by the pioneering work of Ranson and his co-workers (e.g., Hetherington and Ranson, 1942) and of Hess (1949). Dramatic effects on feeding, drinking, sexual activity, and other aspects of motivated behaviors have been produced, especially with lesions and stimulation of the hypothalamus and limbic system. The interpretation of these experiments and the models that emerged were strongly influenced by the prevailing theoretical views in physiology and in psychology. Typically the effects of lesions and stimulation were considered in terms of disrupting or activating drive mechanisms. The view that drives result from biological deficits, such as the need for water or food, was compatible with the physiological concept of homeostasis (Cannon, 1932) and with the view that motivated behavior is adaptive and self-regulatory (Richter, 1944). It was also consistent with the popular psychological theory of motivation and learning based on the principle of drive reduction (Hull, 1943). Accordingly, as indicated in Section II, motivational processes were considered to be the drive mechanisms that intervene between deficit stimuli and the motor system.

It was soon pointed out that a good deal of motivated behavior, particularly in animals with more highly developed brains, does not depend on biological deficits (Harlow, 1953; Hebb, 1955). For example, there are four or five "thirsts" in the sense that drinking (under multifactor control: Adolph et al., 1954), may be initiated in a variety of ways, and "All are not necessarily regulatory" (Stellar, 1973, p. V). Motivated behavior is initiated by external stimuli and by cognitive processes as well as by primary deficit signals. For a time these ideas had little theoretical impact; the prevailing view was that feeding, drinking, and other motivated behaviors are initiated by internal, deficit signals that activate hypothalamic drive systems.

Recently there has been a general reassessment of this popular approach to physiological mechanisms of motivated behaviors. This resulted in part from changing theoretical views about the psychology of motivation (discussed in Section III) and also from neurochemical and neuroanatomical evidence (outlined in Section IV) which necessitated a reconsideration of the role of the hypothalamus in motivated behavior (Mogenson, 1974a; Morgane, 1975). These developments, as indicated in Section V, are having far reaching effects on current approaches to the study of the physiological mechanisms of motivated behavior and, more generally, on our understanding of how the brain is organized and how it functions.

The term motivation includes a broad spectrum of behaviors, and we have found it necessary to limit the discussion. Accordingly, in this article, we deal primarily with feeding, drinking, and brain self-stimulation. This seems appropriate since much of the work on the neural mechanisms of motivated behavior in the earlier years was concerned with feeding and drinking, and it has continued to be a vigorous field of research. Brain self-stimulation was a major discovery which has had a significant impact on theoretical ideas. We have included brain self-stimulation in the discussion because the eventual understanding of the neural mechanisms of central reinforcement is likely to have important implications for our understanding of motivated behaviors in general. Major emphasis is given to the role of catecholaminergic pathways in feeding, drinking, and self-stimulation, and we have tried to consider the evidence and raise questions from a broad perspective keeping in mind current theoretical views about motivation.

II. Neurobiology of Motivated Behavior: Major Developments in the 1950s and 1960s

Physiological psychology was one of the most vigorous subdisciplines of psychology and of neurobiology in the 1950s and 1960s. Hebb's (1949) "Organization of Behavior" provided a bridge between psychologists and neurobiologists and showed not only that the study of brain–behavior relationships is legitimate and important, but that psychological theory depends in a vital way on neuropsychological concepts.[1] Dramatic discoveries soon

---

[1] In the search for neural mechanisms that subserve behavior, "it is necessary to study physiology and behavior conjointly" (Weiskrantz, 1973, p. 514). It is the behavior of the whole animal that tells us what sort of mechanism to look for. Unfortunately, all too frequently in the past, "... studies have repeatedly been made of behavior while ignoring the brain and the body, of the body while ignoring the brain and behaviors, and of the brain neglecting the fact that the brain commands and regulates both internal and external environments" (LeMagnen, 1971, p. 207). When this happens, the result, according to LeMagnen, is "A Decapitated Physiology and a Bodiless Psychology."

followed, on the reticular activating system (Moruzzi and Magoun, 1949), on central reinforcement systems (Delgado *et al.*, 1954; Olds and Milner, 1954), and the neural mechanisms for aggression (Brady and Nauta, 1953; Schreiner and Kling, 1953). The study of brain and behavior became a fruitful and exciting endeavor.

At the beginning of this period two theories were formulated concerning the physiological substrates of motivated behavior, one stressing the hypothalamus and multiple-drive systems (Stellar, 1954) and the other the reticular formation and a single-drive or arousal system (Hebb, 1955). During the next 10 or 15 years much of the research on the neurobiology of motivated behavior was stimulated by and provided a test of these theoretical models.

A. THE DRIVE MECHANISM MODEL

The model illustrated in Fig. 1 assumed that the strength of motivated behavior is a direct function of "the amount of activity in certain excitatory centers in the hypothalamus" (Stellar, 1954, p. 6). The publication of the drive mechanisms model was very opportune. It integrated previous work on feeding, drinking, and other drives and stimulated considerable new research on the neural basis of motivated behavior. For 10 or 15 years, as indicated above, the empirical findings and the model were mutually reinforcing. Although the subject of several recent reviews (Stevenson, 1969; Epstein, 1971) a brief description of the major findings will provide an essential perspective from which to consider more recent developments in the neurobiology of motivated behavior.

Lesions of the ventromedial hypothalamus (VMH) cause hyperphagia and obesity (Brobeck *et al.*, 1943) whereas lesions of the lateral hypothalamus (LH) cause aphagia, weight loss, and even death in many cases if the animals are not force-fed (Anand and Brobeck, 1951). According to the early workers and to the drive mechanism model, VMH lesions destroy a satiety system and LH lesions destroy a hunger or appetite system. The VMH and LH were thought to serve as a dual mechanism with the LH appetite system being inhibited by the VMH satiety system. It was assumed that the LH integrates signals from reduced glucose utilization and other primary, as well as secondary, "hunger" and "thirst" signals. Subsequently it was reported that rats with LH lesions show a deficit in response to reduced glucose utilization, hypovolemia, and hyperosmolality (Epstein, 1971). Similarly the VMH was thought to contain satiety receptors, such as glucoreceptors, which monitor the rate of glucose utilization (Mayer, 1953), or that integrate satiety signals, such as those from gastric distention (Anand and Pillai, 1967) or from body fat stores (Kennedy, 1953).

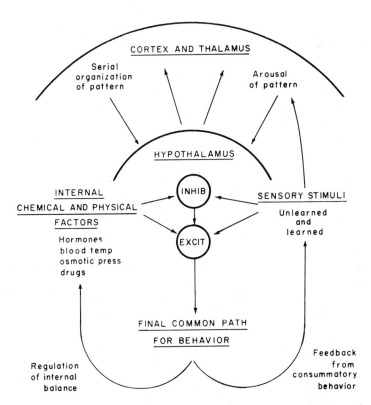

FIG. 1. Diagrammatic representation of physiological factors contributing to the control of motivated behavior. Each drive or type of motivated behavior depends on the activity of various sets of excitatory centers in the hypothalamus. These centers are influenced by sensory stimuli, hormones and other chemical factors, and influences from higher levels of the nervous system (from Stellar, 1954). Copyright 1954 by the American Psychological Association. Reprinted by permission.

According to the model, "There are different centers in the hypothalamus responsible for the control of different kinds of basic motivation" (Stellar, 1954, p. 18). This proposal was supported by experiments demonstrating that lesions of the hypothalamus may also disrupt drinking (Teitelbaum and Stellar, 1954; Montemurro and Stevenson, 1957), sexual behavior (Brookhart and Dey, 1941), sleep (Nauta, 1946), and activity (Gladfelter and Brobeck, 1962). The hypothalamic areas associated with feeding and drinking overlap, but appropriately placed lesions can produce adipsia with little or no change in food intake (Montemurro and Stevenson, 1957), and typically the disturbance in water intake outlasts the disturbance in food intake (Teitelbaum and Epstein, 1962).

If the hypothalamus contains drive systems, as suggested by the lesion data, it should be possible to initiate motivated behaviors with electrical stimulation. This has, in fact, been demonstrated by several investigators; feeding (Delgado and Anand, 1953; Miller, 1960; Hoebel, 1969), drinking (Greer, 1955; Andersson and Wyrwicka, 1957; Mogenson and Stevenson, 1966), copulation (Caggiula and Hoebel, 1966), and other motivated behaviors (Glickman and Schiff, 1967) were elicited by electrical stimulation of the hypothalamus. It is of particular interest that electrical stimulation of the LH initiates feeding, an effect opposite to LH lesions, whereas stimulation of the VMH inhibits feeding (Hoebel, 1969), an effect opposite to lesions of this area. Thus, the electrical stimulation and lesion experiments appeared to provide clear-cut evidence for a dual-mechanism model (see Fig. 1).

Whether electrical stimulation of the hypothalamus elicits discrete drinking and feeding behaviors has been a matter of controversy in recent years (Valenstein et al., 1968; Roberts, 1969; Mogenson, 1973). Although electrical stimulation of the hypothalamus has been reported to elicit feeding only and drinking only (Mogenson, 1971; Mogenson et al., 1971; Huang and Mogenson, 1972; Cioé and Mogenson, 1974), there are a number of examples of multiple responses elicited from the same electrode site and of elicited feeding responses being switched to drinking and vice versa (Mogenson and Morgan, 1967; Valenstein et al., 1968). The latter observations have been widely interpreted as evidence of plasticity of neural systems which subserve feeding and drinking and as support for the activation of a single-drive or arousal system (the model described in Section II,B). However, these observations are also consistent with the view that there are discrete but overlapping systems that subserve drinking and feeding (Mogenson, 1973).

Other evidence in support of the hypothalamic drive system model comes from studies in which chemical substances were applied to the hypothalamus by means of chronic intracranial cannula. The first studies were by Andersson (1953), who elicited drinking in the goat by administering hypertonic saline into the ventricles and directly into the hypothalamus. This was the first evidence for a "thirst center" in the hypothalamus. Later, Grossman (1962) initiated drinking by applying carbachol, a cholinergic compound, to the hypothalamus of rats suggesting that the thirst system contained cholinergic neurons (Miller, 1965). Feeding was elicited by the local application of norepinephrine (NE), suggesting that it was a transmitter for the feeding system.

Electrophysiological studies have also implicated the hypothalamus in feeding and drinking and have provided evidence that the LH and VMH constitute a dual mechanism for the control of ingestive behaviors. Several authors have reported that the discharge of hypothalamic neurons is altered by changing blood glucose levels and by osmotic stimulation (Anand et al., 1961; Brown and Melzack, 1969). The reciprocal relationship of LH and VMH, which had been suggested by lesion and stimulation studies, has been supported by electrophysiological experiments; when LH neurons are discharging slowly VMH neurons discharge rapidly and vice versa (Oomura *et al.*, 1964). These responses may have functional significance since it has been reported that the intravenous infusion of glucose increases multiunit activity of the VMH and decreases such activity in the LH (Brown and Melzack, 1969). For further details about electrophysiological studies of the neural mechanisms that subserve drinking and feeding, see a recent review by Mogenson (1975).

Feeding, drinking, and other motivated behaviors are also altered by lesions and stimulation outside the hypothalamus, particularly in limbic forebrain structures and in the midbrain (for reviews of this work, see Grossman, 1968; Mogenson and Huang, 1973). In many cases the effects of lesions and stimulation have been small and variable. However, some of the changes have been quite dramatic, such as the hyperdipsia following septal lesions (Harvey and Hunt, 1965; Wishart and Mogenson, 1970), the aphagia and hyperphagia following lesions of the amygdala (Grossman and Grossman, 1963; Fonberg, 1969), and the hypersexuality following lesions of the amygdaloid region (Schreiner and Kling, 1953).

It was frequently suggested that the primary mechanisms for the control of feeding, drinking, and sexual behavior are not altered or influenced by lesions or stimulation of limbic structures. Since the effects are often weak or variable and because of the numerous interconnections of limbic structures and hypothalamus, a popular view is that limbic structures exert modulatory influences on the hypothalamic systems that have a primary role in the control of feeding, drinking, and other motivated behaviors (Gloor *et al.*, 1969; Stevenson, 1969; Mogenson and Huang, 1973). For several years, therefore, results of this sort were interpreted in terms of the hypothalamic drive mechanism model, the modulatory influences from limbic structures being considered examples of excitatory and inhibitory influences from other regions of the brain, referred to by Stellar in his classic paper (see Fig. 1).

B. A GENERAL DRIVE OR AROUSAL MODEL

A very different theoretical approach to motivated behaviors was proposed by Hebb (1955, 1958). He maintained that an analysis of motivation based on specific drive systems was oversimplified and based on outdated conceptions of the nervous system. He was especially critical of the "peripheralism" that characterized much of psychological thought in the early 1950s, the stimulus–response analysis of behavior which ignored the role of attention, cognition, and other complex neuropsychological processes. Hebb (1958) objected to "biological hedonism," the "position that identified motivation with biologically primitive hunger, pain and sex" (p. 458) and emphasized instead that many aspects of motivated behavior do not result from homeostatic imbalance. Exploratory, investigatory, and manipulatory behaviors occur in the absence of biological deficits.

As an alternative to the multidrive model, Hebb (1955) proposed that there is a single-drive or arousal system whose neural substrate is the brain stem reticular system (Fig. 2). The brain stem arousal system receives various sensory stimuli and projects diffusely to the higher levels of the brain maintaining behavioral vigilance. In addition to internal deficit stimuli, it also receives external stimuli and projections from the cerebral cortex. Arousal level results from an interaction between internal states and external cues and is influenced by higher cognitive functions. According to Hebb, motivated

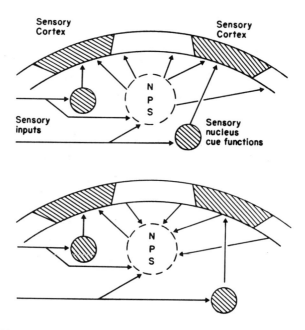

FIG. 2. Diagrammatic representation showing the relationship of the reticular activating system (NPS, nonspecific projection system) to sensory input and to the higher cortical levels of the central nervous system. At top it is shown that sensory inputs go to the reticular activating system as well as to the thalamic sensory nuclei and sensory cortex. The reticular activating system projects diffusely to the cerebral cortex and, as shown at the bottom, the cerebral cortex projects back to the reticular activating system. The latter projections make it possible for higher mental processes to influence neural arousal as well as sensory inputs (from Hebb, 1955). Copyright 1955 by the American Psychological Association. Reprinted by permission.

behaviors occur in order to maintain an optimal level of arousal. Behavioral performance deteriorates when arousal is either too low or too high.

The arousal model represented a different view of motivated behavior than the multidrive model and also a different conception of how the brain functions. The model suggests that the animal does not merely passively react to deficit signals, it seeks stimulation to maintain arousal. Especially in animals with more complex brains, investigatory and manipulatory behaviors are quite characteristic. As shown by the McGill sensory deprivation studies (e.g., Thompson and Heron, 1954), the brain is not a passive switchboard mechanism, but rather it requires sensory input in order to function properly. Furthermore, the nervous system habituates to sensory stimulation so that sensory input must be varied. Learning and cognitive processes are important determinants of the initiation of motivated behavior as well as its direction.

The arousal model and the research it stimulated has had an important impact over the years on theoretical ideas about motivated behaviors. It has been one of the major factors leading to the shift from emphasizing internal, deficit signals as initiators of feeding, drinking, and other motivated behaviors to recognizing the role of incentive stimuli, expectancy, and various cognitive factors. These recent developments in the theoretical interpretations of motivated behaviors are considered in some detail in Section III.

C. BRAIN SELF-STIMULATION

As indicated earlier, the 1950s was a period of dramatic discoveries in the neurobiology of motivated behaviors. One of these which deserves special consideration is the serendipitous observation, made in the course of an attempt to stimulate the reticular activating system, that the rat will actively seek electrical stimulation of its brain (Olds and Milner, 1954). There was immediate excitement about this impressive phenomenon since it appeared that the neural substrate for reinforcement had been discovered. It would now be possible to deal directly with the central mechanisms for behavioral reinforcement.

Many investigators turned their attention to the investigation of self-stimulation and of the mechanisms of central reinforcement, and a large number of papers on the subject appeared during the next few years (for reviews, see Olds, 1962; Milner, 1970, 1975; Mogenson and Cioé, 1975). Several of the reports indicated apparent dissimilarities between central and conventional reinforcers: acquisition of an operant response and its extinction occurred more quickly when reinforced with brain stimulation than with a conventional reinforcer (Olds and Milner, 1954; Seward *et al.,* 1959; Deutsch and Howarth, 1963); animals did not perform normally on a partial reinforcement schedule (Brodie *et al.,* 1960; Culberson *et al.,* 1966); secondary reinforcement was not established (Seward *et al.,* 1959; Mogenson, 1965) when brain stimulation was used. Later it was shown that such differences between central and conventional reinforcers were largely due to procedural differences, particularly in the delay of reinforcement and the deprivation state of the animal (Trowill *et al.,* 1969). The central reinforcement subserving self-stimulation apparently involves the same mechanisms that subserve conventional reinforcers.

It is not surprising that brain self-stimulation was interpreted initially from the viewpoint of the then popular drive-reduction theory. Reinforcing brain stimulation, as Olds (1956) suggested, "must excite some of the nerve cells that would be excited by the satisfaction of the basic drives—hunger, thirst, sex and so forth" (p. 15). In accordance with the drive-reduction theory, Olds was assuming that the reinforcement of an operant response was due to the brain stimulation activating a neural system concerned with reducing one of the basic biological drives. However, observations were made a few years later which suggested just the opposite; feeding (Hoebel and Teitelbaum, 1962; Margules and Olds, 1962), drinking (Mogenson and Stevenson, 1966), and sexual behavior (Herberg, 1963; Caggiula and Hoebel, 1966) were elicited from electrode sites highly effective for brain self-stimulation. It was paradoxical, from the viewpoint of the drive reduction theory of reinforcement, that an animal pressed a lever to stimulate its hypothalamus when the stimulation apparently made it hungry or thirsty.

Attempts to resolve this paradox made it clear that the terms drive and drive-reduction do not have an exclusive role in explaining motivated behaviors. Feeding and drinking elicited by hypothalamic stimulation (as well as normal spontaneous feeding and drinking) do not necessarily result from the activation of neural systems that transmit or integrate deficit signals. Feeding and drinking may result from the brain stimulation mimicking incentive stimuli ("appetite-whetting" stimuli) associated with ingestive behaviors. Certain sensory stimuli, such as salty and sweet solutions, are very effective reinforcers (Young, 1959; Pfaffmann, 1960) even in the absence of biological needs and deficits; a sensory stimulus "can function as a reinforcer in its own right" (Pfaffmann, 1960, p. 207). From this point of view it is not a paradox that animals self-stimulate "feeding sites" and "drinking sites"; the brain stimulation is activating neural systems that transmit incentive stimuli associated with drinking, feeding, and other motivated behaviors (see Section III,C).

Campbell (1971) has demonstrated that various species of fish, amphibians, reptiles, and mammals will self-stimulate to obtain peripheral stimuli. With fish and crocodiles, for example, a goal-post electrode assembly placed in the water tank permitted the animal to turn on electrical stimulation by breaking a light beam to a photocell. These animals swam back and forth in order to stimulate skin receptors which send signals to the "central reward pathways." Campbell suggested that such peripheral self-stimulation has much in common with intracranial self-stimulation.

The results of experiments by Pfaffman and Young, as well as those from Campbell's peripheral self-stimulation experiments, suggest that brain self-stimulation is the consequence of activating pathways of the brain that transmit signals from natural reinforcers. These include inputs from taste and smell and other exteroceptive stimuli, but also, as we indicate later (Section V), may include proprioceptive and interoceptive inputs. In higher species the "central reward pathways" are also activated by cognitive activities. Campbell (1971), after noting the pleasure one gets from mathematics, science, chess, or crossword puzzles, maintains: "Only in the human brain can thinking activate the limbic pleasure areas." It appears that in man and other animals with complex brains, reinforcement and motivated behaviors depend on neural processes concerned with higher cognitive functions as well as those that process exteroceptive, interoceptive, and proprioceptive inputs.

In the next section we expand on the role of incentive stimuli in motivated behavior. Then, after discussing the role of noradrenergic and dopaminergic pathways in feeding, drinking, and self-stimulation in Section IV, we consider in Section V what is known about the neural mechanisms of incentive motivation. In brief, Section V is an attempt to relate what is dealt with in Section IV to Sections II and III.

III. Changing Theoretical Views of the Psychology of Motivation and Their Implications for the Neurobiology of Motivated Behavior

An important task of the physiological psychologist and of other neuroscientists, as indicated earlier, is to elucidate the neural mechanisms that subserve motivated behaviors. However, since it is the behavior of the animal that indicates what neural mechanisms to look for (Weiskrantz, 1973), it is necessary to consider motivated behavior from the psychological point of view. In this section we indicate how our theoretical ideas about the psychology of motivation have changed in recent years. This change in emphasis has important implications when we consider in later sections the role of central catecholaminergic pathways in drinking, feeding, and other motivated behaviors.

A. HISTORICAL PERSPECTIVE

Fifteen or twenty years ago the emphasis was almost exclusively on internal, deficit signals as initiators of drinking and feeding and other motivated behaviors (see Section II). This emphasis was due in part to the popularity of the drive-reduction theory and to the view that motivated behaviors are elicited by biological deficits and imbalances of homeostasis that produce such drives as hunger and thirst (Hull, 1943). Because of the general acceptance of this view, reports of motivated behaviors not initiated by imbalances of homeostasis (Harlow, 1953; Hebb, 1955) were virtually ignored.

In more recent years the popularity of the drive-reduction theory and the stress on internal deficit signals have declined. This has resulted in part from the inability of the drive-reduction theory to deal with various aspects of motivated behaviors (Appley, 1970), in part because of the impact of arousal theory (Malmo, 1959), in part from studies of brain self-stimulation (Mogenson and Cioé, 1975), and especially from the emergence of incentive motivation (Bindra, 1968; Bolles, 1972) as a viable alternative. The view that has emerged is that motivated behavior results not only from the *"push" of internal, deficit signals* but also from the *"pull" of external, incentive stimuli.* Furthermore, since mammalian behavior is characterized by the ability to adapt to an ever-changing environment, brain mechanisms have developed, especially in higher species with more complex nervous systems, which enable the animal to make adaptive, behavioral responses that anticipate homeostatic deficits (LeMagnen, 1967; Fitzsimons, 1972; Mogenson and Huang, 1973). Contemporary analysis of motivated behavior must account for anticipatory behavior both as it relates to the expectation of reward (incentive motivation) and to the more long-range modifications of consummatory patterns which are acquired in anticipation of homeostatic deficits. According to Oatley (1973), animals are able to make responses that are purposive and that anticipate their needs because they utilize mental processes that "represent within the brain the nature of the outside world" (p. 12).

B. ANTICIPATORY FEEDING AND DRINKING

In a recent comprehensive review, Fitzsimons (1972) has concluded that animals normally do not drink in response to water-deficit signals; thirst occurs only as an emergency mechanism. "When food and water are freely available, when climatic conditions are stable, and when the animal's activities remain the same from one day to the next, thirst is probably never experienced. In normal circumstances drinking is largely anticipatory of future needs for water and seems to be governed by oropharyngeal cues from the diet, by habit, and by an innate circadian rhythm; it is not dependent on a present need for water" (Fitzsimons, 1972, p. 548).

In order to demonstrate that normal drinking is not signaled by water deficit, Fitzsimons (1972) administered water by continuous infusion via a gastric fistula. Although the rats received their normal water requirements in this way, they still drank an appreciable volume of water. Rats typically drink more than is needed to maintain water balance (Dicker and Nunn, 1957; Evered and Mogenson, 1974), and apparently, as indicated above, drinking to deficit signals may occur only under emergency conditions.

A good demonstration that an animal may feed in anticipation of its needs is a study by LeMagnen (1959). Rats were given three 1-hour meals per day spaced 7 hours apart. When one of the meals was withdrawn, food intake increased initially for the meal that followed the 15-hour time gap. However, within a few days food intake increased substantially for the meal that preceded this gap. The results of this study indicate that the feeding responses of animals tend to anticipate their needs.

It has been reported that rats fed two meals a day engage in running behavior prior to the meal (Bolles and Moot, 1973). These investigators have concluded that this anticipatory running is controlled not by a need state but by temporal stimuli that enable the animal to anticipate the availability of food. Oatley (1973) suggested that, for such nonhomeostatic ingestive behavior, the animal utilizes representational processes of the characteristics of the environment "deployed not in the feedback mode so that deficits are corrected, but in a feed-forward mode so that they can be anticipated" (p. 221).

Although the behavioral evidence makes it clear that behavioral responses may anticipate homeostatic deficits, there has been little interest (beyond suggesting that different neural substrates are involved, Kissileff, 1973) in investigating the neural systems that subserve such anticipatory responses. Typically the effects of lesions or stimulation on feeding and drinking behavior have been interpreted in terms of a deficit or homeostatic model. It is especially appropriate, therefore, to describe the results of some recent experiments that implicate a neural pathway which projects through the zona incerta in nonregulatory drinking (Fig. 3).

Small bilateral lesions of the zona incerta (ZI) were shown to reduce ad libitum water intake in rats by 20–25% with food intake remaining unchanged (Huang and Mogenson, 1974). This hypodipsia could not be attributed to a deficit in the drinking response to signals of water need. Tests with hypertonic saline and polyethylene glycol demonstrated that ZI lesions did not reduce drinking to osmotic and hypovolemic signals (Evered and Mogenson, 1973, 1974). Although lesioned animals drank slightly less than controls after various periods of water deprivation, the difference in intake was independent of the length of water deprivation; in fact, rats with lesions of the ZI seem to regulate their water intake more precisely according to need (Evered and Mogenson, 1973). Since lesions of the ZI did not disrupt regulatory drinking it was decided to investigate the possibility that neural systems that contribute to nonregulatory drinking were damaged (Evered and Mogenson, 1974). Rats were placed on a liquid diet that met their nutritional and water requirements. They were in good health and continued to gain

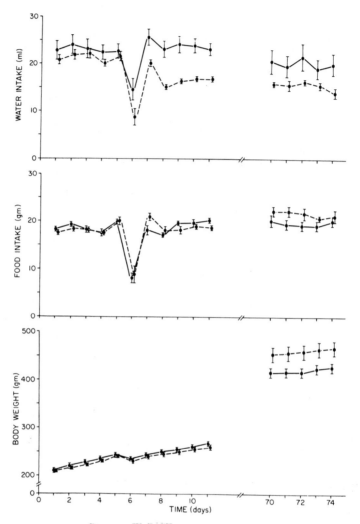

FIG. 3. Effects of bilateral lesions of the zona incerta on water intake, food intake, and body weight. Lesions were made on day 6. Note the decrease in water intake immediately after the lesion and also two months later. Food intake was not depressed, ---, lesion; ——, sham (from Evered and Mogenson, 1974).

weight. However, as reported by other investigators they continued to drink 7–8 ml of water per day when water was available (see Table I, column 1). After lesions of the ZI, this extra drinking did not occur. It is concluded that (1) rats typically overdrink and in this way water intake anticipates water needs, and (2) a pathway through the ZI contributes to this nonregulatory or anticipatory drinking.

TABLE I

EFFECT OF ZONA INCERTA (ZI) LESIONS ON DAILY
WATER INTAKE IN RATS ON LIQUID AND REGULAR
SOLID DIET[a]

| Group | Liquid diet | | Solid diet after lesion |
	Before lesion	After lesion	
ZI lesions	6.8 ± 2.0	0.9 ± 0.4^b	24.1 ± 0.7^b
($N = 7$)			
Sham lesions	7.2 ± 1.9	7.9 ± 1.3	37.4 ± 2.2

[a]Liquid diet was designed to meet all water requirements so that water intake occurring beyond this could be considered excessive. Values are daily water intake (mean ± SEM) in milliliters.

[b]$p < 0.01$.

In another experiment the requirements for water, and therefore the amount of regulatory drinking, were varied by changing the concentration of protein in the diet (Evered and Mogenson, 1974). Water intake was increased substantially when rats were given a high-protein diet. Rats with lesions of the ZI also increased their water intake, but it remained lower than that of the controls. After ZI lesions it appears that rats drink more in accordance with need because the nonregulatory or anticipatory component of water intake has been eliminated.

C. INCENTIVE MOTIVATION

Troland (1928) and Young (1936) were among the first to argue that animals have an innate preference for stimuli such as sweet taste and biologically significant odors. Appropriate stimuli of this sort initiate drinking and feeding in the absence of water and energy deficits. In addition to their affinity for chemosensitive stimulation (Sheffield and Roby, 1950; Long and Tapp, 1967), a number of species have evidenced a strong need to engage in exploratory and manipulatory behavior (Berlyne, 1950; Butler, 1953; Harlow, 1953; Montgomery, 1953). Higher primates are motivated by puzzles and other tasks requiring cognitive skills (Harlow, 1953), and this trend culminates in man, who derives pleasure from such cognitive activities as chess, mathematics, philosophy, and science (Hebb, 1955). These examples, as indicated earlier, stress the need for a model of motivation that emphasizes the role of sensory stimulation and cognitive processes as an alternative to one based solely on reduction of deficit and noxious stimuli.

During the last few years, psychological theorists have given increasing attention to external, nondeficit signals and to cognitive factors in motivated behaviors, including the role of imagery (Mowrer, 1960; Pribram, 1971). One of the leading theoretical approaches is designated incentive motivation, and the views of one of its leading exponents will be outlined. According to Bolles (1972) incentive motivation is derived from the association of certain salient stimuli with the presentation of rewards (i.e., food or other goal objects); these incentive stimuli may be situational cues characteristic of the place in which the goal object was located, or specific features of the goal object, such as its smell. Bolles has suggested that what is learned in most learning situations is that "certain events, cues (S), predict certain other biologically important events, consequences (S*). An animal may incidentally show new responses, but what it learns is an expectancy that represents and corresponds to the S-S* contingency" (p. 402). A link or association is established between stimuli which precede acquisition of the goal object and the object itself. Once incentive properties are acquired stimuli can initiate behavior by enabling the animal to anticipate the consequences of its action. This is because a second type of association is established—a link (R-S*) between the animal's behavior (R) and the consequences of that behavior (S*).

Many stimuli have only the capacity to signal the presence and location of food, a potential mate, or other biologically significant objects. This cue function (S) depends primarily on prior experience and the strength of previous associations (S–S*). However, certain stimuli, particularly those transmitted by chemical sensory systems, possess both S and S* properties. They not only signal the presence and location of goal objects, but also provide positive feedback that maintains the consummatory behavior once the goal objects have been attained. According to Pfaffmann (1960), such stimuli are projected directly to limbic and other structures concerned with reinforcement, and it is activation of reinforcement systems that makes them biologically significant. Internal, deficit signals are not considered by Bolles to have a unique role, as they did in the drive-reduction theory. However, the central states they initiate influence gating mechanisms which permit appropriate sensory inputs to activate reinforcement systems of the brain (Valenstein, 1966; Bindra, 1968).

Finally, it should be stressed that these changing theoretical views have implications for the study of the neural mechanisms of feeding, drinking, and other motivated behaviors. In future experiments more consideration should be given to the possibility that lesions disrupt and stimulation activates neural systems that deal with incentive stimuli for feeding and drinking. Previously the usual practice has been to consider only the possibility that a lesion disrupts feeding or drinking by destroying mechanisms concerned with deficit signals. Similarly feeding and drinking elicited by electrical stimulation has typically been attributed to the activation of neural pathways which transmit or integrate deficits. As indicated earlier, feeding and drinking may anticipate

deficits. The animal utilizes memory and other cognitive processes to anticipate its deficits for food and water. Although the addition of incentive
motivation, expectancy, and anticipatory feeding and drinking to regulatory
ingestive behaviors may appear unduly complicated, it appears foolish to
continue to sacrifice understanding on the altar of parsimony. Many aspects
of motivation can be accounted for only in terms of associative and cognitive
processes, and it will be necessary to direct attention to the neural mechanisms underlying these functions.

IV. Chemical Neuroanatomy: Catecholamine Pathways and Motivated Behavior

The vigorous investigation of brain mechanisms of motivated behaviors that
was undertaken in the 1950s and 1960s has continued up to the present.
After initial focusing on hypothalamic mechanisms subserving feeding, drinking, and other motivated behaviors (see Section II), the scope of the studies
soon expanded to include other brain sites, particularly limbic forebrain
structures. For some time, however, the theoretical analysis remained essentially unchanged with the exception that limbic forebrain structures were
considered to exert modulatory influences on hypothalamic drive systems
(Mogenson, 1973). It was not until a new chemical anatomy of the brain,
based on mapping transmitter-specific pathways with histochemical and histofluorescence techniques, and other developments (discussed elsewhere,
Mogenson, 1974a) forced a reassessment of the role of the hypothalamus and
other neural structures in motivated behaviors that a revision of our theoretical ideas occurred. The impact of chemical neuroanatomy on studies of the
neurobiology of motivated behaviors will now be considered.

A. CATECHOLAMINE PATHWAYS

During the 1960s neurochemical and histochemical studies showed that
catecholamine (CA) pathways project from the midbrain and lower brain
stem through the region of the lateral hypothalamus to forebrain structures.
Using biochemical assays a group of workers in Chicago demonstrated that
the levels of norepinephrine and other biogenic amines were lower in telencephalic structures following lesions of the lateral hypothalamus (Heller and
Harvey, 1963; Heller and Moore, 1965, 1968). Their results suggested that an
ascending monaminergic pathway followed the medial forebrain bundle.
Swedish workers have used the techniques of histofluorescence (Falck *et al.,*
1962), immunohistochemistry (Fuxe *et al.,* 1970), and microspectro-
fluorimetry (Björklund *et al.,* 1968) to identify the cell bodies of catecholaminergic neurons, mainly located in the midbrain, pons, and medulla oblon-

gata (Dahlström and Fuxe, 1964), and to demonstrate their fiber projections. These techniques, in combination with lesions and pharmacological manipulations, have permitted the detailed description of the course of catecholamine systems through the brain (Andén *et al.*, 1966; Jacobowitz and Palkovits, 1974; Lindvall and Björklund, 1974; Palkovits and Jacobowitz, 1974; Ungerstedt, 1971a). The pathways, shown in Fig. 4, are primarily ascending, projecting from the midbrain and brain stem to a variety of diencephalic and telencephalic structures including the hypothalamus, septum, hippocampus, striatum, and cerebral cortex.

Initial reports emphasized that the ascending noradrenergic (NA) fibers were distributed in dorsal and ventral pathways, the former originating mainly from the dorsolateral region of the locus coeruleus (Olson and Fuxe, 1971; Ungerstedt, 1971a) and the latter from subcoeruleus cell bodies (Olson and Fuxe, 1972) and nuclei in the medulla oblongata (A1–A5, A7) (Fuxe *et al.*, 1970; Ungerstedt, 1971a). The ascending dorsal NA bundle projects diffusely to the cerebral cortex and hippocampus by a number of different routes. Tohyama and co-workers (1974) have recently described three different ways by which these NA fibers enter into the cerebral cortex: (1) by way of the internal capsule, (2) via a pathway through the external capsule, and (3) by a pathway through the anterior septal region. The NA terminals originating from the locus coeruleus are located throughout the neocortical areas and most of the older cortical areas (Lindvall *et al.*, 1974a). Fibers from the locus coeruleus reach the hippocampal formation by way of the medial forebrain bundle, where they ascend to the anterior septal region before turning caudalward in the cingulum as far as the retrosplenial area, from where they project to the hippocampus. A previously undescribed component of the dorsal NA bundle also appears to give rise to extensive projections to thalamic, metathalamic, and pretectal areas. The thalamic projections include ventral, lateral, and anterior nuclear complexes as well as the geniculate bodies (Lindvall *et al.*, 1974b).

There appears to be some confusion as to whether the subcoeruleus and medullary projections of the ventral NA bundle are separate systems as they appear to innervate different regions of the diencephalon. In fact, Maeda and Shimizu (1972) have proposed a distinct intermediate pathway originating in the subcoeruleus area and projecting mainly to the periventricular and medial preoptic regions of the hypothalamus. Recently it has been suggested that these subcoeruleus axons may be quite different in amine metabolism from those of the medullary component of the ventral NA bundle, which is a major source of hypothalamic projections (Tohyama *et al.*, 1974). This medullary aspect is thought to innervate the basolateral areas of the hypothalamus and preoptic nuclei as well as the ventral stria terminalis (Olson and Fuxe, 1972).

In addition to these major pathways, ascending NA pathways have also

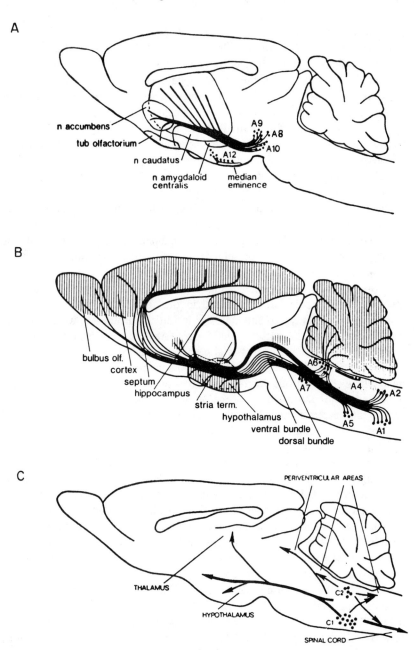

FIG. 4. Sagittal section of the brain showing (A) the ascending dopaminergic pathways, (B) the ascending noradrenergic pathways (from Ungerstedt, 1971a), and (C) the ascending adrenergic pathways (from Hökfelt *et al.*, 1974a).

been identified, using the more sensitive glyoxylic acid method. This procedure has revealed a NA component of the dorsal longitudinal fasciculus that has been called the dorsal periventricular bundle. This system originates in an elongated region located in the dorsal raphe, mesencephalic central gray, and periventricular gray of the caudal thalamus, an area designated as A11. Fibers in this system form a thalamic and hypothalamic periventricular system, projecting to medial and midline thalamic, epithalamic, and pretectal areas. A ventral periventricular bundle has also been identified in the supramamillary region and coursing rostrally into the dorsomedial nucleus where it joins the dorsal periventricular bundle to form an ascending hypothalamic periventricular NA fiber system (Lindvall *et al.*, 1974b).

The cell bodies of the dopaminergic (DA) pathways have been localized, by means of histochemical (Andén *et al.*, 1966; Dahlström and Fuxe, 1964) and silver staining techniques (Hedreen and Chalmers, 1972) to regions in the hindbrain. One of the most prominent regions (A9) is the zona compacta of the substantia nigra, and some cell bodies have been found to extend over and into the medial aspect of the medial lemniscus (Palkovits and Jacobowitz, 1974). DA cell bodies are also found in the area dorsolateral to the interpeduncular nucleus (A10) and caudally in the cell group A8, which extends dorsolaterally into the nucleus cuneiformis (A8). Axons arising from the A9 cell bodies form the nigroneostriatal pathway, which projects rostrally within the medial forebrain bundle through the dorsolateral region of the hypothalamus, where they fan out dorsolaterally before entering the caudate-putamen. A second major DA bundle, the mesolimbic pathway, originates in the A10 region and ascends medial to the nigroneostriatal pathway in the dorsal reaches of the medial forebrain bundle. After bifurcating at the level of the anterior commissure, part of the mesolimbic system innervates the nucleus accumbens and another aspect projects ventrolaterally to the olfactory tubercle (Ungerstedt, 1971a). In addition to these well established DA projections, the existence of DA terminals in the limbic and cerebral cortices has recently been demonstrated (Thierry *et al.*, 1973, 1974; Hökfelt *et al.*, 1974b; Squires, 1974). The DA terminals in the cerebral cortex have been confirmed histochemically after destruction of ascending NA pathways (Berger *et al.*, 1974; Lindvall *et al.*, 1974a). Dopaminergic innervation is localized in the frontal cortex, the anterior cingulate cortex, the ventral aspect of the entorhinal cortex, and the transition zone along the rhinal fissure. This dense and localized innervation is in contrast to the diffuse cortical projections of the dorsal NA system. As to the origin of these DA terminals, Lindvall and co-workers (1974a) have shown that lesions restricted to the lateral portions of the substantia nigra deplete DA terminals in the ipsilateral anterior cingulate cortex while sparing the frontal cortex. Conversely, bilateral destruction of the dorsal and caudal aspects of the A10 cell group results in denervation of DA fibers in the frontal cortex, but not in the anterior cingulate. It is of interest to note that these authors have characterized all dopaminergic neuron systems in the brain as having "topographically ordered and restricted projections" (p. 330) and that the neocortical innervation conforms to this pattern.

On the basis of this brief review of the neuroanatomy of central CA pathways, it is obvious that a complex picture is emerging. Furthermore, the recent localization of epinephrine-containing neurons by immunohistofluorescence which appear identical to some of the CA cell bodies and terminals previously identified by the Falck-Hillarp technique (Hökfelt et al., 1974a), add to the complexity. Two epinephrine containing nerve cell groups have been located, the larger situated in the rostral medulla oblongata, lateral to the olivary complex. These epinephrine cells are distributed through the same rostral area of the nucleus reticularis lateralis as the CA neurons in the rostral part of the A1 cell group. A second group of cells is found in the dorsal region of the reticular formation ventral and medial to the vestibular nuclei. The caudal aspect of this cell group is located ventromedial to the nucleus tractus solitarius in close proximity to the A2 cell bodies. An axon bundle from these adrenergic cell groups appears to ascend with part of the ventral NA bundle in the reticular formation. Further mapping of the ascending adrenergic pathways will have to await lesion experiments, but in the meantime, it is important to consider that some of the functions ascribed to NA pathways may well be subserved by epinephrine systems. In fact, a constant reappraisal of the functional correlates of monamine systems will be essential if we are to benefit fully from the advances in chemical neuroanatomy.

B. CATECHOLAMINE PATHWAYS AND INGESTIVE BEHAVIORS

Several years ago it was reported that the application of norepinephrine (NE) to the LH-initiated feeding in rats implicating noradrenergic (NA) neurons in the control of food intake (Grossman, 1962). Later it was shown that lesions of the LH reduce the levels of NE in the forebrain (Heller and Moore, 1965) and that the aphagia from lesions of the LH is reversed by infusing NE into the ventricles (Berger et al., 1971). When the projections of transmitter-specific pathways were mapped with the histofluorescence technique, as described above, it was apparent that NA as well as DA pathways projected through the regions of the hypothalamus which, from lesion studies, were known to be associated with aphagia and adipsia.

The pioneering study of Ungerstedt (1971b), in which destruction of the nigrostriatal DA pathway with the neurotoxic compound 6-hydroxydopamine (6-OH-DA; 2,4,5-trihydroxyphenylethylamine) produced severe aphagia and adipsia, was a major development. Not only did this study introduce a procedure which, when properly used, permitted selective destruction of catecholaminergic neurons, but it also indicated for the first time the possible role of DA neurons in ingestive behaviors. Interestingly, the aphagia and adipsia in Ungerstedt's animals appeared more severe than that observed in the classical syndrome following LH lesions. This was confirmed a few months later in a report by Oltmans and Harvey (1972), who compared the effects of bilateral electrolytic lesions of the nigrostriatal pathway and of the medial forebrain bundle as they pass through the lateral hypothalamus; the locus of the site of the lesions was confirmed by assaying catecholamine levels of telencephalic tissue samples. Again nigrostriatal damage produced more severe effects.

More recent studies (Fibiger *et al.*, 1973; Marshall and Teitelbaum, 1973) have also compared the effects of damaging neurons in the nigrostriatal pathway with the effects of damaging the LH area associated with the classical LH syndrome. Marshall and Teitelbaum (1973) observed aphagia and adipsia following bilateral administration of 6-OH-DA to the substantia nigra (the origin of the DA nigrostriatal fibers). The animals were impaired in feeding to injections of 2-deoxy-D-glucose and in drinking to cellular dehydration or hypovolemia. Also they recovered the control of food and water intake in the same sequence of stages as usually observed in rats with lesions of the LH. Similar results were obtained by Fibiger *et al.* (1973); neurotoxic lesions of the substantia nigra resulted in reduced water intake, prandial drinking, finickiness, and failure to drink after injection of hypertonic saline, all deficits produced by electrolytic lesions of the LH. In this latter study, the effects of the different lesion techniques on catecholamine (CA) activity was measured at a variety of subcortical sites permitting the correlation of regulatory deficits with decreases in CA levels. Bilateral destruction of DA neurons in the substantia nigra was accompanied by a 93% reduction in striatal tyrosine hydroxylase activity. Interestingly, several of the regulatory deficits were greater in rats with LH electrolytic lesions even though they had less damage to the nigrostriatal pathway than rats with neurotoxic lesions of the substantia nigra. It was concluded that the effects of LH lesions cannot be attributed solely to damage of the nigrostriatal pathway as has been suggested by other researchers (Ungerstedt, 1971b; Oltmans and Harvey, 1972; Zigmond and Stricker, 1974). The validity of this conclusion is further emphasized by the recent finding that extrahypothalamic lesions of central trigeminal structures produce aphagia, adipsia, and finickiness. These observations have been interpreted as suggesting that some aspects of the LH syndrome are due to incidental damage to trigeminal fibers of passage (Zeigler and Karten, 1974).

Several investigators have studied the effects of damage to catecholaminergic neurons on ingestive behaviors following intraventricular administration of 6-OH-DA (Zigmond and Stricker, 1972; Breese *et al.*, 1973; Fibiger *et al.*,

1973). Two distinct syndromes have been observed, which appear to be correlated with the amount of depletion of striatal dopamine levels. With moderate reduction of DA levels but large depletion of NE levels animals appear indistinguishable from controls unless subjected to acute homeostatic imbalance produced by glucoprivation, hypovolemia, or exposure to cold (Zigmond and Stricker, 1974). Although physiological compensation to these challenges is normal, the animals do not make appropriate ingestive responses to them. With severe depletion of striatal dopamine levels, produced by pretreating animals with a monoamine oxidase inhibitor prior to 6-OH-DA administration, there are both acute and chronic impairments of ingestive behavior. Unless the animals are given liquid diet by stomach tube, they soon succumb to the effects of the 6-OH-DA. If striatal dopamine is depleted by 98% or more the animals never recover from the aphagia or adipsia, but with 90–98% depletion there is gradual recovery of feeding and drinking in a manner similar to that of rats with electrolytic lesions of the LH (e.g., Epstein and Teitelbaum, 1964), and they progress through the same stages of recovery. Recovery of ingestive behaviors in animals with a permanent 90–98% depletion of striatal dopamine is attributed by Zigmond and Stricker to a functional recovery of damaged DA fibers and to increased synthesis and release of DA from undamaged neurons.

Recently it has been reported that lesions of the orbitofrontal cortex of rats cause severe aphagia and adipsia similar to that produced by lesions of the lateral hypothalamus and DA nigrostriatal pathway (Kolb and Nonneman, 1975). Since DA levels are relatively high in this region of the frontal cortex (Hökfelt *et al.*, 1974b), this interesting observation raises the possibility that damage to some DA fibers which project to the frontal cortex is responsible for these regulatory deficits.

Although aphagia and adipsia are clearly associated with damage to the DA nigrostriatal pathway, a major consideration is whether feeding and drinking are subserved exclusively by this system. In recent reviews of their work in this field, Zigmond and Stricker (1974, and this volume) have concluded that damage to DA neurons is responsible for the disruption of motivated ingestive behavior and Ungerstedt (1974) has reached a similar conclusion. On the other hand, Marshall *et al.* (1974) were reluctant to attribute aphagia and adipsia exclusively to damage to the DA nigrostriatal pathway even though they injected 6-OH-DA into the substantia nigra. Since telencephalic norepinephrine levels were depleted as much as dopamine in the striatum (both by 89%), a possible contribution of noradrenergic pathways could not be excluded.

It is important to note that most of the permanent regulatory deficits to acute homeostatic imbalance are also observed when NE levels are preferentially suppressed. This raises the possibility that NA pathways are involved in ingestive behavior initiated by deficit signals. However, if NA fibers contribute to ingestive behaviors it seems unlikely that the different pathways subserve similar functions. In fact the ventral NA pathway may be associated with satiety rather than the initiation of feeding; it has been reported that, after destruction of the ventral NA pathway, rats become hyperphagic and obese (Ahlskog and Hoebel, 1973; Kapatos and Gold, 1973). It appears that these effects traditionally ascribed to damage to the classical VMH satiety center may be attributed to destruction of the ventral NA bundle which projects along the lateral edge of the VMH (Gold, 1973).

More studies involving discrete lesions of the ascending CA fiber pathways are needed. It would also be profitable to selectively stimulate these pathways, especially if small-diameter electrodes and low current levels are used to increase specificity. This would appear to be especially true in view of the recent demonstration that intraventricular injections of 6-OH-DA produce a severe disruption of stimulation-induced feeding (Phillips and Fibiger, 1973a). Attempts to elicit ingestive behavior with electrical stimulation of the substantia nigra have proved to be unsuccessful although "rebound-feeding" was observed upon termination of the stimulus (Phillips and Fibiger, 1973b). Cioé and Mogenson (1974) were also unable to elicit ingestive behavior from the substantia nigra but when electrodes were directed to the region of the dorsal NA bundle, strong feeding responses were elicited in the absence of stimulation-induced drinking. The latter observation is of particular interest since it has been reported recently that electrical stimulation of the locus coeruleus, the site of origin of the dorsal NA pathway, elicits feeding (Micco, 1974).

C. Catecholamine Pathways and Brain Self-Stimulation

Although self-stimulation is obtained from a variety of hypothalamic, limbic, and extrapyramidal sites, it is well known that the fastest response rates and presumably the strongest central reinforcement are obtained from the region of the lateral hypothalamus-medial forebrain bundle (LH-MFB). For a time it appeared that this might be because of the association of this region with drive systems, such as feeding and drinking (Hoebel, 1969; Mogenson, 1969). However, as we shall see later, more recent evidence suggests that this region is highly effective for self-stimulation because of stimulating ascending noradrenergic and dopaminergic fibers, which are densely concentrated here.

For a number of years there was a good deal of interest in the possibility that the LH-MFB was a central focus for self-stimulation and in determining its relationship with other sites that typically were associated with lower rates of self-stimulation. Several studies involved the investigation of the effects of lesions of the MFB on self-stimulation of rostral sites. Later attempts were made to trace pathways from the LH-MFB focus using microelectrode recording techniques to identify neurons that were activated by stimulation of the LH-MFB (Huang and Routtenberg, 1971; Ito and Olds, 1971; Rolls, 1971a,b), and using histological techniques to trace degenerating fibers from lesions placed at self-stimulation sites in the LH-MFB (Huang and Routtenberg, 1971; Routtenberg, 1971).

The studies that implicated the LH-MFB as a focus for central reinforcement and tested the hypothesis that self-stimulation of limbic forebrain sites involves caudal projections along the MFB (Olds and Olds, 1964; Lorens, 1966; Valenstein and Campbell, 1966; Olds and Olds, 1969) were equivocal. Although decrements in self-stimulation were produced by lesions posterior to the stimulation sites, it was not possible to draw definitive conclusions because of the complexity of the MFB (Millhouse, 1969). Furthermore, a deficit in self-stimulation could result from the lesion damaging rostrally projecting fibers as well as caudally projecting fibers. The histological and electrophysiological results were also equivocal. For example, stimulation of the LH-MFB was shown to activate neurons in the amygdala, an important limbic forebrain structure (Rolls, 1972), as well as in the midbrain (Rolls, 1971a).

The recent interest in chemical neuroanatomy, and in particular with the role of catecholaminergic pathways in central reinforcement, has shifted emphasis from caudally to rostrally projecting pathways associated with self-stimulation. These important developments, which provide a promising lead to understanding the mechanisms of central reinforcement, will now be reviewed.

It was, in fact, several years ago that the suggestion was made that ascending NA neurons are involved in self-stimulation (Dreese, 1966, 1967). However, the significance of this proposal was not appreciated until the new chemical neuroanatomy, based on the mapping of transmitter-specific pathways, began to influence the thinking of investigators concerned with the neural basis of self-stimulation and other motivated behaviors.

There are now several lines of evidence to indicate that NA fibers are associated with self-stimulation. The relevant literature has been reviewed in detail by German and Bowden (1974). The most direct evidence is that self-stimulation is obtained with stimulation of the locus coeruleus (Cooper and Rolls, 1974; Crow, 1972, Crow et al., 1972; Ritter and Stein, 1973), the site from which dorsal NA fibers orginate. Self-stimulation also occurs with electrodes in the ventral NA pathway (Ritter and Stein, 1974) although for a time its role in central reinforcement was uncertain (Arbuthnott et al., 1970, 1971; Clavier and Routtenberg, 1974; German and Bowden, 1974; Stinus and Thierry, 1973). It is of interest to note that self-stimulation occurs at sites in the mesencephalic reticular formation which causes the release of norepinephrine and decreased dopamine release (Arbuthnott et al., 1971). This suggests an interaction between NA and DA systems, specifically the possibility of inhibitory projections from NA self-stimulation sites to DA nigrostriatal neurons to influence activity in extrapyramidal systems.

Neuropharmacological studies provide additional evidence for the role of catecholaminergic pathways in brain self-stimulation. Drugs that inhibit catecholamine synthesis, such as α-methyl-p-tyrosine, and those that deplete catecholamine stores, such as reserpine, produce a decrement in self-stimulation (Olds et al., 1956; Stein, 1962; Poschel and Ninteman, 1966; Cooper et al., 1971). Conversely, self-stimulation is facilitated by drugs that increase catecholamine levels, such as monoamine oxidase inhibitors (Poschel, 1969) or which increase the synaptic release and block the reuptake of catecholamines, such as amphetamine or cocaine (Horovitz et al., 1962; Stein, 1962, 1964; Crow, 1970, Olds, 1970; Domino and Olds, 1972).

On the basis of such pharmacological evidence, Stein has proposed an NA hypothesis of reward, which in turn has received support from a series of elegant perfusion and central injection experiments (Stein and Wise, 1969; Wise and Stein, 1969). More recent evidence of a severe reduction in self-stimulation after destruction of central catecholamines by intraventricular injections of 6-OH-DA has also been interpreted in light of the NA hypothesis (Breese et al., 1971; Stein and Wise, 1971). Inhibition of self-stimulation by phentolamine, an alpha-adrenergic antagonist, but not by the beta-adrenergic blocker propanolol, suggests the mediation of self-stimulation by the alpha-adrenergic system (Hastings and Stutz, 1973).

Despite the evidence in favor of the NA hypothesis, it is becoming apparent that it represents only a partial explanation of the neurochemistry of reward as DA pathways have also been associated with self-stimulation (for a recent review, see German and Bowden, 1974). It was reported by Arbuthnott et al., (1970) that stimulation of sites that were shown in other experiments to be associated with self-stimulation caused the release of dopamine as demonstrated with the fluorescence technique. Self-stimulation has been obtained from a number of sites known to contain DA neurons, such as the substantia nigra (A9) (Routtenberg and Malsbury, 1969; Crow, 1972; Phillips and Fibiger, 1973b), the nucleus accumbens (Rolls, 1971b), and the area adjacent to the intrapenduncular nucleus (A10) (Dreese, 1966, 1967). Since the d- and l-isomers of amphetamine are thought to have differential effects on NA and DA neurons (Coyle and Snyder, 1969; Snyder, 1974), it is possible to identify by pharmacological means the NA and DA substrates of self-stimulation. It was shown that d-amphetamine was approximately ten times more potent than l-amphetamine in increasing self-stimulation with electrodes in an NA pathway whereas the two isomers were equipotent with stimulation of DA neurons of the zona compacta of the substantia nigra (Phillips and Fibiger, 1973c). Similar results were obtained with stimulation of the dorsal

NA pathway and the DA fibers of the nucleus accumbens (Fibiger and Phillips, 1975). Additional pharmacological evidence for DA involvement comes from studies with neuroleptic drugs, which act as relatively selective blockers of DA receptors when given at low doses. Both pimozide and haloperidol produce a large decrease in self-stimulation (Wauquier and Niemegeers, 1972; Liebman and Butcher, 1973). In addition, rats will self-administer apomorphine via a jugular cannula (Baxter *et al.*, 1974). The administration of apomorphine, which is a central dopamine receptor stimulant, in this way is apparently reinforcing because it activates DA (and possibly NA) synapses of the "central reward system."

The effect of 6-OH-DA on self-stimulation was originally thought to provide strong evidence for the NA hypothesis, but these data may also be reinterpreted as supporting DA involvement in self-stimulation. Lippa *et al.* (1973) have reported that 6-OH-DA at doses which destroy a significantly greater number of NA neurons than DA neurons, produces only a temporary depression in self-stimulation. In these studies, the critical variable appears to be pretreatment with a monoamine oxidase inhibitor, such as pargyline. When 6-OH-DA is given in combination with pargyline, whole brain levels of both norepinephrine and dopamine are reduced by 90%, and this in turn results in a sustained decrement in self-stimulation (Phillips *et al.*, 1975). Treatment with 6-OH-DA alone results in a very temporary depression of bar pressing for brain stimulation, confirming Lippa *et al.* (Fig. 5). Lippa *et al.* (1973) also

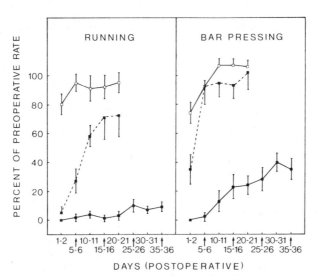

FIG. 5. Mean postinjection self-stimulation rates in Shuttlebox (left panel) and Skinner Box (right panel) for control group (□———□), 6-hydroxydopamine group (■----■), and 6-hydroxydopamine + pargyline group (■———■).

presented additional evidence that is at variance with the NA hypothesis. Neither the alpha-adrenergic blocker phentolamine nor FLA-63, a potent inhibitory of dopamine-β-oxidase, had a significant effect on self-stimulation at electrode sites in the hypothalamus, suggesting an exclusive role for DA.

In summary, the stimulation and neuropharmacological studies reviewed in this section clearly support the role of catecholaminergic (CA) pathways in central reinforcement, and it appears that the DA nigrostriatal, the dorsal and ventral NA pathways are all associated with self-stimulation.[2] Regions of the brain, such as the medial forebrain bundle, where CA neurons are the most densely concentrated are associated with the highest rates of self-stimulation (German and Bowden, 1974).

Although in this section rostrally projecting DA and NA pathways have been emphasized, we do not intend to imply that other transmitter-specific pathways may not be involved in brain self-stimulation. Furthermore, the pathways may not all be rostral ones. A few years ago there was considerable interest in caudal projections, and recently, using microelectrode recording techniques in conjunction with chronic stimulation of self-stimulation sites, Rolls and Cooper (1974) have identified a possible pathway that originates in the frontal cortex and projects to the brain stem, passing near the central gray. A good deal of work remains to be done before the pathways for brain self-stimulation are completely demonstrated.

V. Catecholamine Pathways and Motivated Behaviors: Implications and Future Prospects

It was shown in the preceding sections that DA and NA pathways are associated with drinking, feeding, and brain self-stimulation. We now consider some of the implications of this association in the context of the theoretical developments discussed in Sections II and III. We speculate about the direction of future research and raise questions that need to be answered.

At the outset it should be pointed out that we are not suggesting that motivated behaviors can be explained entirely by studies of DA and NA

[2] It should be noted that a recent electrophysiological study involving, among a number of sites in pons and medulla, microelectrode recordings from locus coeruleus failed to provide evidence of direct activation of ascending NA neurons during self-stimulation of the lateral hypothalamus (Cooper and Rolls, 1974). Although some neurons in the locus coeruleus were activated transsynaptically from the self-stimulation sites, none were activated antidromically. As suggested by Cooper and Rolls, this could mean that direct activation of the dorsal NA neurons is not necessary for self-stimulation to occur. Alternatively, the results may indicate that self-stimulation was due to activation of neurons of the dorsal NA pathway not recorded from, or to activation of fibers of the ventral NA pathway or the DA nigrostriatal pathway.

pathways. In fact there is a danger that the current intense interest in CA pathways will divert attention away from other neural mechanisms. Future research is likely to implicate other transmitter-specific pathways. Also pathways that project caudally from limbic structures and the frontal cortex to the hypothalamus and the midbrain have been shown to have at least a modulatory role in motivated behaviors (Mogenson, 1973).

Our goal, which has been implicit in the discussion of the preceding section, is merely to consider the role of DA and NA pathways in the initiation of feeding, drinking, and self-stimulation.

A. MOTIVATED BEHAVIORS INITIATED BY DEFICIT STIMULI

More than a decade ago, Morgane (1961) suggested that aphagia and adipsia resulting from hypothalamic lesions might be due to destruction of fiber pathways rather than integrative sites. It is only recently, however, that this idea has been taken seriously. Since the pioneering study of Ungerstedt (1971b), there has been increasing interest in the role of catecholaminergic pathways in feeding and drinking. From the results of several studies, reviewed in the preceding section, it is clear that NA and DA pathways have an important role in feeding, drinking, and self-stimulation.[3]

It is tempting to merely substitute pathways for centers (e.g., LH appetite center and VMH satiety center) and to think of the neural mechanisms much as before. However, this would be a serious mistake; an important goal of future research is to determine the complete neural circuitry of which DA and NA pathways are a part. On the input side we need to know whether the specific DA and NA pathways are activated by primary deficit signals for hunger and thirst or by incentive stimuli that initiate drinking and feeding. On the response side it is necessary to determine the relationship of DA and NA pathways to the neural systems for motor control. We also need to consider the possible role of these CA pathways in memory and other cognitive processes and the possibility that they contribute to ingestive responses that depend on experience and habit. What is the role of DA and NA pathways in drinking and feeding behaviors which anticipate water and energy deficits?

In most of the discussions of the role of DA and NA pathways in ingestive behaviors, there has been an implicit assumption that they are involved in regulatory feeding and drinking. Indeed, as pointed out earlier, there is a

---

[3] Another approach to investigating pathways involved in ingestive behaviors has been the use of knife cuts (Albert and Storlien, 1969; Gold, 1970; Sclafani and Grossman, 1969). The results of these studies have been particularly valuable in providing new ideas about the role of the ventromedial nucleus of the hypothalamus and in suggesting important connections between limbic and hypothalamic sites.

deficiency in responding to water and energy deficit signals following damage to CA and, in particular, DA pathways. Furthermore, neuropharmacological evidence suggests that CA, and particularly DA, pathways are concerned with the drinking response to extracellular thirst stimuli related to angiotensin, whereas drinking initiated by intracellular thirst is mediated by cholinergic pathways (Setler, 1973). Therefore, it is understandable that a great deal of emphasis has been given to the possible role of these pathways in transmitting or integrating signals from receptors that monitor the depletion or repletion of body water or lipids or amino acids or rate of intracellular glucose utilization. However, feeding and drinking are initiated in a variety of ways, and deficits in ingestive behavior following damage to CA pathways do not necessarily mean a disruption of mechanisms that are limited to regulatory feeding and drinking.

B. Motivated Behaviors Initiated by Incentive Stimuli

Ingestive behaviors may also be initiated by incentive stimuli. If deficit signals and homeostatic, regulatory systems are primarily emergency mechanisms, as suggested above, incentive stimuli for anticipatory drinking and feeding may be very important in ensuring an appropriate intake of water and food. Therefore, in future studies it will be necessary to consider the role of DA, NA, and other transmitter-specific pathways in drinking and feeding subserved by incentive stimuli.

A prominent effect of lesions of the nigrostriatal DA pathway, as indicated earlier, is sensory neglect (Marshall and Teitelbaum, 1973; Ungerstedt, 1974). Therefore, failure to feed and drink following such lesions may be due, in part at least, to a deficit in responding to incentive stimuli that initiate ingestive behaviors.

According to Bolles, external incentive cues (S) become associated with biologically significant events (S*). In the laboratory this might be a tone that has been paired with food; in a natural setting a variety of potential stimuli could elicit an expectancy of food. A relatively permanent trace of the association of S and S* is established in the central nervous system, and this stored association (memory trace) can subsequently initiate behavioral responses. An expectancy has been established and the animal may utilize this expectancy when it initiates a feeding response or some other motivated behavior.

What is being suggested by this formulation of incentive motivation is that memory contributes to the initiation of motivated behavior. Although the neural substrates of memory have proved to be elusive over the years, the results of many studies suggest that the most complex structures of the brain are involved, including cerebral cortex, hippocampus, and reticular formation (Jasper and Doane, 1968).

In a series of ingenious experiments, Olds and his colleagues have used electrophysiological techniques in chronic animals to study neurons involved in the transcription and storage of information that permits an animal to anticipate a biologically significant event. In the initial experiments rats were trained to remain motionless while awaiting a food reward. During this period of food anticipation neurons of the hippocampus increased their rate of discharge (Olds, 1965, 1967). In subsequent experiments recordings were also made from "anticipatory neurons" in the midbrain; these neurons accelerated their discharge rate in the time period immediately preceding the presentation of food (Olds et al., 1969; Olds and Hirano, 1969). Some animals were trained to three different auditory stimuli (S) each of which was followed by a different S* (food, water, no reward). By manipulating deprivation conditions, it was shown that neurons of the midbrain discharged faster in response to the tone signaling the S* appropriate to the deprivation (Phillips and Olds, 1969).

Recently M. E. Olds (1973) has reported that neurons in the hypothalamus also increase their rate of discharge when anticipating food. She suggested that these changes " . . . are viewed as signifying a participation of the hypothalamic region in the cognitive processes, not as the primary 'informational process' but as a region where input-output sequences are related to positive reinforcements" (p. 95). When the animal begins to feed the hypothalamic units are inhibited (Hamburg, 1971).

It would be of great interest to utilize Olds' techniques and to record from DA neurons in the substantia nigra or NA neurons in the locus coeruleus. There is only suggestive evidence, from self-stimulation experiments (see Section V,E), that DA and NA pathways are involved in transmitting incentive stimuli. Experiments utilizing the Olds techniques would provide direct evidence by showing whether DA and NA neurons respond to incentive stimuli.

The possible role of CA pathways in incentive motivation raises another set of intriguing questions, which awaits future investigation. The importance of memory processes in incentive motivation has been repeatedly emphasized, and this in turn leads one to consider the possible role of DA and/or NA pathways in the association of incentive cues (S) with biologically significant events (S*) and furthermore leads one to consider how these pathways contribute to the permanent storage of the association. Recently, Crow (1973) has made the interesting suggestion that external incentive cues activate the nigrostriatal DA pathway and that biologically significant events activate the dorsal NA pathway. It will also be necessary to consider whether the DA and/or NA pathways are involved when this S–S* association is utilized to initiate a feeding response or some other goal-directed behavior. With respect to the role of ascending CA pathways in the consolidation of memory, recent experiments have implicated the nigrostriatal DA pathway. When this pathway was stimulated immediately after the acquisition of a passive avoidance response there was a marked retention deficit 24 hours later (Routtenberg and Holzman, 1973). A similar effect on retention of a one-trial appetitive response was also produced by stimulation of the nigrostriatal DA pathway (Phillips *et al.*, 1975). The role of the ascending NA pathways in memory consolidation awaits experimental investigation, as does the role of the NA and DA pathways in the initiation of goal-directed behaviors by S–S* associations.

C. The Initiation of Behavior

It should be pointed out that CA pathways may not be involved exclusively with feeding and drinking or, for that matter, with any specific motivated behavior. In fact, from recent neuropharmacological studies of tranquilizing drugs it would appear that CA pathways have as much to do with schizophrenia as they do with ingestive behaviors (Hökfelt *et al.*, 1974b; Matthysse, 1974; Snyder, 1974). In this section we consider alternatives to the view that the deficits following damage to CA pathways are specific to responses initiated by primary or secondary hunger and thirst stimuli. Evidence is considered which suggests that the deficits may be the result of disrupting motor functions, sensory functions, sensory–motor integration or behavioral alertness and arousal.

The DA nigrostriatal pathway has been implicated for some time in motor functions. It is well known that Parkinsonian patients, in whom this DA pathway is diseased, have difficulty in translating the "intention to respond" (e.g., pick up a glass from the table) into a specific response, although they may be perfectly capable of making prompt reflexive movements (e.g., grabbing the glass as it topples from the table). Recent evidence indicates that the DA fibers project diffusely to the cerebral cortex as well as to the striatum (Thierry *et al.*, 1973; Hökfelt *et al.*, 1974b). The dorsal NA pathway also projects diffusely to the cerebral cortex and hippocampus (Olson and Fuxe, 1971). Jouvet (1972) has suggested that the nigrostriatal DA and dorsal NA pathways may be concerned with the maintenance of behavioral arousal and with mediating cortical activation, respectively. When the substantia nigra, the origin of the DA nigrostriatal pathway, was lesioned, cats showed akinesia and a lack of behavioral arousal and responsiveness (Jones *et al.*, 1973). Some showed a failure to drink and feed and had to be force-fed. In general the behavioral deficits were similar to those observed by Ungerstedt

(1971b) in the rat. When the locus coeruleus and other sites of NA neurons were lesioned, the cat spent more time sleeping as indicated by continuous EEG recording. A similar synchronization of the EEG was observed in the rat after lesions of the ascending dorsal NA pathway (Lidbrink, 1974). Lesions of the ventral NA pathway with 6-OH-DA have also been recorded to induce somnolence (Panksepp et al., 1973), although in this study there was some damage to the dorsal NA pathway as well.

Hyperactivity (A. G. Phillips and H. C. Fibiger, unpublished observations) and occasionally induced feeding (Evetts et al., 1972) and induced drinking (Myers and Martin, 1973) are observed following damage of catecholaminergic projections using 6-OH-DA. As a result of the hyperactivity, rats may lose as much as 50 gm during the first 24 hours. These behavioral effects are due apparently to the initial release of catecholamines from nerve terminals since the chronic effects of the 6-OH-DA are characterized by a general hypoactivity. Zigmond and Stricker (1974) observed failure to groom, arched back, and difficulty in initiating movements. Myers and Martin (1973) reported increased sleepiness following the administration of 6-OH-DA to the hypothalamus, and for 2–4 weeks "apparent muscle weakness and atonia together with a lack of activity" (p. 332). These symptoms were particularly severe in rats that did not recover and finally succumbed to the treatment. Following 6-OH-DA lesions of the DA nigrostriatal pathway, Ungerstedt (1971b) reported hypoactivity, difficulty in initiating activity and loss of exploratory activity and curiosity (Fig. 6).

Behavioral arousal or vigilance is an important dimension of motivated behavior. In an earlier section Hebb's arousal theory, which emphasized the importance of an optimal level of arousal, was outlined. Some of the behavioral effects of damaging or destroying CA pathways, particularly the dorsal NA pathway and the nigrostriatal DA pathway, may be the result of disrupting activation of higher levels of the nervous system and behavioral arousal. It is possible that CA pathways respond to and transmit "hunger and thirst signals" or make a specific contribution to feeding and drinking behaviors. However, they may also contribute to a variety of external behaviors as well as to the control of the endocrine and autonomic nervous systems.

In his classic paper that directed attention to the role of CA pathways in ingestive behaviors Ungerstedt expressed doubt that the DA nigrostriatal pathway was concerned specifically with regulating drinking and feeding. "When considering the curious hypokinesia, lack of exploratory behavior and difficulty to initiate activity that occurs after selective lesions of the nigrostriatal system it is more probable that the DA system and the striatum control a general arousal or drive level that is necessary for performing a number of activities where eating and drinking deficits are noticed only because they are easily measured by the observer and disastrous to the

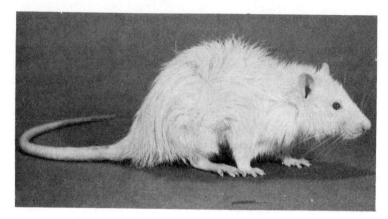

FIG. 6. Long-term effects of bilateral injections of 6-hydroxydopamine (4 mg) into the substantia nigra. The animal, 5 months after the injection, maintains body weight on Purina Chow pellets and water ad libitum at approximately preoperative level (280 gm).

animal" (Ungerstedt, 1971b, p. 116). More recently, Ungerstedt (1974) emphasized the importance of the DA nigrostriatal pathway in sensorimotor integration and attributed the behavioral deficits (sensory neglect, disruption of feeding, drinking, and self-stimulation) following lesions of this pathway to disruption in "the ability to perceive and respond to sensory stimuli" (p. 701). The inattention to visual, tactile, and proprioceptive stimuli (sensory neglect) on the opposite side of the body, which was reported initially for lateral hypothalamic lesions (Marshall *et al.*, 1971) and more recently for lesions of the DA nigrostriatal pathway (Marshall and Teitelbaum, 1973) is, according to Kornhuber (1974), similar to the akinetic mutism well known in the clinical literature.

In future research it will be important to determine the precise role of each of the CA pathways in ingestive and other motivated behaviors. In most of the studies reported it is unlikely that 6-OH-DA has selectively damaged only one of the ascending CA pathways.[4] There have been a number of studies of the deficits following damage to the DA nigrostriatal pathway, but further

---

[4] The problem of the possible widespread biochemical effects of 6-OH-DA treatment was emphasized by Panksepp and co-workers (1973) who damaged the dorsal NA pathway and medial serotonergic systems as well as the ventral NA pathway when the neurotoxic compound was administered to the ventral NA pathway. Marshall *et al.* (1974) severely damaged the nigrostriatal pathway by injecting 6-OH-DA into the substantia nigra but also observed an 89% depletion of norepinephrine in the telencephalon apparently because the neurotoxin also damaged the dorsal NA pathway. Because of failure to damage one of the CA pathways selectively, they were unable to conclude from their results whether destruction of the DA nigrostriatal pathway is sufficient to disrupt feeding and drinking or whether " . . . aphagia and adipsia result only when both noradrenergic and dopaminergic systems are interrupted" (Marshall *et al.*, 1974, p. 328).

work is needed. Although technically difficult, significant advances will be made when each pathway is lesioned selectively and the deficits that result are characterized completely. Tests for anticipatory or nonregulatory feeding and drinking should be included as well as those for the responses to deficit stimuli. It will also be of interest to observe the behavioral effects of selective stimulation of the various CA pathways.

There is some indication that lesions of the ventral NA pathway selectively influence feeding behavior. It has been reported that, after lesions of this pathway, rats become hyperphagic and obese (Ahlskog and Hoebel, 1973; Kapatos and Gold, 1973). Hyperphagia as a result of lesions of the ventral NA pathway has been confirmed by Mogenson and co-workers (Mogenson, 1974b). Since these observations suggest that the ventral NA pathway is involved in satiety, it will be of interest to see whether selective stimulation of this pathway suppresses feeding. It will also be necessary to investigate whether repletion and other satiety signals project to ventral NA neurons. An example of an attempt to stimulate specific CA pathways is a recent study by Cioé and Mogenson (1974). They elicited feeding in the absence of drinking when stimulating the region of the dorsal NA pathway consistent with the report of feeding from electrical stimulation of the locus coeruleus, the origin of dorsal NA fibers (Micco, 1974).

D. NEURAL MECHANISMS FOR MOTOR CONTROL

The DA nigrostriatal pathway and the dorsal NA pathway project to the striatum, the cerebral cortex, and the cerebellum (see Section IV,A), structures which make important contributions to the initiation and motor control of behavior. Since these pathways also contribute to feeding, drinking, and other goal-directed behaviors (see Sections IV,B and IV,C), it may be suggested that they are at the interface between neural systems concerned with the "intention to respond" and those concerned with "motor control." In this section we consider briefly what is known about motor systems of the brain and how the anatomical and functional relationship of the CA pathways to these systems might provide some clues about their contributions to motivated behaviors.

Motor control depends on complex interrelationships among a number of structures, as shown in Fig. 7. According to Kemp and Powell (1971), neural events for the initiation of movements originate in association cortex[5] and important contributions to the programming and execution of the movements are made by the striatum and the cerebellum. As shown in Fig. 7A, the

[5] Recordings of a "readiness potential" over much of the cerebral surface 500–800 msec before the onset of a movement (Deecke et al., 1969) is consistent with the view that widespread areas of association cortex provide signals for the initiation of movements.

A

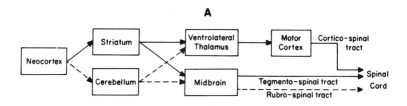

B

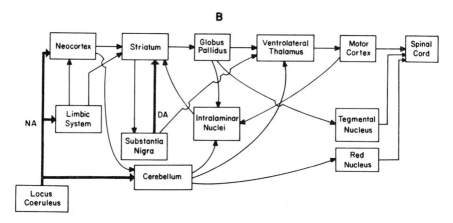

FIG. 7. The dopaminergic nigrostriatal pathway (DA) and the dorsal noradrenergic pathway (NA) are shown in relation to key structures involved in the motor control of behavior. (A) Parallel systems project from the neocortex to the lower motor neurons of the spinal cord via the striatum and cerebellum. The major contributions of the cerebellar route are to provide subroutines for the intended movement and to contribute to error detection through projections to the motor cortex. The striatum route contributes to the initiation of movement. (B) The substantia nigra projects to the striatum via the dopaminergic nigrostriatal pathway and to the ventrolateral nucleus of the thalamus. The dorsal noradrenergic pathway projects to the cerebral cortex and hippocampus. The evidence from lesion, electrophysiological, and behavior studies reviewed in Section V,C indicate that these pathways make important contributions to the electrical activity of the cerebral cortex and other higher levels of the central nervous system and to behavioral arousal. It is hypothesized that they also have an important role in the translation of the "intention to respond" into the command signals for the "motor control" (based on Kemp and Powell, 1971; Evarts and Thach, 1969).

signals from the cortex utilize parallel systems, of which the striatum and cerebellum are important components, in projecting to the motor cortex (via the ventrolateral thalamus) and to the spinal cord (the striatum via the globus pallidus and tegmental nucleus and the cerebellum via the red nucleus). The striatum, which samples the activity of several areas of the brain, is believed to be one of the key structures in the motor control of behavior (Fig. 7B). In addition to the topographical projections from sensory and association areas of the cerebral cortex, it receives inputs from the motor cortex and cerebellum, the latter two via the intralaminar nuclei of the thalamus. It also receives projections from limbic forebrain structures directly, as well as indirectly, via frontal association cortex. The striatum is in a good position, therefore, to contribute to the translation of the "intention to respond" into the appropriate "command signals" for the initiation and control of movements. The cerebellum is believed to be involved more with the execution of movement contributing to error detection. However, it has been suggested recently that the cerebellum might also be involved in the initiation of movement as well as in the execution (Allen and Tsukahara, 1974).

It should be noted that models to account for the motor control of behavior typically have not included the DA nigrostriatal pathway and the dorsal NA pathway. Since a major deficit of Parkinson patients, in whom the nigrostriatal pathway is diseased, is in the initiation of movement, this pathway should be included in such models. The dorsal NA pathway would also seem to deserve a place since it projects to the cerebral cortex which, according to the above analysis, is the initiator of voluntary movements. Therefore, these two pathways have been included in Fig. 7B, and we now turn to a consideration of what their contribution might be to the initiation and motor control of motivated behavior.

The fibers of the DA nigrostriatal and dorsal NA pathways exert inhibitory effects on the striatum, cerebral cortex, hippocampus, and cerebellum (Conner, 1970; Curtis and Crawford, 1969; Segal and Bloom, 1974). How then are these pathways responsible for cortical activation and behavioral arousal (Jones et al., 1973; Jouvet, 1972)? This could come about if the DA and NA axon terminals inhibited inhibitory interneurons, thereby causing the disinhibition of neurons concerned with motor control. A proposal of this sort has been made recently by Roberts (1974). He assumes that the central nervous system consists of " . . . genetically pre-programmed circuits which are released for action by neurons (command neurons) that are strategically located at junctions in neuronal hierarchies dealing with both sensory input and effector output" (p. 127). A number of investigators have suggested that such preprogrammed circuits for biting, chewing, swallowing, etc., are represented in the brain stem (e.g., Glickman and Schiff, 1967). Roberts suggests that "segmental command neurons, like the circuits they control, are largely inhibited from above, and that a decrease in inhibition allows command neurons to fire, thereby releasing the pre-programmed circuits over whose activity they preside" (p. 128).

There is evidence that NA fibers inhibit inhibitory γ-aminobutyric acid (GABA) interneurons in the upper layers of the cerebral cortex, thereby influencing EEG cortical arousal and behavior (Roberts, 1974). There are also inhibitory GABA interneurons in the basal ganglia which tonically inhibit preprogrammed neural circuits for patterned postural control and movements and which could be inhibited by the DA nigrostriatal neurons.

> Afferent inputs to the nigral neurons may release patterns of firing. In analogy to the activating effects of noradrenergic input to the cortex, the nigro-fugal fibers release dopamine in the caudate and putamen, inhibiting the indigenous tonically inhibitory GABA neurons and, acting together with excitatory and/ or disinhibitory inputs from the thalamus and cortex, release specific coded neural patterns in a sequential manner. The results of this activity are communicated to the pallidum and thence to regions in the thalamus where integration with other incoming information takes place. The final postural instructions are then sent to the appropriate regions of the motor cortex, where after further refinement the activity of appropriate pyramidal neurons is released to signal the effectors (Roberts, 1974, p. 139).

It should also be noted that the NA fibers which project to the cerebellum synapse on, and inhibit, Purkinje cells, which themselves are inhibitory neurons. However, the functional significance of this arrangement for behavioral disinhibition has not been considered.

In summary, it is suggested that the DA nigrostriatal pathway and the dorsal NA pathway contribute to motivated behavior by inhibiting inhibitory interneurons in neural structures that make important contributions to the initiation and motor control of behavior (Fig. 8). Disinhibition may be an important principle of CNS function, serving as the mechanism for the release of preprogrammed circuits representing components of behavior. In the final section, we consider how neural disinhibition by catecholamine pathways

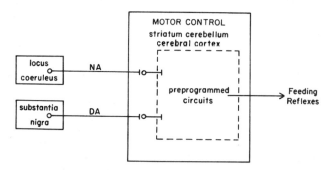

FIG. 8. The neurons of the dorsal noradrenergic pathway (NA) and of the nigrostriatal dopaminergic pathway (DA) inhibit inhibitory neurons in the cerebral cortex and striatum. In this way the catecholaminergic neurons disinhibit preprogrammed circuits for feeding and other behaviors (from Mogenson, 1976. Reproduced by permission of Raven Press).

may also account for self-stimulation of the brain as well as goal-directed behaviors to obtain food, water, or other rewards.

E. BRAIN SELF-STIMULATION

Recently, as indicated in Section IV,C, it has been shown that central reinforcement is associated with stimulation of brain catecholamine pathways. We now consider the implications of this discovery for understanding the neural mechanisms of brain self-stimulation.

Previous attempts to explain self-stimulation have emphasized the role of sensory systems, drive mechanisms, and motor output. The first alternative suggests that self-stimulation results from the activation of neural pathways relaying the sensory consequences of natural reinforcers and incentive stimuli (Pfaffmann, 1960; Trowill et al., 1969). The second alternative is based on the association of self-stimulation with central drive systems (Hoebel, 1969; Mogenson, 1969). The third alternative, that self-stimulation results from activation of neural systems associated with motor control, is based on reports that self-stimulation is obtained from extrapyramidal motor structures (Routtenberg and Malsbury, 1969) and elicits species-specific behaviors (Glickman and Schiff, 1967). The role of catecholamine pathways in self-stimulation will be considered in turn from these three points of view.

Certain gustatory stimuli, such as saccharin, and many odors have inherent reinforcing properties (S*); animals will work for such rewards even when they do not satisfy biological needs. Other stimuli (S) acquire incentive properties when associated with biologically significant events (see Section III,C). Many incentive stimuli are in the external environment and serve to guide the animal's behavior toward that which is "beneficial" and away from objects and events that are "harmful." Although all exteroceptive sensory systems may transmit incentive stimuli, the olfactory system is particularly suited to this function and may be the prototype system for analyzing sensory stimuli. It is of interest, therefore, that self-stimulation of olfactory structures has been reported (Olds and Milner, 1954; Wurtz and Olds, 1961; Valenstein and Campbell, 1966), including the olfactory bulbs (Phillips and Mogenson, 1969).

There are other sources of sensory information about biologically significant events. The consequences of natural reinforcers (S*) may involve proprioceptive and interoceptive systems as well as exteroceptive systems. Behaviors such as copulation and aggression, for example, depend a good deal on proprioceptive feedback. Central reinforcement may be the result of activating neural pathways and integrative structures for proprioceptive stimuli as well as pathways subserving exteroceptive and interoceptive stimuli.

Recently, Crow (1973) suggested that stimulation of the DA nigrostriatal pathway is reinforcing for brain self-stimulation because it is associated with the processing of incentive stimuli. According to Crow, signals from olfactory receptors project to the habenular nucleus and then to the interpeduncular nucleus where they influence DA neurons. Self-stimulation of the DA pathway, therefore, is attributed to the activation of fibers that normally transmit olfactory, incentive signals. This hypothesis could be investigated electrophysiologically by recording the discharge of DA neurons when olfactory stimuli are presented or when the olfactory bulb is stimulated directly. Other exteroceptive stimuli, as well as interoceptive and proprioceptive stimuli, might also be used because of the suggested role of various exteroceptive, interoceptive, and proprioceptive stimuli in self-stimulation.

Crow also hypothesized that the dorsal NA bundle is the substrate for central reinforcement based on drive reduction. He cites anatomical and physiological evidence in support of this proposal, in particular the close relationship between dorsal NA neurons in the locus coeruleus and the nucleus tractus solitarius which receives gustatory input from the oral cavity. Crow suggests that since gustatory stimuli are closely associated with the termination of ingestive behavior the dorsal NA bundle is activated by stimuli associated with drive reduction. Although Crow limits the analysis to gustatory stimuli, other stimuli might also be involved. For example, the solitary nucleus receives interoceptive inputs via the vagus nerve and self-stimulation is markedly inhibited by vagotomy (Ball, 1974).

Crow's views concerning the role of CA pathways in self-stimulation are in line with the two theoretical approaches that have been most popular for a number of years—central reinforcement from the viewpoint of incentive motivation and drive reduction. His proposal is also somewhat similar to that of Deutsch (Deutsch and Howarth, 1963) with the exception that, whereas Deutsch assumed that both incentive and drive pathways had to be stimulated concurrently, Crow implies that central reinforcement is the result of stimulating either the incentive pathway or the drive pathway. Although this may be an acceptable neuropsychological model, its validity may depend more on the theoretical predilections of the investigators than on neuroanatomical and neurophysiological evidence regarding the basic mechanisms of central reinforcement. We turn, therefore, to the third approach, which considers the role of CA pathways in brain self-stimulation from the viewpoint of their anatomical and physiological relationship with neural systems concerned with the motor control of behavior.

As indicated in Section V,D, the DA nigrostriatal pathway and the dorsal NA pathway project to and have inhibitory effects on the striatum, cerebral cortex, and cerebellum, structures which make important contributions to motor control (Fig. 7). The DA and NA neurons inhibit inhibitory neurons in the striatum, cerebral cortex, and cerebellum and thereby, according to

Roberts (1974), disinhibit preprogrammed neural circuits for motor responses. These inhibitory effects of the catecholamine pathways not only contribute to motor function, but may also be a key to understanding self-stimulation and central reinforcement (Milner, 1975).

It is well known that a novel stimulus can interrupt ongoing behavioral responses. Milner attributes this to the activation of a response inhibitory system in the cerebral cortex. This disruption of ongoing behavior by various stimuli encountered in the environment does not occur if the behavior is reinforced (e.g., by a conventional reinforcer or by brain stimulation). The ongoing responses are protected and maintained as goal-directed behavior. According to Milner, this is the result of the inhibitory catecholamine pathways suppressing the response inhibitory system.[6]

Milner's hypothesis is quite ingenious since it suggests a mechanism common to both conventional reinforcement and central reinforcement. Reinforcement, from activation of catecholamine pathways either by natural reinforcers or by stimulating them directly, disinhibits behavior because of inhibitory effects on a response-inhibitory system in the cerebral cortex (and possibly the striatum). As a result the behavior is repeated. Not only does this hypothesis provide a role for drive and incentive stimuli as activators of the catecholamine "reward" pathways, but it also links these pathways with neural systems for motor control. Experimental investigation of this model promises to be a fruitful approach to understanding the neural mechanisms of reinforcement and more generally the role of CA pathways in behavior.

VI. Summary

Physiological psychology is a relative newcomer to neurobiology, and it is in the study of the neural basis of feeding, drinking, and other motivated behaviors that physiological psychologists and neurobiologists have interacted and collaborated most extensively during the last 15 or 20 years. Lesion and stimulation of the hypothalamus and other deep structures of the brain in unanesthetized animals, with the aid of the stereotaxic procedure, led to the demonstration of a number of dramatic effects on motivated behaviors. Most

---

[6] The increased activity and greater persistence of exploratory behavior following lesions of certain regions of the cerebral cortex and hippocampus indicates that these structures are part of a response inhibitory system. Milner suggests that "arousal of any cortical activity produces a transient response inhibition" so that "the immediate effect of the presentation of a new stimulus is to interrupt any ongoing response" (p. 13). Activation of the catecholaminergic pathways, by food or other conventional reinforcers or by central stimulation, protects the animal's preceding, goal-directed responses from suppression by inhibiting the response-inhibitory system (I). "Thus, food, for a hungry animal not only elicits approach, chewing, swallowing, and so on, but sends inhibitory input to I to ensure cortical outflow does not interfere with the performance" (p. 15).

of these observations were consistent with a model that postulated multiple
hypothalamic drive systems, and, because this model was readily compatible
with the drive reduction theory of behavior as well as with the concepts of
homeostasis and biological adaptation, it was widely accepted by psychologists and neurobiologists alike.

Lesion and stimulation, as well as electrophysiological and histological,
techniques also implicated limbic forebrain and midbrain structures in the
control of motivated behaviors. For a time, however, the hypothalamus
retained its dominant position in the thinking of most investigators and the
other structures were considered to have a secondary role, exerting modulatory influences on the hypothalamic drive systems.

In recent years there has been a reassessment of the popular views about the
mechanisms of motivated behaviors. Many investigators have emphasized that
a good deal of motivated behavior, including feeding and drinking, is not
initiated by deficit signals, and they cautioned against reliance on an exclusively homeostatic model. There has been an increasing stress on the importance of external stimuli, of cognitive factors, and of incentive motivation
and a deemphasis of the role of the hypothalamus and of internal, deficit
signals. At the same time, histochemical and histofluorescence techniques are
providing the basis for a new chemical anatomy of the brain based on
biogenic amine systems. Noradrenergic, dopaminergic, and other transmitter-
specific pathways originating in the midbrain and lower in the brain stem
were shown to project through the hypothalamus to the septum, hippocampus, and other limbic structures, to the striatum, and to the cerebral
cortex. It has been reported that lesioning these pathways either electro-
lytically or more selectively with neurotoxins disrupts feeding, drinking and
other motivated behaviors. Other fibers whose transmitters are unknown
project from forebrain structures, some terminating in the hypothalamus, but
many continuing to the midbrain area. Clearly the hypothalamus is not the
center for motivated behaviors and currently vigorous investigations are being
undertaken to determine the essential pathways and the integrative mechanisms which subserve both internal and external signals as well as memory
and other cognitive processes that are involved in the initiation of motivated
behaviors.

Along with the deemphasis on the role of deficit stimuli and of drive states
in motivated behaviors there has been an increasing stress on the importance
of expectancy and of anticipatory behaviors. When investigating the role of
DA, NA, and other transmitter-specific pathways in drinking and feeding, it
will be necessary to consider their possible role in mediating incentive stimuli
and expectancies as well as ingestive behaviors in response to deficit signals.
Neurons which discharge in anticipation of food or water rewards have been

identified in the brain stem of behaving animals using chronic single unit recording techniques. Further studies are needed to relate these "anticipatory neurons" to transmitter-specific pathways.

It is obvious that the problems associated with the neurobiology of motivated behaviors have taken on greater complexity. Recent experimental evidence from studies utilizing a variety of techniques (histological, neurochemical, neuropharmacological, electrophysiological, behavioral) have challenged accepted models based on oversimplified views of behavior and of fragmentary evidence about brain function. Hypothalamic and homeostatic mechanisms alone cannot account for motivated behaviors such as drinking and feeding. In the search for physiological substrates of motivation it is necessary to tackle mechanisms that subserve associative and cognitive processes—the most complex functions performed by the brain. There is no other way if the neurobiologist adheres to the principle that the behavior of the whole animal indicates the kind of neural mechanism to look for. One of our objectives has been to illustrate with examples from current research that physiology and behavior must be studied conjointly in searching for the physiological substrates of motivated behavior.

Recent experimental evidence, particularly from studies of the role of transmitter specific pathways, does not fit readily into the neurobiological models of motivation of the 1950's and 1960's. An important current issue is whether the dual mechanism model and its more recent modification incorporating the concept of limbic modulatory influences will have to be abandoned or whether it can be revised and expanded to incorporate the evidence from chemical neuroanatomy. The emphasis on the functional role of transmitter-specific pathways and with the wiring diagram of neural systems that subserve goal-directed behaviors will undoubtedly continue for several years. Until we have a better idea of the neural circuitry which initiates actions, particularly actions that are purposive and goal-directed, it may be premature to formulate models for motivated behaviors.

Acknowledgments

The manuscript was read by Blanche Box, Jan Cioé, Mark Evered, Chris Fibiger, John Kucharczyk, and Tom Wishart, who made a number of valuable suggestions. We also acknowledge the assistance of Anne Baxter, Marianne Jeffery, and Iris Morrison, who patiently typed the various versions of the article, Rebecca Woodside, who prepared the illustrations, and Blanche Box, who painstakingly attended to the technical details of editing. During the preparation of this article the authors were supported by grants from the National Research Council of Canada.

References

Adolph, E. F., Barker, J. P., and Hoy, P. A. (1954). Multiple factors in thirst. *American Journal of Physiology* 178, 538–562.

Ahlskog, J. E., and Hoebel, B. D. (1973). Overeating and obesity from damage to a noradrenergic system in the brain. *Science* 182, 166–168.

Albert, D. J., and Storlien, L. H. (1969). Hyperphagia in rats with cuts between the ventromedial and lateral hypothalamus. *Science* 165, 599–600.

Allen, G. I., and Tsukahara, N. (1974). Cerebrocerebellar communication systems. *Physiological Reviews* 54, 957–1006.

Anand, B. K., and Brobeck, J. R. (1951). Hypothalamic control of food intake in rats and cats. *Yale Journal of Biology and Medicine* 24, 123–140.

Anand, B. K., and Pillai, R. V. (1967). Activity of single neurons in the hypothalamic feeding centres: Effect of gastric distention. *Journal of Physiology (London)* 192, 63–77.

Anand, B. K., Dua, S., and Singh, B. (1961). Electrical activity of the hypothalamic "feeding centres" under the effect of changes in blood chemistry. *Electroencephalography and Clinical Neurophysiology* 13, 54–59.

Andersson, B. (1953). The effect of injections of hypertonic NaCl-solutions into different parts of the hypothalamus of goats. *Acta Physiologica Scandinavica* 28, 188–201.

Andén, N. E., Dahlström, A., Fuxe, K., Larsson, K., Olson, L., and Ungerstedt, U. (1966). Ascending monamine neurons to the telencephalon and diencephalon. *Acta Physiologica Scandinavica* 67, 313–326.

Andersson, B., and Wyrwicka, W. (1957). The elicitation of a drinking motor conditioned reaction by electrical stimulation of the hypothalmic "drinking area" in the goat. *Acta Physiologica Scandinavica* 41, 194–198.

Appley, M. H. (1970). Derived motives. *Annual Review of Psychology* 21, 485–518.

Arbuthnott, G. W., Crow, T. J., Fuxe, K., Olson, L., and Ungerstedt, U. (1970). Depletion of catecholamines *in vivo* induced by electrical stimulation of central monoamine pathways. *Brain Research* 24, 471–483.

Arbuthnott, G., Fuxe, K., and Ungerstedt, U. (1971). Central catecholamine turnover and self-stimulation behaviour. *Brain Research* 27, 406–413.

Ball, G. G. (1974). Vagotomy: Effect on electrically elicited eating and self-stimulation in the lateral hypothalamus. *Science* 184, 484–485.

Baxter, L., Gluckman, M. I., Stein, K., and Scerni, A. (1974). Self-injection of apomorphine in the rat: positive reinforcement by a dopamine receptor stimulant. *Pharmacology, Biochemistry and Behavior* 2, 387–391.

Berger, B., Tassin, J. P., Blanc, G., Moyne, M. A., and Thierry, V. (1974). Histochemical confirmation for dopaminergic innervation of the rat cerebral cortex after destruction of the noradrenergic ascending pathways. *Brain Research* 81, 332–337.

Berger, B. D., Wise, C. D., and Stein, K. (1971). Norepinephrine: Reversal of anorexia in rats with lateral hypothalamic damage. *Science* 172, 281–284.

Berlyne, D. E. (1950). Novelty and curiosity as determinants of exploratory behavior. *British Journal of Psychology* 41, 68–80.

Bindra, D. (1968). Neuropsychological interpretation of the effects of drive and incentive-motivation on general activity and instrumental behavior. *Psychological Review* 75, 1–22.

Björklund, A., Ehinger, B., and Falck, B. (1968). A method for differentiating dopamine from noradrenaline in tissue sections by microspectrofluorometry. *Journal of Histochemistry and Cytochemistry* **16**, 263–270.

Bolles, R. C. (1972). Reinforcement, expectancy, and learning. *Psychological Review* **79**, 394–409.

Bolles, R. C., and Moot, S. A. (1973). The rat's anticipation of two meals a day. *Journal of Comparative and Physiological Psychology* **83**, 510–514.

Brady, J. V., and Nauta, W. J. H. (1953). Subcortical mechanisms in emotional behaviour: Affective changes following septal forebrain lesions in the albino rat. *Journal of Comparative and Physiological Psychology* **46**, 339–346.

Breese, G. R., Howard, J. L., and Leahy, J. P. (1971). Effect of 6-hydroxydopamine on electrical self stimulation of the brain. *British Journal of Pharmacology* **43**, 255–257.

Breese, G. R., Smith, D., Cooper, R., and Grant, L. D. (1973). Alterations in consummatory behavior following intracisternal injection of 6-hydroxydopamine. *Pharmacology, Biochemistry and Behavior* **1**, 319–328.

Brobeck, J. R., Tepperman, J., and Long, C. N. H. (1943). Experimental hypothalamic hyperphagia in the albino rat. *Yale Journal of Biology and Medicine* **15**, 831–853.

Brodie, D. A., Moreno, O. M., Malis, J. L., and Brodie, J. J. (1960). Rewarding properties of intracranial stimulation. *Science* **131**, 929–930.

Brookhart, J. M., and Dey, F. L. (1941). Reduction of sexual behavior in male guinea pigs by hypothalamic lesions. *American Journal of Physiology* **133**, 551–554.

Brown, K. A., and Melzack, R. (1969). Effects of glucose on multi-unit activity in the hypothalamus. *Experimental Neurology* **24**, 363–373.

Butler, R. A. (1953). Discrimination learning by rhesus monkeys to visual-exploration motivation. *Journal of Comparative and Physiological Psychology* **46**, 95–98.

Caggiula, A. R., and Hoebel, B. G. (1966). "Copulation-reward site" in the posterior hypothalamus. *Science* **153**, 1284–1285.

Campbell, J. J. (1971). Pleasure-seeking brains: artificial tickles, natural joys of thought. *Smithsonian* **2**, 14–23.

Cannon, W. (1932). "The Wisdom of the Body." Norton, New York.

Cioé, J., and Mogenson, G. J. (1974). Effects of electrical stimulation and lesions in the region of the dorsal noradrenergic (NA) pathway on feeding behavior. *Federation Proceedings, Federation of American Societies for Experimental Biology* **33**(3), 342 (Abstract No. 777).

Clavier, R. M., and Routtenberg, A. (1974). Ascending monoamine-containing fiber pathways related to intra-cranial self-stimulation: histochemical fluorescence study. *Brain Research* **72**, 25–40.

Connor, J. D. (1970). Caudate nucleus neurones: correlation of the effects of substantia nigra stimulation with iontophoretic dopamine. *Journal of Physiology (London)* **208**, 691–703.

Cooper, B. R., Black, W. C., and Paolino, R. M. (1971). Decreased septal-forebrain and lateral hypothalamic reward after alpha-methyl-p-tyrosine. *Physiology & Behavior* **6**, 425–429.

Cooper, S. J., and Rolls, E. T. (1974). Relation of activation of neurones in the pons and medulla to brain-stimulation reward. *Experimental Brain Research (Berlin)* **20**, 207–222.

Coyle, J. T., and Snyder, S. H. (1969). Catecholamine uptake by synaptosomes in homogenates of rat brain: Stereospecificity in different areas. *Journal of Pharmacology and Experimental Therapeutics* **170**, 221–231.

Crow, T. J. (1970). Enhancement by cocaine of intra-cranial self-stimulation in the rat. *Life Sciences* **9**, 375–381.

Crow, T. J. (1972). A map of the rat mesencephalon for electrical self-stimulation. *Brain Research* **36**, 265–273.

Crow, T. J. (1973). Catecholamine-containing neurones and electrical self-stimulation. II. A theoretical interpretation and some psychiatric implications. *Psychological Medicine* **3**, 66–73.

Crow, T. J., Spear, P. J., and Arbuthnott, G. W. (1972). Intracranial self-stimulation with electrodes in the region of the locus coeruleus. *Brain Research* **36**, 275–287.

Culberson, J. L., Kling, J. W., and Berkley, M. A. (1966). Extinction responding following ICS and food reinforcement. *Psychonomic Science* **5**, 127–128.

Curtis, D. R., and Crawford, J. M. (1969). Central synaptic transmission–microelectrophoretic studies. *Annual Review of Pharmacology* **9**, 209–240.

Dahlström, A., and Fuxe, K. (1964). Localization of monoamines in the lower brain stem. *Experientia* **20**, 398.

Deecke, L., Scheid, P., and Kornhuber, H. H. (1969). Distribution of readiness potential, pre-motion positivity, and motor potential of the human cerebral cortex preceding voluntary finger movement. *Experimental Brain Research (Berlin)* **7**, 158–168.

Delgado, J. M. R., and Anand, B. K. (1953). Increase of food intake induced by electrical stimulation of the lateral hypothalamus. *American Journal of Physiology* **172**, 162–168.

Delgado, J. M. R., Roberts, W. W., and Miller, N. E. (1954). Learning motivated by electrical stimulation of the brain. *American Journal of Physiology* **179**, 587–593.

Deutsch, J. A., and Howarth, C. I. (1963). Some tests of a theory of intracranial self-stimulation. *Psychological Review* **70**, 444–460.

Dicker, S. E., and Nunn, J. (1957). The role of the antidiuretic hormone during water deprivation in rats. *Journal of Physiology (London)* **136**, 235–248.

Domino, E. F., and Olds, M. E. (1972). Effects of d-amphetamine, scopolamine, chlordiazepoxide, and diphenylhydantoin on self-stimulation behavior and brain acetycholine. *Psychopharmacologia* **23**, 1–16.

Dreese, A. (1966). Importance du système mésencéphalo-telencephalique noradrenergique comme substratum anatomique du comportement d'autostimulation. *Life Sciences* **5**, 1003–1014.

Dreese, A. (1967). Contribution expérimentale à l'étude du mecanisme d'action des neuroleptiques. These d'Agrégation de l'Enseignement Superieur, Univ. de Liège, Liège.

Epstein, A. N. (1971). The lateral hypothalamic syndrome: Its implications for the physiological psychology of hunger and thirst. *In*"Progress in Physiological Psychology" (E. Stellar and J. M. Sprague, eds.), Vol. 4, pp. 263–317. Academic Press, New York.

Epstein, A. N. (1973). Epilogue: retrospect and prognosis. *In* "The Neuropsychology of Thirst" (A. N. Epstein, H. R. Kissileff, and E. Stellar, eds.), pp. 315–332. Winston, New York.

Epstein, A. N., and Teitelbaum, P. (1964). Severe and persistent deficits in thirst produced by lateral hypothalamic damage. *In* "Thirst" (M. J. Wayner, ed.), pp. 395–406. Macmillan, New York.

Evarts, E. V., and Thach, W. T. (1969). Motor mechanisms of the CNS: Cerebrocerebellar interrelations. *Annual Review of Physiology* **31**, 451–498.

Evered, M. D., and Mogenson, G. J. (1973). Water intake in rats with lesions of the zona incerta. *Proceedings of the Canadian Federation of Biological Societies* **16**, 113.

Evered, M. D., and Mogenson, G. J. (1974). Nature of the hypodipsia following lesions of the zona incerta. *Proceedings of the International Conference on the Physiology of Food and Fluid Intake, Fifth, Jerusalem,* p. 57.

Evetts, K. D., Fitzsimons, J. T., and Setler, P. E. (1972). Eating caused by 6-hydroxy-dopamine-induced release of noradrenaline in the diencephalon of the rat. *Journal of Physiology (London)* **223**, 35–47.

Falck, B., Hillarp, N. A., Thieme, G., and Torp, A. (1962). Fluorescence of catecholamines and related compounds condensed with formaldehyde. *Journal of Histochemistry and Cytochemistry* **10**, 348–354.

Fibiger, H. C., and Phillips, A. G. (1975). The role of dopamine and norepinephrine in the chemistry of reward. *In* "Catecholamines and their Enzymes in the Neuropathology of Schizophrenia" (S. S. Kety and S. Matthysse, eds.). Pergamon, New York. In press.

Fibiger, H. C., Zis, A. P., and McGeer, E. G. (1973). Feeding and drinking deficits after 6-hydroxydopamine administration in the rat: Similarities to the lateral hypothalamic syndrome. *Brain Research* **55**, 135–148.

Fitzsimons, J. T. (1971). The physiology of thirst: A review of the extraneural aspects of the mechanisms of drinking. *In* "Progress in Physiological Psychology" Vol. 4, pp. 119–201. Academic Press, New York.

Fitzsimons, J. T. (1972). Thirst. *Physiological Reviews* **52**, 468–561.

Fonberg, E. (1969). The role of the hypothalamus and amygdala in food intake, alimentary motivation and emotional reactions. *Acta Biologiae Experimentalis (Warsaw)* **29**, 335–358.

Fuxe, K., Goldstein, M., Hökfelt, T., and Joh, T. H. (1970). Immunohistochemical localization of dopamine-β-hydroxylase in the peripheral and central nervous system. *Research Communications in Chemical Pathology and Pharmacology* **1**, 627–636.

German, D. C., and Bowden, D. M. (1974). Catecholamine systems as the neural substrate for intracranial self-stimulation: A hypothesis. *Brain Research* **73**, 381–419.

Gladfelter, W. E., and Brobeck, J. R. (1962). Decreased spontaneous locomotor activity in the rat induced by hypothalamic lesions. *American Journal of Physiology* **203**, 811–817.

Glickman, S. E., and Schiff, B. B. (1967). A biological theory of reinforcement. *Psychological Review* **74**, 81–109.

Gloor, P., Murphy, J. T., and Dreifuss, J. J. (1969). Electrophysiological studies of amygdalo-hypothalamic connections. *Annals of the New York Academy of Sciences* **157**, 629–641.

Gold, R. M. (1970). Hypothalamic hyperphagia produced by parasagittal knife cuts. *Physiology & Behavior* **5**, 23–25.

Gold, R. M. (1973). Hypothalamic obesity: The myth of the ventromedial nucleus. *Science* **182**, 488–490.

Greer, M. A. (1955). Suggestive evidence of a primary "drinking center" in hypothalamus of the rat. *Proceedings of the Society for Experimental Biology and Medicine* **89**, 59.

Grossman, S. P. (1962). Direct adrenergic and cholinergic stimulation of hypothalamic mechanisms. *American Journal of Physiology* **202**, 872–882.

Grossman, S. P. (1968). Hypothalamic and limbic influences on food intake. *Federation Proceedings, Federation of American Societies for Experimental Biology.* **27**, 1349–1360.

Grossman, S. P., and Grossman, L. (1963). Food and water intake following lesions or electrical stimulation of the amygdala. *American Journal of Physiology* **205**, 761–765.

Hamburg, M. D. (1971). Hypothalamic unit activity and eating behavior. *American Journal of Physiology* **220**, 980–985.

Harlow, H. F. (1953). Mice, monkeys, and motives. *Psychological Review* **60**, 23–32.

Harvey, J. A., and Hunt, H. F. (1965). Effect of septal lesions on thirst in the rat as indicated by water consumption and operant responding for water and reward. *Journal of Comparative and Physiological Psychology* **59**, 49–56.

Hastings, L., and Stutz, R. M. (1973). The effect of alpha- and beta-adrenergic antagonists on the self-stimulation phenomenon. *Life Sciences* **13**, 1253–1259.

Hebb, D. O. (1949). "Organization of Behavior." Wiley, New York.

Hebb, D. O. (1955). Drives and the C.N.S. (Conceptual Nervous System). *Psychological Review* **62**, 243–254.

Hebb, D. O. (1958). Alice in wonderland or psychology among the biological sciences. *In* "Biological and Biochemical Bases of Behavior" (H. R. Harlow and C. N. Woolsey, eds.), pp. 451–467. Univ. of Wisconsin Press, Madison.

Hedreen, J. C., and Chalmers, J. P. (1972). Neuronal degeneration in rat brain induced by 6-hydroxydopamine: A histological and biochemical study. *Brain Research* **47**, 1–36.

Heller, A., and Harvey, J. A. (1963). Effect of CNS lesions on brain norepinephrine. *Pharmacologist* **5**, 264.

Heller, A., and Moore, R. Y. (1965). Effect of central nervous system lesions on brain monoamines in the rat. *Journal of Pharmacology and Experimental Therapeutics* **150**, 1–9.

Heller, A., and Moore, R. Y. (1968). Control of brain serotonin content and norepinephrine by specific neural systems. *Advances in Pharmacology* **6**, 191–206.

Herberg, L. J. (1963). Seminal ejaculation following positively reinforcing electrical stimulation of the rat hypothalamus. *Journal of Comparative and Physiological Psychology* **56**, 679–685.

Hess, W. R. (1949). "Das Zwischenhirn." Schwabe, Basel.

Hetherington, A. W., and Ranson, S. W. (1942). The spontaneous activity and food intake of rats with hypothalamic lesions. *American Journal of Physiology* **136**, 609–617.

Hoebel, B. G. (1969). Feeding and self-stimulation. *Annals of the New York Academy of Sciences* **157**, 758–778.

Hoebel, B. G., and Teitelbaum, P. (1962). Hypothalamic control of feeding and self-stimulation. *Science* **135**, 375–377.

Hökfelt, T., Fuxe, K., Goldstein, M., and Johansson, O. (1974a). Immunohistochemical evidence for the existence of adrenaline neurons in the rat brain. *Brain Research* **66**, 235–251.

Hökfelt, T., Ljungdahl, Å., Fuxe, K., and Johansson, O. (1974b). Dopamine nerve terminals in the rat limbic cortex: Aspects of the dopamine hypothesis of schizophrenia. *Science* **184**, 177–179.

Horovitz, Z. P., Chow, M. I., and Carlton, P. L. (1962). Self-stimulation of the brain by cats: Effects of imipramine, amphetamine, and chlorpromazine. *Psychopharmacologia* **3**, 455–462.

Huang, Y. H., and Mogenson, G. J. (1972). Neural pathways mediating drinking and feeding in rats. *Experimental Neurology* **37**, 269–286.

Huang, Y. H., and Mogenson, G. J. (1974). Differential effects of incertal and hypothalamic lesions on food and water intake. *Experimental Neurology* **43**, 276–280.

Huang, Y. H., and Routtenberg, A. (1971). Lateral hypothalamic self-stimulation pathways in *Rattus norvegicus*. *Physiology & Behavior* 7, 419–432.

Hull, C. L. (1943). "Principles of Behavior." Appleton, New York.

Ito, M., and Olds, J. (1971). Unit activity during self-stimulation behavior. *Journal of Neurophysiology* 34, 263–273.

Jacobowitz, D. M., and Palkovits, M. (1974). Topographic atlas of catecholamine and acetylcholinesterase-containing neurons in the rat brain. 1. Forebrain (telencephalon, diencephalon). *Journal of Comparative Neurology* 157, 13–28.

Jasper, H. H., and Doane, B. (1968). Neurophysiological mechanisms in learning. *In* "Progress in Physiological Psychology" (E. Stellar and J. M. Sprague, eds.), Vol. 2, pp. 79–117. Academic Press, New York.

Jones, B. E., Bobillier, P., Pin, C., and Jouvet, M. (1973). The effect of lesions of catecholamine-containing neurons upon monamine content of the brain and EEG and behavioral waking in the cat. *Brain Research* 58, 157–177.

Jouvet, M. (1972). Some monoaminergic mechanisms controlling sleep and waking. *In* "Brain and Human Behavior" (A. G. Karczmar and J. C. Eccles, eds.), pp. 131–161. Springer-Verlag, Berlin and New York.

Kapatos, G., and Gold, M. (1973). Evidence for ascending noradrenergic mediation of hypothalamic hyperphagia. *Pharmacology, Biochemistry and Behavior* 1, 81–87.

Kemp, J. M., and Powell, T. P. S. (1971). The connexions of the striatum and globus pallidus: Synthesis and speculation. *Philosophical Transactions of the Royal Society of London, Series B* 262, 441–457.

Kennedy, G. C. (1953). The role of depot fat in the hypothalamic control of food intake in the rat. *Proceedings of the Royal Society, Series B* 140, 578–592.

Kissileff, H. R. (1973). Nonhomeostatic controls of drinking. *In* "The Neuropsychology of Thirst" (A. M. Epstein, H. R. Kisileff, and E. Stellar, eds.), pp. 163–198. Winston-Wiley, New York.

Kolb, B., and Nonneman, A. J. (1975). Prefrontal cortex and the regulation of food intake in the rat. *Journal of Comparative and Physiological Psychology* 88, 806–815.

Kornhuber, H. H. (1974). Cerebral cortex, cerebellum, and basal ganglia: An introduction to their motor functions. *In* "The Neurosciences, Third Study Program" (F. O. Schmitt and F. W. Worden, eds.), pp. 267–280. MIT Press, Cambridge, Massachusetts.

LeMagnen, J. (1959). Étude d'un phénomène d'appétit provisionnel. *Comptes Rendus Hebdomadaires des Séances de l'Académie des Sciences*, 249, 2400–2402.

LeMagnen, J. (1967). Habits and food intake. *In* "Handbook of Physiology, Section 6: Alimentary Canal, Vol. 1: Control of Food and Water Intake" (C. F. Code, ed.), pp. 11–30. Amer. Physiol. Soc., Washington, D.C.

LeMagnen, J. (1971). Advances on studies of the physiological control and regulation of food intake. *In* "Progress in Physiological Psychology" (E. Stellar and J. M. Sprague, eds.), Vol. 4, pp. 203–261. Academic Press, New York.

Lidbrink, P. (1974). The effect of lesions of ascending noradrenaline pathways on sleep and waking in the rat. *Brain Research* 74, 19–40.

Liebman, J. M., and Butcher, L. L. (1973). Effects on self-stimulation behavior of drugs influencing dopaminergic neurotransmission mechanisms. *Naunyn-Schmiedebergs Archiv für Pharmakologie und Experimentelle Pathologie* 277, 305–318.

Lindvall, O., and Björklund, A. (1974). The organization of the ascending catecholamine neuron systems in the rat brain as revealed by the glyoxylic acid fluorescence method. *Acta Physiologica Scandinavica, Supplementum* 412, 1–48.

Lindvall, O., Björklund, A., Moore, R. Y., and Stenevi, U. (1974a). Mesencephalic dopamine neurons projecting to the neocortex. *Brain Research* 81, 325–331.

Lindvall, O., Björklund, A., Nobin, A., and Stenevi, V. (1974b). The adrenergic innervation of the rat thalamus as revealed by the glyoxylic acid fluorescence method. *Journal of Comparative Neurology* 154, 317–348.

Lippa, A. S., Antelman, S. M., Fisher, A. E., and Canfield, D. R. (1973). Neurochemical mediation of reward: A significant role for dopamine? *Pharmacology, Biochemistry and Behavior* 1, 23–28.

Livingston, R. B. (1967). Brain circuitry relating to complex behavior. *In* "The Neurosciences, A Study Program" (G. C. Quarton, T. Melnechuk, and R. O. Schmitt, eds.), pp. 499–515. Rockefeller Univ. Press, New York.

Long, C. J., and Tapp, J. T. (1967). Reinforcing properties of odors for the albino rat. *Psychonomic Science* 7, 17–18.

Lorens, S. A. (1966). Effect of lesions in the central nervous system on lateral hypothalamic self-stimulation in the rat. *Journal of Comparative and Physiological Psychology* 62, 256–262.

Maeda, T., and Shimizu, N. (1972). Projections ascendantes du locus coeruleus et d'autres neurones aminergiques pontiques au niveau du prosencéphale du rat. *Brain Research* 36, 19–35.

Malmo, R. B. (1959). Activation: A neuropsychological dimension. *Psychological Review* 66, 367–386.

Margules, D. L., and Olds, J. (1962). Identical "feeding" and "rewarding" systems in the lateral hypothalamus of rats. *Science* 135, 374–375.

Marshall, J. F., and Teitelbaum, P. (1973). A comparison of the eating in response to hypothermic and glucoprivic challenges after nigral 6-hydroxydopamine and lateral hypothalamine electrolytic lesions in rats. *Brain Research* 55, 229–233.

Marshall, J. F., Turner, B. H., and Teitelbaum, P. (1971). Sensory neglect produced by lateral hypothalamic damage. *Science* 174, 523–525.

Marshall, J. F., Richardson, J. S., and Teitelbaum, P. (1974). Nigrostriatal bundle damage and the lateral hypothalamic syndrome. *Journal of Comparative and Physiological Psychology* 87, 808–830.

Matthysse, S. (1974). Schizophrenia: Relationships to dopamine transmission, motor control, and feature extraction. *In* "The Neurosciences, Third Study Program" pp. 733–737. (F. O. Schmitt and F. W. Worden, eds.), MIT Press, Cambridge, Massachusetts.

Mayer, J. (1953). Glucostatic mechanism of regulation of food intake. *New England Journal of Medicine* 249, 13–16.

Micco, D. J., Jr. (1974). Complex behaviors elicited by stimulation of the dorsal pontine tegmentum in rats. *Brain Research* 75, 172–176.

Miller, N. E. (1960). Motivational effects of brain stimulation and drugs. *Federation Proceedings, Federation of American Societies for Experimental Biology* 19, 846–854.

Miller, N. E. (1965). Chemical coding of behavior in the brain. *Science* 148, 328–338.

Millhouse, O. E. (1969). A Golgi study of the descending medial forebrain bundle. *Brain Research* 15, 341–363.

Milner, P. M. (1970). "Physiological Psychology." Holt, New York.

Milner, P. M. (1975). Motivation and reinforcement. II. Theory. *In* "Handbook of Psychopharmacology" (L. L. Iversen, S. D. Iversen, and S. H. Snyder, eds.). Plenum, New York. In press.

Mogenson, G. J. (1965). An attempt to establish secondary reinforcement with rewarding brain stimulation. *Psychological Reports* 16, 163–167.
Mogenson, G. J. (1969). General and specific reinforcement systems for drinking
behavior. *Annals of the New York Academy of Sciences* 157, 779–797.
Mogenson, G. J. (1971). Stability and modification of consummatory behaviors elicited
by electrical stimulation of the hypothalamus. *Physiology & Behavior* 6, 255–260.
Mogenson, G. J. (1973). Hypothalamic limbic mechanisms in the control of water
intake. *In* "The Neuropsychology of Thirst" (A. N. Epstein, H. Kissileff, and E.
Stellar, eds.), pp. 119–142. Winston, New York.
Mogenson, G. J. (1974a). Changing views of the role of the hypothalamus in the control
of ingestive behaviors. *In* "Recent Studies of Hypothalamic Function" (K. Lederis
and K. E. Cooper, eds.), pp. 268–293. Karger, Basel.
Mogenson, G. J. (1974b). Changing views concerning the neural mechanisms that
subserve drinking and feeding behavior. (Invited lecture.) *Proceedings of the Interna-
tional Congress of Physiological Sciences, 26th, New Delhi*, pp. 50–51.
Mogenson, G. J. (1975). Electrophysiological studies of the mechanisms that initiate
ingestive behaviours with special emphasis on water intake. *In* "Neural Integration of
Physiological Mechanisms and Behavior" (G. J. Mogenson and F. R. Calaresu, eds.),
pp. 248–266. Univ. of Toronto Press, Toronto.
Mogenson, G. J. (1976). Neural mechanisms of hunger: current status and future prospects.
In "Hunger: Basic Mechanisms and Clinical Implications" (D. Novin, W. Wyrwicka, and
G. Bray, eds.), pp. 473–485. Raven, New York.
Mogenson, G. J., and Cioé, J. (1975). Central reinforcement: A bridge between brain
function and behavior. *In* "Operant Conditioning" (W. K. Honig and J. Staddon,
eds.). Appleton, New York. In press.
Mogenson, G. J., and Huang, Y. H. (1973). The neurobiology of motivated behavior.
Progress in Neurobiology 1, 53–83.
Mogenson, G. J., and Morgan, C. W. (1967). Effects of induced drinking on self-stimula-
tion of the lateral hypothalamus. *Experimental Brain Research (Berlin)* 3, 111–116.
Mogenson, G. J., and Stevenson, J. A. F. (1966). Drinking and self-stimulation with
electrical stimulation of the lateral hypothalamus. *Physiology & Behavior* 1, 251–
254.
Mogenson, G. J., Gentil, C. G., and Stevenson, J. A. F. (1971). Feeding and drinking
elicited by low and high frequencies of hypothalamic stimulation. *Brain Research* 33,
127–137.
Montemurro, D. G., and Stevenson, J. A. F. (1957). Adipsia produced by hypothalamic
lesions in the rat. *Canadian Journal of Biochemistry and Physiology* 35, 31–37.
Montgomery, K. C. (1953). The effect of the hunger and thirst drives upon exploratory
behavior. *Journal of Comparative and Physiological Psychology* 46, 315–319.
Morgane, P. J. (1961). Medial forebrain bundle and "feeding centers" of the hypothalamus. *Journal of Comparative Neurology* 117, 1–25.
Morgane, P. J. (1975). Anatomical and neurobiochemical bases of the central nervous
control of physiological regulations and behaviour. *In* "Neural Integration of Physiological Mechanisms and Behavior" (G. J. Mogenson and F. R. Calaresu, eds.), pp.
24–67. Univ. of Toronto Press, Toronto.
Moruzzi, G., and Magoun, H. W. (1949). Brain stem reticular formation and activation of
the EEG. *Electroencephalography and Clinical Neurophysiology* 1, 455–473.
Mowrer, O. H. (1960). "Learning Theory and Behavior." Wiley, New York.
Myers, R. D., and Martin, G. E. (1973). 6-OHDA lesions of the hypothalamus: Inter-

240   G. J. Mogenson and A. G. Phillips

action of aphagia, food palatability, set-point for weight regulation and recovery of feeding. *Pharmacology, Biochemistry and Behavior* **1**, 329–345.

Nauta, W. J. H. (1946). Hypothalamic regulation of sleep in rats. An experimental study. *Journal of Neurophysiology* **9**, 285–316.

Oatley, K. (1972). "Brain Mechanisms and Mind." Dutton, New York.

Oatley, K. (1973). Simulation and theory of thirst. *In* "The Neuropsychology of Thirst" (A. N. Epstein, H. R. Kissileff, and E. Stellar, eds.), pp. 199–223. Winston-Wiley, New York.

Olds, J. (1956). Neurophysiology of drive. *Psychiatric Research Reports* **6**, 15–22.

Olds, J. (1962). Hypothalamic substrates of reward. *Physiological Reviews* **42**, 554–604.

Olds, J. (1965). Operant conditioning of single unit responses. *Proceedings of the International Congress of Physiological Sciences, 23rd, Tokyo.* Excerpta Medica International Congress Series No. 87, pp. 372–380.

Olds, J. (1967). The limbic system and behavioral reinforcement. *Progress in Brain Research* **27**, 141–167.

Olds, J., and Hirano, T. (1969). Conditioned responses of hippocampal and other neurons. *Electroencephalography and Clinical Neurophysiology* **26**, 159–166.

Olds, J., and Milner, P. (1954). Positive reinforcement produced by electrical stimulation of septal area and other regions of rat brain. *Journal of Comparative and Physiological Psychology* **47**, 419–427.

Olds, J., and Olds, M. E. (1964). The mechanisms of voluntary behavior. *In* "The Role of Pleasure in Behavior" (R. G. Heath, ed.), pp. 23–53. Harper, New York.

Olds, J., Killam, K. F., and Bach-y-Rita, P. (1956). Self-stimulation of the brain used as a screening technique for tranquilizing drugs. *Science* **124**, 265–266.

Olds, J., Mink, W. D., and Best, P. J. (1969). Single unit patterns during anticipatory behavior. *Electroencephalography and Clinical Neurophysiology* **26**, 144–158.

Olds, M. E. (1970). Comparative effects of amphetamine, scopolamine, chlordiazepoxide, and diphenylhydantoin on operant and extinction behavior with brain stimulation and food reward. *Neuropharmacology* **9**, 519–532.

Olds, M. E. (1973). Short-term changes in the firing pattern of hypothalamic neurons during Pavlovian conditioning. *Brain Research* **58**, 95–116.

Olds, M. E., and Olds, J. (1969). Effects of lesions in medial forebrain bundle on self-stimulation behavior. *American Journal of Physiology* **217**, 1253–1264.

Olson, L., and Fuxe, K. (1971). On the projections from the locus coeruleus nordrenaline neurons: The cerebellar innervation. *Brain Research* **28**, 165–171.

Olson, L., and Fuxe, K. (1972). Further mapping out of central noradrenaline neuron systems: Projections of the "subcoeruleus" area. *Brain Research* **43**, 289–295.

Oltmans, G. A., and Harvey, J. A. (1972). LH syndrome and brain catecholamine levels after lesions of the nigrostriatal bundle. *Physiology & Behavior* **8**, 69–78.

Oomura, Y., Kimura, K., Ooyama, H., Maeno, T., Iki, M., and Kuniyoshi, M. (1964). Reciprocal activities of the ventromedial and lateral hypothalamic area of cats. *Science* **143**, 484–485.

Palkovits, M., and Jacobowitz, D. M. (1974). Topographic atlas of catecholamine and acetylcholinesterase-containing neurons in the rat brain. *Journal of Comparative Neurology* **157**, 29–42.

Panksepp, J., Jalowiec, J. E., Morgane, P. J., Zolovick, A. J., and Stern, W. C. (1973). Noradrenergic pathways and sleep-waking states in cats. *Experimental Neurology* **41**, 233–245.

Pfaffmann, C. (1960). The pleasures of sensation. *Psychological Review* **67**, 253–268.

Phillips, A. G., and Fibiger, H. C. (1973a). Deficits in stimulation-induced feeding after intraventricular administration of 6-hydroxydopamine in rats. *Behavioral Biology* 9, 749–754 (Abstract No. 314).

Phillips, A. G., and Fibiger, H. C. (1973b). Substantia nigra: Self-stimulation and poststimulation feeding. *Physiological Psychology* 1, 233–236.

Phillips, A. G., and Fibiger, H. C. (1973c). Dopaminergic and noradrenergic substrates of positive reinforcement: Differential effects of d- and l-amphetamine. *Science* 179, 575–577.

Phillips, A. G., and Mogenson, G. J. (1969). Self-stimulation of the olfactory bulb. *Physiology & Behavior* 4, 195–197.

Phillips, A. G., Brooke, S., and Fibiger, H. C. (1975). Re-examination of the effect of 6-hydroxydopamine on intra-cranial self-stimulation. *Pharmacology, Biochemistry and Behavior*. In press.

Phillips, M. I., and Olds, J. (1969). Unit activity: Motivation-dependent responses from midbrain neurons. *Science* 165, 1269–1271.

Poschel, B. P. H. (1969). Mapping of rat brain for self-stimulation under monoamine oxidase blockade. *Physiology & Behavior* 4, 325–331.

Poschel, B. P. H., and Ninteman, F. W. (1966). Hypothalamic self-stimulation: Its suppression by blockade of norepinephrine biosynthesis and reinstatement with methamphetamine. *Life Sciences* 5, 11–16.

Pribram, K. H. (1971). "Languages of the Brain: Experimental Paradoxes and Principles in Neuropsychology." Prentice-Hall, Englewood Cliffs, New Jersey.

Richter, C. P. (1944). Total self-regulatory functions in animals and human beings. *Harvey Lectures* 38, 63–103.

Ritter, S., and Stein, L. (1973). Self-stimulation of noradrenergic cell group (A6) in locus coeruleus of rats. *Journal of Comparative and Physiological Psychology* 85, 443–452.

Ritter, S., and Stein, L. (1974). Self-stimulation in the mesencephalic trajectory of the ventral noradrenergic bundle. *Brain Research* 81, 145–157.

Roberts, E. (1974). Disinhibition as an organizing principle in the nervous system—the role of gamma-aminobutyric acid. *In* "Proceedings of the Second Canadian-American Conference on Parkinson's Disease" (F. McDowell and A. Barbeau, eds.), pp. 127–143, (Advances in Neurology, Vol. 5, c. 1974). Raven Press, New York.

Roberts, W. W. (1969). Are hypothalamic motivational mechanisms functionally and anatomically specific? *Brain, Behavior and Evolution* 2, 317–342.

Rolls, E. T. (1971a). Involvement of brainstem units in medial forebrain bundle self-stimulation. *Physiology & Behavior* 7, 297–310.

Rolls, E. T. (1971b). Contrasting effects of hypothalamic and nucleus accumbens septi self-stimulation on brain stem single unit activity and cortical arousal. *Brain Research* 31, 275–285.

Rolls, E. T. (1972). Activation of amygdaloid neurones in reward, eating and drinking elicited by electrical stimulation of the brain. *Brain Research* 45, 365–381.

Rolls, E. T., and Cooper, S. J. (1974). Connection between the prefrontal cortex and pontine brain-stimulation reward sites in the rat. *Experimental Neurology* 42, 687–699.

Routtenberg, A. (1971). Forebrain pathways of reward in *Rattus norvegicus. Journal of Comparative and Physiological Psychology* 75, 269–276.

Routtenberg, A., and Holzman, N. (1973). Memory disruption by electrical stimulation of substantia nigra, pars compacta. *Science* 181, 83–85.

Routtenberg, A., and Malsbury, C. (1969). Brainstem pathways of reward. *Journal of Comparative and Physiological Psychology* 68, 22–30.

Schreiner, L., and Kling, A. (1953). Behavioral changes following rhinencephalic injury in cat. *Journal of Neurophysiology* 16, 643–659.

Sclafani, A., and Grossman, S. P. (1969). Hyperphagia produced by knife cuts between the medial and lateral hypothalamus in the rat. *Physiology & Behavior* 4, 533–538.

Segal, M., and Bloom, F. E. (1974). The action of norepinephrine in the rat hippocampus. II. Activation of the input pathway. *Brain Research* 72, 99–114.

Setler, P. E. (1973). The role of catecholamines in thirst. *In* "The Neuropsychology of Thirst" (A. N. Epstein, H. R. Kissileff, and E. Stellar, eds.), pp. 279–291. Winston-Wiley, New York.

Seward, J. P., Uyeda, A., and Olds, J. (1959). Resistance to extinction following cranial self-stimulation. *Journal of Comparative and Physiological Psychology* 52, 294–299.

Sheffield, F. D., and Roby, T. B. (1950). Reward value of a non-nutritive sweet taste. *Journal of Comparative and Physiological Psychology* 43, 471–481.

Snyder, S. H. (1974). Catecholamines as mediators of drug effects in schizophrenia. *In* "The Neurosciences, Third Study Program" (F. O. Schmitt and F. W. Worden, eds.), pp. 721–732. MIT Press, Cambridge, Massachusetts.

Squires, R. F. (1974). Effects of noradrenalin group blockers on its uptake by synaptosomes from several brain regions: additional evidence for dopamine terminals in the frontal cortex. *Journal of Pharmacy and Pharmacology* 26, 264–267.

Stein, L. (1962). Effects and interactions of imipramine, chlorpromazine, reserpine, and amphetamine on self-stimulation: Possible neurophysiological basis of depression. *In* "Recent Advances in Biological Psychiatry" (J. Wortis, ed.), pp. 288–308. Plenum, New York.

Stein, L. (1964). Self-stimulation of the brain and the central stimulant action of amphetamine. *Federation Proceedings, Federation of American Societies for Experimental Biology* 23, 836–850.

Stein, L., and Wise, C. D. (1969). Release of norepinephrine from hypothalamus and amygdala by rewarding medial forebrain bundle stimulation and amphetamine. *Journal of Comparative and Physiological Psychology* 67, 189–198.

Stein, L., and Wise, C. D. (1971). Possible etiology of schizophrenia: Progressive damage to the noradrenergic reward system by 6-hydroxydopamine. *Science* 171, 1032–1036.

Stellar, E. (1954). The physiology of motivation. *Psychological Review* 61, 5–22.

Stellar, E. (1973). Introduction. *In* "The Neuropsychology of Thirst" (A. N. Epstein, H. R. Kissileff, and E. Stellar, eds.), pp. xiii–xv. Winston-Wiley, New York.

Stevenson, J. A. F. (1969). Neural control of food and water intake. *In* "The Hypothalamus" (W. Haymaker, E. Anderson, and W. J. H. Nauta, eds.), pp. 524–621. Thomas, Springfield, Illinois.

Stinus, L., and Thierry, A-M. (1973). Self-stimulation and catecholamines. II. Blockade of self-stimulation by treatment with alpha-methylparatyrosine and the reinstatement by catecholamine precursor administration. *Brain Research* 64, 189–198.

Teitelbaum, P., and Epstein, A. N. (1962). The lateral hypothalamic syndrome: Recovery of feeding and drinking after lateral hypothalamic lesions. *Psychological Review* 69, 74–90.

Teitelbaum, P., and Stellar, E. (1954). Recovery from the failure to eat produced by hypothalamic lesions. *Science* 120, 894–895.

Thierry, A-M., Blanc, G., Sobel, A., Stinus, L., and Glowinski, J. (1973). Dopaminergic terminals in the rat cortex. *Science* 182, 499–501.

Thierry, A-M., Hirsch, J. C., Tassin, J. P., Blanc, G., and Glowinski, J. (1974). Presence of dopaminergic terminals and absence of dopaminergic cell bodies in the cerebral cortex of the cat. *Brain Research* 79, 77–88.

Thompson, W. R., and Heron, W. (1954). Effects of restriction early in life on problem-solving ability in dogs. *Canadian Journal of Psychology* **8**, 17–31.

Tohyama, M., Maeda, T., and Shimizu, N. (1974). Detailed noradrenaline pathways of locus coeruleus neuron to the cerebral cortex with use of 6-hydroxydopa. *Brain Research* **79**, 139–144.

Troland, L. T. (1928). "The Fundamentals of Human Motivation." Van Nostrand, New York.

Trowill, J. A., Panksepp, J., and Gandelman, R. (1969). An incentive model of rewarding brain stimulation. *Psychological Review* **76**, 264–281.

Ungerstedt, U. (1971a). Stereotaxic mapping of the monoamine pathways in the rat brain. *Acta Physiologica Scandinavica, Supplementum* **367**, 1–48.

Ungerstedt, U. (1971b). Adipsia and aphagia after 6-hydroxydopamine induced degeneration of the nigrostriatal dopamine system. *Acta Physiologica Scandinavica, Supplementum* **367**, 95–122.

Ungerstedt, U. (1974). Brain dopamine neurons and behavior. *In* "The Neurosciences, Third Study Program" (F. O. Schmitt and F. W. Worden, eds.), pp. 695–703. MIT Press, Cambridge, Massachusetts.

Valenstein, E. S. (1966). The anatomical locus of reinforcement. *In* "Progress in Physiological Psychology" (E. Stellar and J. M. Sprague, eds.), Vol. 1, pp. 149–190. Academic Press, New York.

Valenstein, E. S., and Campbell, J. F. (1966). Medial forebrain bundle-lateral hypothalamic area and reinforcing brain stimulation. *American Journal of Physiology* **210**, 270–274.

Valenstein, E. S., Cox, V. C., and Kakolewski, J. W. (1968). Modification of motivated behavior elicited by electrical stimulation of the hypothalamus. *Science* **159**, 1119–1121.

Wauquier, A., and Niemegeers, C. J. E. (1972). Intracranial self-stimulation in rats as a function of various stimulus parameters. II. Influence of haloperidol, pimozide and pipamperone on medial forebrain bundle stimulation with monopolar electrodes. *Psychopharmacologia* **27**, 191–202.

Weiskrantz, L. N. (1973). Problems and progress in physiological psychology. *British Journal of Psychology* **64**, 511–520.

Wise, C. D., and Stein, L. (1969). Facilitation of brain self-stimulation by central administration of norepinephrine. *Science* **163**, 299–301.

Wishart, T. B., and Mogenson, G. J. (1970). Effects of food deprivation on water intake in rats with septal lesions. *Physiology & Behavior* **5**, 1481–1486.

Wurtz, R. H., and Olds, J. (1961). Chronic stimulation of amygdaloid complex. *Federation Proceedings, Federation of American Societies for Experimental Biology* **20**, 336 (Abstract).

Young, P. T. (1936). "Motivation of Behavior." Wiley, New York.

Young, P. T. (1959). The role of affective processes in learning and motivation. *Psychological Review* **66**, 104–125.

Zeigler, H. P., and Karten, H. J. (1974). Central trigeminal structures and the lateral hypothalamic syndrome in the rat. *Science* **186**, 636–638.

Zigmond, M. J., and Stricker, E. M. (1972). Deficits in feeding behavior after intraventricular injection of 6-hydroxydopamine in rats. *Science* **177**, 1211–1214.

Zigmond, M. J., and Stricker, E. M. (1974). Ingestive behavior following damage to central dopamine neurons: Implications for homeostasis and recovery of function. *In* "Neuropsychopharmacology of Monoamines and Their Regulatory Enzymes" (E. Usdin, ed.), pp. 385–402. Raven, New York.

The Evolution of Intelligence and Access to the Cognitive Unconscious[1]

Paul Rozin

Department of Psychology,
University of Pennsylvania,
Philadelphia, Pennsylvania

I. Introduction

A. ABSTRACT

In this paper, I shall consider intelligence as a phenotype, subject to the same biological principles and evolutionary forces as any other phenotype. As is the case with virtually all complex biological systems, intelligence should be organized in a hierarchical manner, out of component "subprograms." Within an evolutionary framework, these subprograms, which can be called *adaptive specializations,* usually originate as specific solutions to specific problems in survival, such as prey detection. These specializations, functionally defined, may be simple programs or circuits, or clusters of these, and may contain

[1] I thank Norman Adler, Henry Gleitman, Elisabeth Rozin, and W. John Smith for helpful comments on the manuscript, and James W. Kalat for participation in the development of some of the ideas presented here. The preparation of this paper and some of the research reported in it were supported by National Science Foundation Grant GB 8013 to the author.

both plastic and prewired elements. They form the building blocks for higher level intelligence.

At the time of their origin, these specializations are tightly wired into the functional system they were designed to serve and are thus inaccessible to other programs or systems in the brain. I suggest that in the course of evolution these programs become more *accessible* to other systems and, in the extreme, may rise to the level of consciousness and be applied over the full realm of behavior or mental function. Accessibility can be gained by establishment of a physical connection of one system to another or by duplication of one system's circuitry in another part of the brain by use of the appropriate genetic blueprint. I maintain that the notion of accessibility, or *levels of accessibility*, is useful in understanding the development and dissolution of intelligence, as well as its evolution. This paper is devoted to supporting and elaborating these claims and exploring the implications of this position for a psychology of learning and education. It is suggested that part of the process of learning and education can be considered as bringing to consciousness some of the limited-access programs, the "cognitive unconscious," already in the head.

B. AN EXAMPLE

Karl von Frisch (1967) has described the remarkable system used by some species of honey bees to exploit food sources. Having discovered a food source (e.g., a clump of flowers), a bee remembers some of the surrounding landmarks and flies back to the hive. On the basis of information gathered on the flight to and from the source, the bee now has information on the distance from the hive to the food source and on the direction, measured as an angle with respect to the sun's position. This information allows the bee to return to the food source and also to communicate its location to other bees in the hive.

Since the sun moves across the sky in the course of the day, the bearing taken relative to the sun would be accurate only for a particular time. But the bee brain, despite its pinhead size, contains mechanisms that can compensate for sun movement. It adjusts the angle with respect to the sun as a function of time, so that the flight from the hive to food would always be direct. In other words, the bee essentially has a set of astronomical (e.g., sun arc) data in its head, plus a "clock," as well as a scheme for relating these.

Even from this greatly oversimplified sketch of how bees locate food sources, one cannot help but be impressed by the complexity, adaptability, and appropriateness of this system. In a very reasonable sense, it is a type of intelligent behavior. This example suggests three general points: (1) the existence of adaptive specializations related to intelligence, (2) the important contribution of prewired components in intelligence, and (3) the inaccessibility of adaptive specializations (that is, the limitation of use of the bee's impressive navigational communication abilities to certain well defined situations, such as food foraging). I shall consider each of these issues in turn.

II. Adaptive Specializations

A. INTRODUCTION

In the honey bee example, a variety of behaviors and capacities, some quite specific and complex, all fit together to accomplish the successful exploitation of a food source. The cluster of behaviors and capacities is quite comparable in origin and basic biological nature to other clusters contributing to survival in nonbehavioral systems, such as adaptations to conserve body water, regulate blood pressure, or manufacture red blood corpuscles. Since biologists refer to these latter clusters as adaptive specializations, I see no objection to extending the term to "behavioral clusters," such as the bee navigation system. Use of this term serves to put intelligence in a biological-evolutionary context, which psychologists rarely do. Faced with the discovery that the fearsome wolf bitch behaves in a tender and loving manner to her cubs, psychologists or other people are neither surprised nor at a loss for explanation. One can simply say that the circuitry or programs for both aggressive and nurturant behaviors exist in the wolf brain (or, for those behavioristically inclined, in the wolf's repertoire), but have separate connections and are activated under different circumstances. However, many have been reluctant to apply this same logic to intelligent behaviors. These can be viewed as specific adaptations to specific problems rather than as the outputs of a superior, unitary, general intelligence system.

This general view, insofar as it stresses the fit between behavior and environmental demands, has been ably championed in modern times by the ethologists, particularly Tinbergen (1951), Lorenz (1965), and later Hinde (1970) and Manning (1972) (see also Shettleworth, 1971; Hinde and Stevenson-Hinde, 1973; Seligman and Hager, 1972; Rozin and Kalat, 1972). From my point of view, the critical notion is that all adaptive specializations, whether involving intelligent behaviors or red blood corpuscle manufacture, are successful attempts at problem solving. I would like to illustrate this point.

B. FOOD SELECTION

In the late 1930s and early 1940s, Curt Richter (1943) and his colleagues conclusively demonstrated the ability of the rat (*Rattus norvegicus*) to select foods that would correct a variety of nutritional imbalances. This ability, of obvious value to an omnivore, seems for the most part to be accounted for by a unique adaptive specialization, which allows rats to learn what foods make them sick or well, and thus avoid or recover from almost any possible deficiency. The unique, real-world properties of foods and their metabolic consequences are clearly reflected in this system (Rozin and Kalat, 1971, 1972; Rozin, 1976a).

In the real world, there tend to be causal connections between things that enter the mouth and events that occur in the gut or other viscera; this is mirrored in the rat by a strong tendency to "associate" tastes (e.g., as opposed to lights and sounds) with gastrointestinal and some other types of visceral events (Garcia and Koelling, 1966; Rozin, 1967; Garcia and Ervin, 1968). This has been called "belongingness" or preparedness (Seligman, 1970). Correspondingly, exteroceptive cues associate preferentially with exteroceptive events, such as pain emanating from the skin. It would indeed be folly to associate the pain produced by stepping on a tack with what was just eaten (tasted).

In the real world, there is an inherent delay imposed by the digestive system between food ingestion and its metabolic consequences. In order to learn about the significant consequences of foods and thus avoid poisons, adjust amount eaten to energy needs, and select nutritious foods, a system would have to bridge this delay. And, in contrast to other systems, where close temporal contiguity between stimuli is a prerequisite to their association, delays of hours can support learning in the feeding system, involving associations between tastes (e.g., saccharine solutions) and visceral consequences (e.g., nausea) (Garcia et al., 1966; Smith and Roll, 1967; Revusky and Garcia, 1970; Rozin, 1969a; Rozin and Kalat, 1971). Learning about the aversive (as opposed to positive) consequences of foods (e.g., poisons) occurs especially rapidly. Usually, one pairing of a new food with an aversive gastrointestinal event, even with delays of an hour or more, is adequate to produce a strong aversion which may be remembered over many months.

In the real world of the rat, which might mean a garbage dump, there are often many foods simultaneously available. The special belongingness and long-delay learning mechanisms are not, in themselves, capable of leading the rat to adaptive food selection in this complex situation. But they are complemented by some important, often built-in, aspects of the food selection system, which help sort out the various foods. The belongingness principle effectively limits the important stimuli to foods. The food world of the rat seems to be clearly divided into the familiar (experienced at least once) and the new. At any point in time, a rat may have already learned about the positive, neutral, or negative consequences of some of the available food. Needless to say, among such foods the rat avoids those that have had aversive consequences. In the presence of new foods, in addition to the above, rats are quite suspicious, and eat primarily familiar, safe foods, especially if they have had previous aversive (poisoning or deficiency) experiences (Richter, 1953; Rozin, 1968). However, new foods are eventually sampled, rather tentatively, in a "testing" manner (Rzoska, 1953).

Rats are particularly inclined to associate new foods with "new" consequences. If a rat consumes a familiar safe food along with a new food, and then becomes ill, it subsequently avoids the new food rather than the familiar food (Revusky and Bedarf, 1967; Kalat and Rozin, 1973). The adaptive value of this feature should be obvious. When faced with a variety of new foods, the rat's natural feeding pattern unconfounds the complex situation. Rats tend to eat well defined "meals," separated by rather long time periods. Furthermore, within meals, they tend to eat only one type of food. Thus, by exposing themselves to one food at a time, they optimize the operation of the long-delay learning-belongingness abilities in evaluating the consequences of ingesting each food. Just as a normal rat's tendency to avoid new foods in the presence of safe foods is exaggerated in deficiency, the normal rat's tendency to sample one food at a time is exaggerated (Rozin, 1969b).

It should be clear from this brief description that rats come equipped with an impressive set of special learning abilities that dovetail neatly with natural feeding patterns to successfully solve the food selection problems and form a well-defined adaptive specialization.

C. IMPRINTING

In order to breed successfully, adult organisms must possess some form of species recognition and species-specific displays. Since identifying character-istics of any particular species are usually distinctive and very low in variabil-ity, a sensible solution is to build in the appropriate perceptual recognition or performance system. However, for reasons that are not entirely clear, an important learning component, imprinting, appears in many species as a solution to the problem. The advantages of imprinting, insofar as it is almost foolproof, are that it can accommodate local variations within a species and may be more efficient in that it "saves" the genetic coding material that would be needed to completely specify the perceptual or behavior systems. The process will be illustrated by Marler's (1970) superb studies of the acquisition of species-specific song in white-crowned sparrows.

Adult white-crowned sparrows have a characteristic song, displayed in Fig. 1. Marler studied birds singing three different dialects of this song, depending on which part of the San Francisco area they came from (Fig. 1, A, B, C). The dialects are distinct, but all have the basic form of white-crowned sparrow song. In brief, Marler found that if birds were raised in isolation from

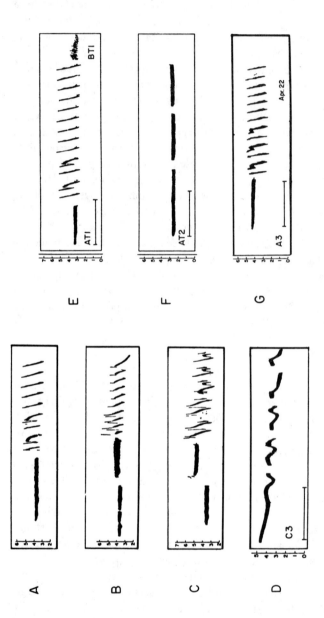

FIG. 1. Imprinting of bird song in white-crowned sparrows (composite figure made from several figures in Marler, 1970). (A–C) Samples of normal adult male songs of three white-crowned sparrows from the San Francisco Bay area: (A) the Marin dialect, (B) the Berkeley dialect, and (C) the Sunset Beach dialect. (D) Song of an adult male raised from nestling stage without hearing an adult song. This represents the "crude template" of the white-crowned sparrow song.

(E and F). Taped white-crowned sparrow song (E) and Harris' sparrow song (F) played 2 hours, twice a day to white-crowned sparrows over the age range of 35–56 days. These young birds were not exposed to the species song before or after this period. (G) Resulting adult song, in one white-crowned sparrow exposed to the conditions described under (E) and (F).

a few days after birth, they would not sing a well-developed white-crowned sparrow song when adult, but would sing a very crude song which had some of the basic structure of white-crowned sparrow song (Fig. 1D). If birds reared in isolation were exposed to tape recordings of a particular dialect of white-crowned sparrow song somewhere in the period of about 10 to 50 days of age, they would then sing in adulthood (more than 6 months later) the appropriate full-blown white-crowned sparrow song of the dialect they heard. If exposed to the same songs outside of this critical period, they would behave like completely isolated birds, and sing only the crude song. If during the critical period, they heard both a dialect of white-crowned sparrow song and some other bird song, for equal periods of time, (Fig. 1, E and F), they behave just as the group that hears only the white-crowned sparrow song (Fig. 1,G).

In short, this type of "learning" has three salient characteristics that differentiate it from most types of learning and are uniquely suited to the problem at hand:

1. It occurs during a critical period, early in life, when the probability is very high that the animal will be selectively exposed to the species song (or, in other cases of imprinting, other aspects of the parents). Clearly, later in life, close exposure to other species is much more likely.

2. The set of stimuli on which the animal can imprint is constrained. Even with a close parental tie, a young animal is exposed to many stimuli other than those emanating from the parents. Thus, some focusing or narrowing down seems appropriate. In this case, only songs with the general structure of white-crowned sparrow song fit the crude song template in the bird's head, and thus can modify it. So the crude form is inherited, and the detailed form, including the particular dialect, is learned through imprinting.

3. The imprinted "memory" or template lasts for the life of the organism and is highly resistant to extinction. The young white-crowned sparrow flies around for 6 months or more without singing the song, hears very little of its own species song during the winter, and in its first autumn and the subsequent spring hears the songs of many other species. Yet, it sings a full-blown appropriate song by the following spring.

These specific characteristics are manifested only in *certain* behaviors; other types of learning in white-crowned sparrows are presumably not characterized by "templates," critical periods, and the like. The imprinting "package" is limited in application or accessibility to certain stimuli at certain times.

Furthermore, the female white-crowned sparrow, who does not sing, seems to develop a sensory representation of its appropriate dialect, so that it can recognize local males. This representation or template is apparently temporarily unavailable to the motor system. However, after injection with testosterone, access is achieved, and the appropriate dialect is sung (Konishi, 1965).

D. Unusual, Isolated Memory Abilities

There are a number of instances of outstanding memorial achievements in species far from distinguished for their learning or memory capacity. These include, in addition to the bees already referred to, the memory of salmon for their home-stream odors (Hasler, 1966) and the memory of digger wasps (*Ammophila campestris*) for the location and state of food supply of a number of holes containing its eggs or larvae (Baerends, 1941; described in Tinbergen, 1951). Usually in such cases, in the life pattern of the species, there is one problem requiring memory for stimuli that cannot be genetically programmed, since the particular stimuli depend on characteristics that vary in different localities. For example, Aronson (1951) has shown that certain gobiid fish can find their way from one tidepool to another, at low tide, by jumping accurately over rocks. Random jumps would harm them or leave them stranded on rocks. In fact, the fish behave without error. Aronson eliminated obvious sources of direct sensory information on the location of neighboring pools. Furthermore, when placed in an unfamiliar pool, the fish will not jump. It appears that during high tide, the fish swims above and into the rock crevices and forms an accurate map of the area, which is stored in memory and utilized at low tides.

III. The Significant Contribution of Prewired Components

Most of what the bee does in navigation and communication is mediated by built-in circuitry. Representations of the basic features of the sun arc and possibly other astronomical variables, plus the clock mechanism, seem genetically determined in that they are independent of specific early experience and constant within races of a species. Obviously, the particular location of the sun with respect to today's food source is given by experience. Furthermore, given changes in the sun arc both with season and with the latitude at which a particular bee happens to find itself, it would be folly to genetically program the specific parameters of the arc. In fact, some experience observing a piece of the sun arc is critical to adequate navigation (Lindauer, 1961). However, the bee need not have observed the sun in a particular part of the day, in the past, in order to orient correctly to food when first released at that time. By and large, it seems that those aspects of the system (including the communication code and fundamental navigational principles) which are quite constant are prewired, while those that vary from day to day contain a more plastic, experiential component. In this system, environmental input often has the function of calibrating a prewired system.

The division between experiential components and genetic programming is seen most clearly in the navigational systems of some fish (Hasler and Schwassman, 1960), which are also based on orientation to the sun. In one species which lives in only one hemisphere, the direction of sun movement across the sky is genetically coded within the navigational system. In a related species that straddles the equator, the direction of sun movement is not prespecified, but is acquired by experience.

When intelligence is viewed in the context of problem solving, the relative importance of genetic and experiential components in the solution depends on the type of problem. Each has inherent advantages. Experience does not necessarily provide more successful or more complex solutions.

The bee example represents a class of adaptations that have been described by Lorenz (1965) as "calibration of aiming mechanisms, adjustment of computers, and setting of internal clocks." I shall use the term calibrational learning for all these, meaning to imply that there is an elaborate prewired system, which is capable of producing fairly precise adjustments of an animal to its environment. The main function of environment, experience, or memory, in these instances is to provide reference points, so that the precise function inherent in the organism can be calibrated. Calibrational mechanisms tend to be found in navigational, homeostatic, and perceptual systems.

Space perception in humans provides an example of such a system. When displacing prisms are worn, subjects misjudge the location of seen targets when they reach for them with their hands. This makes sense, since the elaborate "isomorphism" between points in visual and kinesthetic space (be that innate or acquired) has been systematically disturbed. What is remarkable (Harris, 1965) is that, after only a few minutes of reaching practice, the subjects can reach accurately. Brief "practice," lasting minutes and involving possibly only a small portion of the total visual and kinesthetic fields, may lead to a general readjustment of relationship between the arm and the eye. It is as though two "maps" of the world each remained intact, but were sliding with respect to each other. This can easily be described as a recalibration.

The contribution of prewired circuitry to the complex behavior that we often describe as intelligent has been generally underrated. This may result, in part, from emphasis by American learning psychologists on a few powerful and well-documented learning paradigms, in which plasticity has a dominant role, and the contributions of complex prewired circuitry are not salient. The bee navigation example is at the opposite extreme: the "intelligence," or, for that matter, "interest" in the phenomenon comes largely from the prewired circuitry. If a full astronomical table were built into the bee, so that environmental calibration was not required, the bee's behavior and its underlying mechanism would be just as fascinating and would certainly still seem intelligent.

Most animal behavior with a plastic component fits somewhere between the extremes of traditional learning paradigms and calibrational phenomena. The adaptive specializations already described illustrate some of the various types of interactions of plastic and prewired components. For example, the prewired crude song template in the white-crowned sparrow is as critical a component of song learning as the plastic mechanism that shapes it into a specific dialect.

In short, the biological framework espoused here and by the ethologists allows for a wide variety of plastic mechanisms, and a wide variety of interactions between them and prewired circuitry. The only limitations are what is feasible, given the properties of the basic neuronal building blocks, and the constraints of a gradual evolution in which intermediate forms must be expected to have some selective value.

IV. The Inaccessibility of Adaptive Specializations

Adaptive specializations, by their nature as solutions to specific problems, tend to manifest themselves only in the narrow set of circumstances related to the problem that directed their evolution. The same navigationally brilliant bees may perform poorly in a simple conditioning experiment and do not show highly sophisticated computerlike capacities in all other types of behavior. For most of a bee's problems, the navigational system would be of little use, so that it might be an evolutionary waste of resources to program the "hardware" to make it generally available. In other words, bees cannot use their navigational computer for other purposes for the same reason that Boeing 747s cannot roll over on the ground. There are no advantages for certain capacities in certain contexts. Similar restrictions in accessibility would hold for the white-crowned sparrow's template matching machinery, the goby's visual memory, and the rat's long-delay learning system. I describe this restrictive feature of adaptive specializations by saying that they are *inaccessible* to other systems. As I will indicate later in this paper, I consider the concept of inaccessibility, and the understanding of the circumstances under which inaccessible programs can be made accessible, of central importance in psychology and biology.

A particularly clear example of inaccessibility comes from low-level inferential systems in visual perception. Highly complex and sophisticated, "intelligent" systems seem to pervade the visual system. These systems are inaccessible to consciousness and are probably tightly wired into the visual system. Much of their sophisticated circuitry would appear to be built in. The phenomenon of size constancy is an example. The fact that a given object appears equal in size at different distances from the eye, and hence with different-sized retinal images, requires a rather complex explanation. It can be partially explained as a compensation mechanism that trades off distance and retinal size reciprocally. This, of course, requires a measure of retinal size, which seems straightforward enough, and a measure of distance or depth, which is arrived at by a complex process (Hochberg, 1973). One factor in the calculation of distance is convergence: the angle between the major axes of the two eyes varies (becomes larger) the closer the object, since the image of the focal object projects on the fovea of both retinas. Hence, a measure of convergence could supply distance information, and with retinal size information, lead to a size-constancy effect. Such a compensatory system could well be built in; at least it appears to be operating in children of 70—85 days of age (Bower, 1964). However, experience must play some role, if for no other reason than that the interocular distance (critical in determining amount of convergence) obviously increases with age, and therefore must be recalibrated.

In fact, a full determination of depth involves many factors other than convergence, such as texture, texture occlusion (how much of the texture or "grain" is occluded by the object), aerial perspective, familiar size. Familiar size is clearly a clue that heavily involves experience. Only acquired knowledge of the "real" size of an object can account for its superiority in size constancy to an unfamiliar object. In some complex way, various depth cues, such as those listed above, combine into a total distance estimate. Weighed against retinal size, and influenced by familiar size and other factors, the result is size constancy. The whole elaborate information gathering and evaluation process, and others like it, were named "unconscious inference" by Helmholtz (1867). Clearly, this system is inaccessible to consciousness and "tightly wired" into the visual system. Otherwise, how could it be that classical training of artists involved, in part, "learning the rules for portraying depth which are actually the depth cues themselves" (Hochberg, 1973).

Another example comes from the perception of motion. When subjects observe an illuminated dot on the circumference of an invisible and rotating circle, the path of the dot appears to be forward moving and "bouncing" off an invisible floor (see Fig. 2, top) (Wallach, 1959). If now the same movement sequence of the dot is repeated, but with a light at the center of the circle, the dot on the circumference, describing the same objective course, is interpreted as rotating around the hub of a wheel (Fig. 2, bottom). Thus, in a complex way, contextual information is integrated to provide a reasonable, relatively simple, and consistent interpretation of a pattern of objective movement. This, and many other examples from perception of motion (Hochberg, 1973) imply the operation of systems which take many factors into account, integrating over space and/or time, and usually resulting in a consistent, unitary perception. The processes involved are clearly inaccessible (again, Helmholtz's unconscious inference), and seem to be geared toward deciding on the simplest interpretation of an array.

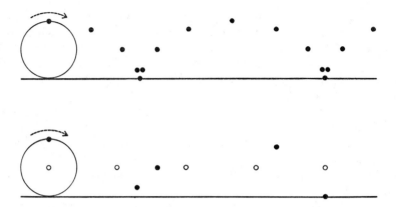

FIG. 2. Different experiences in the observer are caused by the same objective motion of light on the rim of a rolling wheel. At top, the perceived motion (on a cycloidal curve) fits the objective motion. However, if the hub is lighted (bottom), this perceived motion gives way to a compound motion: the light on the rim now seems to rotate about the hub as the wheel rolls from left to right.

V. Accessibility and the Organization and Evolution of Intelligence

The notion of accessibility leads to a theory of the organization and evolution of intelligence. Since all reasonably complex animals have quite a few sophisticated circuits or programs (adaptive specializations) in their brains, I suggest that a major route to increasing flexibility and power over the environment, surely hallmarks of intelligence, would be to make these more generally available or accessible. This would have adaptive value when an area of behavioral function could profit from programs initially developed for another purpose.

Using a computer analogy, it is as though there are specific circuits wired to only certain inputs and/or outputs. Thus, only numbers entered in a certain register might contact the addition program. If this program were now connected into other inputs (made more accessible), the additive power of the machine would be extended. Similarly, if separate addition and logarithmic conversion circuits in the same computer could be connected to each other, a multiplication ability would emerge.

I call all the specific, tightly wired, limited-access machinery in the brain the cognitive unconscious. Part of progress in evolution toward more intelligent organisms could then be seen as gaining access to or emancipating the cognitive unconscious. Minimally, a program (adaptive specialization) could be wired into a new system or a few new systems. In the extreme, the program could be brought to the level of consciousness, which might serve the purpose of making it applicable to the full range of behaviors and problems.[2]

Intelligent function, in this scheme, is conceived in terms of a hierarchy, in which specific components become available to more and more systems. As Simon (1967) has pointed out, complex systems should almost always be hierarchical, since it would be extremely difficult to build (evolve or develop) them otherwise. A single error in the nonhierarchical assembly of a complex system could destroy the whole system, whereas in a hierarchical system, only the subcomponent involved would be destroyed. For this reason, as Simon points out, the watchmaker who assembles component sections of the watch, and then joins these together, is much more likely to end up with a watch than his compatriot who sequentially assembles the whole thing. If the second watchmaker drops the watch at any point, he is likely to have to begin all over again. In organic evolution, there would be yet further pressures for hierarchical organization, since each subcomponent must not only be stable, but have some adaptive value. The watchmaker need not worry that a particular assembled component on his bench have any time-keeping properties.

Given that behavioral adaptive specializations exist, it seems natural that these stable systems should be components in more complex systems. And indeed, one often sees common mechanisms at work in different behavior systems. How much more reasonable that the common elements in such systems were "invented" only once, and simply reapplied (accessed) in other situations.

The increased-accessibility view of the evolution of intelligence contrasts with the general-process view, which probably has more adherents among American learning psychologists. In this view, intelligence is considered in

---

[2] Jerison's (1973) interesting ideas on the evolution of the brain and intelligence, although focused on interpretation of changes in brain size, make potential contact with the view presented here. He sees intelligence and related measures of brain size as related to complexity of information-processing capacity and ability to construct a satisfactory model of the real world. This involves, among other things, interrelation of the major sensory systems. He makes the point that the reptiles, largely visual animals, perform a great deal of their visual processing peripherally, that is, in the eye (what I would call a place rather inaccessible to other systems in the brain). The originally nocturnal mammals relied more on other sensory systems, such as audition, with processing carried out more centrally. With invasion of diurnal niches, some groups of mammals (e.g., primates) utilized visual information much more, but corticalized much of the visual processing, on the model of audition. In Jerison's view, the location of all these programs for vision, audition, etc., within the same part of the brain faciliated integration of the systems. In the terms used here, the corticalization of visual processing allowed mutual accessing of the auditory, visual, and other sensory systems.

terms of learning capacity, and the evolution of intelligence as gradual accretion of new learning capacities (Bitterman, 1965).

One critical contrast between the two views hinges on the importance of new abilities, for the adaptive specialization-accessibility view focuses on reapplication of old abilities. It seems unlikely that a new capacity, at its inception, would be broadly available, as implied by a general process view, since broad availability involves more connections, programming, and reorganization than would be necessary. Under the reasonable assumption that environmental problems are usually the immediate selecting force for a particular ability, the simplest, most efficient, and least disorganizing approach would be to wire the new circuit into the relevant program.[3]

Another critical contrast between the two views concerns the emphasis by Bitterman and others on learning as *the* critical component in intelligence. Although "plasticity" is clearly a fundamental component of intelligence, as argued above, it is only one component. Consider an animal with an enormously complicated built-in program to handle one specific problem. It might advance greatly in power (intelligence) if it could apply that sophistication to another problem. This application might involve a learned or evolved connection into a new system. However, from the point of view of intelligence, the new program being accessed would be at least as interesting as the process of accessing it. In the same sense, plugging one computer program into another is not adequately described by examining the plug. The adaptive specialization-accessibility view sees traditional learning as one of a wider set of plastic mechanisms (e.g., calibration mechanisms) sensitive to environmental factors, which, in varying combinations with genetically determined programs, leads to successful solutions to problems.

The accessibility view causes difficulty for traditional attempts to arrange animals on a ladder of increasing levels of intellectual capacity. Looking at peak performance, for example, bees come out extremely high. To say the "mammals" are more intelligent than "fish" because mammals show X type of learning and fish (or more correctly, a few, particular species of fish) do not (Bitterman, 1965) is not satisfactory for two reasons. First it arbitrarily selects skills of importance within the framework of traditional learning theory as critical determinants of intelligence. Second, it assumes that, because some fish do not show a particular type of learning in a situation selected by an experimenter, they are incapable of such learning. Clearly,

---

[3] However, it must be recognized that though individual problems have unique characteristics, there are also common elements in many situations, as a result of the physical nature of the world. For example, the general forward-moving temporal sequence of causality in the physical world seems sensibly reflected by a general property of learning: forward (as opposed to backward) conditioning.

testing must be done in a situation where the behavior in question might have some adaptive value.

However, the work of Bitterman, Gonzalez, and others (e.g., Gonzalez *et al.*, 1963; Behrend *et al.*, 1965; see also discussion in Gleitman and Rozin, 1971) has quite clearly shown that the few species of fish studied are not capable of performing well on some relatively complex tasks in the *laboratory*, such as habit reversal, which at least some mammal species can rather easily master.[4]

The general issue is not with the truth of these interesting results of Bitterman, Gonzalez, and their colleagues, but with their interpretation. My interpretation is that some mammals can demonstrate the abilities in question in a wider range of circumstances, including the laboratory situation. In other words, the circuits needed for performing these tasks are more accessible in the mammals studied. For the case of habit reversal, this view is supported by the fact that habit reversal effects have occasionally been obtained in fish within a yet to be specified narrow range of conditions. Mammals (or at least some species of mammals) may differ from most other animals not so much in the complexity and plasticity of their behavior in any particular situation, as in the *range* within which they can apply their complex, plastic programs. This conception could apply to the basic learning "paradigms" themselves.[5] That is, classical and instrumental learning are rather easy to discover in a wide variety of functional systems or situations in mammals studied in the

---

[4] A more general difference between the two classes (as inferred from a small sample of species) is suggested by recent work (e.g., Pert and Gonzalez, 1974). Some fish (and one reptile) species show a very simple and straightforward relationship between magnitude of reinforcement and the strength of reinforced behavior. For example, resistance to extinction *increases* as magnitude of reinforcement in training increases for goldfish and one turtle species (*Chrysemys picta picta*), while resistance to extinction *decreases* in rats and other mammals studied under the same circumstances. This finding, and some related findings on contrast effects have led Pert and Gonzales (1974) to suggest that ". . . the behavior of fish is regulated in terms of the strict principle of reinforcement (Hull . . . , Thorndike . . .) . . . according to this principle, reward acts directly to strengthen the functional connections between stimuli and responses—while the behavior of rats is regulated in terms of the learning about and subsequent anticipation of reward."

However, this conception must be qualified by the observation that learning about foods (taste-aversion learning, see Section II,B) in rats seems to fit more with the simpler "fish" model. It does not show some of the higher-order effects (e.g., "blocking") which are seen in other areas of rat learning and have led to the view of the rat as anticipator of events or information processor (Seligman, 1970; Seligman and Hager, 1972; Kalat and Rozin, 1972). Nonetheless, a modified distinction of the type described by Gonzalez and his colleagues may hold true: phenomena requiring notions like anticipation or expectancy may not be found in the poikilothermic vertebrates.

[5] The possibility of placing learning paradigms within the accessibility framework was suggested by Richard Katz (personal communication).

laboratory. It is presumably for this reason that these basic paradigms seem to describe general learning processes. On the other hand, one may find clear instances of this type of learning only in specific, well defined situations in other groups of animals, such as insects. These paradigmatic learning properties may initially appear as adaptive specializations in well defined situations, and become more generally accessible in mammals. The emphasis of the ethologists on the confinement of learning to specific situations may come in part from their concentration on groups other than mammals, in contrast to the psychologists, who came up with general learning "laws" based primarily on the study of mammals.

One could be led to conclude, as Schwartz (1974) has suggested, that, "It is odd, but perhaps reassuring, to think that by studying the behavior of pigeons in arbitrary situations, one learns nothing about the principles which govern the behavior of pigeons in nature, but a good deal about the principles which govern the behavior of people." The Skinner box presents a type of "abstract" task in which "emancipated" humans can perform well, since they can apply many programs over a wide variety of situations. Strangely enough, then, the adaptive specialization notion leads to a definition of intelligence along the lines of concrete (limited, specific applicability) to abstract. This concrete-abstract dimension is reminiscent of what many psychologists mean by intelligence. In some sense, g is a measure of accessibility.

VI. Mechanisms of Increasing Accessibility

Let us consider only extending the domain of a program, X, tightly wired into a system A, into a new system B. There are two ways in which X is represented in such an organism: first, as a genetic blueprint and, second, as a set of circuits in the brain. In evolution, one way to extend X to B is to reduplicate the X circuit in conjunction with the B system. That is, the program for execution of a given circuit must exist in the genome of every cell, and hence in every part of the nervous system. Although we do not know, in any detail, how a neural circuit unfolds under the guidance of a genetic program, we can be reasonably confident that a genetic blueprint, coded into units like operons, exists, and can be repressed or released in the appropriate environment. Under this view, a specialization (circuit) could be extended by releasing (or derepressing) the appropriate genetic program at the appropriate time in the appropriate neural context. Such extensions have probably occurred many times in the evolution of organisms.

Without such a mechanism, one would be forced to assume that such frequently utilized adaptions as feedback or homeostatic control systems were repeatedly created *de novo*. Surely, such a widespread mechanism should become generally accessible through the process of genetic reduplication. Similarly, the size constancy "component" in the visual system, with its compensating trade-off of size and distance (see Section IV), has some formal resemblance to the compensatory system that seems to be involved in Piagetian tasks such as conservation of mass or volume (see Section VIII). In this case, it is highly unlikely, given the probable location of these two programs in the head, that they share any physical circuitry. However, it is conceivable that a shared genetic program is involved. In other cases of common mechanisms, the possibility of reduplicated genetic programs as opposed to shared physical circuitry (or, a third possibility, independent origins) is not clearly decidable. For example, the possible common mechanisms involved in scanning the visual world and the scanning of memory could result from reduplication, shared circuitry, or independent evolution of parallel structures.

A second method of increasing accessibility is to use the same physical X circuitry and somehow connect B into it. That is, X evolves to satisfy some contingencies faced by system A, but now that it is present, it has adaptive value within system B. At the level of evolution, situations like this have been described as preadaptation (Mayr, 1960). Thus, for example, the mammalian middle ear bones originated, in primitive fish, as part of the jaw articulation. Pressure for powerful chewing ability led to an increased articulation surface, and gradually to a new articulation in addition to and more substantial than the original one. The new articulation removed the old one from selection pressure directed toward chewing. The old articulation, which was already well suited for transmission of sound, then came under the selective control of the auditory system and, as it happened, ceased to function in articulation. The result was the middle ear bones. Here we have a transfer rather than an extension of function, but the mechanism would be the same in either case. Of course, genetic modifications would be required.

Thinking now of the establishment of the B–X connection within the animal's lifetime, we immediately run up against present ignorance of the physiology of learning. I, at least, find a primitive connectionistic neurology of learning as reasonable as anything here, so that the analog of plugging an old program into new inputs would hold. Whatever the precise mechanism, if the B–X connection had survival value, any genetic change that made the *learned* establishment of the connection easier would be selected for. Most simply, this could involve increasing the number of potential synaptic contacts between the components. The earliest stages of accessing in evolution could often be the potentiality of some kind of learned "connection." Note that if B–X had significant survival value, continued selection for easier connection (learning) could take place, and this could conceivably lead ultimately to a genetically determined connection (Waddington, 1957). Connection into existing programs as a result of experience would seem to be an important form of learning and an important mode of increasing accessibility. It is discussed below in Sections VIII and IX, with particular reference to acquisition of initial reading skills.

There are, then, at least two models for increased access: an evolutionary mechanism, based on duplication of the physical program itself in development by appropriate activation of the genetic blueprint, or preservation of a single physical program, and increasing connections to it by genetic programming or acquisition in the course of an individual lifetime.

VII. Increased Accessibility Applied to Human Function: Development, Dissolution, and Pathology

The hallmark of the evolution of intelligence notion put forward here is that a capacity first appears in a narrow context and later becomes extended into other domains. This seems to be quite a reasonable interpretation of cognitive development as described, for example, within a Piagetian framework. The general Piagetian scheme (Piaget, 1955; Flavell, 1963) involves movement from concrete to abstract, which means, in this context, specific-inaccessible to general-accessible. Thus, programs are at work in the young child which are not yet usable in all situations, available to consciousness, or statable. In the adaptive specialization framework, one would expect a gradual extension of a specialization, first to additional concrete situations, with a possible ultimate extension into consciousness (abstract conception). Piaget represents just such a process, using the term *décalage* to describe it. Thus, conservation involves the logical capacity that "appreciates" the notions of reversibility (if A → B → A then B is equivalent to A) and compensation (reciprocal relationship between measures such as height and width of a vessel, which incidentally bears an obvious parallel to the size—distance trade-off in size constancy). This "program" is initially only accessible in the limited domain of numbers. At age 6, children understand that there are the same *number* of marbles whether spread out or clumped together, but cannot yet apply the same logic to water vessels of different shape, or equivalent clay masses of different shapes. Gradually through the process of horizontal décalage, the "conservation circuitry" extends through mass to volume conservation and finally to area conservation. In general, then, in early stages, intelligence is manifested as unconnected, separate capacities. In support of this type of conception, Lewis and McGurk (1972) comment in a recent review: " . . . infant intelligence is not a general, unitary trait, but is rather, a composite of skills and abilities that are not necessarily covariant" (p. 1176). Through development, the capacities are extended and connected together. In the final Piagetian stage of formal operations, some capacities become fully emancipated and hence conscious and statable. It does appear that, in this case, ontogeny recapitulates phylogeny.

J. Hughlings Jackson (1884) has pointed out that neuropathology has regressive consequences, so that the dissolution of function tends to mirror its evolution and development. This relationship seems to appear most clearly in cases where brain function is systemically depressed, as in atherosclerosis or concussions. Within the framework discussed here, dissolution could be seen as *loss of access* to the most recently "acquired" programs. Indeed, a few studies of the dissolution of cognitive function in senility suggest a gradual return to the limited Piagetian capacities of the child, with the order of disappearance (loss of access) roughly reversing the order of appearance (de Ajuriaguerra *et al.,* 1964; Feldman *et al.,* 1975). There are also reasons to believe that, in recovery of function, the ontogenetic sequence is respected; for example, the stages of development of food and water ingestion and regulation systems in the infant rat clearly parallel the stages of recovery of these same functions following damage to the lateral hypothalamus (Teitelbaum *et al.,* 1971; Teitelbaum, 1973).

Some of the puzzling achievements of seniles, or children for that matter, are easily understood within an accessibility framework. For example, the linguistic fluency of both in the face of poor logical-cognitive function is easily interpretable as the function of a language system disconnected from much of the rest of intelligence-generating circuitry. In general, neurologists disagree as to the extent to which the pathology of higher mental function results from destruction of programs or processing centers as opposed to disconnection of intact systems. Certainly both must occur, but Geschwind (1965a,b) has argued persuasively that many cognitive defects consequent on brain damage can be explained by disconnection of processing centers, which translates into loss of access. A clear example is a variety of acquired alexia [originally described by Dejerine and recently confirmed by Geschwind (1962)]. In the few cases on record, there is sudden loss of ability to read, associated with blindness in the right visual field, but normal visual perception in the left visual field. The lesion, produced by occlusion of a cerebral blood vessel, involves extensive destruction of the left occipital cortex *and* destruction of the posterior portion of the corpus callosum. The result is that the intact occipital cortex has been cut off from its principal connection to the linguistic hemisphere, and processing of orthographic material is blocked. The loss of *capacity* in this case, is not loss of processing centers as much as loss of access. Disconnection syndromes, or loss of access, are particularly common, as pointed out by Geschwind (1965a,b) because the fiber tract connections between brain areas are much more compact than the brain areas themselves. Hence, the tracts are more easily compromised by spatially contiguous lesions, as produced for example, by strokes, bullets, or tumors. Thus, loss of access may be a primary explanation of pathology.

An example of this, in addition to acquired alexia, is the frequent preservation of short-term memory, as measured by digit span, in the face of severe cognitive regression in senility (see Rozin, 1976b, for a general discussion of this issue). The failure of digit span to regress to childhood levels while other functions do can be puzzling, since the superior digit span of adults may be partly attributed to *intelligent* functions, such as grouping or organization. After all, digit span is part of many standard adult intelligence tests, and correlates rather highly with other, more common-sense measures of intelligence. A loss of access view explains this phenomenon by assuming that senility has not resulted in elimination of organization-chunking and other "intelligent" processes, but rather their confinement to a narrow area of function, which may include some short-term memory processes.[6]

VIII. Language and the Acquisition of Reading

The usefulness of the notion of levels of accessibility, and some problems it raises about the process of education, will be discussed in these final sections on language and reading.

Human language is an adaptive specialization. It is particularly valuable for my purposes because it highlights the notion of *inaccessibility,* since learning to read involves gaining access to parts of the language system. Language has been in use for tens of thousands of years in our species and obviously serves many adaptive functions. It is remarkable how this incredibly complex system, which deservedly merits a special academic field for its study, seems to develop so easily in almost all members of the species. After 4 to 5 years of life, without explicit organized instructions, children demonstrate remarkable linguistic facility. They are able to generate new sentences that they have never heard, and understand complicated constructions. Only in the last few decades have linguists made major advances in unraveling the phonological, syntactic, and semantic principles underlying this performance. That is, the rules of sentence production or comprehension, which are obviously present in the head of virtually all 5-year-olds, have escaped a satisfactory description for thousands of years. Language seems to be represented by a sophisticated set of programs in the brain, which are inaccessible to conscious reflection

---

[6] There are other instances of loss of access in normal function. Forgetting itself is often described as loss of access. The process of automatization may be another example. Highly practiced tasks or capacities (e.g., perception of letters in words, bicycle riding), though often acquired in terms of well-defined units, become smoothly perceived or executed routines, in which the components are ultimately difficult to recover. In some sense, these component skills may have lost their access to consciousness.

[although not entirely inaccessible, even in children—see Gleitman *et al.* (1973)] . It is indeed striking how a child who cannot appreciate the simplest logical relationships, such as overlap of classes, can show high level mastery over this incredibly complicated system. The precocious linguistic performance of children has prompted a number of leading investigators to assume that, with respect to language function, there is a considerable amount of innate prestructuring in the brain (Chomsky, 1965; Lenneberg, 1967).

Much of the evidence favoring an important role for genetic determination in human language, and for language as an adaptive specialization, has been reviewed by Lenneberg (1967). The major lines are as follows.

1. The complexity of linguistic behavior far outstrips most other sorts of conceptual behavior in children.

2. The biological-genetic regularity of language development: Early language development unfolds in a pattern quite similar to motor development (e.g., walking), that is, as though it were a maturational phenomenon (Lenneberg, 1967). The universality of certain features of all languages (e.g., existence of word categories, such as noun or verb) and the regular development in stages support a highly biologically determined system.

3. Specializations in speech production and reception: Certain anatomical features of the human speech production (Lieberman, 1973) and speech reception systems (Liberman *et al.*, 1967) seem to have been specially and uniquely evolved to handle material like speech.

4. Hemispheric specialization for language: Data from split-brain and other patients have demonstrated that a significant portion of linguistic function, most clearly that having to do with speech production, usually lies in only one cerebral hemisphere (Sperry *et al.*, 1969, Gazzaniga, 1970; Milner, 1973; Levy, 1974). Thus, we can talk about a physical location for some of the circuitry. Geschwind *et al.* (1968) have reported a patient who suffered severe brain damage, which resulted in destruction of the brain tissue surrounding the areas in the left hemisphere that subserve language. This patient was a talking machine: he would repeat everything said to him, yet there was no evidence that the material presented made any contact with any nonlinguistic functions. Therefore an anatomically identifiable functional speech reception and production system exists. It can perform the incredibly complicated task of converting the pattern of sound waves representing a particular utterance, as represented in the auditory system, into a set of "equivalent" commands to the articulatory apparatus.

5. A final argument for language as an adaptive specialization has to do with the inaccessibility of the phonological system. I will discuss it below, in the context of understanding reading.

It is striking that reading, unlike speech, is rarely acquired spontaneously, and almost always requires systematic and extended instruction. More interesting is the fact that many children who master English speech without any apparent difficulty have great difficulty in learning to read. Yet reading seems to be much the easier task: spoken language mastery has already occurred, and the only problem for English speakers seems to be to learn an additional mapping of some 26 symbols onto the already learned sounds of speech.

Reading is a very new event in our species, since writing is at most 5000 years old, and literacy was an accomplishment of a very select few until this century. Valuable as reading skill is now, one could say that it has not yet had time to evolve as an adaptive specialization. My thesis is that reading the English alphabet involves gaining access to the *phonological system,* which is tightly wired into the auditory-speech system. The problem then is accessing the phonological system: pulling it out of the cognitive unconscious, or at least connecting it somehow into the visual system (this view is expressed in Rozin and Kalat, 1972; Gleitman and Rozin, 1973a,b, 1976; Rozin and Gleitman, 1976; Mattingly, 1972; Savin, 1972; Liberman *et al.,* 1974).

One might ask what aspects of the phonological system are so hard to connect into the visual system? Since writing systems have unfolded in an historically orderly way, this order might be a clue to the different components of reading and writing, and the relative complexity of each (Gelb, 1952). Earliest systems are varieties of "picture writing" schemes (semasiography) in which ideas rather than words are represented (e.g., *"man eat corn"* would be represented by a picture of a man eating corn). Later, schemes for the representation of the words of speech (logography) by characters with some visual resemblance to the meaning of the word were invented (e.g., "man eat corn" would be represented by the sequence of pictures: man eat corn). This type of logographic system is approximated by present day Chinese and has the critical characteristic that the sound of the language does not mediate between the orthography and the meaning. Later systems of writing gradually became more and more dependent on the sound stream of speech (a process called *phoneticization*). In earlier stages, the unit of the sound stream represented in writing was the syllable. Many *syllabaries* were developed independently in ancient times (e.g., Sumerian cuneiform), and some exist today. According to our best information (Gelb, 1952), the *alphabet,* which essentially maps a smaller unit of speech, the phoneme, was invented only once and spread from its Mediterranean origin to much of the world (see Gleitman and Rozin, 1976, for an extended discussion of this material).

Logographic systems do not require tapping into the sound system of speech, so according to this view they should not be terribly difficult to learn. After all, learning to assign the name "car" to a certain shaped thing in the real world and "dog" to a different thing is not very different from calling one written character car and another dog. In fact, this appears to be relatively easy for children: almost all children easily learn at least a few words by sight. Even children having great difficulty learning to read English can easily learn a substantial number (30) of Chinese characters and their English spoken translations (Rozin et al., 1971). In fact, many inner city children in the third or fourth grade, after years of schooling in reading seem only to have learned a modest number of whole words and their spoken equivalents, even when taught by "phonics" methods.

The main difficulty seems to arise at the level of phoneticization, and in the particular unit or level of phoneticization. Lila Gleitman and I believe that the major problem concerns the level of the unit of phoneticization: the alphabet maps into phonemes, and these units are deeply embedded in the specialized speech system. Evidence for this position comes from two quarters: speech perception and reading instruction. For a more extensive discussion of these issues, see Gleitman and Rozin (1973a,b; 1976), Rozin and Gleitman (1976), Mattingly (1972), Savin (1972), Liberman et al. (1974), and the volume edited by Kavanagh and Mattingly (1972).

Recent work, done largely by Liberman and his colleagues at the Haskins Laboratory (Liberman et al., 1967) indicates clearly the nature of the problem. The work shows that contrary to what might be called common sense, the sound stream of speech is not divisible into separate elements (phonemes) that correspond to the separate alphabetic letters. There are not, in other words, three separate or separable sound events in the spoken word bag. It does appear that in the organization of the speech system in the brain there are three separate elements in the word (see Fig. 3) bag. According to Chomsky and Halle (1968) and others, at the deepest level these are represented as "systematic phonemes," which become converted through a series of rules peculiar to the particular language, into sequential commands for b, a, and g, which are sent down from the brain into the articulatory apparatus. However, the musculature of the mouth, pharynx, etc., responds sluggishly, so that, for example, the g command arrives in the mouth while the muscles are still following the a instruction. Furthermore, the shape of the vocal cavity, which largely determines the quality of the sound, will be quite different when the g command arrives in the word bag as opposed to big, so that the same g command to the same set of muscles will produce different events in the mouth. As a result of this (see Fig. 3), the isolatable phonemes of the articulatory commands overlap in a complex way in the sound stream. Liberman has referred to this overlapping effect as "shingling." What the reader of the alphabet must learn is that at some underlying level, represented in the phonological system but not clearly in the sound stream, speech utterances can be segmented to the phonemic level. And yet this segment cannot always be clearly illustrated, since some consonants cannot be pronounced in isolation. Thus, for example, the stop consonants like d or p

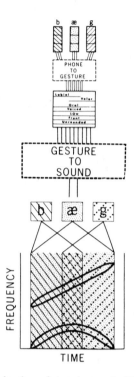

FIG. 3. Scheme for the production of speech sounds. This display is a representation of what happens at the various levels in the speech system during the utterance of a single syllable *baeg*. Time is represented on the horizontal axis, and levels of the speech system (from neural command to articulatory movements) are represented vertically. The figure illustrates two fundamental transitions in speech production. The first is the transition from commands to the articulatory apparatus from the brain (top level) to the actual movements in the articulatory apparatus (middle level). Note that separate commands for each of the three phonemes in *baeg* are assumed to be sent down from the brain, in the appropriate temporal order. At this level, the phoneme is isolatable. These commands interact in a complex way with the speech apparatus, depending on its previous state and further anticipated states. A second transition from gesture (movements of the articulatory apparatus) to sound, adds much complexity and shingling, since it is the shape of the oral cavity and other such features that determine the characteristics of the sound uttered. The net result of the two transitions is a complex sound pattern (bottom level), in which the three basic phonemes can no longer be isolated, because of overlapping (Liberman, 1970).

cannot be pronounced without appending a weak vowel, called the schwa, yielding *duh* or *puh*. Children are often instructed to blend the word dog, for example, by combining the three elements, *duh, o, guh*. If they dutifully follow instructions, they will get *duh-o-guh*, no matter how fast they blend. This can be shown by combining the three segments on a tape recorder and playing them rapidly. The reason is simply that there is no *duh* in dog. The *d* command does different things to the mouth in the context of a following *uh* or *o* command. This can be seen in Fig. 4, which shows the sound patterns necessary to produce two common English syllables, *di* and *du*. Note that there is no clean break corresponding to the *d* and *i* or *u*.

One might think that one could extract the *d* from a tape of the *di* syllable by clipping off the *i*. If this is tried, by gradually cutting off the end of the tape, one hears a shorter and shorter *i* in *di*, and then suddenly a chirping sound which has no particular resemblance to speech. There is no pure *d* isolated in the sound stream. Furthermore, it is extremely difficult to understand, on the basis of examining the *sound patterns* of various syllables with initial *d*, for example, what common characteristics lead to the perception of *d* (Liberman *et al.*, 1967).

But our speech system is built to make just such categorical phoneme distinctions. The upshot of the Haskins work is that the smallest sound unit

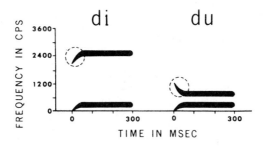

FIG. 4. Sound patterns sufficient to produce the perception of the syllables *di* and *du*. The abscissa (horizontal axis) represents time in milliseconds. Thus the time taken for the utterance *di* is about 300 msec, or 0.3 second. The ordinate (vertical axis) represents frequency of sound in cycles per second. The dark bands on the graph represent the presence of energy at the indicated frequency and time. Thus, for the syllable *di* all but the beginning 50 msec consists of two steady bands of acoustic energy, one at a few hundred cycles per second, and one at about 2400 cycles per second. The first 50 msec consist of a gradual rise in frequency to the level of the two steady frequency bands. As indicated in the text, it is tempting to assume that the initial 50 msec, involving changes in the two basic frequencies, represent *d*. However, if only these segments of the sound are presented, people hear a "bird chirp," not resembling *d* at all. If more sound is added, including some of the two steady frequencies, the bird chirp abruptly changes to a short *di*. Note also that the sound patterns at the beginning of the two syllables look grossly different, even though both are heard by the human ear as the same sound category, *d*. The sound spectrograms (visual representations of sound patterns over time) shown here are idealizations. They do indeed sound like the appropriate syllables to the human ear, but the actual utterance of these sounds by humans is much more complex. The bands shown in this figure actually form the areas of relative concentration of sound energy (Liberman, 1970).

that is relatively context independent and separately pronounceable is the syllable. Although the two sounds in *to* cannot be separately pronounced and easily blended, the two syllables in *today* are both easily pronounced and blended.

A second line of evidence for phoneme inaccessibility comes from reading research. Reading teachers are aware of the difficulty of getting children to blend phoneme "sounds" into recognizable words, or getting children to understand that *dog* and *dig* start with the same *d* sound. Children have great difficulty in understanding this notion, even though they have no trouble discriminating words like *dog, dig, pig,* and *big*. This has been shown nicely in an experiment by Blank (1968). She confirmed a previous finding that children with reading backwardness performed poorly on the Wepman test (1958), in which a child must judge whether two consecutively spoken words were the same or different. The word pairs either differ in one phoneme (e.g., *web-wed*) or are the same. Children who claimed that particular pairs of different words were the same were later asked to repeat these same words when each was spoken by the experimenter. They made the appropriate responses, clearly distinguishing, in this imitation task, between words that they had claimed were the same. Clearly, they could hear the differences, but not *talk about* them.

FIG. 5. Conceptual outline of the syllabary curriculum. In the first stage, semasiography, children learn to interpret pictures and thus get to meanings directly from the page. In the second step, logography, they learn picture-symbols that stand for words and construct simple sentences with them. In the third stage, phoneticization, direct orthographic representation of the sounds of speech rather than the meanings is introduced. Attention is called to sound segmentation of speech by a "speaking slowly" game, in which long words are broken into syllables and pronounced slowly (e.g., *hos-pi-tal*). The children must guess the word they hear. To exemplify the idea that symbols can represent sounds, they play a nonsense noise game. A few odd and entertaining noises (such as "clucking" with the tongue or whistles) are each given a symbol equivalent. Children then learn to read off symbol sequences by making the proper noise sequences. Rebuses (e.g., can, saw) are used to emphasize the use of words for their sound value. Blends of two words (syllables) that form new words are also introduced in a game format. In the fourth stage, an English syllabary consisting of about 70 common English syllables and the words made by blending these syllables, is introduced. Wherever possible, pictorial symbols are provided along with the written form of each syllable to help in identifying and remembering them. However, for some of the more abstract items (e.g., *er, the*), no pictorial aids are provided for obvious reasons. Children progress through this syllabary primarily by playing word construction games with the syllabic elements and reading 15 progressively more difficult story books. The segmentation cues separating the syllables are gradually made less salient (see also Fig. 6). Once some fluency in this syllabary is gained, the fifth stage, introduction to the alphabet, begins. Alphabetic (phonemic) elements are introduced gradually, beginning with initial *s,* a sound relatively easy to pronounce in isolation. It is blended onto the already learned syllabic elements (Rozin and Gleitman, 1974).

CONCEPTUAL OUTLINE OF THE SYLLABARY CURRICULUM

	SEMASIOGRAPHY	LOGOGRAPHY	PHONETICIZATION	SYLLABARY	INTRODUCTION TO THE ALPHABET
DESCRIPTION	Reading for meaning through pictures	Mapping between spoken words and visual symbols	Focusing on sound rather than meaning by developing awareness of sound segmentation	Constructing and segmenting meaningful words and sentences in terms of syllables	Segmenting and blending initial consonant sounds
ACTIVITIES	Interpretation of pictures	Reading material of the form: 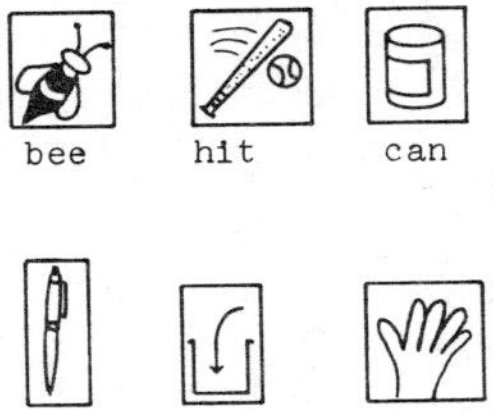 bee, hit, can, pen, in, hand	"Speaking slowly" game; Nonsense noise game  — goo la la goo; Rebus homonyms 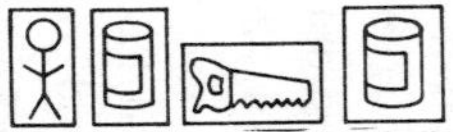 — man can saw can; Concrete blends  — = rainbow	Basic blends of meaningful syllables  = sandwich; sand witch; Addition of meaningless syllables (e.g. terminal y, er, ing) 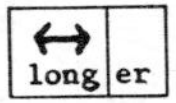 — long er; Partial fading of segmentation cues  — be•ing	Blends using initial consonant sounds: s•ing; s•and

FIG. 5

271

The notion that phonemes are less accessible than syllables is supported by data on different orthographies. Syllabaries have been invented many times in history whereas the alphabet seems to have been invented only once (Gelb, 1952). This implies that syllabic segmentation is easier to discover. There are also reports of rapid and easy acquisition of current or recent syllabic orthographies. The Cherokee language, written in the last century in syllabic notation, was widely read; literacy rates in the Cherokee compared favorably to those of neighboring white settlers (Walker, 1969). A significant part of modern Japanese is written as a syllabary, mixed with Chinese-type logographic characters. It is striking that there is virtually no reading disability in Japan (Sakamoto and Makita, 1973). Furthermore, the syllabic aspect of Japanese writing is often learned spontaneously by preschool Japanese children (Sakamoto and Makita, 1973).

In light of these considerations, Lila Gleitman and I (Gleitman and Rozin, 1973a,b; Rozin and Gleitman, 1976) have tried to introduce English reading by recapitulating the history of writing, moving from accessible to inaccessible. We have devised a curriculum (outlined in Fig. 5) in which we begin with semasiography; children learn to interpret pictures that represent an action or story, thus gaining meanings directly from the pictures. We follow this with construction of simple sentences from iconic symbols (logography), then introduce the idea of phoneticization with rebuses and other devices, and then move from accessible sound units (syllables) to inaccessible ones (phonemes) (Gleitman and Rozin, 1973a; Rozin and Gleitman, 1974). Children learn to read and blend common English syllables before introduction of phonemic units. Thus, they learn about phoneticization (e.g., the rebus) and the notion of building large sound units from smaller ones. They practice this by learning to read a simple English syllabary. Only after they have understood the notion of phoneticization and can fluently blend syllables, are they exposed to the more abstract alphabetic-phonemic units. (The conceptual stages of this syllabary curriculum are illustrated in Figs. 5 and 6). We can report that inner city first grade children with a poor prognosis for reading can acquire the basic skills of syllable blending and reading of syllabic materials quite easily (Rozin and Gleitman, 1976; Gleitman and Rozin, 1973a). This success presumably occurs because we have separated three components (phoneticization, blending, and the phonemic units) which are ordinarily taught simultaneously. A syllabary *avoids* the abstract unit problem, and concentrates on phoneticization and blending. But since our writing system is alphabetic, and English does not lend itself to transcription with a modest number of syllables, we are still faced with the ultimate problem of the accessibility of the phoneme. Note that this problem is not inherently related to the writing system: it could as well be described in terms of speech

sandwich

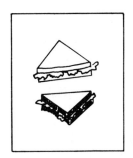

sand   wich

sand wich

sandwich

FIG. 6. Successive stages in presentation of syllabic elements of the word "sandwich." The initial stage involves blending of concrete representation of syllables (*sand* and *wich*) to produce a new whole (*sandwich*) with an emergent meaning. In later stages, the concrete representations are supplemented by their printed equivalent. Then, the spatial segmentation between the syllables and the concrete representation are gradually eliminated, as indicated in the bottom two representations.

segmentation (see Rosner, 1972). And it is a problem for which we do not have a ready solution. We know of no basic principles of learning that offer helpful guidance in achieving access to something that is already in the head. We only know that almost all nonreaders do not have access to the phoneme concept, while virtually all fluent readers of English have achieved it, and in fact, consider the principle so obvious that they find it difficult to believe that it is a stumbling block in reading acquisition.

IX. Education and Accessibility

Difficulty with teaching the conception of the phoneme raises the general issue of the role of access to the cognitive unconscious in the process of education. The need to learn what is already in the head, as is the case in reading acquisition, seems to arise often in education. For example, teaching the rules of grammar, which are at best imperfect representations of a much more sophisticated system actually in the head, can easily be described as learning what is already known. Similarly, mnemonic devices, often *taught*, are in part expressions of the normal, though usually unconscious, operation of the memory, which spontaneously organizes and connects presented materials.

In general, what is taught in the process of education can be described as either gaining access to knowledge already in the head, or revealing relationships in the outside world (i.e., understanding the Copernican system). Since a significant amount of learning seems to be about what is already inside, it would seem worthwhile to describe the circumstances and principles underlying access to the cognitive unconscious. To my knowledge, the problem has not been stated in this way before, so it is not too surprising that there have been no systematic attempts to solve it. The physiology or psychology of learning, memory, or cognition do not address this problem as such. Yet it seems to be quite fundamental; it is, possibly, a different type of learning. It of course resembles what is sometimes called generalization and transfer, but differs in that the reference material or ability, instead of being put into the brain by a training procedure itself, is part of the basic circuitry of the brain.

In the absence of systematic theoretical guidance, common sense appears to be the best short-term guide in dealing with actual problems in education. It was basically common sense that led Lila Gleitman and myself to approach the problem of access to the phoneme the way we did. We attempted to *isolate* the access problem, by separately teaching related concepts that did not involve this difficulty (phoneticization and blending). By teaching a more concrete and accessible reading system involving syllabic segmentation, we hoped to provide motivation in children, as they would experience success in one type of reading system. We presumed that whatever happens in access to the phoneme, time spent attending to the problem would favor acquisition. After all, most children do seem to gain access by the time-honored procedure of "practice makes perfect"; that is, steady drill, often of the form of *buh-a-tuh- but*. But most critically, we assumed that the way to approach the small and abstract unit was through a more concrete, more easily comprehendible unit which shared many properties with the inaccessible unit. The approach was to gradually approximate the phoneme, using a syllabic base, and to go from the most context insensitive phonemes to those phonemes least pronounceable and most context dependent. In this respect, our program is similar to Rosner's (1972) independently devised approach of phonological awareness. Rosner has dealt directly with the sound segmentation problem and does not involve writing—reading at all in teaching this fundamental concept. As we do, he moves from concrete to abstract. Children begin by imitating patterns of sound, such as hand claps, which have clear boundaries and definitions. He then moves the children through smaller units, from words through syllables to phonemes. Children deal with these materials in a variety of ways, including repetition of patterns and manipulation of patterns. For example, they are asked to repeat patterns deleting an element: Repeat *I am home* without *home,* or repeat *slit* without the *l* sound. This sensible procedure seems to have had some success in increasing ability to deal with alphabetic—phonemic units (Rosner, 1974).

There is other support for the general efficacy of movement from concrete to abstract to achieve increased accessibility. It comes from the area of clinical neurology and was called to my attention by Philip Teitelbaum. I have pointed out that both phonemic segmentation and recovery of function can be described as instances of increased access. If this parallel holds (see Teitelbaum, 1973, for a discussion of recovery—development parallels), then the principles of recovery of function and the techniques used to achieve it may become relevant to reading and other educational processes. A study on recovery of independent finger movement in people with spastic paralysis is particularly instructive (Lauretana *et al.,* 1959). Marked improvement has been produced by facilitating movements that the patient is incapable of making on his own. For example, at one stage, patients can flex all fingers simultaneously, but cannot flex individual fingers. Individual fingers of the patient are extended, thus facilitating flexion (via the stretch reflex) in these particular fingers. It is not surprising that with this aid the patient can flex individual fingers. What is surprising is that this exercise significantly facilitates recovery. Teitelbaum (1973) has described this procedure as facilitating the highest intact center in a damaged hierarchy. This notion provides a new and refreshing approach to the process of education, using recovery of function as a model. Adapted to reading acquisition, it maps onto the procedure I have described: working at the most abstract unit the child can handle, and practicing at this level, while constantly probing the next level. This is one sensible approach to solving the problem. It may or may not work. If it works, its mechanism of operation will have to be understood. Meanwhile, we must patiently wait in the hope that more of the secrets locked in our cognitive unconscious can be harnessed to serve our daily intellectual lives.

References

Aronson, L. (1951). Orientation and jumping in the gobiid fish *Bathygobius soporator*. *American Museum Novitates* **1486**, 1–22.

Baerends, G. P. (1941). Fortpflanzungsverhalten und orientierung der grabwespe *Ammophila campestris* Jur. *Tijdschrift voor Entomologie* **84**, 68–275.

Behrend, E. R., Domesick, V. B., and Bitterman, M. E. (1965). Habit reversal in the fish. *Journal of Comparative and Physiological Psychology* **60**, 407–411.

Bitterman, M. E. (1965). The evolution of intelligence. *Scientific American* **212**, 92–100.

Blank, M. (1968). Cognitive processes in auditory discrimination in normal and retarded readers. *Child Development* **39**, 1091–1101.

Bower, T. G. R. (1964). Discrimination of depth in premotor infants. *Psychonomic Science* **1**, 368.

Chomsky, N. (1965). "Aspects of the Theory of Syntax." MIT Press, Cambridge, Massachusetts.

Chomsky, N., and Halle, M. (1968). "The Sound Pattern of English." Harper, New York.

de Ajuriaguerra, J., Bellet-Muller, M. R., and Tissot, R. (1964). A propos de quelques problèmes posés par le déficit opératoire des vieillards atteints de démence dégénérative en début d'evolution. *Cortex* **1**, 103–132, 232–256.

Feldman, H., Gelman, R., and Rozin, P. (1975). Cognitive dysfunction in senile dementia. In preparation.

Flavell, J. H. (1963). "The Developmental Psychology of Jean Piaget." Van Nostrand-Reinhold, Princeton, New Jersey.

Garcia, J., and Ervin, F. R. (1968). Gustatory-visceral and telereceptor-cutaneous conditioning–adaptation to internal and external milieus. *Communications in Behavioral Biology, A* **1**, 389–415.

Garcia, J., and Koelling, R. A. (1966). Relation of cue to consequence in avoidance learning. *Psychonomic Science* **4**, 123–124.

Garcia, J., Ervin, F. R., and Koelling, R. A. (1966). Learning with prolonged delay of reinforcement. *Psychonomic Science* **5**, 121–122.

Gazzaniga, M. S. (1970). "The Bisected Brain." Appleton, New York.

Gelb, I. J. (1952). "A Study of Writing." Univ. of Chicago Press, Chicago, Illinois.

Geschwind, N. (1962). The anatomy of acquired disorders of reading. *In* "Reading Disability" (J. Money, ed.), pp. 115–130. Johns Hopkins Press, Baltimore, Maryland.

Geschwind, N. (1965a). Disconnexion syndromes in animals and man. Part I. *Brain* **88** (2), 237–294.

Geschwind, N. (1965b). Disconnexion syndromes in animals and man. Part II. *Brain* **88** (3), 585–644.

Geschwind, N., Quadfasel, F. A., and Segarra, J. M. (1968). Isolation of the Speech Area. *Neuropsychologia* 6, 327–340.

Gleitman, H., and Rozin, P. (1971). Learning and memory. *In* "Fish Physiology" (W. S. Hoar and D. J. Randall, eds.), Vol. 6, pp. 191–278. Academic Press, New York.

Gleitman, L. R., and Rozin, P. (1973a). Teaching reading by use of a syllabary. *Reading Research Quarterly* 8, 447–483.

Gleitman, L. R., and Rozin, P. (1973b). Phoenician go home? (A response to Goodman). *Reading Research Quarterly* 8, 494–501.

Gleitman, L. R., and Rozin, P. (1976). The structure and acquisition of reading. I. Relations between orthographies and the structure of language. *In* "Reading: The CUNY Conference" (A. S. Reber and D. Scarborough, eds.). Erlbaum, Hillsdale, New Jersey. In press.

Gleitman, L. R., Gleitman, H., and Shipley, E. (1973). The emergence of the child as grammarian. *Cognition* 1, 137–164.

Gonzalez, R. C., Eskin, R. M., and Bitterman, M. E. (1963). Further experiments on partial reinforcement in the fish. *American Journal of Psychology* 76, 366–375.

Harris, C. S. (1965). Perceptual adaptation to inverted, reversed, and displaced vision. *Psychological Review* 72, 419–444.

Hasler, A. D. (1966). "Underwater Guideposts. Homing of Salmon." Univ. of Wisconsin Press, Madison.

Hasler, A. D., and Schwassman, H. O. (1960). Sun orientation in fish at different latitudes. *Cold Spring Harbor Symposia on Quantitative Biology* 25, 429–441.

Helmholtz, H. (1962). "Treatise on Physiological Optics." [Translated from the 3rd German Edition (1867), J. P. C. Southall, ed.] Dover, New York.

Hinde, R. A. (1970). "Animal Behavior: A Synthesis of Ethology and Comparative Psychology," 2nd Ed. McGraw-Hill, New York.

Hinde, R. A., and Stevenson-Hinde, J., eds. (1973). "Constraints on Learning: Limitations and Predispositions." Academic Press, New York.

Hochberg, J. (1973). Perception. II. Space and Movement. *In* "Woodworth and Schlossberg's Experimental Psychology. Vol. 1: Sensation and Perception" (J. W. Kling and L. A. Riggs, eds.), 3rd Ed., Ch. 13. Holt, New York.

Jackson, J. H. (1884). Croonian lectures on evolution and dissolution of the nervous system. *British Medical Journal* 1, 591. [Reprinted in Taylor, J., ed. (1958). "Selected Writings of John Hughlings Jackson," Vol. 2. Staples Press, London.]

Jerison, H. J. (1973). "Evolution of the Brain and Intelligence." Academic Press, New York.

Kalat, J. W., and Rozin, P. (1972). You can lead a rat to water but you can't make him think. *In* "Biological Boundaries of Learning" (M. E. P. Seligman and J. Hager, eds.), pp. 115–122. Appleton, New York.

Kalat, J. W., and Rozin, P. (1973). "Learned safety" as a mechanism in long-delay taste-aversion learning in rats. *Journal of Comparative and Physiological Psychology* 83, 198–207.

Kavanagh, J. F., and Mattingly, I. G., eds. (1972). "Language by Ear and by Eye." MIT Press, Cambridge, Massachusetts.

Konishi, M. (1965). The role of auditory feedback in the control of vocalization in the white-crowned sparrow. *Zeitschrift für Tierpsychologie* 22, 770–783.

Lauretana, M. M., Partan, D. L., and Twitchell, T. E. (1959). Rehabilitation of the upper extremity in infantile spastic hemiparesis. *American Journal of Occupational Therapy* 13, 264–267.

Lenneberg, E. H. (1967). "Biological Foundations of Language." Wiley, New York.

Levy, J. (1974). Psychobiological implications of bilateral asymmetry. *In* "Hemisphere Function in the Human Brain" (S. Dimond and J. G. Beaumont, eds.), pp. 121–183. Paul Flek, London.

Lewis, M., and McGurk, H. (1972). Evaluation of infant intelligence. *Science* **178**, 1174–1177.

Liberman, A. M. (1970). The grammars of speech and language. *Cognitive Psychology* **1**, 301–323.

Liberman, A. M., Cooper, F. S., Shankweiler, D. P., and Studdert-Kennedy, M. (1967). Perception of the speech code. *Psychological Review* **74**, 431–461.

Liberman, I. Y., Shankweiler, D., Fischer, F. W., and Carter, B., (1974). Explicit syllable and phoneme segmentation in the young child. *Journal of Experimental Child Psychology* **18**, 201–212.

Lieberman, P. (1973). On the evolution of language: a unified view. *Cognition* **2**, 59–94.

Lindauer, M. (1961). "Communication among Social Bees." Harvard Univ. Press, Cambridge, Massachusetts.

Lorenz, K. (1965). "Evolution and the Modification of Behavior." Univ. of Chicago Press, Chicago, Illinois.

Manning, A. (1972). "An Introduction to Animal Behavior." 2nd Ed. Addison-Wesley, Reading, Massachusetts.

Marler, P. (1970). A comparative approach to vocal learning; song development in white crowned sparrows. *Journal of Comparative and Physiological Psychology, Monograph* **71** (2), Part 2, 1–25.

Mattingly, I. G. (1972). Reading, the linguistic process, and linguistic awareness. *In* "Language by Ear and By Eye" (J. F. Kavanagh and I. G. Mattingly, eds.), pp. 133–148. MIT Press, Cambridge, Massachusetts.

Mayr, E. (1960). The emergence of evolutionary novelties. *In* "Evolution after Darwin. Vol. 1. The Evolution of Life" (S. Tax, ed.), pp. 349–380. Univ. of Chicago Press, Chicago, Illinois.

Milner, B. (1973). Hemispheric specialization: scope and limits. *In* "The Neurosciences; Third Study Program" (F. O. Schmitt and F. G. Worden, eds.), pp. 75–89. MIT Press, Cambridge, Massachusetts.

Pert, A., and Gonzalez, R. C. (1974). Behavior of the turtle (*Chrysemys picta picta*) in simultaneous, successive, and behavioral contrast situations. *Journal of Comparative and Physiological Psychology* **87**, 526–538.

Piaget, J. (1955). Les stades du developpement intellectuel de l'enfant et de l'adolescent. *In* "Le Problème des Stades en Psychologie de l'Enfant" (P. Osterrieth *et al.*, eds.), pp. 33–113. Presses Univ. France, Paris.

Revusky, S. H., and Bedarf, E. W. (1967). Association of illness with prior ingestion of novel foods. *Science* **155**, 219–220.

Revusky, S. H., and Garcia, J. (1970). Learned associations over long delays. *In* "The Psychology of Learning and Motivation: Advances in Research and Theory" (G. H. Bower, ed.), Vol. 4, pp. 1–84. Academic Press, New York.

Richter, C. P. (1943). Total self regulatory functions in animals and human beings. *Harvey Lecture Series* **38**, 63–103.

Richter, C. P. (1953). Experimentally produced reactions to food poisoning in wild and domesticated rats. *Annals of the New York Academy of Sciences* **56**, 225–239.

Rosner, J. (1972). The development and validation of an individualized perceptual skills curriculum. *Learning Research and Development Center, University of Pittsburgh, Publication 7.*

Rosner, J. (1974). Auditory analysis training with prereaders. *Reading Teacher* 27, 379–384.

Rozin, P. (1967). Specific aversions as a component of specific hungers. *Journal of Comparative and Physiological Psychology* 64, 237–242.

Rozin, P. (1968). Specific aversions and neophobia as a consequence of vitamin deficiency and/or poisoning in half-wild and domestic rats. *Journal of Comparative and Physiological Psychology,* 66, 82–88.

Rozin, P. (1969a). Central or peripheral mediation of learning with long CS-US intervals in the feeding system. *Journal of Comparative and Physiological Psychology* 67, 421–429.

Rozin, P. (1969b). Adaptive food sampling in vitamin deficient rats. *Journal of Comparative and Physiological Psychology* 69, 126–132.

Rozin, P. (1976a). The selection of foods by rats, humans, and other animals. *In* "Advances in the Study of Behavior" (C. G. Beer, R. A. Hinde, J. S. Rosenblatt, and E. Shaw, eds.), Vol. 6. Academic Press, New York. In press.

Rozin, P. (1976b). The psychobiological approach to human memory. *In* "Neural Mechanisms of Learning and Memory" (E. L. Bennett and M. R. Rosenzweig, eds.), MIT Press, Cambridge, Massachusetts. In press.

Rozin, P., and Gleitman, L. R. (1974). "Syllabary." (An introductory reading curriculum). Published in pilot edition by Curriculum Development Associates, Washington, D.C.

Rozin, P., and Gleitman, L. R. (1976). The structure and acquisition of reading. II. The reading process and the acquisition of the alphabetic principle. *In* "Reading: The CUNY Conference" (A. S. Reber and D. Scarborough, eds.). Erlbaum, Potomac, Maryland. In press.

Rozin, P., and Kalat, J. (1971). Specific hungers and poison avoidance as adaptive specializations of learning. *Psychological Review* 78, 459–486.

Rozin, P., and Kalat, J. (1972). Learning as a situation-specific adaptation. *In* "Biological Boundaries of Learning " (M.E.P. Seligman and J. Hager, eds.), pp. 66–97. Appleton, New York.

Rozin, P., Poritsky, S., and Sotsky, R. (1971). American children with reading problems can easily learn to read English represented by Chinese characters. *Science* 171, 1264–1267.

Rzoska, J. (1953). Bait shyness, a study in rat behavior. *British Journal of Animal Behavior* 1, 128–135.

Sakamoto, T., and Makita, K. (1973). Japan. *In* "Comparative Reading: Cross-National Studies of Behavior and Processes in Reading and Writing" (J. Downing, ed.), pp. 440–465. Macmillan, New York.

Savin, H. (1972). What the child knows about speech when he starts to learn to read. *In* "Language by Ear and by Eye" (J. F. Kavanagh and I. G. Mattingly, eds.), pp. 319–326. MIT Press, Cambridge, Massachusetts.

Schwartz, B. (1974). On going back to nature: a review of Seligman's and Hager's Biological Boundaries of Learning. *Journal of the Experimental Analysis of Behavior* 21, 183–198.

Seligman, M. E. P. (1970). On generality of the laws of learning. *Psychological Review* 77, 406–418.

Seligman, M. E. P., and Hager, J., eds. (1972). "The Biological Boundaries of Learning." Appleton, New York.

Shettleworth, S. (1971). Constraints on learning. *In* "Advances in the Study of Behavior" (D. S. Lehrman, R. A. Hinde, and E. Shaw, eds.), Vol. 4. Academic Press, New York.

Simon, H. A. (1967). The architecture of complexity. *Proceedings of the American Philosophical Society* **106**, 467–482.

Smith, J. C., and Roll, D. L. (1967). Trace conditioning with x-rays as an aversive stimulus. *Psychonomic Science* **9**, 11–12.

Sperry, R. W., Gazzaniga, M. S., and Bogen, J. E. (1969). Interhemispheric relationships: the neocortical commissures; syndromes of hemisphere disconnection. *In* "Handbook of Clinical Neurology" (P. J. Vinken and G. W. Bruyn, eds.), Vol. IV, pp. 273–290. North-Holland Pub., Amsterdam.

Teitelbaum, P. (1973). The physiological analysis and synthesis of behavior; the parallel between development and recovery of nervous function. *Society for Research in Child Development, Philadelphia, Pa.*

Teitelbaum, P., Cheng, M. F., and Rozin, P. (1971). Starvation retards the development of food and water regulations. *Journal of Comparative and Physiological Psychology* **76**, 206–218.

Tinbergen, N. (1951). "The Study of Instinct." Oxford Univ. Press (Clarendon), London and New York.

von Frisch, K. (1967). "The Dance Language and Orientation of Bees." Belknap Press, Cambridge, Massachusetts.

Waddington, C. H. (1957). "The Strategy of the Genes." Allen, London.

Walker, W. (1969). Notes on native writing systems and the design of native literacy programs. *Anthropological Linguistics* **11**, 148–166.

Wallach, H. (1959). The perception of motion. *Scientific American* **201**, 56–60.

Wepman, J. M. (1958). "Wepman Auditory Discrimination Test." Language Research Associates, Chicago, Illinois.

Author Index

Numbers in italics refer to the pages on which the complete references are listed.

A

Abadi, R., 97, *116*
Adamson, L., 36, *58*
Adolph, E. F., 190, *232*
Aghajanian, G. K., 148, 168, *174, 179*
Agid, Y., 125, 142, 151, *172, 179, 184*
Ahlskog, J. E., 125, *172*, 212, 223, *232*
Albe-Fessard, D., 139, 142, *172, 179*
Albert, D. J., 122, 131, *172*, 217, *232*
Algeri, S., 125, 157, *173*
Allen, G. I., 225, *232*
Allman, J. M., 31, 33, *60*
Altman, J., 38, *58*
Amassian, V. E., 139, *172*
Anand, B. K., 121, 122, 166, *172,* 192, 194, *232, 234*
Andén, N. E., 122, 138, 140, 148, *172,* 206, 208, *232*
Andersen, H. T., 19, *24*
Andersson, B., 1, *25,* 130, *172,* 194, *232*
Andrews, D. P., 76, *111*
Andriessen, J., 95, 97, *112*
Angeletti, P. U., 168, *186*
Anokhin, P. K., 139, *172*
Antelman, S. M., 143, *174,* 215, 216, *238*
Appley, M. H., 200, *232*
Arbuthnott, G. W., 213, 214, *232, 234*
Ariëns Kappers, C. U., 39, *58*
Aronson, L., 252, *276*
Atz, J., 33, *58*
Avar, A., 143, *173*
Axelrod, J., 151, 153, 159, *177, 178, 186*

B

Bach-y-Rita, P., 214, *240*
Baerends, G. P., 252, *276*
Baillie, P., 143, *173*
Balagura, S., 143, 145, 168, *173, 175, 177*
Balinska, H., 145, 169, *173*
Ball, G. G., 228, *232*
Banerjee, S. P., 144, *184*
Baresova, O., 169, *173*
Barker, J. P., 190, *232*
Barlow, H. B., 70, 72, 73, 74, 76, 77, 81, 105, *111*

Bartholini, G., 150, 169, *173, 179*
Bartoshuk, L. M., 17, 18, 23, *25, 26*
Baxter, L., 215, *232*
Becker, G., 146, *187*
Behrend, E. R., 259, *276*
Beidler, L. M., 1, 2, 4, 21, *25, 26*
Bellet-Muller, M. R., 263, *276*
Berger, B., 208, *232*
Berger, B. D., 168, *173,* 209, *232*
Berkley, M. A., 81, 82, 83, 84, 85, 86, 89, 91, 95, 96, 97, 99, 100, 101, *111, 114, 116, 119,* 197, *234*
Berlucchi, G., 98, *111*
Berlyne, D. E., 203, *232*
Bernard, R. A., 1, 21, *25, 27*
Berner, C. N., 137, *184*
Besson, M. J., 146, 147, *173*
Best, P. J., 219, *240*
Bilge, M., 102, *112*
Bindra, D., 200, 204, *232*
Bingle, A., 102, *112*
Bishop, P. O., 97, 101, 102, 105, 107, *112, 115, 117, 118, 119*
Bisti, S., 88, 91, 92, 93, 94, *112*
Bitterman, M. E., 34, *58,* 258, 259, *276, 277*
Bjerre, B., 168, *173*
Björklund, A., 47, *61,* 124, 125, 138, 155, 168, *173, 179, 180,* 205, 206, 208, *232, 237, 238*
Bjur, R., 146, *187*
Black, S. L., 137, *173*
Black, W. C., 214, *233*
Blake, R., 87, 88, 91, 93, 104, 106, *112, 114*
Blakemore, C., 97, 104, 105, 106, *111, 112, 117, 118*
Blanc, G., 208, 220, *232, 242*
Blank, M., 270, *276*
Blass, E. M., 136, 137, *173*
Bliss, E. L., 146, *173*
Blondaux, C., 142, 156, *173, 182*
Bloom, F. E., 123, 125, 140, 157, *173, 178,* 225, *242*
Blough, P. M., 52, *58*

281

Ernst, A. M., 140, *176*
Ervin, F. R., 248, *276*
Ervin, G. N., 160, *184*
Eskin, R. M., 259, *277*
Evarts, E. V., 224, *234*
Evered, M. D., 201, 202, 203, *234*
Everitt, A. V., 163, *177*
Evetts, K. D., 221, *235*
Evinger, C., 83, 85, 86, *111*

F

Falck, B., 205, *232, 235*
Farnebo, L. O., 148, *176*
Feldman, H., 263, *276*
Feldman, S. M., 127, 140, *176, 182*
Feltz, P., 155, *176*
Fibiger, H. C., 122, 123, 136, 142, 151, *176, 180,* 210, 211, 212, 214, 215, *235, 240, 241*
Fifkova, E., 169, *173*
Finch, L., 155, *176*
Fink, R. P., 34, 45, *59*
Finger, S., 168, *176*
Fiorentini, A., 82, 85, 86, 89, 93, 97, 100, 106, *112, 116*
Fisher, A. E., 215, 216, *238*
Fisher, G. L., 20, *26*
Fishman, I. Y., 1, 2, *25*
Fitch, M., 95, *114*
Fitzhugh, R., 70, 74, 76, 77, 81, *111*
Fitzsimons, J. T., 200, 221, *235*
Flavell, J. H., 262, *276*
Fleming, W. W., 146, 149, 154, *176*
Fletcher, G. V., 42, *61*
Fonberg, E., 133, 144, 145, *176, 183,* 195, *235*
Fox, R., 104, 106, *114*
Frank, M., 17, 24, *25*
Freeman, R., 92, *117*
French, J. D., 139, 142, *176*
Friedman, E., 168, *176*
Friedman, M. I., 134, 162, 163, 169, *176, 185*
Frigyese, T. L., 142, *176*
Froment, J. L., 142, *182*
Fukada, Y., 82, *114*
Fukuda, Y., 102, *118*
Funakoshi, M., 19, 21, 23, *24, 25, 26*
Fuxe, K., 122, 124, 138, 139, 140, 148, 155, 169, *172, 174, 175, 176, 179, 182,* 205, 206, 207, 208, 209, 211,

213, 214, 220, *232, 234, 235, 236, 240*

G

Galey, D., 125, *184*
Galifret, Y., 36, *59*
Ganchrow, J., 20, *26*
Gandelman, R., 198, 227, *243*
Ganson, R., 79, *113*
Ganz, L., 95, *114*
Garcia, J., 248, *276, 278*
Gardner, E. L., 155, *181*
Gaze, R. M., 34, *59*
Gazzaniga, M. S., 265, *276, 280*
Gelb, I. J., 266, 272, *276*
Gelman, R., 263, *276*
Gentil, C. G., 194, *239*
German, D. C., 213, 214, 216, *235*
Gerold, M., 125, *177*
Gershon, S., 168, *176*
Geschwind, N., 263, *276, 277*
Geyer, M. A., 149, 168, *176*
Gibbs, J., 166, *184*
Gladfelter, W. E., 193, *235*
Glavcheva, L., 145, *176*
Gleitman, H., 259, 265, *277*
Gleitman, L. R., 265, 266, 267, 270, 272, *277, 279*
Glick, S. D., 168, *176, 177*
Glickman, S. E., 194, 225, 227, *235*
Glickstein, M., 101, *114*
Gloor, P., 195, *235*
Glowinski, J., 125, 142, 146, 147, 151, 159, *172, 173, 177, 179, 184, 185,* 208, 220, *242*
Gluckman, M. I., 215, *232*
Gold, M., 212, 223, *237*
Gold, R. M., 122, 125, 127, 163, *177, 179,* 212, 217, *235*
Goldstein, M., 205, 206, 207, 209, *235, 236*
Gonzalez, R. C., 259, *277, 278*
Goodman, D. C., 47, *59*
Gordon, G., 1, 2, 18, *26*
Gordon, R., 146, *177, 184*
Graham, C., 106, *114*
Granda, A. M., 34, *59*
Granit, R., 70, 76, 77, 79, *114*
Grant, L. D., 125, 136, 143, 145, 151, *174, 175,* 210, *233*
Grastyan, E., 139, *177*

Subject Index

A

Adaptive specializations, 247–252
  food selection, 247–249
  imprinting, 249–251
  inaccessibility of, 254–255
  unusual, isolated memory abilities, 252
Affect, brain catecholamines and, 144–145
Anticipatory feeding and drinking, 200–203
Arousal, brain catecholamines and, 138–143
Arousal model, of motivation, 195–197

B

Behavior, initiation of, 220–223
Binocular vision
  cyclopean, 103–106
  visual fields and, 100–103
Birds
  importance for understanding vertebrate evolution, 34–35
  selection for study of visual system, 34–35
  visual system of
    anatomy and physiology of, 36–38
    coarse discriminations and, 40–47
    in normal pigeons, 47–54
    in pigeons with lesions, 54–56
Brain catecholamines
  biochemical regulation of, 146–149
  function of, 138–145
  lateral hypothalamic syndrome and, 123–138
  motivation and, see Motivation
Brain self-stimulation, 197–199
  catecholamine pathways and, 212–216, 227–229

C

Cat
  visual psychophysics of, see Visual psychophysics
  visual system
    compared with man, 106–107

    photometry and, 107–111
Catecholamines, see Brain catecholamines
Chorda tympani, gustatory coding in, 1–27
Coding, gustatory, 1–27
Cognitive unconscious, accessibility of, 245–280
  adaptive specializations and, 247–252, 254–255
  development, dissolution, and pathology in humans, 262–264
  education and, 274–276
  language and reading and, 264–274
  mechanisms of, 260–262
  organization and evolution of intelligence and, 256–260
  prewired components in, 252–254
Color vision, light sensitivity and, 79–81
Contrast sensitivity function, spatial, 91–94
Critical fusion frequency, 81–83
Cyclopean vision, 103–106

D

Dark adaptation, 73–75
Deficit stimuli, motivated behaviors initiated by, 217–218
Discrimination, visual system and, 40–47
Drinking, anticipatory, 200–203
Drive mechanism model, 192–195

E

Education, accessibility of cognitive unconscious and, 274–276
Equivalence, evolution of visual system and, 32–34
Evolution
  of intelligence, 256–260
  of visual system, 32–34
Extrapyramidal motor function, brain catecholamines and, 143–144

F

Feeding, anticipatory, 200–203
Food selection, as adaptive specialization, 247–249

294